HANDBOOK ON
BULLYING
PREVENTION

A LIFE COURSE PERSPECTIVE

Catherine P. Bradshaw, Editor

NASW PRESS

National Association of Social Workers
Washington, DC 20002-4241

Darrell P. Wheeler, PhD, MPH, ACSW
President

Angelo McClain, PhD, LICSW
Chief Executive Officer

Cheryl Y. Bradley, *Publisher*
Stella Donovan, *Acquisitions Editor*
Julie Gutin, *Project Manager*
Julie Palmer-Hoffman, *Copyeditor*
Sue Harris, *Proofreader*
Lori Holtzinger, *Indexer*

Cover by Suzani Pavone, Eye to Eye Design Studio, LLC
Interior design, composition, and eBook conversion by Xcel Graphic Services
Printed and bound by Sheridan

First impression: July 2017

Library of Congress Cataloging-in-Publication Data

Names: Bradshaw, Catherine P. (Catherine Pilcher), 1975- editor.
Title: Handbook on bullying prevention : a life course perspective /
    Catherine P. Bradshaw, editor.
Description: 1 Edition. | Washington, DC : NASW Press, [2017] | Includes
    bibliographical references and index.
Identifiers: LCCN 2016059036 (print) | LCCN 2017005599 (ebook) | ISBN
    978-0-87101-500-6 (pbk.) | ISBN 978-0-87101-501-3 (ebook)
Subjects: LCSH: Bullying. | Bullying—Prevention. | Bullying in schools.
Classification: LCC BF637.B85 H346 2017 (print) | LCC BF637.B85 (ebook) | DDC
    302.34/3—dc23
LC record available at https://lccn.loc.gov/2016059036

Printed in the United States of America

I would like to dedicate this book to my parents, John and Matilda Bradshaw. Thank you for your support and encouragement across my life course.

Table of Contents

Acknowledgments

I would like to thank the many colleagues who contributed to this book, both directly and indirectly, with particular appreciation to Tracy Waasdorp, Lindsey O'Brennan, Elise Pas, Katrina Debnam, Sarah Lindstrom Johnson, Jessika Bottiani, Phil Leaf, and Nick Ialongo. I also appreciate the research support and collaboration with my colleagues at the Johns Hopkins Center for the Prevention of Youth Violence and the Johns Hopkins Center for Prevention and Early Intervention. I am especially grateful to my doctoral students at the University of Virginia Curry School of Education, Elizabeth Bistrong and Hillary K. Morin, who assisted with several aspects of this book. And many thanks to my mentor, Jim Garbarino, who helped me develop an early interest in bullying prevention research.

About the Editor

Catherine Bradshaw, PhD, MEd, is a professor and the associate dean for research and faculty development at the Curry School of Education, University of Virginia; she is also the deputy director of the Centers for Disease Control and Prevention (CDC)–funded Johns Hopkins Center for the Prevention of Youth Violence and codirector of the National Institute of Mental Health (NIMH)–funded Johns Hopkins Center for Prevention and Early Intervention. She holds a doctorate in developmental psychology from Cornell University and a master's of education in counseling and guidance from the University of Georgia. Her research focuses on issues related to bullying and school climate; the development of aggressive and problem behaviors; and the design, evaluation, and implementation of evidence-based prevention programs in schools. She has coauthored over 200 journal articles and book chapters. She has considerable experience leading federally funded randomized trials of school-based prevention programs, including Positive Behavioral Interventions and Supports and social-emotional learning curricula. Her research has been funded by federal grants from the NIMH, National Institute on Drug Abuse, CDC, National Institute of Justice, U.S. Department of Education, and the Institute of Education Sciences, as well as foundation awards from the William T. Grant Foundation and Spencer Foundation. She has also consulted with the National Education Association, National Academy of Sciences, the United Nations, and the World Bank on issues related to bullying, mental health, and school-based prevention. She is a former associate editor for the *Journal of Research on Adolescence*, the editor of *Prevention Science*, and coeditor of the *Handbook of School Mental Health*.

About the Contributors

Paul Arnold, MD, PhD, is the inaugural director of the Mathison Centre for Mental Health Research & Education, an associate professor in the Departments of Psychiatry and Medical Genetics, and Alberta Innovates Health Solutions Translational Health Chair in Child and Youth Mental Health at the University of Calgary. His research focuses on the neurobiology of childhood neuropsychiatric disorders and risk and resilience factors in childhood mental health.

Elizabeth Bistrong, MEd, is a doctoral student in clinical psychology at the University of Virginia. Her research focuses on bystander reactions to bullying in middle and high school students.

Sarah J. Blakely-McClure, MA, is a doctoral student in the clinical psychology program at the University at Buffalo, the State University of New York. Her research interests include the development of self-concept and its association with aggressive behavior.

Chloe Campbell, PhD, is senior research fellow on the Psychoanalysis Unit at University College London. She has published widely on school violence, prevention of bullying in schools and the workplace, and innovative methods for managing the school climate.

Tina Cheng, MD, MPH, is the chair of pediatrics at Johns Hopkins Bayview, vice-chair of the Johns Hopkins Department of Pediatrics, and a professor of public health. She received her MD from Brown University and her MPH from the University of California. Her clinical, teaching, and research efforts focus on child health disparities, violence prevention, and primary care models to promote positive youth development and family health.

Erin Cook, MA/AC, NCSP, is completing her doctoral degree at the University at Buffalo, the State University of New York. She is a graduate assistant at the Alberti Center for Bullying Abuse Prevention, and her research interests include bullying among students with disabilities and school crisis prevention and intervention.

Dewey Cornell, PhD, is a forensic clinical psychologist who holds the Bunker Chair in Education at the Curry School of Education, University of Virginia. His research interests include bullying, school climate and safety, threat assessment, and youth violence prevention.

Wendy Craig, PhD, is professor and head of the Department of Psychology at Queen's University, Kingston, Ontario, Canada. Her research program focuses on healthy relationships, bullying and victimization, and knowledge mobilization.

Joanne Cummings, PhD, is a registered child clinical psychologist in Toronto, Ontario, Canada, and she is the knowledge mobilization director of PREVNet (Promoting Relationships and Eliminating Violence Network). With PREVNet, her work focuses on translating knowledge and brokering partnerships between university researchers and youth-serving organizations, governments, and corporations to promote healthy social development for Canada's youth.

Jeffrey Duong, PhD, holds a doctorate from the Johns Hopkins Bloomberg School of Public Health and is currently in medical school at the University of California, Davis, School of Medicine. His research focuses on child and adolescent development, with an emphasis on bullying among sexual minority youth.

Dorothy L. Espelage, PhD, is a professor of psychology at the University of Florida in Gainesville. She has conducted research on bullying, homophobic teasing, sexual harassment, and dating violence for the last 22 years.

Erika D. Felix, PhD, is an assistant professor in the Department of Counseling, Clinical, and School Psychology at the University of California, Santa Barbara. She is an expert in promoting adaptive recovery for youth following disasters, youth victimization (including bullying) and its consequences, and research and evaluation to improve community-based services.

Katherine Figiel-Miller, EdM, is a practitioner of educational interventions. She is currently the assistant director of service-learning at Loyola University Maryland.

Peter Fonagy, PhD, is Freud Professor of Psychoanalysis at University College London, with extensive publications on school violence, prevention of bullying in schools and the workplace, and innovative methods for managing the school climate.

Michael J. Furlong, PhD, is a professor at the University of California, Santa Barbara, affiliated with the International Center for School-Based Youth Development. He is a fellow of the American Psychological Association (Division 16, School Psychology) and the American Educational Research Association. His research focuses on youth psychological well-being, assessment of positive psychology self-schemas, resilience, school violence, and bullying.

James Garbarino, PhD, holds the Maude Clark Chair in Humanistic Psychology and is senior faculty fellow at the Center for the Human Rights of Children at Loyola University Chicago. His most recent book is *Listening to Killers*.

Cynthia Germanotta, MA, is the cofounder and president of Born This Way Foundation, which she founded with her daughter, Lady Gaga, to empower youth and inspire bravery.

Sara E. Gonzalez, MA, is a doctoral student at the University of Nebraska–Lincoln, involved in research on bullying.

Jennifer Greif Green, PhD, is an associate professor of special education in the School of Education at Boston University. Her research focuses on school-based mental health service provision and bullying prevention, with a particular emphasis on survey methods.

Danielle Guttman, PhD, NCSP, is a school psychologist working for the Aldine Independent School District, Houston, Texas. Formerly, she was a postdoctoral research associate at the Alberti Center for Bullying Abuse Prevention at the University at Buffalo, the State University of New York. Her research interests include schoolwide prevention approaches related to social-emotional issues.

Anna Heilbrun, MA, is a doctoral candidate in clinical psychology at the Curry School of Education, University of Virginia. Her research interests include disciplinary practices, school safety, and threat assessment.

Zephyr Horowitz-Johnson is a clinical research assistant at the Children's Hospital of Philadelphia. Her research interests surround promoting positive school climate in underserved communities.

Michelle Howell-Smith, PhD, is a research assistant professor at the Nebraska Academy for Methodology, Analytics, and Psychometrics.

Saida B. Hussain, PhD, is a graduate of the community psychology doctoral program at the University of Virginia. Her broad research interests include the examination of race-related experiences among marginalized youth and their relationships with supportive adults.

Nicholas Ialongo, PhD, is a professor in the Johns Hopkins Bloomberg School of Public Health, where he has directed a number of large-scale evaluations of elementary school-based preventive intervention trails.

Kimberly E. Kamper-DeMarco, PhD, is a postdoctoral associate at the Research Institute on Addictions, University at Buffalo, the State University of New York. Her research interests center on the development of aggression, victimization, and related psychosocial outcomes.

Stephen S. Leff, PhD, is professor of clinical psychology in pediatrics and codirector of the Violence Prevention Initiative at the Children's Hospital of Philadelphia and the Perelman School of Medicine at the University of Pennsylvania. His research focuses on aggression and bullying prevention programming, relational aggression, and using a community-based participatory research process of working with school and community stakeholders to integrate their perspectives into best practice programming.

Susan P. Limber, PhD, MLS, is the Dan Olweus Professor in the Institute on Family and Neighborhood Life within the Department of Youth, Family, and Community Studies at

Clemson University. She is a developmental psychologist who also holds a master's of legal studies. Dr. Limber's research and writing have focused on psychological and legal issues related to bullying among children, as well as youth participation and children's rights.

Sarah Lindstrom Johnson, PhD, is an assistant professor in the School of Social and Family Dynamics at Arizona State University. She received her PhD in public health from the Johns Hopkins School of Public Health. Her work takes a positive youth development perspective in reducing youth involvement in violence for which she partners with pediatricians, community-based organizations, and schools.

John E. Lochman, PhD, ABPP, is professor and Doddridge Saxon Chair in Clinical Psychology at the University of Alabama and director of the Center for the Prevention of Youth Behavior Problems. He has over 370 publications on risk factors and intervention research with aggressive children.

Patricia McDougall, PhD, serves as the vice-provost, teaching and learning, at the University of Saskatchewan and is an associate professor in the Department of Psychology. She conducts research on social relationships in childhood and adolescence, including such topics as friendship and social status, with a particular focus on studying the long-term impact of bullying and victimization.

Theresa McKinney, MA, is a mixed methods consultant and MAXQDA software trainer. She received her MA in quantitative, qualitative, and psychometric methods from the University of Nebraska–Lincoln.

Hillary K. Morin, PhD, MEd, holds a doctorate in clinical psychology at the University of Virginia. Her research focuses on adjustment outcomes associated with bullying victimization. She is currently a postdoctoral fellow at New York University.

Zachary R. Myers, MA, is a doctoral student at the University of Nebraska–Lincoln involved in research on bullying.

Amanda B. Nickerson, PhD, NCSP, is a professor of school psychology at the University at Buffalo, the State University of New York, where she directs the Alberti Center for Bullying Abuse Prevention. Her research focuses on school crisis prevention and intervention, with a particular emphasis on violence and bullying and the role of parents, peers, and educators in building the social-emotional strengths of children and adolescents.

Lindsey O'Brennan, PhD, is a postdoctoral fellow at the University of South Florida, Department of Educational and Psychological Studies. Her research focuses on the development and evaluation of school-based intervention and prevention programs that reduce youth violence, increase school connectedness, and improve the overall climate of the school.

Dan Olweus, PhD, is a professor of psychology, University of Bergen, Bergen, Norway. He conducted in Sweden what is generally recognized as the first scientific study on bullying in the world in 1973. The book was published in the United States in 1978 under the title *Aggression in the Schools: Bullies and Whipping Boys.*

Jamie M. Ostrov, PhD, is a professor of psychology in the clinical psychology program at the University at Buffalo, the State University of New York. His research focuses on the development and prevention of relational and physical aggression.

Debra J. Pepler, PhD, is a distinguished professor of psychology at York University, Toronto, Ontario, Canada, and a senior executive member of the LaMarsh Centre for Research on Violence and Conflict Resolution. Her current research examines aggression and victimization among adolescents, with a focus on the processes related to these problems over the life span. She is a codirector of PREVNet.

Kelly Petrunka, MS, is the executive director of PREVNet, headquartered at Queen's University, Kingston, Ontario, Canada. She has over 25 years of project management experience and child-related research experience.

Nicole Powell, PhD, MPH, has been a research psychologist at the Center for the Prevention of Youth Behavior Problems at the University of Alabama since 2003. In this position, she has been involved in delivering the Child and Parent Components of the Coping Power Program as well as training and supervising others in the implementation of the program. Dr. Powell received her doctorate in clinical psychology from the University of Alabama in 2000 and completed internship training at Children's Memorial Hospital in Chicago. She is a licensed psychologist, specializing in children and families.

Chad A. Rose, PhD, is an assistant professor in the Department of Special Education at the University of Missouri. He earned his PhD in 2010 from the University of Illinois at Urbana-Champaign. Dr. Rose's research focuses on the intersection of disability labels and special education services within the bullying dynamic, unique predictive and protective factors associated with bullying among students with disabilities, and social and emotional learning as a vehicle to reduce bullying among youth who receive special education services.

Carleigh Sanderson, MA, is a doctoral student working under the supervision of Dr. Tracy Vaillancourt at the University of Ottawa. Her research uses electroencephalography and event-related potential to examine peer victimization.

Heather Schwartz, MA, is a doctoral student at the University of Nebraska–Lincoln involved in research on bullying.

Jenna Strawhun, PhD, received her doctorate from the University of Nebraska–Lincoln and is currently a postdoctoral research fellow at the University of Nebraska Medical Center. Her research focuses on the relations between bullying and hazing.

Susan M. Swearer, PhD, is a professor of school psychology at the University of Nebraska–Lincoln. She is the codirector of the Bullying Research Network and the director of the Empowerment Initiative. She is the chair of the Research Advisory Board for the Born This Way Foundation.

Stuart W. Twemlow, MD, is a retired professor of psychiatry at the Baylor College of Medicine in Houston, Texas. Much of his research and publication history focuses on school violence, prevention of bullying in schools and the workplace, and innovative methods for managing the school climate.

Tracy Vaillancourt, PhD, is a Canada Research Chair in Children's Mental Health and Violence Prevention at the University of Ottawa, where she is cross-appointed as a full professor in Counselling Psychology and the School of Psychology. She is also an elected member of the College of the Royal Society of Canada. Her research examines the links between bullying and mental health, with a particular focus on social neuroscience. She is currently funded by the Canadian Institutes of Health Research.

Tracy Evian Waasdorp, PhD, MSEd, is a research scientist at the Children's Hospital of Philadelphia and an associate research scientist at the Johns Hopkins University School of Public Health. Her research interests include aggression and bullying, peer relationships, and school-based bullying prevention and intervention.

Joanna Lee Williams, PhD, is an associate professor in the Department of Leadership, Foundations, and Policy in the Curry School of Education at the University of Virginia. Her research interests focus on race and ethnicity as social contexts for youth development.

Joseph Wright, MD, is the chair of the Department of Pediatrics at Howard University and a professor of medicine. He received his MD from Rutgers University and is a practicing Emergency Department physician. His primary areas of academic interest include emergency medical services, injury prevention, and the needs of the underserved.

Foreword

James Garbarino

From time to time, issues emerge out of our collective experience to become a factor in our collective public and professional consciousness. Bullying has seen a significant shift in public and professional awareness and programmatic efforts to respond. What child growing up in the 1950s, and what teenager reaching adolescence in the 1960s, was a stranger to bullying—as a victim, as a perpetrator, or as a bystander? Having grown up back then, I know that bullying was all around us in school and in the community, whether from peers, siblings, or adults. But it was a silent epidemic and one that did not register as "serious" because it was thought to be psychologically insignificant. When I look back with professional eyes, I see things differently. I see the pain and suffering caused by the bullying that was all around me. My mentor, Urie Bronfenbrenner, was fond of saying, "What is most difficult? That, which you think is easiest—to see what is before your eyes." Indeed.

What was the catalyst for transforming the raw historical experience of kids (and, in point of fact, adults) into the current issue of bullying? I believe the precipitating factor was the rash of school shootings that began in the 1990s, particularly the attack on Columbine High School by Dylan Klebold and Eric Harris in April of 1999. In the wake of these lethally violent outbursts, a growing chorus of observers (including the FBI and the Secret Service) identified bullying as a factor. For these observers, bullying was at the heart of the dynamics that led these troubled boys to make war against their schools and the world of their peers. The reactive nature of these attacks highlighted the fact that the combination of troubled boys and a negative social climate could lead to outbreaks of homicide and suicide—particularly in a society in which the cultural, psychological, and physical availability of guns made transforming rage and hurt into wounded and killed kids (and adults) so efficient. In the wake of this, bullying became a prominent issue for anyone who cared about or studied kids.

It is testimony to the progress made that half a century after I was a teenager and nearly two decades after the Columbine school shooting, there is sufficient serious scholarly and clinical work to permit the publication of a handbook on bullying, and that such a book could be taken seriously intellectually and programmatically. Catherine Bradshaw and her colleagues have done just that, and the result is excellent (as is much of the work Dr. Bradshaw has accomplished in her career). The *Handbook on Bullying Prevention* is comprehensive in its coverage and excellent in its attention to scientific and clinical detail, and should become a benchmark volume.

Introduction

A Life Course Perspective on Bullying Prevention

Catherine P. Bradshaw

Bullying is a complex phenomenon with significant impacts across the life course. Although recent data suggest a slight decline in the rates of victimization by bullying among school-age youth (Rivara & Le Menestrel, 2016; Robers, Zhang, Morgan, & Musu-Gillette, 2015), this issue continues to be of great public health concern for the vast majority of youth, including those directly involved and those who serve as bystanders. There is also a growing body of literature documenting the significant impact of bullying, which may even outrank other forms of abuse (Lereya, Copeland, Costello, & Wolke, 2015). These effects include not only immediate harm but also lasting effects on social-emotional functioning, educational outcomes, mental health, as well as physical health more generally (Farrington & Ttofi, 2011; Lereya et al., 2015). There is compelling evidence that these effects can "get under the skin," such as by affecting the physiological stress system, telomere length, and systemic inflammation (see, for example, Carney, Hazler, Oh, Hibel, & Granger, 2010; Copeland et al., 2014). The vast majority of research on bullying has focused on school-age youth, with most studies more narrowly focused on middle schoolers, where the risk for involvement in bullying appears to be greatest. Although bullying can occur at any point in the life course—ranging from early childhood through late adulthood—we know relatively little about risk factors, impacts, and preventive intervention approaches relevant across the life course (Bradshaw, 2015; Sourander et al., 2016).

The goal of this book is to provide a comprehensive yet concise review of research on bullying with an orientation toward prevention and intervention across the life course. The chapters synthesize the latest research on bullying among children, adolescents, and adults and provide recommendations for prevention and early intervention in bullying situations involving youth and adults, as well as collections of individuals (for example, schools, communities).

We used a life course framework (see, for example, Elder, 1994; Rutter, 1996) to conceptualize bullying as a behavior that occurs across the life course, not just in youth. This framing is a bit controversial, as some may question the extent to which the term "bullying" even applies to adult populations or circumstances. However, we contend that there is a certain degree of heterotypic continuity. Although bullying takes slightly different forms in adulthood (for example, hazing, intimate partner violence, workplace bullying, adult bullying of children), we argue that the underlying features of intentionality, the repeated nature, and the power differential are consistent across the ages. Thus, there may be a thin line between these behaviors across the life course.

We also leverage bioecological theories of human development, which highlight the transactional and bidirectional influences between individuals and groups across environmental and social settings (Bronfenbrenner & Morris, 1998). Recent variations on the diathesis–stress model, including differential susceptibility theory, are also relevant, as they emphasize variation in vulnerability to environmental and social experiences, such as bullying (Swearer & Hymel, 2015), as well as intervention. Consistent with life course and bioecological frameworks, we consider developmental perspectives on risk factors as well as consequences, in addition to developmentally relevant prevention programming (Kellam & Rebok, 1992).

Drawing on these and other theoretical frameworks, the book is broken into five interrelated sections. We begin by considering some foundational issues in bullying, such as definitions, measurement, and development roots of bullying in childhood. The second section considers potential impacts of bullying across the life course, including biological as well as psychological, social, and mental health effects. Recent technological advances have provided a new medium and venue for engagement in bullying, which are considered and contrasted to traditional and relational forms of bullying. The third section focuses on bullying among youth, with a deeper dive into cultural and contextual considerations. We examine some of the emerging research linking bullying in adolescence with involvement in sexual harassment and intimate partner violence in adolescence and adulthood. We also consider special populations of youth, such as sexual minorities, ethnic minorities, and youth with disabilities, in light of research indicating that they are at increased risk for involvement in bullying. The fourth section of the book addresses the often "undiscussable" topic of adults who bully, be they college students who bully their peers or teachers who bully their students.

In the fifth and final section of the book, we consider multiple approaches to prevention, starting with an ecological focus on school climate. We then review specific prevention frameworks that have demonstrated significant impacts on bullying and related forms of aggression (see Bradshaw, 2015). Yet meta-analyses of school-based prevention programs suggest that, at best, the extant research-based models may reduce perpetration of bullying by only 23 percent and victimization by 20 percent (Ttofi & Farrington, 2011). This illustrates the need for additional research focused on issues related to implementation, which in turn may explain some of the variation in program effectiveness. The increasing focus on a multitiered system of supports also highlights the lack of intensive and targeted prevention programs for youth and adults who are frequently involved in and suffering the consequences of bullying (Bradshaw, 2015). The movement toward ecological approaches to bullying prevention emphasizes the critical role of peers and adults (for example, teachers, education support professionals, community members, physicians) as well as social media and policy in bullying prevention. Despite the increased awareness of the significance of bullying in higher education and the workplace, there has been very little rigorous research focused on preventing bullying and related forms of aggression and abuses of power in these settings (Rivara & Le Menestrel, 2016).

It is our collective hope that this book challenges the current conceptualization of bullying as a problem only affecting youth. Furthermore, we will explore a range of provocative and understudied topics related to bullying. Together, this collection of thought-provoking chapters will advance our understanding of this complex issue and inform bullying prevention approaches across the life course.

REFERENCES

Bradshaw, C. P. (2015). Translating research to practice in bullying prevention. *American Psychologist, 70*, 322–332.

Bronfenbrenner, U., & Morris, P. (1998). The ecology of developmental processes. In W. Damon (Ed.), *Handbook of child psychology: Vol. 1. Theoretical models of human development* (pp. 993–1028). New York: Wiley.

Carney, J.-L., Hazler, R. J., Oh, I., Hibel, L. C., & Granger, D. A. (2010). The relationships between bullying exposures in middle childhood, anxiety, and adrenocortical activity. *Journal of School Violence, 9*, 194–211.

Copeland, W. E., Wolke, D., Lereya, S. T., Shanahan, L., Worthman, C., & Costello, E. J. (2014). Childhood bullying involvement predicts low-grade systemic inflammation into adulthood. *PNAS, 111*(21), 7570–7575. doi:10.1073/pnas.1323641111

Elder, G. (1994). Time, human agency, and social change: Perspectives on the life course. *Social Psychological Quarterly, 57*, 4–15.

Farrington, D. P., & Ttofi, M. M. (2011). Bullying as a predictor of offending, violence and later life outcomes. *Criminal Behaviour and Mental Health, 21*, 90–98.

Kellam, S. G., & Rebok, G. W. (1992). Building developmental and etiological theory through epidemiologically based preventive intervention trials. In J. McCord & R. E. Tremblay (Eds.), *Preventing antisocial behavior: Interventions from birth through adolescence* (pp. 162–195). New York: Guilford Press.

Lereya, S. T., Copeland, W. E., Costello, E. J., & Wolke, D. (2015). Adult mental health consequences of peer bullying and maltreatment in childhood: Two cohorts in two countries. *Lancet Psychiatry, 2*(6), 524–531. doi:10.1016/S2215-0366(15)00165-0

Rivara, F., & Le Menestrel, S. (2016). *Preventing bullying through science, policy, and practice.* Washington, DC: National Academies of Science.

Robers, S., Zhang, A., Morgan, R. E., & Musu-Gillette, L. (2015). *Indicators of School Crime and Safety: 2014* (NCES 2015-072/NCJ 248036). Washington, DC: National Center for Education Statistics, U.S. Department of Education.

Rutter, M. (1996). Transitions and turning points in developmental psychopathology: As applied to the age span between childhood and mid-adulthood. *International Journal of Behavioral Development, 19*, 603–626.

Sourander, A., Gyllenberg, D., Klomek, A. B., Sillanmäki, L., Ilola, A. M., & Kumpulainen, K. (2016). Association of bullying behavior at 8 years of age and use of specialized services for psychiatric disorders by 29 years of age. *JAMA Psychiatry, 73*, 159–165. doi:10.1001/jamapsychiatry.2015.2419

Swearer, S. M., & Hymel, S. (2015). Understanding the psychology of bullying: Moving toward a social-ecological diathesis–stress model. *American Psychologist, 7*, 344–353.

Ttofi, M. M., & Farrington, D. P. (2011). Effectiveness of school-based programs to reduce bullying: A systematic and meta-analytic review. *Journal of Experimental Criminology, 7*(1), 27–56.

Part I
Foundational Research on Bullying

Defining and Measuring Bullying across the Life Course

Jennifer Greif Green, Michael J. Furlong, and Erika D. Felix

Despite the prominence of the word "bullying" in educational settings and popular media, the term has been inconsistently defined. Many researchers and policymakers have called for greater precision in definition (Cornell & Bandyopadhyay, 2010; Felix, Sharkey, Green, Furlong, & Tanigawa, 2011; Furlong, Sharkey, Felix, Tanigawa, & Green, 2010), and some have questioned whether the term should be eliminated altogether (Finkelhor, Turner, & Hamby, 2012). The lack of consensus in defining bullying has implications for laws and policies that use varying definitions of the term (Stuart-Cassel, Bell, & Springer, 2011). This is further complicated for assessment tools that, because of their inconsistency, have made it difficult to generate precise data on trends in bullying involvement across time and settings (Gladden, Vivolo-Kantor, Hamburger, & Lumpkin, 2014).

Initially, research and discourse related to bullying were dominated by discussions about the elementary and secondary school contexts. Seminal research on bullying in Europe (for example, Olweus, 1978) was designed to understand a specific form of peer aggression among youth that often occurred within schools. In the United States, deeper interest and a larger volume of scholarly research on bullying emerged in the mid-1990s out of reports that linked a history of bullying victimization to several school shootings. Recently, research has expanded to focus on both bullying of children in nonschool contexts (for example, neighborhoods) and bullying in adulthood. For example, the first journal articles on workplace bullying (the main context in which bullying has been studied in adulthood) were not published until the mid-1990s. Research on bullying among adults has still primarily been conducted in Europe and has not been as widely studied as school-based bullying. In addition, although bullying is generally conceptualized as peer-to-peer aggression, more recent studies have considered the possibility of bullying between adults and children (Twemlow, Fonagy, Sacco, & Brethour, 2006), as well as between siblings (Menesini, Camodeca, & Nocentini, 2010). These expansions on the concept of bullying naturally evoke questions about the definition of the term, the extent to which the concept is relevant and useful across the life course, the intersection of bullying with other related life experiences (for example, harassment, hazing, intimate partner violence), and the extent to which narrowly and broadly defined conceptualizations of bullying are useful for improving policy and practice. In this chapter, we first review definitions of bullying and discuss issues that arise in their application across the life course. Second, we describe measurement strategies and the relevance of these strategies across life course stages. Finally, we highlight examples of measures of bullying that practitioners might find useful in their work with children, adolescents, and adults.

DEFINITIONS OF BULLYING ACROSS THE LIFE COURSE

Efforts to define bullying have been guided by the foundational work of Dan Olweus, who is widely considered the pioneer of bullying research. He defined *bullying* as direct and indirect aggression that (a) is intentional, (b) is repeated, and (c) involves a power differential between the aggressor and the target (Olweus, 1978). These qualities were designed to distinguish bullying from the broader category of aggression, which might include playful behavior, one-time acts, and aggression between two equals. This definition is the most widely adopted one by both researchers and policymakers (Green, Felix, Sharkey, Furlong, & Kras, 2013); however, a number of questions have been raised about the effective use of this definition. For example, how is it determined whether there is a power differential between the aggressor and the target? Although this criterion was included to categorize cases in which the target cannot defend him- or herself, in reality it can be difficult to identify different sources of power in relationships, particularly when relationships are in flux.

There have been several recent efforts to expand and update the original definition proposed by Olweus, the most significant of which was initiated by the U.S. Centers for Disease Control and Prevention (CDC). In 2011, the CDC established a panel to develop a uniform definition of bullying, specifically for youth, with the goal of reducing discrepancies in methods for defining and measuring bullying. The CDC defines *bullying* as

> any *unwanted aggressive behavior(s)* by another youth or group of youth who are not siblings or current dating partners that involves an *observed or perceived power imbalance and is repeated multiple times or is highly likely to be repeated.* Bullying may inflict harm or distress on the targeted youth including physical, psychological, social, or educational *harm.* (Gladden et al., 2014, p. 7; emphasis in original)

This definition expands the subset of behaviors that can be defined as bullying to include a power differential that is either *observed or perceived* and aggression that is not actually repeated but is *highly likely to be repeated.* However, this definition of bullying is also restricted to relationships among youth (not adults) and specifies that those youth are not siblings or current dating partners. It is not yet clear how this revised definition is being integrated into and influencing practice, policy, and assessment.

Researchers defining bullying have further categorized aggression into direct (overt) and indirect (covert) forms (Gladden et al., 2014; Van der Wal, De Wit, & Hirasing, 2003). Bullying that is direct includes physical and verbal aggression (for example, hitting, shoving, name-calling) that transpires in the presence of the target. Indirect bullying is characterized as aggression that occurs through a third party (for example, exclusion, rumors, gossip) or when the target is not present and is typically designed to decrease social status.

Some studies have found that the experience of victimization by indirect bullying is more strongly associated with poor psychosocial outcomes than victimization that occurs by direct bullying (Van der Wal et al., 2003). Common types of bullying include physical, verbal, and relational aggression, destruction of theft or property, and cyberbullying (Breivik & Olweus, 2015; Crick & Grotpeter, 1995; Gladden et al., 2014).

At the core of debates about the definition of bullying are questions about the purpose and importance of clearly defining bullying. What began as a term developed to define a unique subset of victimization and aggression among children has steadily expanded into other contexts and relationships, such as workplace bullying and teenage dating violence. At what point is a term defined too broadly (or too narrowly) to be useful for research and practice? Is there a set of bullying experiences that are homogenous enough to be accurately classified under one name? Researchers studying bullying in either very young children or adulthood have needed to be particularly thoughtful about these definitional issues. In the following sections, we discuss critical definitional issues that arise in three life course stages: early childhood, school age, and adulthood.

Early Childhood

In early childhood, the primary challenges to defining bullying are determining the age at which it is possible for bullying to first emerge and identifying whether bullying can be effectively distinguished from other forms of aggression. Some studies have suggested that peer-directed aggression can be identified in children as young as 12 months old (for example, taking toys, pushing or hitting others; Hanish, Kochenderfer-Ladd, Fabes, Martin, & Denning, 2004). As children enter preschool, many experiment with cause and effect in relationships, trying out aggressive and exclusionary roles for brief periods of time. As such, involvement in peer aggression and victimization in this age group is commonly brief and unstable. Given the fluidity of social relationships among this age group and the continued development of core social skills, researchers are hesitant to label this behavior "bullying" (Hanish et al., 2004). In particular, because of yet-to-be-developed cognitive complexity, young children might not have sufficient perspective-taking skills to anticipate the emotional or physical harm caused by their behaviors or to sufficiently understand harm that they inflict. When this is the case, can behaviors be considered "intentional"?

Despite the definitional challenges, these early experiences of peer aggression can be significant and increase risk for later peer victimization (Godleski, Kamper, Ostrov, Hart, & Blakely-McClure, 2015), which suggests the importance of intervening in peer aggression in early childhood settings. Although not all aggressive young children will go on to behave as bullies, it seems reasonable to suggest that the majority of children who engage in bullying behaviors had some history of practice enacting aggression in preschool. Whether to call this behavior "bullying" or "pre-bullying" might depend on whether the term serves a useful purpose for an individual child or a school. Particularly in early childhood, it might be sufficient to address all aggressive behavior as a social learning opportunity, rather than labeling behavior as bullying specifically.

School Age

The majority of research on bullying has been conducted among school-age children and adolescents and has focused specifically on their experiences in the context of schools. In this age group, definitional issues have focused on the extent to which bullying overlaps with other forms of violence or victimization and the distinction among forms of bullying behaviors. Youth experiencing multiple forms of victimization (for example, bullying and victimization at home) have worse psychological and academic outcomes than those who have experienced only one type of victimization (for example, just bullying; Holt, Finkelhor, & Kantor, 2007). Furthermore, among those who have been bullied, having experienced multiple forms of bullying (for example, physical and verbal bullying) is associated with poorer outcomes (Bradshaw, Waasdorp, & Lindstrom Johnson, 2015). These results are reminiscent of the broader literature on polyvictimization that consistently finds that exposure to a greater number of adverse events is associated with worse psychosocial and health outcomes (Finkelhor et al., 2007). Findings suggest the importance of defining bullying as a distinct phenomenon from other forms of aggression, so that it can be considered in relation to other victimization experiences. Similarly, definitions of bullying will be most useful when they incorporate the broad range of possible manifestations of bullying. For example, when Crick and Grotpeter (1995) introduced the concept of relational aggression (that is, aggression designed to damage peer relationships, such as rumor spreading and social exclusion), research and policy on bullying expanded to incorporate the aggression that girls tend to engage in more frequently than physical aggression (Espelage & Swearer, 2003).

One form of bullying that has recently received particular attention is cyberbullying (that is, bullying that uses electronic forms of contact; Smith et al., 2008). Researchers have generally defined *cyberbullying* as a type of aggression that, just as other forms of bullying, requires repetition, intentionality, and a power differential (Menesini & Nocentini, 2009). However, some of these definitional qualities can be difficult to identify in the context of cyberbullying. For example, is a single message posted on social media considered repetition if it can be viewed indefinitely by a broad audience (Menesini & Nocentini, 2009)? Furthermore, defining the power differential in an online setting can be difficult. For example, some targets of cyberbullying do not know the identity of aggressors. Can a power difference be assumed?

Adulthood

Although the impact of bullying involvement into adulthood is well documented (for example, Copeland, Wolke, Angold, & Costello, 2013; Holt et al., 2014), the study of bullying behaviors among adults is relatively new. A primary question to address is whether bullying among adults is fundamentally the same concept as bullying among children or adolescents. The fact that some studies have found evidence of continuity in bullying involvement from childhood through emerging adulthood (for example, Chapell et al., 2005) suggests that there might be some stability in the experience. The literature on bullying in adults contends with similar difficulties in terms of defining bullying, differentiating it from other forms of aggression, and identifying effective measurement tools (Hershcovis, 2011). For example, research on workplace aggression identifies several constructs, including bullying, incivility, abusive supervision, social undermining, and interpersonal conflict (Hershcovis, 2011). Many of these terms can be subtly differentiated on the basis of certain features of their definition, such as perceived intent, intensity, frequency, the relationship between the aggressor and victim, whether the behavior is overt or covert, and the outcomes of the aggression (Hershcovis, 2011). Even within the field of workplace bullying per se, investigators have used definitions of bullying (Nielsen et al., 2009) that vary on the degree to which they include different forms of aggression, harassment, and incivility.

Some researchers of adult bullying based their definition on the commonly used Olweus definition (Nielsen, Matthiesen, & Einarsen, 2010), stressing the repetition, chronicity, and perceived power imbalance of bullying. In their description of bullying, Nielsen and associates (2010) specifically excluded behaviors that are sexual in nature in order to differentiate bullying from sexual harassment. They also suggest that bullying among adults is largely nonviolent, perhaps to differentiate it from assault. However, both of these exclusions are open to debate.

CONSIDERATIONS IN MEASURING BULLYING ACROSS THE LIFE COURSE

Approaches to defining bullying have direct implications for measurement. Given disagreement over definitions of bullying and distinctions in how bullying manifests at different ages, a range of methodological strategies have been used to identify bullying involvement. Ultimately, the selection of a measurement strategy and tool should be guided both by the purpose of the assessment and by the age of individuals involved in the assessment. In particular, bullying measures may be used for monitoring and safety planning, identifying individuals who might be involved in bullying relationships (as targets, aggressors, bystanders), and providing information to inform clinical intervention efforts. The nature and structure of each of these forms of assessment vary.

First, methods for monitoring and safety planning typically use brief self-report measures that can be completed easily by large numbers of people to obtain prevalence estimates and track changes in those estimates over time. For example, the Olweus Bullying Scale uses these response options: "it hasn't happened in the past couple of months," "it has only happened once or twice," "2 or 3 times a month," "about once a week," and "several times a week" (Breivik & Olweus, 2015), with a frequency of two to three times a month or more indicating bullying. Many schools conducting schoolwide assessments use anonymous assessment methods for this purpose because of the greater likelihood that students will provide honest responses. Self-report measures that directly ask students if they have been bullied are, however, reliant on self-perceptions of bullying-involved youth who might or might not perceive aggression to be "bullying" and identify themselves as an involved student (Sharkey et al., 2015). To address this issue, some surveys do not use the term "bullying" and instead ask students to indicate whether they have experienced aggression that is repeated, is intentional, and involves an imbalance of power (Felix et al., 2011). The vast majority of bullying measures have been developed and used for this purpose—to track trends in bullying and to evaluate the effectiveness of bullying prevention and intervention efforts (for example, does the prevalence of bullying decrease following the administration of a bullying prevention program?).

Second, in contrast, efforts to identify individuals involved in bullying will by necessity be nonanonymous. In addition to self-report measures, schools often use peer nominations for this purpose, which ask students to nominate classmates who match a definition or description of bullying involvement. Using peer nominations eliminates some concerns that self-report methods might be inaccurate when children are reluctant to identify themselves as involved in bullying (Cornell & Bandyopadhyay, 2010). However, studies indicate that peer nomination and self-report methods identify different groups of students as being involved in bullying. For example, in a study of middle school students, Branson and Cornell (2009) found that approximately 5 percent of students were categorized as bullies on the basis of their own self-report, whereas 11 percent were identified as bullying others when using peer nominations. Both self-report and peer nomination were significantly and independently associated with aggressive attitudes and negative school outcomes. These results suggest that using these measurement strategies in combination might be the most effective way to identify students at risk for poor outcomes (Cornell & Bandyopadhyay, 2010).

Finally, whereas self-report surveys typically assess whether an individual was involved in bullying, those in clinical practice may want more information to understand an individual's experience and design intervention efforts. Our team has developed a structured interview that is part of a multigating procedure to be used in schools to identify and respond to students involved in bullying. This interview, the California Bullying Victimization Scale—Gate 2 (Furlong, Felix, Sharkey, Green, & Tanigawa, 2006), is designed to be administered by mental health providers in a one-on-one interview with students previously identified by a schoolwide survey. Mental health providers ask about the frequency of different forms of victimization and then follow up with specific prompts (for example, was the aggression carried out "in a mean way"?) to determine intentionality and the presence of a power differential. Mental health providers also ask a series of questions about the impact of bullying on student well-being, reasons students believe they were involved, and help-seeking behaviors. This interview is designed to (a) facilitate a conversation in which mental health providers can assess bullying involvement and (b) obtain information that will provide actionable steps for interventions to address the bullying and respond to the impact of bullying on the student (Furlong et al., 2006).

Although we focus in this chapter on strategies for assessing bullying specifically, it is important to note that for intervention purposes, additional assessment of the impact of bullying, characteristics of individuals involved, and the broader landscape of those individuals' strengths and well-being is critical. As an example, for clinicians intervening with a person involved in bullying it might be less important to understand the details of the aggression experienced than to identify how that aggression influenced self-perception, mental health, social support, and intrapersonal strengths (Sharkey et al., 2015). Ideally, studies of bullying across the life course would include longitudinal measurement to identify the continuity of bullying and differential impact as individuals. However, with some exceptions (for example, Sourander, Helstelä, Helenius, & Piha, 2000), most longitudinal studies of bullying focus only on one life course stage (for example, childhood; Pellegrini & Long, 2002). Longitudinal studies are challenging to conduct, in part because measurement approaches vary by age. In the sections below, we describe critical issues in assessing bullying at different stages in the life course.

Early Childhood

Assessing bullying among young children presents a unique challenge. As described by Monks, Smith, and Swettenham (2003), the reliability of self-reported aggression among young children is questionable and researchers disagree about whether young children can effectively nominate involved peers. When asked directly, young children provide broader and less nuanced definitions of bullying than their older peers, often ignoring issues of repetition, intentionality, and power differential and focusing on the outcome of the action (Monks & Smith, 2010). For this reason, it can be particularly difficult to distinguish bullying from other forms of aggression and victimization among young children. Furthermore, although teachers can provide reliable reports, they might have limited knowledge of student involvement in aggression, particularly as targets (Monks et al., 2003).

Researchers of peer aggression in early childhood have therefore developed alternative strategies to study behaviors and identify involved students. For example, some studies have used live observers or audiovisual recordings to collect data on instances of physical and relational aggression in child interaction and then coded observations (Godleski et al., 2015). These methods provide the advantage of data collection in naturalistic settings and the opportunity to use trained and unbiased observers. However, they are limited in their documentation only to behaviors that are observable (for example, Godleski et al. found ratings of physical aggression more reliable than ratings of relational aggression). Furthermore, observational methods can be time-consuming and require prior training, making it more likely that they are used for research purposes than in practice. Collecting information from multiple informants (for example, observational methods, parent and teacher report, as well as student self-report) is particularly important because of measurement challenges among this age group. Ultimately, practitioners involved in assessing bullying behaviors among preschoolers need to determine whether it is useful to label behavior as "bullying" or if reported behavior is suggestive of children learning interpersonal and problem-solving approaches that could lead to bullying or other, less than optimal, developmental outcomes.

School Age

Bullying assessment among school-age children and adolescents has been widely studied, and a large number of tools are available that include self-report, peer nomination, and teacher–parent report (for recent reviews, see Cornell & Bandyopadhyay, 2010; Furlong et al., 2010). In 2011, the CDC published a compendium of assessment tools measuring bullying victimization, perpetration, and bystander experiences (Hamburger, Basile, & Vivolo, 2011). Debate continues on questions about the choice of informant source (Cornell & Bandyopadhyay, 2010), decisions about whether to use the term "bullying" in assessments (Felix et al., 2011), and how to effectively measure an imbalance of power (Green et al., 2013).

Similar to the issues in early childhood measurement, efforts to examine the extent to which measurement approaches consistently identify youth involved in bullying (Green et al., 2013) have generally found that different measurement tools identify different groups of bullying-involved youth. Without a "gold standard" measure of bullying, it is difficult to determine the relative validity of different approaches. A series of studies by Cornell and colleagues (for example, Cornell & Mehta, 2011) have used interviews conducted by school counselors to confirm the status of students identified as being involved in bullying by either self-report or peer nomination methods. Still, there is no clear way for schools and researchers to identify the "true" set of bullying-involved youth because (a) the nature of bullying is that of a dynamic peer relationship, (b) defining bullying is reliant on student perceptions (for example, of intentionality and power), and (c) many forms of bullying are not equally observable to all potential reporters (for example, students might not tell their parents about bullying). Studies seeking to determine the true population of bullying-involved youth, such as the approach by Cornell and colleagues, are critical to moving research and practice in bullying assessment forward.

Adulthood

Conceptual overlap and definitional issues also affect measurement of adult bullying for both victims and aggressors (Hershcovis, 2011). This can have an impact on prevalence rates (Nielsen et al., 2010) and associations with mental health, postsecondary success, and work-related outcomes (Hershcovis, 2011). There is a wide variety of methods to assess and understand the nature of bullying among adults, and the choice of method depends on the purpose (for a review, see Cowie, Naylor, Rivers, Smith, & Pereira, 2002). The purpose of assessment can include the goal of understanding a target's experience, establishing prevalence of bullying on a college campus or in a workplace, discerning whether culture and climate is conducive to bullying, elucidating interpersonal dynamics associated with bullying, and evaluating intervention success (Cowie et al., 2002). Self-report surveys are a popular, cost-effective, and efficient way to collect information from large groups of adults. Paralleling the discussion in the child literature, there is debate over the best self-report methods—questions about a series of behaviors experienced or a one-item question asking whether a person has ever been bullied (Nielsen et al., 2010). This one item can be given with or without a definition of bullying, with implications for prevalence rates. Nielsen and associates (2010) found the lowest prevalence rates for self-labeled bullying victimization when a definition was given and higher rates for self-labeling when no definition was presented. Thus, the choice of measure has implications to be considered.

IMPLICATIONS FOR PRACTICE AND POLICY

Practitioners are better prepared to meaningfully engage in bullying assessment when they are aware of the challenges researchers have faced in developing measures. In some ways, "bullying" is defined by the instrument that is used; hence, it is important to examine a specific measure's content and decide whether it is appropriate for its intended application, particularly when it is considered that a recent review identified 27 youth self-report bullying instruments alone (Vessey, Strout, DiFazio, & Walker, 2014). Having stated this, such nuanced critiques of bullying measurement are not as critical in applied practice because a practitioner's primary interest is to identify individuals who are experiencing social or psychological distress and to address their needs. However, measuring bullying specifically adds an increased awareness of the role that interpersonal power differences might play in aggression, recognizing that this type of victimization is associated with poor developmental outcomes across the life course (Ttofi, Farrington, & Lösel, 2012). Given the large number of bullying instruments available, we suggest the following four considerations:

1. Be familiar with a range of bullying assessments, keeping in mind the life course context and your assessment needs. The CDC compendium (Hamburger et al., 2011) is a readily available resource that is updated periodically. Other comprehensive reviews are provided for bullying and cyberbullying (Vessey et al., 2014; Vivolo-Kantor, Martell, Holland, & Westby, 2014), as well as workplace bullying (Galanaki & Papalexandris, 2013).
2. Recognize that the optimal use of bullying assessments is within the context of a coordinated approach that collects information to inform ongoing prevention and intervention efforts. Totten, Quigley, and Morgan (2004) provide a detailed best practice guide on how to administer and use bullying assessments within schools.
3. Be mindful of special populations, such as children with disabilities (for example, Fink, Deighton, Humphrey, & Wolpert, 2015), youth and adults who identify as lesbian, gay, bisexual, transgender, or queer (for example, Kosciw, Greytak, Palmer, & Boesen, 2014), and college-age young adults (Holt et al., 2014). Measurement strategies should be considered in the context of the population assessed and modified or supplemented to effectively address specific needs.

Table 1.1: Commonly Used Measures of Bullying

Resource	Grade or Age Group	Description and Access
Authoritative School Climate Survey (Cornell, 2014)	Grades 3–5 and 6–12	**Self-report:** This measure was developed to assess an Authoritative School Climate model. Psychometrically supported subscales address the prevalence of bullying, reactions to bullying, aggressive attitudes, and victim experiences. There is also a staff version. **Availability:** http://curry.virginia.edu/resource-library/authoritative-school-climate-survey-and-school-climate-bullying-survey
Bully Survey (Swearer & Cary, 2003)	Grades 3–12	**Self-report:** Section A assesses the type, frequency, location, perpetrator, and reasons that the student attributes to being victimized. Section B asks about bullying observed at school. Section C asks whether students have engaged in bullying others. Section D inquires about general attitudes toward bullying. Individual sections could be used for program evaluation and counseling purposes. Staff and parent versions are available. **Availability:** Centers for Disease Control and Prevention. http://www.cdc.gov/violenceprevention/pub/measuring_bullying.html An online administration system is published by H & H Publishing. http://www.bullysurvey.com/description_.html
Olweus Bullying Questionnaire (Solberg & Olweus, 2003)	Grades 3–12	**Self-report:** The Olweus Bullying Questionnaire is available with the Olweus Bullying Prevention Program. This is the most widely used bullying assessment worldwide. **Availability:** Hazelden Publishing. http://www.hazelden.org/itemquest/search.view?srch=Y&start=0&HAZLWEB_STORE_SELECTED=EDU&kw=olweus+bullying+questionnaire
PREVNet Bullying Evaluation and Strategies Tool (BEST; Pepler & Craig, n.d.)	Grades K–12	**Self-report:** The PREVNet (Promoting Relationships & Eliminating Violence Network) assessment system includes instruments for Grades 4–12. In addition, a K–3 version includes an audio component and interactive graphics so that the young child does not need to read the questions in order to respond. This comprehensive online system includes parents and teacher instruments and a principal reporting option. **Availability:** http://www.prevnet.ca/resources/assessment-tool

(continues)

Table 1.1: Commonly Used Measures of Bullying (*Continued*)

Resource	Grade or Age Group	Description and Access
Student School Survey (Williams & Guerra, 2007)	Ages 10–17	**Self-report:** This 70-item instrument assesses school climate. In particular, items 17–38 ask about bullying victimization, perpetrator, and bystander behaviors. Items 53–70 inquire about moral disengagement from aggression and peer victimization. **Availability:** Centers for Disease Control and Prevention. http://www.cdc.gov/violenceprevention/pub/measuring_bullying.html
Modified Peer Nomination Inventory (Perry, Kusel, & Perry, 1988)	Ages 10–14	**Peer nomination:** Within this instrument, 7 items measure aggression (e.g., "He makes fun of people") and 7 measure victimization (e.g., "He gets picked on"). Students identify classmates fitting each behavior. This source has been widely cited. **Availability:** Centers for Disease Control and Prevention. http://www.cdc.gov/violenceprevention/pub/measuring_bullying.html
Child Social Behavior Questionnaire (Warden, Cheyne, Christie, Fitzpatrick, & Reid, 2003)	Ages 9–10	**Peer nomination:** An interview style presents 24 items to students, asking them to indicate whether they have observed any of 8 randomly selected classmates engaging in behavior (e.g., "Pushing or tripping"). Parallel self-report and teacher report forms are available. **Availability:** Centers for Disease Control and Prevention. http://www.cdc.gov/violenceprevention/pub/measuring_bullying.html
Negative Acts Questionnaire—Revised (Einarsen, Hoel, & Notelaers, 2009)	Ages 18+	**Self-report:** This 22-item instrument asks employees to indicate exposure to work-related bullying (e.g., "Having your opinions ignored"), person-related bullying (e.g., "Persistent criticism of your errors"), and physically intimidating bullying (e.g., "Intimidating behaviours such as finger-pointing, invasion of personal space"). **Availability:** Bergen Bullying Research Group. http://www.uib.no/en/rg/bbrg/44045/naq

4. Advances in bullying assessment are ongoing. New assessment resources are available (for example, Morrow, Hubbard, Barhight, & Thomson, 2014), including innovative computer-aided assessments (for example, Verlinden et al., 2014). Finally, there is a range of measurement strategies used in bully instruments; however, the dominant methods are self-report (used in 85 percent of research) followed by peer nominations (12 percent; Vivolo-Kantor et al., 2014). Table 1.1 lists some of the best developed and most widely used self-report and peer nomination instruments.

Practitioners using surveys to evaluate the need for or success of bullying interventions should consider the advice of Olweus, the pioneer of bullying research and prevention:

> There currently exist several questionnaires that purport to measure bullying and may even be named "bullying questionnaires" but do not involve the three key criteria through a definition or by other means. . . . Such instruments are likely to measure aggression in general rather than the special subcategory of bullying. (Breivik & Olweus, 2015, p. 9)

Survey selection should be based on a match between item content and practical need, not the title of the instrument.

REFERENCES

Bradshaw, C. P., Waasdorp, T. E., & Lindstrom Johnson, S. (2015). Overlapping verbal, relational, physical, and electronic forms of bullying in adolescence: Influence of school context. *Journal of Clinical Child & Adolescent Psychology, 44*, 494–508. doi:10.1080/15374416.2014.893516

Branson, C., & Cornell, D. (2009). A comparison of self and peer reports in the assessment of middle school bullying. *Journal of Applied School Psychology, 25*, 5–27.

Breivik, K., & Olweus, D. (2015). An item response theory analysis of the Olweus Bullying Scale. *Aggressive Behavior, 41*(1), 1–13. doi:10.1002/AB.21571

Chapell, M. S., Hasselman, S. L., Kitchin, T., Lomon, S. N., MacIver, K. W., & Sarullo, P. L. (2005). Bullying in elementary school, high school, and college. *Adolescence, 41*(164), 633–648.

Copeland, W. E., Wolke, D., Angold, A., & Costello, E. J. (2013). Adult psychiatric outcomes of bullying and being bullied by peers in childhood and adolescence. *JAMA Psychiatry, 70*, 419–426. doi:10.1001/jamapsychiatry.2013.504

Cornell, D. G. (2014). *The Authoritative School Climate Survey and School Climate Bullying Survey: Description and research summary.* Charlottesville: University of Virginia, Virginia Youth Violence Project.

Cornell, D. G., & Bandyopadhyay, S. (2010). The assessment of bullying. In S. R. Jimerson, S. M. Swearer, & D. L. Espelage (Eds.), *Handbook of bullying in schools: An international perspective* (pp. 265–276). New York: Routledge.

Cornell, D., & Mehta, S. B. (2011). Counselor confirmation of middle school student self-reports of bullying victimization. *Professional School Counseling, 14*, 261–270. doi:10.5330/PSC.n.2011-14.261

Cowie, H., Naylor, P., Rivers, I., Smith, P. K., & Pereira, B. (2002). Measuring workplace bullying. *Aggression and Violent Behavior, 7*, 33–51. doi:10.1080/09585192.2012.725084

Crick, N. R., & Grotpeter, J. K. (1995). Relational aggression, gender, and social-psychological adjustment. *Child Development, 66*, 710–722. doi:10.1111/j.1467-8624.1995.tb00900.x

Einarsen, S., Hoel, H., & Noetelaers, G. (2009). Measuring exposure to bullying and harassment at work: Validity, factor structure and psychometric properties of the Negative Acts Questionnaire-Revised. *Work & Stress, 23*, 24–44. doi:10.1080/02678370902815673

Espelage, D. L., & Swearer, S. M. (2003). Research on school bullying and victimization: What have we learned and where do we go from here? *School Psychology Review, 32*, 365–383.

Felix, E. D., Sharkey, J. D., Green, J. G., Furlong, M. J., & Tanigawa, D. (2011). Getting precise and pragmatic about the assessment of bullying: The development of the California Bullying Victimization Scale. *Aggressive Behavior, 37*, 234–247. doi:10.1016/j.sbspro.2012.05.281

Fink, E., Deighton, J., Humphrey, N., & Wolpert, M. (2015). Assessing the bullying and victimisation experiences of children with special educational needs in mainstream schools: Development and validation of the Bullying Behaviour and Experience Scale. *Research in Developmental Disabilities, 36*, 611–619. doi:10.1016/j.ridd.2014.10.048

Finkelhor, D., Ormrod, R. K., Turner, H. A., Avery-Leaf, S., Cascardi, M., O'Leary, K. D., et al. (2007). Polyvictimization and trauma in a national longitudinal cohort. *Development and Psychopathology, 19*, 149–166. doi:10.1017/S0954579407070083

Finkelhor, D., Turner, H. A., & Hamby, S. (2012). Let's prevent peer victimization, not just bullying. *Child Abuse & Neglect, 36*, 271–274. doi:10.1016/j.chiabu.2012.10.006

Furlong, M. J., Felix, E. D., Sharkey, J. D., Green, J. G., & Tanigawa, D. (2006). *Development of a multi-gating bullying victimization assessment: Final report to the Hamilton Fish Institute.* Center for School-Based Youth Development, University of California, Santa Barbara.

Furlong, M. J., Sharkey, J. D., Felix, E., Tanigawa, D., & Green, J. (2010). Bullying assessment: A call for increased precision of self-reporting procedures. In S. R. Jimerson, S. M. Swearer, & D. L. Espelage (Eds.), *Handbook of bullying in schools: An international perspective* (pp. 329–346). New York: Routledge.

Galanaki, E., & Papalexandris, N. (2013). Measuring workplace bullying in organisations. *International Journal of Human Resource Management, 24*, 2107–2130. doi:10.1080/09585192.2012.725084

Gladden, R. M., Vivolo-Kantor, A. M., Hamburger, M. E., & Lumpkin, C. D. (2014). *Bullying surveillance among youths: Uniform definitions for public health and recommended data elements, version 1.0.* Atlanta: National Center for Injury Prevention and Control, Centers for Disease Control and Prevention; U.S. Department of Education.

Godleski, S. A., Kamper, K. E., Ostrov, J. M., Hart, E. J., & Blakely-McClure, S. J. (2015). Peer victimization and peer rejection during early childhood. *Journal of Clinical Child & Adolescent Psychology, 44*, 380–392. doi:10.1080/15374416.2014.940622

Green, J. G., Felix, E. D., Sharkey, J. D., Furlong, M. J., & Kras, J. E. (2013). Identifying bully victims: Definitional versus behavioral approaches. *Psychological Assessment, 25*, 651–657. doi:10.1037/a0031248

Hamburger, M. E., Basile, K. C., & Vivolo, A. M. (Eds.). (2011). *Measuring bullying victimization, perpetration, and bystander experiences: A compendium of assessment tools.* Atlanta: Centers for Disease Control and Prevention, National Center for Injury Prevention and Control, Division of Violence Prevention.

Hanish, L. D., Kochenderfer-Ladd, B., Fabes, R. A., Martin, C. L., & Denning, D. (2004). Bullying among young children: The influence of peers and teachers. In D. L. Espelage & S. M. Swearer (Eds.), *Bullying in American schools: A social-ecological perspective on prevention and intervention* (pp. 141–159). Mahwah, NJ: Erlbaum.

Hershcovis, M. S. (2011). "Incivility, social undermining, bullying . . . oh my!": A call to reconcile constructs within workplace aggression research. *Journal of Organizational Behavior, 32*, 499–519. doi:10.1002/job.689

Holt, M. K., Finkelhor, D., & Kantor, G. K. (2007). Multiple victimization experiences of urban elementary school students: Associations with psychosocial functioning and academic performance. *Child Abuse & Neglect, 31*, 503–515. doi:10.1016/j.chiabu.2006.12.006

Holt, M. K., Green, J. G., Reid, G., Dimeo, A., Espelage, D. L., Felix, E., et al. (2014). Associations between past bullying experiences and initial adjustment to college. *Journal of American College Health, 62,* 552–560. doi:10.1080/07448481.2014.947990

Kosciw, J. G., Greytak, E. A., Palmer, N. A., & Boesen, M. J. (2014). *The 2013 National School Climate Survey: The experiences of lesbian, gay, bisexual and transgender youth in our nation's schools.* New York: GLSEN. Retrieved from http://glsen.org/nscs

Menesini, E., Camodeca, M., & Nocentini, A. (2010). Bullying among siblings: The role of personality and relational variables. *British Journal of Developmental Psychology, 28,* 921–939. doi:10.1348/026151009X479402

Menesini, E., & Nocentini, A. (2009). Cyberbullying definition and measurement: Some critical considerations. *Journal of Psychology, 217,* 230–232. doi:10.1027/0044-3409.217 .4.230

Monks, C. P., & Smith, P. K. (2010). Definitions of bullying: Age differences in understanding of the term, and the role of experience. *British Journal of Developmental Psychology, 24,* 801–821. doi:10.1348/026151009X479402

Monks, C. P., Smith, P. K., & Swettenham, J. (2003). Aggressors, victims, and defenders in preschool: Peer, self-, and teacher reports. *Merrill-Palmer Quarterly, 49,* 453–469. doi:10.1353/mpq.2003.0024

Morrow, M. T., Hubbard, J. A., Barhight, L. J., & Thomson, A. K. (2014). Fifth-grade children's daily experiences of peer victimization and negative emotions: Moderating effects of sex and peer rejection. *Journal of Abnormal Child Psychology, 42,* 1089–1102. doi:10.1007/s10802-014-9870-0

Nielsen, M. B., Matthiesen, S. B., & Einarsen, S. (2010). The impact of methodological moderators on prevalence rates of workplace bullying. A meta-analysis. *Journal of Occupational and Organizational Psychology, 83,* 955–979. doi:10.1348/096317909X481256

Nielsen, M. B., Skogstad, A., Matthiesen, S. B., Glasø, L., Aasland, M. S., Notelaers, G., & Einarsen, S. (2009). Prevalence of workplace bullying in Norway: Comparisons across time and estimation methods. *European Journal of Work and Organizational Psychology, 18,* 81–101. doi:10.1080/13594320801969707

Olweus, D. (1978). *Aggression in the schools: Bullies and whipping boys.* Washington, DC: Hemisphere (Wiley).

Pellegrini, A. D., & Long, J. D. (2002). A longitudinal study of bullying, dominance, and victimization during the transition from primary school through secondary school. *British Journal of Developmental Psychology, 20*(2), 259–280. doi:10.1348/026151002166442

Pepler, D., & Craig, W. (n.d.). PREVNet's BEST (Bullying Evaluation and Strategies Tool) [Unpublished measure]. Retrieved from https://www.safeacceptingschools.ca/en/ resources/prevnets-best-bullying-evaluation-and-strategies-tool

Perry, D. G., Kusel, S. J., & Perry, L. C. (1988). Victims of peer aggression. *Developmental Psychology, 24,* 807–814. doi:10.1037/0012-1649.24.6.807

Sharkey, J. D., Ruderman, M. A., Mayworm, A., Green, J. G., Furlong, M. J., Rivera, N., & Purisch, L. (2015). Behavioral strengths and risks of bullied youth who accept versus deny the bullied victim label. *School Psychology Quarterly, 30*(1), 91–104. doi:10.1037/ spq0000077

Smith, P. K., Mahdavi, J., Carvalho, M., Fisher, S., Russell, S., & Tippett, N. (2008). Cyberbullying: Its nature and impact in secondary school pupils. *Journal of Child Psychology and Psychiatry, 49,* 376–385. doi:10.1111/j.1469-7610.2007.01846.x

Solberg, M. E., & Olweus, D. (2003). Prevalence estimation of school bullying with the Olweus Bully/Victim Questionnaire. *Aggressive Behavior, 29,* 239–268. doi:10.1002/ ab.10047

Sourander, A., Helstelä, L., Helenius, H., & Piha, J. (2000). Persistence of bullying from childhood to adolescence: A longitudinal 8-year follow-up study. *Child Abuse & Neglect, 24*, 873–881. doi:10.1016/S0145-2134(00)00146-0

Stuart-Cassel, V., Bell, A., & Springer, J. F. (2011). *Analysis of state bullying laws and policies.* Washington, DC: Office of Planning, Evaluation and Policy Development, U.S. Department of Education.

Swearer, S. M., & Cary, P. T. (2003). Perceptions and attitudes toward bullying in middle school youth: A developmental examination across the bully/victim continuum. *Journal of Applied School Psychology, 19*, 63–79. doi:10.1300/J008v19n02_05

Totten, M., Quigley, P., & Morgan, M. (2004). *Assessment toolkit for bullying, harassment and peer relations at school.* Ottawa, Canada: Canadian Public Health Association.

Ttofi, M. M., Farrington, D. P., & Lösel, F. (2012). School bullying as a predictor of violence later in life: A systematic review and meta-analysis of prospective longitudinal studies. *Aggression and Violent Behavior, 17*, 405–418. doi:10.1016/j.avb.2012.05.002

Twemlow, S. W., Fonagy, P., Sacco, F. C., & Brethour, J. R. (2006). Teachers who bully students: A hidden trauma. *International Journal of Social Psychiatry, 52*, 187–198. doi:10.1177/0020764006067234

Van der Wal, M. F., De Wit, C. A., & Hirasing, R. A. (2003). Psychosocial health among young victims and offenders of direct and indirect bullying. *Pediatrics, 111*, 1312–1317. doi:10.1542/peds.111.6.1312

Verlinden, M., Veenstra, R., Ringoot, A. P., Jansen, P. W., Raat, H., Hofman, A., et al. (2014). Detecting bullying in early elementary school with a computerized peer-nomination instrument. *Psychological Assessment, 26*, 628–641. doi:10.1037/a0035571

Vessey, J., Strout, T. D., DiFazio, R. L., & Walker, A. (2014). Measuring the youth bullying experience: A systematic review of the psychometric properties of available instruments. *Journal of School Health, 84*, 819–843. doi:10.1111/josh.12210

Vivolo-Kantor, A. M., Martell, B. N., Holland, K. M., & Westby, R. (2014). A systematic review and content analysis of bullying and cyber-bullying measurement strategies. *Aggression and Violent Behavior, 19*, 423–434. doi:10.1016/j.avb.2014.06.008

Warden, D., Cheyne, B., Christie, D., Fitzpatrick, H., & Reid, K. (2003). Assessing children's perceptions of prosocial and antisocial peer behaviour. *Educational Psychology, 23*, 547–567. doi:10.1080/0144341032000123796

Williams, K. R., & Guerra, N. G. (2007). Prevalence and predictors of Internet bullying. *Journal of Adolescent Health, 41*, s14–s21. doi:10.1016/j.jadohealth.2007.08.018

2

Developmental Roots of Bullying

Jamie M. Ostrov, Sarah J. Blakely-McClure, and
Kimberly E. Kamper-DeMarco

Understanding the onset, course, and developmental considerations associated with bullying is integral to any attempt to effectively intervene. In this chapter, we adopt a developmental psychopathology framework and recognize the importance of studying and intervening with both typical and atypical populations over time. We further appreciate the role of risk and protective factors across contexts. It is crucial for scholars and practitioners to understand the typical and normative occurrences of aggression in order to better inform our collective understanding of pathology (Sroufe, 2013). From an ecological perspective, we also acknowledge the importance of understanding bullying and peer victimization at multiple levels of influence across home, school, and community settings (Espelage & Swearer, 2003). Furthermore, we recognize that a truly developmental orientation implies that a uniform approach to assessment or intervention will not be efficacious and rather that modifications will be needed when working across different developmental periods and contexts. We examine these issues with regard to various forms of aggression and bullying subtypes (for example, physical and relational). Physical forms of aggression include the use of physical force to hurt others (for example, hitting, kicking, pushing) whereas relational forms use the removal or threat of the removal of the relationship as the means of harm (for example, social exclusion, friendship withdrawal threats such as "I won't be your friend anymore unless . . ."; Crick, Ostrov, & Kawabata, 2007). We adopt the Centers for Disease Control and Prevention (CDC) definition of bullying to include intentional aggressive behavior that occurs within the context of a power imbalance and is repeated or has the strong possibility of repetition (Gladden, Vivolo-Kantor, Hamburger, & Lumpkin, 2014).

Preparation of this manuscript was supported by a grant from the National Science Foundation (BCS-1450777) to Jamie M. Ostrov. Authors thank the UB Social Development Lab members and Dr. Stephanie A. Godleski (now at the Department of Psychology, Rochester Institute of Technology), who has influenced their thinking on the ideas reflected within this chapter. They are also grateful to the directors, teachers, parents, and children that participated in the research described in this chapter.

DEVELOPMENTAL CHANGES FROM CHILDHOOD THROUGH ADOLESCENCE

In this section we consider the developmental changes from childhood through adolescence, focusing on the manifestations of bullying and aggressive behavior during early childhood and preschool, middle childhood, and adolescence. We address issues of continuity (that is, stability) and change. We also consider special developmental considerations, such as children who are aggressive victims or engage in and receive high levels of aggression from peers. Finally, we argue that an ecological perspective is warranted, as the influence of various contexts including the home, school, community, and larger macro forces are apparent in the prediction of the onset and course of aggression from early childhood to adolescence (Hong & Espelage, 2012).

Early Childhood

Limited research exists on the development of bullying and bullying behaviors during early childhood. The available research has confirmed that bullying does exist during early childhood and both physical and relational forms of bullying may be reliably detected among young children. For example, in our laboratory, a preliminary investigation into this question demonstrated that both teachers and observers are able to reliably identify physical and relational bullying among three- to five-year-olds (Ostrov, Godleski, Kamper-DeMarco, Blakely-McClure, & Celenza, 2015). Given the relative lack of current published research on physical and relational bullying for these ages, we focus on the larger aggression literature for this developmental period. Aggression, particularly physical aggression behavior, is normative behavior commonly seen during the preschool period. However, around the age of four to five years, most children show a rapid decline in physically aggressive behavior (National Institute of Child Health and Human Development, Early Child Care Research Network, 2004). This decline is likely due to increased emotion regulation processes and increased expressive language capacity. It also corresponds to the transition to formal school settings and increased sanctions for physically aggressive behavior (especially for physical bullying). A key challenge when conducting observational assessments of physically aggressive behavior among younger children (for example, Ostrov & Keating, 2004) is to rule out rough-and-tumble play (for example, games of chase or wrestling) and social dominance behaviors (for example, "I am the leader, follow me"). Rough-and-tumble play and social dominance or assertion behaviors may promote social competence and are not in keeping with the definition of aggression (Ostrov, Pilat, & Crick, 2006). Moreover, it is a challenge to infer "intent" to harm, and this component is pivotal to the definition of aggression and bullying subtypes (Gladden et al., 2014). These issues have important implications for how we intervene or do not intervene to address behavior among our youngest children.

Currently, the earliest documented onset for relational forms of aggression is 30 months. Given their limited cognitive and social-cognitive capacities, it is unlikely that children younger than this age will display these behaviors (Crick et al., 2006). In early childhood, much like physical aggression, relational aggression is based on in-the-moment interactions. The identity of the perpetrator is typically known and the behaviors are displayed in a direct fashion (Crick et al., 2007). Finally, physical and relational aggressive behaviors are associated with social-psychological adjustment problems (for example, peer rejection, conduct problems) in preschool (for example, Godleski, Kamper, Ostrov, Hart, & Blakely-McClure, 2015).

Scholars have also begun to make the distinction between the forms (for example, physical and relational) and the functions (for example, proactive and reactive) of aggression in early childhood. Proactive aggression is goal oriented and premeditated; whereas reactive aggression is impulsive, retaliatory, and often hostile (Ostrov, Murray-Close, Godleski, & Hart, 2013). There appear to be differential pathways and correlates associated with proactive and reactive physical as well as proactive and reactive relational aggression (for example, Ostrov et al., 2013). These findings have clear implications for intervention efforts. For example, proactive relational aggression uniquely predicted increases in emotion regulation skills, whereas reactive relational aggression was associated with decreases in emotion regulation skills over an academic year. This example of divergent outcomes for proactive and reactive relational aggression suggests that "one size fits all" intervention approaches will not be effective (Ostrov et al., 2013).

Middle Childhood

In middle childhood, physical forms of aggression and bullying are less normative and therefore, if occurring at high levels, may be indicative of more serious problems. In particular, a child who has consistently engaged in high levels of physical aggression from early childhood through middle childhood (and beyond) may be on a "life course–persistent" aggressive pathway, which is arguably more difficult to treat (Moffitt, 1993). With regard to functions of aggression, proactive aggressive behaviors are often associated with indicators of personality pathology in middle childhood and adolescence. For example, children and adolescents high on proactive aggression are often high on psychopathy or callous-unemotional traits, an effect present for both physical and relational forms of proactive aggression (for example, Marsee & Frick, 2007). It is also the case that physical bullying has been uniquely associated with proactive aggression during this developmental period (Prinstein & Cillessen, 2003), and more attention to this link is warranted.

Relational aggression also changes during middle childhood to become more covert and indirect and likely involves other peers. Relational aggression moves from friendship withdrawal threats and social exclusion in early childhood to malicious lies, gossip, and rumor spreading in middle childhood and adolescence (Crick et al., 2007). Relational bullying likely increases during middle childhood and adolescence and is associated with serious adjustment and mental health problems (Bradshaw, Waasdorp, & Lindstrom Johnson, 2015; Crick et al., 2007; Pepler, Jiang, Craig, & Connolly, 2008). However, given that relational aggression may occur among equal status peers with the same levels of power (for example, Grotpeter & Crick, 1996), it is important to ensure that a power differential exists within the friendship dyad or peer group before considering a case of relational aggression as bullying behavior.

Adolescence

In adolescence, a key developmental task is the formation of romantic relationships, and it is interesting to note that this may be one of the first times that boys begin to learn about relational forms of aggression and bullying (Crick et al., 2007). Prior to adolescence, relatively strict gender segregation patterns are in place that may insulate boys from knowledge of these forms of aggression (Crick et al., 2007). By adolescence, relational aggression and bullying is relatively covert and typically involves both online and offline behaviors (Low & Espelage, 2013).

As previously stated, adolescents who continue to engage in physical bullying and have consistently done so at high levels in prior developmental periods are likely on a maladaptive trajectory with a poor prognosis (Moffitt, 1993). However, it is common to see a new pathway emerge during adolescence that represents those individuals who previously did not engage in antisocial behavior but begin to do so in adolescence (that is, "adolescent limited"). These individuals will likely return to an adaptive pathway after adolescence unless they experience "snares" during this period of development (for example, incarceration, pregnancy; Moffitt, 1993). Clinicians must be mindful of the prior developmental history of any adolescent whom they are assessing and treating. Knowing where a child has come from should inform diagnosis and treatment decisions and will probabilistically predict the child's prognosis (Sroufe, 2013).

Stability

Past developmental research has demonstrated evidence for the stability of physical and relational aggression as well as peer victimization (Crick et al., 2007). In addition, bullying status and peer harassment within the context of bullying is often stable across time (for example, Camodeca, Goossens, Meerum, & Schuengel, 2002). Despite the continuity that we typically see with regard to bullying, it is also possible to predict lawful discontinuity or clear changes across time. Often as children develop social-cognitive skills such as language, empathy, and perspective taking, we see decreases in aggressive behaviors. However, these decreases may occur only for those individuals who are engaging in primarily reactive forms of aggression. The proactive aggressor or bully may actually improve his or her capacity to harm others with enhancements in perspective taking or empathy and thus might account for documented iatrogenic effects of some bullying prevention efforts in the field.

Special Considerations

A special consideration for scholars and practitioners is the case of the aggressive victim or provocative victim. These children or adolescents engage in high levels of aggression and receive high levels of peer victimization (Schwartz, 2000). We know that these individuals often present the greatest clinical risk and are likely in need of intervention. These children and adolescents are most likely displaying reactive aggression, and they may have hostile attribution biases or a hostile view of the world that increases their tendency to view even ambiguous provocation situations with hostile intent (Bailey & Ostrov, 2008). From an intervention perspective, it may be effective to address the social-cognitive biases of these individuals in order to reduce their aggressive behavior (Leff et al., 2009). Despite the existence of this special group of aggressors, it is the case that most individuals are either physical or relational perpetrators (Crick & Grotpeter, 1995). In addition, most children are victimized with only one form of aggression (Crick & Bigbee, 1998). However, "double aggressors" (that is, high on both physical and relational aggression) or "double victims" (that is, high on both physical and relational victimization) may be at increased risk as well, and we need to give more theoretical and empirical attention to these special cases (see Prinstein, Boergers, & Vernberg, 2001). Finally, we need to know much more about polyvictimization (that is, being the victim of multiple types of victimization and often in multiple contexts; Finkelhor, Ormrod, & Turner, 2007) and links between multiple forms of victimization (for example, maltreatment, sibling abuse, teenage dating violence, bullying) and prospective links with early forms of aggression and peer victimization.

EARLY EXPERIENCES IN THE HOME AND SCHOOL ENVIRONMENT THAT MAY INCREASE RISK

Despite a plethora of risk and protective factors implicated in the development of bullying and peer victimization, there are several documented early experiences specifically in the home and school context that may place children at greater risk for bullying and victimization. These risk factors at home include child temperament, parent–child interactions, and the child's neighborhood (for example, Cook, Williams, Guerra, Kim, & Sadek, 2010; Hansen, Steenberg, Palic, & Elklit, 2012; Hong & Espelage, 2012). At school these risk factors include friendship status, peer rejection, peer victimization, and school climate factors (for example, Demaray & Malecki, 2003; Hong & Espelage, 2012; Monks et al., 2009).

Influence of Early Experiences in the Home

One early risk factor at home is a child's temperament, which is presumed to have a biological component. Temperament is a child's general way of behaving in the world across multiple contexts (Kagan, 1997). There are mixed findings about which temperament traits might lead to a child becoming a bully or a victim (Hansen et al., 2012). Many researchers have identified emotional dysregulation as a risk factor for both bullying and victimization (for example, Bacchini, Affuso, & Trotta, 2008; Cook et al., 2010). These emotion regulation problems may often be expressed through negative affect (that is, anger and sadness; Bacchini et al., 2008), which may be a risk factor for bullying behavior (Bosworth, Espelage, & Simon, 1999).

Beyond the individual child, risk factors for bullying and victimization can be identified within the parent–child relationship. Generally, those families high in conflict have been identified as at risk for learning bullying behaviors (Pellegrini, 1998; Pepler et al., 2008). Children may be experiencing hostile and conflict-prone communication styles and behavior from their interactions with parents, which they then use in interactions with those outside of their family. Parents' use of aggression and other power assertive techniques to manage child behavior has also been linked with increased risk of bullying (Pellegrini, 1998) because parents convey the message that aggression is acceptable and effective (Bandura, 1973; Schwartz, Dodge, Pettit, & Bates, 1997).

Parent–child interactions also have an impact on the risk for children to become victims of bullying. Parenting styles that are categorized as negative (for example, abuse and neglect, maladaptive parenting, including inconsistent discipline styles and overprotection) have been associated with an increased risk of becoming a victim or an aggressive victim (Bowers, Smith, & Binney, 1994; Lereya, Samara, & Wolke, 2013). Lack of parental involvement and high levels of criticism have also been linked to increased risk for children and youth to be victimized (Holt, Kantor, & Finkelhor, 2009). Overprotective mothers are also a risk factor for victimization with suggestions that this behavior might hinder autonomy for boys and limit connectedness for girls, placing them at greater risk for victimization (Hong & Espelage, 2012). Overall, there are many parent–child factors that increase or decrease the risk of peer victimization.

The attachment relationship is fundamentally linked to parenting and the role it plays in a child's interactions with others. *Attachment* can be defined as a lasting emotional link between infant and caregiver, with the type of attachment developed between an infant and caregiver able to shape future behavior and social interactions (Ainsworth & Bowlby, 1991). A secure or positive attachment is demonstrated when an infant has confidence in the caregiver's availability and ability to respond to the infant's needs. Children with secure attachments use the caregiver as a secure base in which they may then explore their environment. A secure attachment with parents has been found to protect against bullying and victimization (Hong & Espelage, 2012); however, a secure attachment is not always associated with positive outcomes. Secure attachment with a problematic parent (for example, an alcoholic parent) has been found to be associated with negative outcomes such as bullying (Eiden et al., 2010) because of learned maladaptive patterns of behavior and communication.

A child's neighborhood also plays an important role in understanding risk and protective factors for bullying and victimization. In general, low socioeconomic status is a known risk factor for aggressive behavior (Hong & Espelage, 2012). Youth living in impoverished circumstances are more likely to be exposed to violence and to hold more positive attitudes toward violence and aggression (Hong & Espelage, 2012). In general, youth who experience residential instability and those residing in unsafe neighborhoods are likely to be at increased risk of bullying and victimization (Foster & Brooks-Gunn, 2013). Bowes and colleagues (2009) posited that exposure to hostile situations, such as witnessing neighborhood violence, may provide children with models of bullying, which they then reproduce (Bowes et al., 2009). In sum, neighborhood and community factors are important and should be considered when trying to understand the development of bullying and victimization.

Influence of Early Experiences in the School

Risk factors at school for bullying and victimization occur within the context of peer interactions as well as within the larger school climate. Peer rejection (that is, feelings of dislike by peers) has repeatedly been linked to bullying behavior and victimization (Hong & Espelage, 2012). Individuals who are identified as aggressive have been found to be unpopular with other children and tend to be the most rejected members of their peer group (Bosworth et al., 1999). This suggests that not only are rejected peers more likely to be bullies but that their aggressive behaviors may also increase future peer rejection. Children and youth who are rejected are also at greater risk for victimization. Godleski et al. (2015) found that peer rejection predicted increases in relational victimization in early childhood. Furthermore, low levels of acceptance by peers and lack of social support increase the risk of victimization (Demaray & Malecki, 2003).

Children and youth who are victimized are subsequently at risk for displaying future aggressive behaviors. Ostrov (2010) found that experiencing victimization predicted later (that is, at the end of an academic year) aggressive behavior. Previous research has reported that victimized children often imitate those who bullied them (Pellegrini, 1998). Other researchers have also found that victims often display hostile social interactions such as bullying others (Perry, Kusel, & Perry, 1988; Schwartz et al., 1997). Thus, it may be that victims are learning bullying behaviors from their bullies and subsequently displaying similar behaviors.

There are large variations from school to school in the prevalence of bullying. School climate and school connectedness are major considerations in understanding the risks of bullying and victimization (Monks et al., 2009). School connectedness and attachment are associated with risk for bullying and victimization. Boulton and colleagues (2012) identified low school connectedness as an important risk factor for both bullying and victimization. In addition, a poor-quality teacher–child relationship is also associated with increased risk for bullying and victimization (Boulton et al., 2012). Overall, less connectedness to the school and teachers increases the likelihood of bullying and victimization.

In relation to school climate, shared beliefs and attitudes supporting or tolerating bullying are also associated with increased rates of bullying. Disorderly or disorganized schools and classrooms, where this tolerance or support often exists, have higher rates of bullying (Bradshaw et al., 2015; Hong & Espelage, 2012). These disorderly and disorganized schools are perceived as unsafe; they are typically less supportive and less supervised, which increases the frequency of bullying (Bradshaw, Sawyer, & O'Brennan, 2009). The lower level of adult monitoring may also promote peer victimization (Hong & Espelage, 2012). The research seems to clearly demonstrate a number of risk factors across both the home and school contexts, highlighting areas of focus for interventionists.

CONCLUSIONS AND IMPLICATIONS

Considering the aforementioned risk factors, there are clear developmental implications for intervention. Frequently used family-based interventions focus on the parents and their ability to teach the child and shape his or her behaviors (Orpinas & Horne, 2006). These programs also lead to enhancements in the parent–child relationship, a known risk factor for bullying. Specific strategies include promoting positive behaviors rather than concentrating solely on decreasing the negative. Parents learn to model appropriate behaviors and provide instruction for problem solving. Especially during early and middle childhood, parents are believed to be one of the strongest influences on a child. Thus, these strategies are thought to promote the use of positive behaviors in the place of negative behaviors in the home, leading to generalization in school and beyond (Orpinas & Horne, 2006). From a developmental psychopathology framework, we believe that earlier intervention will more likely establish long-lasting effects (Sroufe, 2013). For example, parent–child interaction therapy, an intervention focused on decreasing disruptive behaviors like bullying, is suggested during early childhood (Hembree-Kigin & McNeil, 1995). These early childhood family interventions address risk factors such as the parent–child relationship and harsh or dysfunctional parenting styles, which are more likely to become more and more entrenched as development progresses. It is important to note that family interventions across development have been shown to be effective in decreasing bullying behavior (Healy & Sanders, 2014; Orpinas & Horne, 2006); however, researchers often focus on where the bullying behavior with peers occurs, which is frequently at school.

As previously highlighted, bullying behavior is an interpersonal process, rather than one focused solely on the bully (Pepler, 2006). School-based interventions have increasingly addressed the peer relations of both bullies and victims (Ttofi & Farrington, 2011). We believe that a school-based approach would likely have positive effects across all areas of development. As children progress through school, peers and the school climate have a major influence on their development. This influence or socialization can facilitate the promotion of positive behaviors but could also increase negative behaviors. Numerous school-based intervention programs have been implemented in order to address problems with bullying by capitalizing on these influences and promoting positive change.

The KiVa intervention based in Finland demonstrates the effectiveness of an intervention program implemented not just within certain schools but also across an entire nation (Garadeau, Lee, & Salmivalli, 2014), indicating the growing importance of broad-based intervention. In a 2011 review, Ttofi and Farrington examined the effectiveness of over 40 different intervention efforts. The authors found that the more intensive the intervention, the more successful it was at reducing bullying behavior (Ttofi & Farrington, 2011). When parent and teacher strategies were implemented that centered on discipline for bullying behavior and parents were informed and involved with their children's behaviors at school, interventions were more effective. Similarly, those programs emphasizing supervision and inclusion among peers also showed higher success rates. Thus, when treating bullying behaviors and their wide-ranging and long-lasting effects, it appears that the most intensive treatments that address multiple contexts are most likely to show wide-ranging and long-lasting change.

In conclusion, we argue that developmental and ecological perspectives are critical for effective understanding, identification, and treatment of bullying problems among children and adolescents. An emphasis on the different forms of bullying and the various manifestations of bullying behavior across development will assist clinicians with their challenging work to tailor their intervention efforts to more effectively facilitate positive change.

REFERENCES

Ainsworth, M.D.S., & Bowlby, J. (1991). An ethological approach to personality development. *American Psychologist, 46*, 333–341.

Bacchini, D., Affuso, G., & Trotta, T. (2008). Temperament, ADHD and peer relations among schoolchildren: The mediating role of school bullying. *Aggressive Behavior, 34*, 447–459. doi:10.1002/ab.20271

Bailey, C. A., & Ostrov, J. M. (2008). Differentiating forms and functions of aggression in emerging adults: Associations with hostile attribution biases and normative beliefs. *Journal of Youth and Adolescence, 37*, 713–722. doi:10.1007/s10964-007-9211-5

Bandura, A. (1973). *Aggression: A social learning analysis.* Englewood Cliffs, NJ: Prentice Hall.

Bosworth, K., Espelage, D. L., & Simon, T. R. (1999). Factors associated with bullying behavior in middle school students. *Journal of Early Adolescence, 19*, 341–362. doi:10.1177/0272431699019003003

Boulton, M., Woodmansey, H., Williams, E., Spells, R., Nicholas, B., Laxton, E., & Duke, E. (2012). Associations between peer bullying and classroom concentration: Evidence for mediation by perceived personal safety and relationship with teacher. *Educational Psychology, 32*, 277–294. doi:10.1080/01443410.2011.648903

Bowers, L., Smith, P. K., & Binney, V. (1994). Perceived family relationships of bullies, victims and bully/victims in middle childhood. *Journal of Social and Personal Relationships, 11*, 215–232. doi:10.1177/0265407594112004

Bowes, L., Arseneault, L., Maughan, B., Taylor, A., Caspi, A., & Moffitt, T. E. (2009). School, neighborhood, and family factors are associated with children's bullying involvement: A nationally representative longitudinal study. *Journal of the American Academy of Child & Adolescent Psychiatry, 48*, 545–553. doi:10.1097/CHI.0b013e31819cb017

Bradshaw, C. P., Sawyer, A. L., & O'Brennan, L. M. (2009). A social disorganization perspective on bullying-related attitudes and behaviors: The influence of school context. *American Journal of Community Psychology, 43*, 204–220. doi:10.1007/s10464-9240-1

Bradshaw, C. P., Waasdorp, T., & Lindstrom Johnson, S. (2015). Examining the overlap between verbal, relational, physical, and electronic bullying: The influence of school context. *Journal of Clinical Child and Adolescent Psychology, 44*, 494–508. doi:10.1080/15374416.2014.893516

Camodeca, M., Goossens, F. A., Meerum, T. M., & Schuengel, C. (2002). Bullying and victimization among school-age children: Stability and links to proactive and reactive aggression. *Social Development, 11*, 332–345. doi:10.1111/1467-9507.00203

Cook, C. R., Williams, K. R., Guerra, N. G., Kim, T. E., & Sadek, S. (2010). Predictors of bullying and victimization in childhood and adolescence: A meta-analytic investigation. *School Psychology Quarterly, 25*(2), 65–83. doi:10.1037/a0020149

Crick, N. R., & Bigbee, M. A. (1998). Relational and overt forms of peer victimization: A multiinformant approach. *Journal of Consulting and Clinical Psychology, 66*, 337–347.

Crick, N. R., & Grotpeter, J. K. (1995). Relational aggression, gender, and social-psychological adjustment. *Child Development, 66*(3), 710–722. doi:10.2307/1131945

Crick, N. R., Ostrov, J. M., Burr, J. E., Cullerton-Sen, C., Jansen-Yeh, E., & Ralston, P. (2006). A longitudinal study of relational and physical aggression in preschool. *Journal of Applied Developmental Psychology, 27*(3), 254–268. doi:10.1016/j.appdev.2006.02.006

Crick, N. R., Ostrov, J. M., & Kawabata, Y. (2007). Relational aggression and gender: An overview. In D. J. Flannery, A. T. Vazsonyi, & I. D. Waldman (Eds.), *The Cambridge handbook of violent behavior and aggression* (pp. 245–259). New York: Cambridge University Press.

Demaray, K. M., & Malecki, K. C. (2003). Perceptions of the frequency and importance of social support by students classified as victims, bullies, and bully/victims in an urban middle school. *School Psychology Review, 32*, 471–489.

Eiden, R. D., Ostrov, J. M., Colder, C. R., Leonard, K. E., Edwards, E. P., & Orrange-Torchia, T. (2010). Parent alcohol problems and peer bullying and victimization: Child gender and infant attachment security as moderators. *Journal of Clinical Child and Adolescent Psychology, 39*, 341–350. doi:10.1080/15374411003691768

Espelage, D. L., & Swearer, S. M. (2003). Research on school bullying and victimization: What have we learned and where do we go from here? *School Psychology Review, 32*, 365–383.

Finkelhor, D., Ormrod, R. K., & Turner, H. A. (2007). Polyvictimization and trauma in a national longitudinal cohort. *Development and Psychopathology, 19*, 149–166. doi:10.1017/S0954579407070083

Foster, H., & Brooks-Gunn, J. (2013). Neighborhood, family and individual influences on school physical victimization. *Journal of Youth and Adolescence, 42*, 1596–1610. doi:10.1007/s10964-012-9890-4

Garadeau, C. F., Lee, I. A., & Salmivalli, C. (2014). Inequality matters: Classroom status hierarchy and adolescents' bullying. *Journal of Youth and Adolescence, 43*, 1123–1133. doi:10.1007/s10964-013-0040-4

Gladden, R. M., Vivolo-Kantor, A. M., Hamburger, M. E., & Lumpkin, C. D. (2014). *Bullying surveillance among youths: Uniform definitions for public health and recommended data elements, version 1.0.* Atlanta: National Center for Injury Prevention and Control, Centers for Disease Control and Prevention; U.S. Department of Education.

Godleski, S. A., Kamper, K. E., Ostrov, J. M., Hart, E. J., & Blakely-McClure, S. J. (2015). Peer victimization and peer rejection during early childhood. *Journal of Clinical Child and Adolescent Psychology, 44*, 380–392. doi:10.1080/15374416.2014.940622

Grotpeter, J. K., & Crick, N. R. (1996). Relational aggression, overt aggression, and friendship. *Child Development, 67*, 2328–2338. doi:10.2307/1131626

Hansen, T. B., Steenberg, L. M., Palic, S., & Elklit, A. (2012). A review of psychological factors related to bullying victimization in schools. *Aggression and Violent Behavior, 17,* 383–387. doi:10.1016/j.avb.2012.03.008

Healy, K. L., & Sanders, M. R. (2014). Randomized controlled trial of a family intervention for children bullied by peers. *Behavior Therapy, 45,* 760–777. doi:10.1016/j.beth.2014.06.001

Hembree-Kigin, T. L., & McNeil, C. B. (1995). *Parent-child interaction therapy.* New York: Plenum Press.

Holt, M. K., Kantor, G. K., & Finkelhor, D. (2009). Parent/child concordance about bullying involvement and family characteristics related to bullying and peer victimization. *Journal of School Violence, 8*(1), 42–63. doi:10.1080/15388220802067813

Hong, J. S., & Espelage, D. L. (2012). A review of research on bullying and peer victimization in school: An ecological systems analysis. *Aggression and Violent Behavior, 17,* 331–322. doi:10.1016/j.avb.2012.03.003

Kagan, J. (1997). Temperament and the reactions to unfamiliarity. *Child Development, 68,* 139–143.

Leff, S. S., Gullan, R. L., Paskewich, B. S., Abdul-Kabir, S., Jawad, A. F., Grossman, M., et al. (2009). An initial evaluation of a culturally-adapted social problem solving and relational aggression prevention program for urban African American relationally aggressive girls. *Journal of Prevention and Intervention in the Community, 37*(4), 260–274. doi:10.1080/10852350903196274

Lereya, S. T., Samara, M., & Wolke, D. (2013). Parenting behavior and the risk of becoming a victim and a bully/victim: A meta-analysis study. *Child Abuse & Neglect, 37,* 1091–1108. doi:10.1016/j.chiabu.2013.03.001

Low, S., & Espelage, D. (2013). Differentiating cyber bullying perpetration from non-physical bullying: Commonalities across race, individual, and family predictors. *Psychology of Violence, 3,* 39–52. doi:10.1037/a0030308

Marsee, M. A., & Frick, P. J. (2007). Exploring the cognitive and emotional correlates to proactive and reactive aggression in a sample of detained girls. *Journal of Abnormal Child Psychology, 35,* 969–981. doi:10.1007/s10802-007-9147-y

Moffitt, T. E. (1993). Adolescence-limited and life-course persistent antisocial behavior: A developmental taxonomy. *Psychological Review, 100,* 674–701.

Monks, C. P., Smith, P. K., Naylor, P., Barter, C., Ireland, J. L., & Coyne, I. (2009). Bullying in different contexts: Commonalities, differences and the role of theory. *Aggression and Violent Behavior, 14,* 146–156. doi:10.1016/j.avb.2009.01.004

National Institute of Child Health and Human Development, Early Child Care Research Network. (2004). Trajectories of physical aggression from toddlerhood to middle childhood. *Monographs of the Society for Research in Child Development, 69*(4), 1–146.

Orpinas, P., & Horne, A. M. (2006). Persistent bullying: Family interventions. In *Bullying prevention: Creating a positive school climate and developing social competence* (pp. 203–231). Washington, DC: American Psychological Association. doi:10.1037/11330-009

Ostrov, J. M. (2010). Prospective associations between peer victimization and aggression. *Child Development, 81,* 1670–1677. doi:10.1111/j.1467-8624.2010.01501.x

Ostrov, J. M., Godleski, S. A., Kamper-DeMarco, K. E., Blakely-McClure, S. J., & Celenza, L. (2015). Replication and extension of the early childhood friendship project: Effects on physical and relational bullying. *School Psychology Review, 44,* 445–463.

Ostrov, J. M., & Keating, C. F. (2004). Gender differences in preschool aggression during free play and structured interactions: An observational study. *Social Development, 13*(2), 255–277. doi:10.1111/j.1467-9507.2004.000266.x

Ostrov, J. M., Murray-Close, D., Godleski, S. A., & Hart, E. J. (2013). Prospective associations between forms and functions of aggression and social and affective processes during early childhood. *Journal of Experimental Child Psychology, 116*, 19–36. doi:10.1016/j.jecp.2012.12.009

Ostrov, J. M., Pilat, M. M., & Crick, N. R. (2006). Assertion strategies and aggression during early childhood: A short-term longitudinal study. *Early Childhood Research Quarterly, 21*, 403–416. doi:10.1016/j.ecresq.2006.10.001

Pellegrini, A. D. (1998). Bullies and victims in school: A review and call for research. *Journal of Applied Developmental Psychology, 19*(2), 165–176. doi:10.1016/S0193-3973(99)80034-3

Pepler, D. J. (2006). Bullying interventions: A binocular perspective. *Journal of the Canadian Academy of Child and Adolescent Psychiatry, 15*(1), 16–20.

Pepler, D., Jiang, D., Craig, W., & Connolly, J. (2008). Developmental trajectories of bullying and associated factors. *Child Development, 79*, 325–338. doi:10.1111/j.1467-8624.2007.01128.x

Perry, D. G., Kusel, S. J., & Perry, L. C. (1988). Victims of peer aggression. *Developmental Psychology, 24*, 807–814.

Prinstein, M. J., Boergers, J., & Vernberg, E. M. (2001). Overt and relational aggression in adolescents: Social-psychological adjustment of aggressors and victims. *Journal of Clinical Child Psychology, 30*, 479–491. doi:10.1207/S15374424JCCP3004

Prinstein, M. J., & Cillessen, A.H.N. (2003). Forms and functions of adolescent peer aggression associated with high levels of peer status. *Merrill-Palmer Quarterly, 49*, 310–342. doi:10.1353/mpq.2003.0015

Schwartz, D. (2000). Subtypes of victims and aggressors in children's peer groups. *Journal of Abnormal Child Psychology, 28*, 181–192.

Schwartz, D., Dodge, K. A., Pettit, G. S., & Bates, J. E. (1997). The early socialization of aggressive victims of bullying. *Child Development, 68*, 665–675.

Sroufe, L. A. (2013). The promise of developmental psychopathology: Past and present. *Development and Psychopathology, 25*, 1215–1224. doi:10.1017/S0954579413000576

Ttofi, M. M., & Farrington, D. P. (2011). Effectiveness of school-based programs to reduce bullying: A systematic and meta-analytic review. *Journal of Experimental Criminology, 7*(1), 27–56. doi:10.1007/s11292-010-9109-1

Part II
Potential Impacts of Bullying

3

The Neurobiology of Peer Victimization: Longitudinal Links to Health, Genetic Risk, and Epigenetic Mechanisms

Tracy Vaillancourt, Carleigh Sanderson, Paul Arnold, and Patricia McDougall

Recent research on peer victimization has documented the negative correlates and consequences of bullying, especially for those who are victimized. For example, relative to nonvictimized youth, those who are bullied by peers report lower self-esteem and self-worth and report that they are lonelier and more socially withdrawn as well as more anxious and depressed. Bullied youth also report more headaches, stomachaches, and other somatic complaints, which may reflect stress-related illness (see reviews by Beeson & Vaillancourt, 2016; McDougall & Vaillancourt, 2015).

Prospective studies on peer victimization suggest that the aforementioned inventory of ills is the result of being abused and not a precipitator of poor treatment by peers. This finding is consistent with a robust literature that demonstrates a causal relation between exposure to stressful life events and the onset of health problems such as depression (Kendler, Karkowski, & Prescott, 1999). Longitudinal research also suggests that being bullied does not lead to the same pathological or nonpathological outcome in every individual, a concept termed *multifinality* (Cicchetti & Rogosch, 1996; see McDougall & Vaillancourt, 2015). The shared or common experience of being victimized does not mean individuals end at a single or common outcome; rather, there is marked variability (Cicchetti & Rogosch, 1996). Accordingly, understanding the impact of peer victimization in childhood requires

This work was supported by grants from the Canadian Institutes of Health Research.

an examination of other conditions and attributes that exist within a broader "system" for each child. Of recent interest in the study of peer victimization is the role of an individual's genetic susceptibility. It has been proposed that this genetic susceptibility can make certain individuals more sensitive to negative environmental influences. However, if the environment is supportive and enriched and lacks significant adversity, it may also be associated with better outcomes (Belsky & Pluess, 2009; Boyce & Ellis, 2005). This phenomenon is known as *differential susceptibility*.

MODERATORS

Cross-sectional and longitudinal studies clearly indicate that for many bullied youth, their negative experience with peers causes them harm. This makes sense intuitively, given that the need to belong is a fundamental human motivator (Baumeister & Leary, 1995). However, what is not clear from research on bullying and health is why some youth become ill as a consequence of poor treatment by peers while others do not. To date, most research has focused on environmental characteristics (such as family and school) when trying to explain heterogeneity in outcomes. For example, studies have shown that parental involvement and positive family functioning moderate the relation between being bullied and poor health outcomes—youth with better home environments fare better when bullied than youth with poorer home environments (for example, Flouri & Buchanan, 2002). Classroom context also matters. Huitsing, Veenstra, Sainio, and Salmivalli (2012) showed that victimization can become a focal element of the classroom dynamic when only a handful of students are targeted and perceived as "social misfits." In these instances, the impact of victimization on mental health grows more intense. The moderating role of gender also matters. In one study, peer victimization at age eight was associated with suicide attempts before age 25 for girls and women but not for boys and men (controlling for conduct and depressive symptoms; Klomek et al., 2009).

Far fewer studies have examined the moderating role of biology when examining the link between peer victimization and health, despite compelling evidence from other literatures demonstrating such an effect. These studies suggest that (a) genotypic markers of vulnerability do seem to moderate the relation between psychosocial stressors and poor health (that is, candidate gene by environment [cGxE] interactions), and (b) early adversity is linked to poorer health outcomes as a function of how genes are expressed (that is, epigenetic alterations).

cGxE Interactions and Differential Susceptibility

In 2003, Caspi and colleagues published a seminal study in which they examined the moderating role of a functional polymorphism in the promoter region of the serotonin transporter gene (5-HTTLPR) in the relation between exposure to child maltreatment and depression outcomes at age 26. Results indicated that maltreated individuals were far more likely to be depressed in adulthood if they also had two copies of the short allele (SS) in the 5-HTTLPR. Results also indicated that the long allele (L) was protective against depression for individuals who had been abused in childhood. Although Caspi et al.'s (2003) study was not the first to examine cGxE interactions, it did receive unprecedented attention, owing in part to the strong moderating effect reported and the impact of the journal in which it appeared.

Since its publication, Caspi and colleagues' (2003) article has been cited over 7,000 times and hundreds of similar studies have been published. Most of these studies have focused on candidate genes that have neurobiological evidence supporting their examination. In the case of 5-HTTLPR, serotonin has been implicated in the development of depression, and the short allele in particular has been shown to have lower transcriptional efficiency of the promoter than the long allele (Caspi et al., 2003; Lesch et al., 1996). Other popular candidate genes include catechol-O-methyltransferase (*COMT*), dopamine transporter gene (*DAT1*), dopamine receptor D4 (*DRD4*), and monoamine oxidase A (*MAOA*), which have been linked to mental health problems in relation to being exposed to an environmental stressor. We believe that these candidate genes should also be examined in relation to the often-ignored environmental stressor of being bullied. However, before discussing the merits of their inclusion, it is important to highlight the ongoing controversy surrounding cGxE studies.

Criticisms of cGxE Research

Duncan and colleagues have been especially critical of cGxE studies in psychiatric genetics (Duncan, 2013; Duncan & Keller, 2011; Duncan, Pollastri, & Smoller, 2014; see also Dick et al., 2015). One of their main criticisms relates to the fact that cGxE studies are often not replicated. According to Duncan (2013), 96 percent of the early cGxE studies reported positive interactions and yet only 27 percent of replications were positive, suggesting a notable publication bias. Duncan and colleagues have also suggested that the rate of false discoveries is very high in cGxE studies, an assumption made in part on the basis of two negative meta-analytic findings of 14 studies (Munafò, Durrant, Lewis, & Flint, 2009; Risch et al., 2009). A more recent meta-analysis of 54 studies demonstrating strong evidence that 5-HTTLPR moderates the relation between stress and depression (Karg, Burmeister, Shedden, & Sen, 2011) was, however, dismissed by these researchers for using lax inclusion criteria.

Detractors of Duncan and colleagues (Duncan, 2013; Duncan & Keller, 2011; Duncan et al., 2014) suggested that they failed to consider important reasons for lack of replication, which include the fact that many of the nonreplication studies used notably weaker methodologies, such as the inclusion of brief self-report measures of stress, retrospective accounts of exposure to life stressors, a poorly defined stressor, and the contemporaneous testing of stress and depression (Caspi, Hariri, Holmes, Uher, & Moffitt, 2010). Moreover, critics maintain that differential susceptibility, which also accounts for the role of positive environmental influences when examining the sequelae of illness, is more likely than the diathesis–stress interpretation offered by Duncan and colleagues (Pluess & Belsky, 2012).

It is essential to highlight that even the most ardent critics of cGxE research have stated that "unequivocally, more empirical research is needed to definitively determine the promise of cGxE research" and that replication attempts "should be a high priority" (Duncan et al., 2014, p. 251). However, critics have also cautioned that cGxE research needs to be conducted with particular attention paid to statistical issues such as low power, the correction of multiple testing, the use of cross-product terms, properly controlled confounders, and the estimation of genotype and environment correlations (see Dick et al., 2015). Moreover, consistent with Moffitt and Caspi's (2014) suggestion, the use of longitudinal studies is also needed so that the temporal sequence between cause and effect can be disentangled. A longitudinal approach also allows researchers to examine environmental risk factors as time limited or enduring, an approach that tends to be missing in cGxE research.

It is unquestionable that the development of mental health problems is far from straightforward. For example, although the prevailing hypothesis is that individuals with the risk allele of 5-HTTLPR are more likely to develop depression if they experience a major life stressor, as Moffitt and Caspi (2014) asserted, the minimal criterion to validly test this hypothesis is "a set of measures that can unambiguously establish that the stress came before the depression" (p. 1). Studies that use retrospective accounts of depression or other psychiatric disorders cannot meet this standard, nor can cross-sectional studies. Moreover, as Dick et al. (2015) pointed out, the choice of environment in cGxE research is as important as the choice of gene because "if the wrong form of environment is assessed or if the right form of the environment is assessed poorly" (p. 44), valid cGxE interactions will not be detected. Studies need to also be comprehensive in nature, because according to the differential susceptibility hypothesis, individuals who may be most adversely affected by poor environments (that is, being bullied) may also be the ones who procure the most benefit from supportive environments (Belsky & Pluess, 2009; Boyce & Ellis, 2005).

5-HTTLPR, *MAOA*, *COMT*, *DAT*, and *DRD4*

Several studies have shown that variants within the 5-HTTLPR moderate the relation between exposure to negative environmental influences such as maltreatment in childhood and future health outcomes such as depression (Caspi et al., 2003) and anxiety (Stein, Schork, & Gelernter, 2008). This moderating effect has also been shown to be present for the stressor of peer victimization. Sugden et al. (2010) found that children who carried the SS genotype and were bullied were at greater risk for developing emotional problems than bullied children with the SL or LL genotype. This effect was present even when controlling for pre-victimization emotional problems and other risk factors. Three other published studies have also shown that 5-HTTLPR moderates the relation between health problems and peer victimization (Banny, Cicchetti, Rogosch, Oshri, & Crick, 2013; Benjet, Thompson, & Gotlib, 2010; Iyer, Dougall, & Jensen-Campbell, 2013). Given that these studies were all cross-sectional and included fewer than 157 children, replication is still required. The only well-powered study was Sugden and colleagues' (2010), yet this study is not representative because British twins were recruited from high-risk environments (that is, poor families, young mothers), which conflates the stress of being bullied with other environmental risks (see Lereya, Copeland, Costello, & Wolke, 2015).

The *MAOA* gene encodes the enzyme that metabolizes neurotransmitters like norepinephrine, serotonin, and dopamine and thus genetic variants that alter enzyme metabolism may render these neurotransmitters inactive or cause dysregulation in neurotransmission. There are several studies examining the moderating role of the low- versus high-activity alleles of a variant in the promoter region of *MAOA* on the development of mental health outcomes in relation to environmental stressors like child maltreatment. These studies have typically shown that children with low *MAOA* activity who have been exposed to a negative environmental influence are more likely to have externalizing problems, such as conduct disorder (Caspi et al., 2002; Foley et al., 2004) and attention deficit/hyperactivity disorder (ADHD; Kim-Cohen et al., 2006) than children with high *MAOA* activity. We know of only one published study linking *MAOA* to peer victimization. Whelan, Kretschmer, and Barker (2014) found that harsh parenting was associated with increased peer victimization (and perpetration) via oppositional behavior but that the effect was not moderated by *MAOA* genotype. More research is needed, especially when considering that peer victimization is often associated with the development of conduct problems, including aggression.

For example, in a recent article, bullied children became bullies, but, it is important to note, not all bullied children went on to bully their peers (Haltigan & Vaillancourt, 2014). Understanding this type of heterogeneity is essential for prevention and intervention work.

COMT affects dopamine and other catecholamines and has been used to index differential susceptibility (Belsky & Beaver, 2011; Voelker, Sheese, Rothbart, & Posner, 2009). Specifically, the *COMT* gene encodes the COMT enzyme, which degrades catecholamines such as dopamine, epinephrine, and norepinephrine. A single nucleotide polymorphism that results in a valine (Val) to methionine (Met) amino acid substitution to the protein (*COMT* Val^{158}Met) is the most commonly studied variant in this gene (Sulik et al., 2015). The Met allele results in lower *COMT* efficiency than the Val allele (Lachman et al., 1996; Lotta et al., 1995). Of relevance to the study of peer victimization is research demonstrating a relation between *COMT* Val^{158}Met and internalizing problems (McGrath et al., 2004; Olsson et al., 2005), including a recent meta-analysis demonstrating a link with anxiety traits (Lee & Prescott, 2014). Studies have also shown that Val^{158}Met may index plasticity. For example, Sulik et al. (2015) showed that although parenting was positively associated with inhibitory control for Met–Met boys and for Val–Val or Val–Met girls, it was negatively associated with internalizing symptoms for Met–Met boys. In another study, Laucht et al. (2012) reported that teenagers homozygous for the Met allele engaged in higher drinking activity at age 19 years if their parents were less involved; however, for teenagers with this same polymorphism, having involved parents was associated with reduced drinking activity. No such relation was found in individuals carrying the Val allele. *COMT*'s association with internalizing symptoms and increased problematic behavior makes it a worthy gene to consider when examining the neurobiological underpinnings of peer victimization.

The dopamine transporter gene (*DAT1*, *SLC6A3*) has been implicated in disorders such as ADHD (Cornish et al., 2005) and conduct problems (Lahey et al., 2011). A variable number tandem repeat (VNTR) polymorphism in the 3' untranslated region of *DAT1* has been well studied. The allele frequencies of this *DAT1* polymorphism vary within the population and are related to different mental health outcomes. For example, the presence of two *DAT1* VNTR 10-repeat alleles has been shown to be associated with symptoms of ADHD (Cornish et al., 2005). The moderating role of *DAT1* in the relation between negative environmental influences and mental health outcomes has also been examined. Lahey et al. (2011) reported an inverse relation between levels of positive and negative parenting at four to six years and later conduct disorder symptoms, a result that was found mostly among children with two copies of the nine-repeat allele of the VNTR (Sonuga-Barke et al., 2009). Given the established relation between peer victimization and conduct problems (Haltigan & Vaillancourt, 2014), it seems worthwhile to examine the role of *DAT1* variation in the emergence of these problems.

The dopamine receptor D4 regulates dopamine receptor activity in the brain. The *DRD4* gene contains a 48 base-pair VNTR polymorphism in Exon III, which can take the form of a long (7-repeat) or short (4-repeat) allele. The short allele is the more frequent variant (64 percent versus 20 percent for long allele; Oak, Oldenhof, & Van Tol, 2000). The *DRD4* 7-repeat allele, which has been shown to cause lower intracellular response to dopamine, is associated with disorders such as depression (López León et al., 2005), ADHD (Gizer, Ficks, & Waldman, 2009), and substance abuse (Ray et al., 2009). Externalizing behavior has also been consistently linked to the *DRD4* 7-repeat allele (Boutwell & Beaver, 2008), and *DRD4* has been shown to play a moderating role in the relation between negative environmental influences and mental health outcomes. For example, a sixfold increase in externalizing behavior problems in children exposed to insensitive parenting and carrying the *DRD4*

7-repeat allele was reported (Bakermans-Kranenburg & van IJzendoorn, 2006). Of relevance to the study of peer victimization is a study by Kretschmer, Dijkstra, Ormel, Verhulst, and Veenstra (2013), who examined the moderating role of *DRD4* in the relation between peer victimization and later delinquency in a large Dutch cohort study of youth assessed four times across the ages of 11 to 19. Results indicated that contrary to expectations, carriers of the 4-repeat homozygous variant were more susceptible to the effects of peer victimization on delinquency later in adolescence, even though the 7-repeat allele was expected to be the "risk" allele on the basis of prior studies.

Finally, a study by VanZomeren-Dohm, Pitula, Koss, Thomas, and Gunnar (2015) examined the moderating role of *FKBP5* rs1360780 in the relation between peer victimization and symptoms of depression in post-institutionalized children from 25 countries. *FKBP* is a gene that governs stress response, and the rs1360780 single nucleotide polymorphism is thought to be a functional variant of this gene (Zanner & Binder, 2014, as cited in VanZomeren-Dohm et al., 2015). Results indicated that girls who had the minor allele (TT or CT) were more depressed at higher levels of peer victimization but less depressed at lower levels of peer victimization, consistent with differential susceptibility. For boys, the CC genotype was associated with more symptoms of depression than for girls with the same CC genotype when bullied.

Taken together, studies examining cGxE interactions suggest that poorer mental health outcomes are associated with certain biological risk markers in the context of being bullied. However, in the context of a better environment, these same risk alleles may be associated with better outcomes, consistent with recent work on differential susceptibility.

EPIGENETIC MECHANISMS

DNA methylation is an epigenetic mechanism that "maintains gene activity or changes gene expression by activating or silencing the gene, resulting in the development of phenotypes that are time-dependent and are not determined by the DNA sequence at that locus" (Vaillancourt, Hymel, & McDougall, 2013, pp. 243–244). Epigenetic alterations are believed to function as a biological mechanism in which environmental signals are translated into "organismal molecular events" (Bick et al., 2012, p. 1418). The study of epigenetics in psychiatry and psychology is fairly new, heralded by a seminal study by Meaney and colleagues on maternal care in rats (Weaver et al., 2004; see review by Meaney, 2010). Using an experimental design, newborn pups were randomized to high-quality or low-quality maternal care. Individual differences in stress reactivity of adult rats were found to be influenced by the quality of their early environment, which was associated with epigenetic changes that conferred a risk or protective effect on the rats' stress reactivity. Changes in DNA methylation resulted as a function of early adversity or nurturance, and this change had an effect on later stress reactivity. Following this landmark study, several studies have shown that exposure to adversity influences DNA methylation, which in turn influences a person's health trajectory. For example, epigenetic alterations have been implicated in the emergence of neuropsychiatric disorders (Tsankova, Renthal, Kumar, & Nestler, 2007) and other health outcomes such as cancer (Asting et al., 2014) and diabetes (Diabetes Genetics Initiative of Broad Institute, 2007).

Of particular relevance to the study of peer victimization are studies demonstrating a pathway from early adversity (Heim & Binder 2012; Labonté et al., 2012; Shonkoff et al., 2012; Szyf & Bick, 2013), including peer victimization (Ouellet-Morin et al., 2011), to changes in DNA methylation. For example, Essex et al. (2013) showed that exposure to maternal stress in infancy was associated with differential methylation in adolescence. Tyrka, Price, Marsit, Walters, and Carpenter (2012) found that inadequate early nurturing by caregivers, including maltreatment, was associated with increased methylation to the promoter of the type II glucocorticoid receptor gene. This change was linked to attenuated cortisol responses. This finding is intriguing insofar as several studies have also shown that bullied youth tend to have a blunted cortisol response (Kliewer, 2006; Knack, Jensen-Campbell, & Baum, 2011; Ouellet-Morin et al., 2011; Vaillancourt et al., 2008). We know of only one study that has examined epigenetic changes in relation to peer victimization. Ouellett-Morin et al. (2013) showed that increased DNA methylation of the serotonin transporter gene between ages five and 10 was found for bullied twins but not for nonbullied twins. This finding is also significant because children with higher serotonin DNA methylation had a blunted cortisol response to stress, which has been shown to causally change as a result of being bullied. Ouellett-Morin et al.'s (2013) study needs to be replicated with singletons because assisted reproductive technology, which increases the chances of having a multiple birth, has been linked to epigenetic errors (Niemitz & Feinberg, 2004).

It is clear that more research is needed to examine whether the experience of being bullied "gets under the skin" and is associated with epigenetic alterations, which in turn places youth at risk for poorer health outcomes. Although little is known about how bullying may result in epigenetic alterations that may be linked to the pathogenesis of common diseases, it nevertheless represents an important and logical area of inquiry, considering that the literature on other forms of childhood adversity points convincingly in this direction. A recent technical report published by the American Academy of Pediatrics (Shonkoff et al., 2012) states that "many adult diseases should be viewed as developmental disorders that begin early in life and that persistent health disparities associated with poverty, discrimination, or maltreatment could be reduced by the alleviation of toxic stress in childhood" (p. e232). We suspect that the intrinsic mechanism will be similar for bullied youth—we expect that genome-wide DNA methylation alterations will be induced by being bullied by peers and that these alterations will be associated with detrimental health outcomes.

Our interest in differential susceptibility makes us also question whether "recovery" from being bullied might reverse the influences of this life stress on molecular biological changes associated with detrimental outcomes. That is, can a better social environment positively influence epigenetic mechanisms and improve health? Prevalence estimates of peer victimization show a notable decline as students move into the college or university environment (Chapell et al., 2006). Schäfer et al. (2004) have speculated that the university context might serve as a "corrective experience" for young people with a history of peer victimization. The postsecondary milieu tends to be less hierarchical and more openly structured so that individuals have new opportunities for positive relationships. There is emerging evidence in the areas of physical exercise (Sanchis-Gomar et al., 2012) on epigenetic modulation suggesting that positive genetic adaptations through epigenetic mechanisms are possible.

KEY GAPS IN EVIDENCE

Our review identifies the following key gaps in evidence, which severely disadvantages us when it comes to making policy recommendations or making recommendations about bullying prevention and intervention (that is, the "alleviation of toxic stress in childhood").

Specifically, we know little about (a) why some bullied youth develop significant mental and physical health problems as a consequence of poor peer treatment, while other youth seem to fare better (that is, the moderating role of biology in the bullying–health link is relatively unknown but worthy of more attention); (b) how the experience of being bullied may be related to epigenetic changes and how these changes are related to health outcomes; (c) how the timing, duration, and severity of peer victimization are associated with health outcomes, genetic risk, and epigenetic changes; and (d) the effects of context transitions on trajectories of peer victimization and health (and we know nothing about possible positive epigenetic changes related to transitions).

CONCLUSION

Understanding the neurobiology of peer victimization is pertinent because so many youth are negatively affected by bullying. Peer victimization causes harm to young people by significantly impairing opportunities to develop relationship capacity and by interfering with pathways to adaptive outcomes. Accordingly, we urge researchers to explore a full range of functioning that includes biological risk.

Concerns about bullying have clearly become part of public consciousness and under-score the notion that, as a society, we are no longer willing to stand by and tolerate the poor treatment of others. With this awareness, however, comes the need for accurate facts regarding the long-term impact of peer abuse. As such, it is essential to delve into the complex dynamics that perpetuate bullying in order to delineate paths to better well-being. Indeed, in the absence of a strong scientific knowledge base, we are left with nonsystematic (and occasionally damaging) approaches to intervention and prevention (for example, Merrell, Gueldner, Ross, & Isava, 2008; Ttofi & Farrington, 2011; Vreeman & Carroll, 2007).

REFERENCES

Asting, A. G., Caren, H., Andersson, M., Lonnroth, C., Lagerstedt, K., & Lundholm, K. (2014). COX-2 gene expression in colon cancer tissue related to regulation factors and promoter methylation status. In K. Ayyanathan (Ed.), *Specific gene expression and epigenetics: The interplay between the genome and its environment* (pp. 29–50). Oakville, ON: Apple Academic Press.

Bakermans-Kranenburg, M. J., & van IJzendoorn, M. H. (2006). Gene-environment interaction of the dopamine D4 receptor (DRD4) and observed maternal insensitivity predicting externalizing behavior in preschoolers. *Developmental Psychobiology, 48,* 406–409.

Banny, A. M., Cicchetti, D., Rogosch, F. A., Oshri, A., & Crick, N. R. (2013). Vulnerability to depression: A moderated mediation model of the roles of child maltreatment, peer victimization, and serotonin transporter linked polymorphic region genetic variation among children from low socioeconomic status backgrounds. *Development and Psychopathology, 26,* 599–614.

Baumeister, R. F., & Leary, M. R. (1995). The need to belong: Desire for interpersonal attachments as a fundamental human motivation. *Psychological Bulletin, 117,* 497–529.

Beeson, C.M.L., & Vaillancourt, T. (2016). The short- and long-term health and education outcomes of peer victimization: Implications for educators and clinicians. In B. Haslam

& P. J. Valletutti (Eds.), *From medical and psychosocial problems in the classroom: The teacher's role in diagnosis and management* (5th ed.; pp. 445–468). Austin: PRO-ED.

Belsky, J., & Beaver, K. M. (2011). Cumulative-genetic plasticity, parenting and adolescent self-regulation. *Journal of Child Psychology and Psychiatry, 52*, 619–626.

Belsky, J., & Pluess, M. (2009). Beyond diathesis stress: Differential susceptibility to environmental influences. *Psychological Bulletin, 135*, 885–908.

Benjet, C., Thompson, R. J., & Gotlib, I. H. (2010). 5-HTTLPR moderates the effect of relational peer victimization on depressive symptoms in adolescent girls. *Journal of Child Psychology and Psychiatry, 51*, 173–179.

Bick, J., Naymova, O., Hunter, S., Barbot, B., Lee, M., Luthar, S. S., et al. (2012). Childhood adversity and DNA methylation of genes involved in the hypothalamus-pituitary-adrenal axis and immune system: Whole-genome and candidate-gene associations. *Development and Psychopathology, 24*, 1417–1425.

Boutwell, B. B., & Beaver, K. M. (2008). A biosocial explanation to delinquency abstention. *Criminal Behavior and Mental Health, 18*, 59–74.

Boyce, W. T., & Ellis, B. J. (2005). Biological sensitivity to context: I. An evolutionary–developmental theory of the origins and functions of stress reactivity. *Development and Psychopathology, 17*, 271–301.

Caspi, A., Hariri, A. R., Holmes, A., Uher, R., & Moffitt, T. E. (2010). Genetic sensitivity to the environment: The case of the serotonin transporter gene and its implications for studying complex diseases and traits. *American Journal of Psychiatry, 167*, 509–527.

Caspi, A., McClay, J., Moffitt, T. E., Mill, J., Martin, J., Craig, I. W. et al. (2002). Role of genotype in the cycle of violence in maltreated children. *Science, 297*, 851–854.

Caspi, A., Sugden, K., Moffitt, T. E., Taylor, A., Craig, I. W., Harrington, H., et al. (2003). Influence of life stress on depression: Moderation by a polymorphism in the 5-HTT gene. *Science, 301*(5631), 386–389.

Chapell, M. S., Hasselman, S. L., Kitchin, T., Lomon, S. N., MacIver, K. W., & Sarullo, P. L. (2006). Bullying in elementary school, high school, and college. *Adolescence, 41*, 633–648.

Cicchetti, D., & Rogosch, F. A. (1996). Equifinality and multifinality in developmental psychopathology. *Development and Psychopathology, 8*, 597–600.

Cornish, K. M., Manly, T., Savage, R., Swanson, J., Morisano, D., Butler, N., et al. (2005). Association of the dopamine transporter (DAT1) 10/10-repeat genotype with ADHD symptoms and response inhibition in a general population sample. *Molecular Psychiatry, 10*, 686–698.

Diabetes Genetics Initiative of Broad Institute of Harvard and MIT, Lund University, and Novartis Institutes of BioMedical Research, Saxena, R., Voight, B. F., Lyssenko, V., et al. (2007). Genome-wide association analysis identifies loci for type 2 diabetes and triglyceride levels. *Science, 316*, 1331–1336.

Dick, D. M., Agrawal, A., Keller, M. C., Adkins, A., Aliev, F., Monroe, S., et al. (2015). Candidate gene–environment interaction research: Reflections and recommendations. *Perspectives on Psychological Science, 10*, 37–59.

Duncan, L. E. (2013). Paying attention to all results, positive and negative. *Journal of the American Academy of Child and Adolescent Psychiatry, 52*, 462–465.

Duncan, L. E., & Keller, M. C. (2011). A critical review of the first 10 years of candidate gene-by-environment interaction research in psychiatry. *American Journal of Psychiatry, 168*, 1041–1049.

Duncan, L. E., Pollastri, A. R., & Smoller, J. W. (2014). Mind the gap: Why many geneticists and psychological scientists have discrepant views about gene–environment interaction (G×E) research. *American Psychologist, 69*, 249–268.

Essex, M. J., Boyce, W. T., Hertzman, C., Lam, L. L., Armstrong, J. M., Neumann, S.M.A., & Kobor, M. S. (2013). Epigenetic vestiges of early developmental adversity: Childhood stress exposure and DNA methylation in adolescence. *Child Development, 84*, 58–75.

Flouri, E., & Buchanan, A. (2002). Life satisfaction in teenage boys: The moderating role of father involvement and bullying. *Aggressive Behavior, 28*, 126–133.

Foley, D., Eaves, L., Wormley, B., Silberg, J. L., Maes, H., Kuhn, J., & Riley, B. (2004). Child-hood adversity, monoamine oxidase A genotype, and risk for conduct disorder. *Archives of General Psychiatry, 61*, 738–744.

Gizer, I. R., Ficks, C., & Waldman, I. D. (2009). Candidate gene studies of ADHD: A meta-analytic review. *Human Genetics, 126*, 51–90.

Haltigan, J. D., & Vaillancourt, T. (2014). Joint trajectories of bullying and peer victimization across elementary and middle school and associations with symptoms of psychopathol-ogy. *Developmental Psychology, 50*, 2426–2436.

Heim, C., & Binder, E. (2012). Current research trends in early life stress and depression: Review of human studies on sensitive periods, gene–environment interactions, and epigenetics. *Experimental Neurology, 233*, 102–111.

Huitsing, G., Veenstra, R., Sainio, M., & Salmivalli, C. (2012). "It must be them" or "It could be me?" The impact of the social network position of bullies and victims on victims' adjustment. *Social Networks, 34*, 379–386.

Iyer, P. A., Dougall, A. L., & Jensen-Campbell, L. A. (2013). Are some adolescents differ-entially susceptible to the influence of bullying on depression? *Journal of Research in Personality, 47*, 272–281.

Karg, K., Burmeister, M., Shedden, K., & Sen, S. (2011). The serotonin transporter promoter variant (5-HTTLPR), stress, and depression meta-analysis revisited: Evidence of genetic moderation. *Archives of General Psychiatry, 68*, 444–454.

Kendler, K. S., Karkowski, L. M., & Prescott, C. A. (1999). Causal relationship between stressful life events and the onset of major depression. *American Journal of Psychiatry, 156*, 837–841.

Kim-Cohen, J., Caspi, A., Taylor, A., Williams, B., Newcombe, R., Craig, I. W., & Moffitt, T. E. (2006). MAOA, maltreatment, and gene–environment interaction predicting children's mental health: New evidence and a meta-analysis. *Molecular Psychiatry, 11*, 903–913.

Kliewer, W. (2006). Violence exposure and cortisol responses in urban youth. *International Journal of Behavioral Medicine, 13*, 109–120.

Klomek, A. B., Sourander, A., Niemela, S., Kumpulainen, K., Piha, J., Tamminen, T., et al. (2009). Childhood bullying behaviors as a risk for suicide attempts and completed suicides: A population-based birth cohort study. *Journal of the American Academy of Child and Adolescent Psychiatry, 48*, 254–261.

Knack, J. M., Jensen-Campbell, L. A., & Baum, A. (2011). Worse than sticks and stones? Bullying is linked with altered HPA axis functioning and poorer health. *Brain and Cognition, 77*, 183–190.

Kretschmer, T., Dijkstra, J. K., Ormel, J., Verhulst, F. C., & Veenstra, R. (2013). Dopamine receptor D4 gene moderates the effect of positive and negative peer experiences on later delinquency: The Tracking Adolescents' Individual Lives Survey study. *Development and Psychopathology, 26*, 1107–1117.

Labonté, B., Suderman, M., Maussion, G., Navaro, L., Yerko, V., Mahar, I., et al. (2012). Genome-wide epigenetic regulation by early-life trauma. *Archives of General Psychiatry, 69*, 722–731.

Lachman, H. M., Papolos, D. F., Saito, T., Yu, Y. M., Szumlanski, C. L., & Weinshilboum, R. M. (1996). Human catechol-O-methyltransferase pharmacogenetics: Description of a functional polymorphism and its potential application to neuropsychiatric disorders. *Pharmacogenetics, 6*, 243–250.

Lahey, B. B., Rathouz, P. J., Lee, S. S., Chronis-Tuscano, A., Pelham, W. E., Waldman, I. D., & Cook, E. H. (2011). Interactions between early parenting and a polymorphism of the child's dopamine transporter gene in predicting future child conduct disorder symptoms. *Journal of Abnormal Psychology, 120*, 33–45.

Laucht, M., Blomeyer, D., Buchmann, A. F., Treutlein, J., Schmidt, M. H., Esser, G., et al. (2012). Catechol-O-methyltransferase Val 158 Met genotype, parenting practices and adolescent alcohol use: Testing the differential susceptibility hypothesis. *Journal of Child Psychology and Psychiatry, 53*, 351–359.

Lee, L. O., & Prescott, C. A. (2014). Association of the catechol-O-methyltransferase val158met polymorphism and anxiety-related traits: A meta-analysis. *Psychiatric Genetics, 24*, 52–69.

Lereya, S. T., Copeland, W. E., Costello, E. J., & Wolke, D. (2015). Adult mental health consequences of peer bullying and maltreatment in childhood: Two cohorts in two countries. *Lancet Psychiatry, 2*(6), 524–531.

Lesch, K.-P., Bengel, D., Heilis, A., Sabol, S. Z., Greenberg, B. D., Petri, S., et al. (1996). Association of anxiety-related traits with a polymorphism in the serotonin transporter gene regulatory region. *Science, 274*, 1527–1531.

López León, S., Croes, E. A., Sayed-Tabatabaei, F. A., Claes, S., Van Broeckhoven, C., & van Duijn, C. M. (2005). The dopamine D4 receptor gene 48-base-pair-repeat polymorphism and mood disorders: A meta-analysis. *Biological Psychiatry, 57*, 999–1003.

Lotta, T., Vidgren, J., Tilgmann, C., Ulmanen, I., Melen, K., Julkunen, I., et al. (1995). Kinetics of human soluble and membrane-bound catechol-O-methyltransferase: A revised mechanism and description of the thermolabile variant of the enzyme. *Biochemistry, 34*, 4202–4210.

McDougall, P., & Vaillancourt, T. (2015). The long-term outcomes of peer victimization in school: Pathways to adjustment and maladjustment. *American Psychologist, 70*, 300–310.

McGrath, M., Kawachi, I., Ascherio, A., Colditz, G. A., Hunter, D. J., & De Vivo, I. (2004). Association between catechol-O-methyltransferase and phobic anxiety. *American Journal of Psychiatry, 161*, 1703–1705.

Meaney, M. J. (2010). Epigenetics and the biological definition of gene × environment interactions. *Child Development, 81*, 41–79.

Merrell, K. W., Gueldner, B. A., Ross, S. W., & Isava, D. M. (2008). How effective are school bullying intervention programs? A meta-analysis of intervention research. *School Psychology Quarterly, 23*, 26–42.

Moffitt, T. E., & Caspi, A. (2014). Bias in a protocol for a meta-analysis of 5-HTTLPR, stress, and depression. *BMC Psychiatry, 14*, 1–13.

Munafò, M. R., Durrant, C., Lewis, G., & Flint, J. (2009). Gene × environment interactions at the serotonin transporter locus. *Biological Psychiatry, 65*, 211–219.

Niemitz, E. L., & Feinberg, A. P. (2004). Epigenetics and assisted reproductive technology: A call for investigation. *American Journal of Human Genetics, 74*, 599–609.

Oak, J. N., Oldenhof, J., & Van Tol, H.H.H. (2000). The dopamine D4 receptor: One decade of research. *European Journal of Pharmacology, 405*, 303–313.

Olsson, C. A., Anney, R. J., Lotfi-Miri, M., Byrnes, G. B., Williamson, R., & Patton, G. C. (2005). Association between the COMT Val158Met polymorphism and propensity to anxiety in an Australian population-based longitudinal study of adolescent health. *Psychiatric Genetics, 15*, 109–115.

Ouellet-Morin, I., Danese, A., Bowes, L., Shakoor, S., Ambler, A., Pariante, C. M., et al. (2011). A discordant monozygotic twin design shows blunted cortisol reactivity among bullied children. *Journal of the Academy of Child & Adolescent Psychiatry, 50,* 574–582.

Ouellet-Morin, I., Wong, C.C.Y., Danese, A., Pariante, C. M., Papadopoulos, A. S., Mill, J., & Arseneault, L. (2013). Increased serotonin transporter gene (SERT) DNA methylation is associated with bullying victimization and blunted cortisol response to stress in childhood: A longitudinal study of discordant monozygotic twins. *Psychological Medicine, 43,* 1813–1823.

Pluess, M., & Belsky, J. (2012). Conceptual issues in psychiatric gene-environment interaction research. *American Journal of Psychiatry, 169,* 222–223.

Ray, L. A., Bryan, A., MacKillop, J., McGreary, J., Hesterberg, K., & Hutchison, K. E. (2009). The dopamine D_4 receptor (DRD4) gene exon III polymorphism, problematic alcohol use, and novelty seeking: Direct and mediated genetic effects. *Addiction Biology, 14,* 238–244.

Risch, N., Herrell, R., Lehner, T., Liang, K. Y., Eaves, L., Hoh, J., et al. (2009). Interaction between the serotonin transporter gene (5-HTTLPR), stressful life events, and risk of depression. *JAMA, 301,* 2462–2472.

Sanchis-Gomar, F., Garcia-Gimenez, J. L., Perez-Quilis, C., Gomez-Cabrera, M. C., Pallardo, F. V., & Lippi, G. (2012). Physical exercise as an epigenetic modulator: Eustress, the "positive stress" as an effector of gene expression. *Journal of Strength & Conditioning Research, 26,* 3469–3472.

Schäfer, M., Korn, S., Smith, P., Hunter, S. C., Mora-Merchan, J. A., Singer, M. M., & van der Meulen, K. (2004). Lonely in a crowd: Recollections of bullying. *British Journal of Developmental Psychology, 22,* 379–394. doi:10.1348/0261510041552756

Shonkoff, J. P., Garner, A. S., Siegel, B. S., Dobbins, M. I., Earls, M. F., McGuinn, L., et al. (2012). The lifelong effects of early childhood adversity and toxic stress: Technical report. *Pediatrics, 129,* e232–e246.

Sonuga-Barke, E.J.S., Oades, R. D., Psychogiou, L., Chen, W., Franke, B., Buitelaar, J., et al. (2009). Dopamine and serotonin transporter genotypes moderate sensitivity to maternal expressed emotion: The case of conduct and emotional problems in attention deficit/hyperactivity disorder. *Journal of Child Psychology and Psychiatry, 50,* 1052–1063.

Stein, M. B., Schork, N. J., & Gelernter, J. (2008). Gene-by-environment (serotonin transporter and childhood maltreatment) interaction for anxiety sensitivity, an intermediate phenotype for anxiety disorders. *Neuropsychopharmacology, 33,* 312–319.

Sugden, K., Arseneault, L., Harrington, H., Moffitt, T. E., Williams, B., & Caspi, A. (2010). Serotonin transporter gene moderates the development of emotional problems among children following bullying victimization. *Journal of the American Academy of Child and Adolescent Psychiatry, 49,* 830–840.

Sulik, M. J., Eisenberg, N., Spinrad, T. L., Lemery-Chalfant, K., Swann, G., Silva, K. M., et al. (2015). Interactions among catechol-O-methyltransferase genotype, parenting, and sex predict children's internalizing symptoms and inhibitory control: Evidence for differential susceptibility. *Development and Psychopathology, 27,* 709–723.

Szyf, M., & Bick, J. (2013). DNA methylation: A mechanism for embedding early life experiences in the genome. *Child Development, 84,* 49–57.

Tsankova, N., Renthal, W., Kumar, A., & Nestler, E. J. (2007). Epigenetic regulation in psychiatric disorders. *Nature Reviews Neuroscience, 8,* 355–367.

Ttofi, M. M., & Farrington, D. P. (2011). Effectiveness of school-based programs to reduce bullying: A systematic and meta-analytic review. *Journal of Experimental Criminology, 7*(1), 27–56.

Tyrka, A. R., Price, L. H., Marsit, C., Walters, O. C., & Carpenter, L. L. (2012). Childhood adversity and epigenetic modulation of the leukocyte glucocorticoid receptor: Preliminary findings in healthy adults. *PLoS ONE, 7*, e30148.

Vaillancourt, T., Duku, E., deCatanzaro, D., MacMillan, H., Muir, C., & Schmidt, L. A. (2008). Variation in hypothalamic–pituitary–adrenal axis activity among bullied and non-bullied children. *Aggressive Behavior, 34*, 294–305.

Vaillancourt, T., Hymel, S., & McDougall, P. (2013). The biological underpinnings of peer victimization: Understanding why and how the effects of bullying can last a lifetime. *Theory into Practice, 52*, 241–248.

VanZomeren-Dohm, A. A., Pitula, C. E., Koss, K. J., Thomas, K., & Gunnar, M. R. (2015). *FKBP5* moderation of depressive symptoms in peer victimized, post-institutionalized children. *Psychoneuroendocrinology, 51*, 426–430.

Voelker, P., Sheese, B. E., Rothbart, M. K., & Posner, M. I. (2009). Variations in catechol-O-methyltransferase gene interact with parenting to influence attention in early development. *Neuroscience, 164*, 121–130.

Vreeman, R. C., & Carroll, A. E. (2007). A systematic review of school-based interventions to prevent bullying. *Archives of Pediatrics & Adolescent Medicine, 161*, 78–88.

Weaver, I.C.G., Cervoni, N., Champagne, F. A., D'Alessio, A. C., Sharma, S., Seckl, J. R., et al. (2004). Epigenetic programming by maternal behavior. *Nature Neuroscience, 7*, 847–854.

Whelan, Y. M., Kretschmer, T., & Barker, E. D. (2014). MAOA, early experiences of harsh parenting, irritable opposition, and bullying-victimization: A moderated indirect-effects analysis. *Merrill-Palmer Quarterly, 60*, 217–237.

4

Relational Bullying and Psychosocial Correlates across the Life Course

Hillary K. Morin and Catherine P. Bradshaw

Recent research on bullying has focused on nonphysical forms of aggression that aim to damage peer relationships and social standing through behaviors such as exclusion, withdrawal of friendship, or rumor spreading. There has also been some controversy over the role that gender plays in relational aggression, with studies reporting mixed findings about whether women exhibit more relational aggression or are just more sensitive to relational forms of bullying (Card, Stucky, Sawalani, & Little, 2008; Crick, 1995). Yet, relationally aggressive behavior among both men and women has become a prominent topic of research inquiry and a particular form of bullying of increasing concern among educators, practitioners, and families. Studies have repeatedly shown the distressing qualities and high prevalence of relational aggression (for example, Card et al., 2008). In fact, the damaging effects of relational bullying and aggressive behavior have been noted for both aggressors and victims (Leff & Crick, 2010). However, few studies have considered the adaptive or functional role that relational bullying plays in the lives of youth.

The goal of this chapter is to review various definitions and conceptualizations of relational bullying. We draw heavily on the broader relational aggression literature and leverage it to better understand relational forms of bullying behavior. After first defining the construct of relational bullying and aggression, and reviewing the etymology of the terminology associated with this form of nonphysical aggression, we synthesize the evidence of an association between relational bullying and negative psychosocial outcomes and mental health correlates across the life course. We also explore the somewhat controversial topic of the adaptive function of relational bullying and the extent to which it may serve a functional or instrumental role in adolescence and adulthood. We then consider gender in light of recent research on relational forms of bullying. We conclude with a discussion of some implications for both research and practice.

WHAT IS RELATIONAL BULLYING?

Nonphysical aggression, which is also delineated as indirect aggression, social aggression, or relational aggression, focuses on the psychological harm inflicted on others through verbal and nonverbal means (Underwood, 2003). These three distinct yet overlapping terms have helped elucidate the problematic and harmful impact of nonphysical aggression. Below we consider the nuanced definitions of indirect, social, and relational bullying. Relational aggression and relational bullying are related and overlapping constructs; therefore, the terms are used interchangeably throughout this chapter.

Indirect Aggression and Bullying

Buss (1961) is credited with providing the original definition of *indirect aggression*, which is defined as aggressive behavior that is both subtle and hurtful in nature and avoids a counterattack "by rendering it difficult to identify the aggressor" (p. 8). Whereas direct aggression, such as physical fighting, readily identifies the perpetrator, indirect aggression avoids confrontation and allows the aggressor to remain anonymous. By remaining unidentified, the aggressor can avoid being the target of retaliation while not drawing disapproval from peers or discipline from adults. Indirect aggression can be verbal, such as engaging in rumor spreading, or physical, such as slashing a car tire (Lagerspetz, Bjorkqvist, & Peltonen, 1988).

Social Aggression and Bullying

Social aggression, as defined by Cairns, Cairns, Neckerman, Ferguson, and Gariépy (1989), is "the manipulation of group acceptance through alienation, ostracism, or character defamation" (p. 323). Social aggression often intends to inflict social harm on others by means of social relationship standing, friendships, and peer status. Galen and Underwood (1997) later refined this definition, adding that social aggression is geared toward negatively affecting another's self-esteem or social status. Examples of such behavior include both direct social aggression (the victim is aware of the perpetrator) and indirect social aggression (the aggressor is covert and circuitous) when gossiping, excluding, and manipulating relationships (Underwood, 2003). Taken together, these behaviors all involve the same goal of inflicting social harm on the victim.

Relational Aggression and Bullying

Crick and Grotpeter (1995) proposed a third term relating to nonphysical aggression. They defined *relational aggression* as "harming others through purposeful manipulation and damage of their peer relationships" (p. 711). Relational aggression can be enacted in a covert or secretive manner (for example, gossiping) or overt and blatant manner (for example, threatening to stop being friends). Examples of relationally aggressive behavior include social isolation, exclusion, ignoring, gossiping, or threatening to end a friendship. Unlike social aggression, the construct of relational aggression does not include nonverbal aggressive behavior. For example, mean faces or body language would be considered socially aggressive but not relationally aggressive because these are examples of nonverbal behavior (Vitaro, Brendgen, & Barker, 2006). Whereas social aggression is predominantly nonconfrontational, relationally aggressive behavior can be confrontational in nature, as, for example, when a friend tells another friend directly that he or she is not welcome at an event (for example, a birthday party) (Crick, 1995). Researchers hypothesize that relational aggression may replace physical aggression as youth learn that physically aggressive behavior often leads to discipline and legal sanctions. Relational aggression becomes a safer yet effective alternative method for expressing anger and displeasure (Prinstein, Boergers, & Vernberg, 2001).

RELATIONAL BULLYING AS MALADAPTIVE AND PROBLEMATIC

Several studies have enumerated the negative mental health and social-emotional outcomes associated with relational aggression and bullying (see, for example, Card et al., 2008; Crick, 1995; Galen & Underwood, 1997; Prinstein, Boergers, & Vernberg, 2001). Below we consider the range of internalizing, externalizing, and severe mental health correlates and potential consequences of relational aggression and bullying.

Correlates in Childhood and Adolescence

Research on relational aggression has been continually linked to a host of problems for both aggressors and victims (Leff, Waasdorp, & Crick, 2010). The most notable deficits include internalizing symptoms, such as depression, anxiety, and loneliness. Crick and Grotpeter (1995) first argued that involvement with relational aggression was related to psychological maladjustments and subsequent negative outcomes. Specifically, they found that being a victim of relational bullying was significantly related to psychological distress, including depression, social anxiety, social avoidance, and loneliness. Other studies have substantiated this claim, as relationally victimized youth were more emotionally upset, rejected by peers, and lonely compared with their nonvictimized peers (Crick & Bigbee, 1998). Researchers have similarly found that relationally aggressive youth were lonelier than nonrelationally aggressive youth (Prinstein et al., 2001), had social difficulties, were rejected by peers, and displayed social avoidance (Craig, 1998).

Studies have shown that relational victimization has a unique impact on mental health that is significantly different from the impact of overt victimization. For example, even after controlling for effects of experiences of overt victimization, overt aggression, and relational aggression, experiences of relational victimization have been linked with depression, loneliness, and self-restraint difficulties among school-age youth (Crick & Bigbee, 1998; Crick & Grotpeter, 1995). Teacher-reported experiences of relational victimization also predict subsequent increases in internalizing and externalizing symptoms among elementary school students without a reciprocated best friend (Hodges, Boivin, Vitaro, & Bukowski, 1999). Similarly, relationally victimized teenagers reported higher levels of internalizing symptoms, specifically heightened depression and loneliness and lower global self-worth. Yet relational victimization is also a unique predictor of social anxiety, social avoidance, and loneliness (Crick & Grotpeter, 1995) as well as suicidal ideation (Klomek, Marrocco, Kleinman, Schonfeld, & Gould, 2007).

Depression and Negative Self-Schema

Understanding the underlying mechanisms that promote feelings of depression and loneliness is critical to understanding the cyclical nature of relational victimization. As a result of youth's tendency to derive negative self-evaluations from their social experiences, their own self-schemas and self-perception of competence are negatively affected, often resulting in depression and anxiety (Crick & Dodge, 1994; Haines, Metalsky, Cardamone, & Joiner, 1999; Sacco, 1999). Youth's heightened levels of self-criticism negatively affect their mood. In addition, the reformulation of the social information processing model applied to relational aggression (Crick & Dodge, 1994) posited that youth develop a tendency to interpret ambiguous cues in peer experiences as hostile, therefore altering their behavior among peers and decreasing the rewarding nature of their future social interactions (Rubin & Rose-Krasnor, 1992). Interpretation of these social interactions as a negative appraisal of themselves may serve as the mechanism by which youth develop internalized distress, such as depression, loneliness, and low self-worth (Crick & Bigbee, 1998; Crick, Grotpeter, & Rockhill, 1999).

Because of the overarching tendency to attribute failures in the social realm to internal causes, relationally victimized youth may develop a sense of learned helplessness that can leave them vulnerable to social withdrawal and depression. In addition, this association between social-emotional adjustment difficulties and peer experiences is transactional. Adolescents who experience adjustment difficulties may be more likely to be victimized, whereas victimized youth may be more likely to experience adjustment difficulties. Similarly, prior negative peer experiences, such as being victimized, can reinforce the cognitive bias of social interactions. This may color future peer experiences, resulting in a cyclical relationship between mental health and victimization (Prinstein et al., 2001).

Compounding Effects of Victimization on Mental Health

Studies that have compared the impact of involvement in relational aggression and overt aggression have found that youth who experience both types of victimization have worse mental health outcomes than those who experience only one type of victimization. In contrast to low- or non-victimized adolescents, middle school and high school students who experienced verbal, physical, and relational forms of victimization reported the highest levels of internalizing problems (Bradshaw, Waasdorp, & O'Brennan, 2013). Recent research also suggests that youth who are relationally or indirectly victimized have more difficulty coping (Waasdorp & Bradshaw, 2011). The most intensely maladjusted adolescents with the highest levels of depression, loneliness, and externalizing behaviors were those who were relationally victimized (for example, excluded) as well as overtly (for example, punched) (Prinstein et al., 2001).

Mental Health Correlates in Emerging Adulthood

Although there is a wide range of research on the mental health correlates of relational aggression and victimization during childhood and early adolescence, far less is known about the impact of relational aggression and victimization during late adolescence and adulthood (Schmeelk, Sylvers, & Lilienfeld, 2008). The university setting offers a unique opportunity to examine the impact of relational aggression on social-emotional development. It is often the first time young adults live independent of their families, which may increase the importance of peer relationships and in turn exacerbate the impact of destructive relationally aggressive behavior. Werner and Crick (1999) examined the mental health attributes of college students that were associated with the use of relationally aggressive behaviors with peers. Regression analyses indicated an association between young adults'

($M = 19.5$ years) use of relational aggression and several negative mental health outcomes. Furthermore, relationally aggressive behavior was significantly associated with social-emotional maladjustment. This included problems previously found in younger samples, such as peer rejection and internalizing symptoms (for example, endorsements of feelings of sadness, pessimism about the future, life dissatisfaction) (Werner & Crick, 1999).

Novel forms of maladjustment were also found to be linked to the use of relational aggression among college students, including features of antisocial personality disorder, features of borderline personality disorder, and symptoms of disordered eating (Werner & Crick, 1999). Specifically, women with high levels of relational aggression in the study were found to have significantly higher levels of bulimic behaviors. These symptoms, which are more pathological in nature, are indicative of continued difficulty with affect regulation and impulse control for those young adults behaving in relationally aggressive ways with peers (Werner & Crick, 1999).

Mental Health Correlates in Adulthood

Several recent studies have added to the literature on the impact of relational aggression and victimization among college students. For example, relational victimization has been linked with increased levels of self-defeating behaviors among college students as well as correlated with higher levels of reported depression, anxiety, anger, alcohol problems, loneliness, stress, academic burnout, and social problems due to alcohol consumption (Dahlen, Czar, Prather, & Dyess, 2013; Twenge, Catanese, & Baumeister, 2002). Moreover, after controlling for gender, race, and experiences of relational victimization, college students with heightened anxiety, trait anger, and problems related to alcohol consumption predicted relationally aggressive behavior (Dahlen et al., 2013). These studies of relational aggression among college students further illustrate the link between exposure to relational aggression and poor mental health.

Although there has been relatively limited research on relational bullying in adulthood, results from a national epidemiological study found a significant association between traditional bullying and psychiatric diagnoses among adults (Vaughn et al., 2010). Structured interviews with over 43,000 adults in the United States found that just 6 percent of these adults had a history of bullying others. In addition, there were significant associations between bullying and bipolar disorder, substance use disorders, conduct disorder, and several personality disorders (antisocial, paranoid, and histrionic) (Vaughn et al., 2010). As the study did not specify the type of bullying behavior, additional research is needed to conclude whether these findings are true for relational forms of bullying. Given that adults spend a significant amount of time working, research has also focused on relational aggression in the workplace. Higher levels of relational aggression in the workplace have been shown to be significantly related to negative mental health correlates, including depressed affect, lower self-esteem, physical complaints, and greater alcohol use. (See chapter 12 for more on bullying in the workplace.)

RELATIONAL AGGRESSION AS NORMATIVE AND ADAPTIVE BEHAVIOR

Although considerable research has demonstrated an association between engagement in relational aggression and poor mental health, the normative and adaptive nature of relational aggression is often overlooked. High levels of relationally aggressive behavior are considered problematic; however, developmental psychologists posit that low and moderate levels of relational aggression may be common and normative (Geiger, Zimmer-Gembeck, & Crick, 2004). Envisioning relational aggression along a continuum, from normative to problematic, may help clarify how certain experiences with relational aggression may be considered adaptive or deviant.

The adaptive or maladaptive functions of relational aggression are important as they relate to psychosocial adjustment (Geiger et al., 2004; Salmivalli, Kaukiainen, & Lagerspetz, 2000). For example, gossip can have a benevolent purpose, as it provides an opportunity to discuss a conflict with a third party and can alert others that someone is in need of assistance (Underwood, Galen, & Paquette, 2001). Likewise, gossiping may increase feelings of group inclusion and help to build rapport among friends. Despite this "positive" outcome, it still includes the negative intent to harm the target of the rumor and often leads to adverse consequences, such as upsetting the target (Geiger, Zimmer-Gembeck, & Crick, 2004).

Higher levels of social intelligence are also positively correlated with elevated use of indirect aggression. Relationally aggressive acts require advanced understanding of the social context and an ability to manipulate a social infrastructure (Bjorkqvist, Lagerspetz, & Kaukiainen, 1992). Among a sample of Finnish youth, ages 10–14, indirect aggression but not confrontational aggression was associated with social intelligence (Kaukiainen et al., 1999). Social competence is hypothesized as necessary to appropriately execute relationally aggressive acts. Likewise, researchers have posited that youth who bully may have a superior theory of mind that helps them manipulate and control their targets (Sutton, Smith, & Swettenham, 1999). This advanced theory of mind and social competence is associated with engagement in relational aggression.

Popularity and competence have also been correlated with relational aggression among school-age youth. It may be that competence and popularity precede relationally aggressive behavior, in that individuals use their social competence and popular social standing to enact relational aggression. Among early adolescents ($M = 13.4$ years), risk factors associated with being physically aggressive include low academic competence, low popularity, and low scores of affiliation (for example, "smiles a lot," "friendly"). Verbal aggression was related to low academic competence and low "Olympian" scores (for example, sporting prowess, attractiveness, tendency to win games). In contrast to these poor adjustment scores across domains, social aggression was not associated with any of these risk factors. Moreover, the use of direct relational aggression was correlated with high popularity, Olympian, and affiliation scores (Xie, Swift, Cairns, & Cairns, 2002). These findings demonstrate how relational aggression in early adolescence may award individuals with desired outcomes such as popularity and that relationally aggressive youth may exhibit social competence. Likewise, it may be popularity that affords youth the ability to be relationally aggressive, as it creates a platform from which exclusion and gossip can be particularly damaging to the victim.

There has also been research on the intersection of popularity and likability in relation to aggression. For example, female youth who are more popular but not as well liked are more likely to be relationally aggressive (Lease, Kennedy, & Axelrod, 2002). Similarly, Rose, Swenson, and Carlson (2004) showed that perceived popularity buffers relationally aggressive adolescents against internalizing symptoms. Popularity among relationally aggressive youth and adolescents is likely due to their visibility and impact rather than their likability. It is important to note that the association between relational aggression and popularity has been shown to increase from age 10 to age 14, whereas likability appears to decline over the same time period (LaFontana & Cillessen, 2002).

Given the variation in outcomes across different age groups, it is important to understand the role of development, especially cognitive development, when assessing the adaptive or maladaptive nature of relational aggression and victimization. Although Card and colleagues' (2008) meta-analysis concluded that age did not moderate the relationship between relational aggression and adjustment and maladjustment (implying that there are not specific ages at which relational aggression can be considered exclusively problematic or adaptive), they suggested that relational aggression does continue to move along a continuum throughout development. Age does not appear to moderate the association between relational aggression and adjustment and maladjustment, but longitudinal research suggests that middle school students rated as highly relationally aggressive within a dyadic friendship experienced a significant increase in their perceptions of positive friendship quality one year later (Banny, Heilbron, Ames, & Prinstein, 2011). These results suggest that relationally aggressive behavior may serve to strengthen relationships by functioning as a bonding experience. Although these positive outcomes suggest that relational aggression may be adaptive in some contexts, there are certainly negative correlates associated with increased engagement in relational aggression that deserve further consideration.

WHAT ROLE DOES GENDER PLAY IN RELATIONAL BULLYING?

Past research has largely focused on overt aggression, with relatively few studies on relational aggression before the 1990s (Crick & Grotpeter, 1995). Because overt aggression is less common among women than it is in men, it was often wrongly concluded that women rarely exhibited aggression (Crick, 1995). The field has since shifted to focus more on relational aggression, which was originally considered by some to be a predominantly female behavior (Underwood, 2003). Although involvement in relational aggression has been shown to affect the mental health of both men and women, there have been mixed findings regarding the association between gender and the use of relational aggression. Some studies have suggested that relational aggression is more typical of women than of men (Bjorkqvist et al., 1992; Crick & Grotpeter, 1995); however, two meta-analyses found negligible gender differences in enactment of indirect aggression, thereby providing fairly conclusive evidence that indirect aggression is not a predominantly female behavior (Archer, 2004; Card et al., 2008).

Developmental research does suggest that use of indirect or direct aggression may vary by age. The theoretical developmental model proposed by Bjorkqvist and colleagues (1992) suggests that men typically enact more direct aggression than women; however, as verbal and physical forms of aggression become less socially acceptable in late childhood, both genders use social aggression as their primary aggressive strategy (Card et al., 2008; Vitaro et al., 2006). Studies have also found that girls are more likely than boys to use relational aggression during childhood, but gender differences among adolescents and young adults are less clear (Bailey & Ostrov, 2008). Other research has indicated that there are gender differences in levels of relational aggression for middle school youth but not for younger youth. Among older adolescent and adult samples, more equitable endorsement of relational aggression has been found among men and women, thereby reinforcing the stereotype that relational aggression is a predominantly female behavior (Dahlen et al., 2013).

CONCLUSIONS AND IMPLICATIONS

The aggression literature documents the association between relational aggression and psychosocial adjustment problems as well as some positive correlates (see Card et al., 2008). Relational aggression may be socially helpful and ameliorate some social situations; however, it can also result in negative consequences for mental health. Hawley and Vaughn (2003) summarized this balance well, stating, "it is not so much aggression per se that is adaptive or maladaptive but rather it is the specific functions of aggression that are associated with some proximal gains (status, goal attainment, dominance) or losses" (p. 241). The findings regarding both the negative outcomes and the somewhat adaptive and normative functions of relational bullying illustrate the complexity of this behavior. Given these disparate correlates, there is a need for additional research to better understand why some individuals who engage in relational aggression and bullying develop pathological outcomes whereas others may extract dominance and social status yet not develop severe maladaptive outcomes. It is important to understand this interplay between adaptive and maladaptive uses of nonphysical aggression and to measure it along a continuum. It is particularly important to consider the role of popularity and advanced social information processing when designing interventions for relational aggression. The social skills often addressed in prevention programs may not be relevant to those who do not have deficits in their social skills but rather use their advanced cognitive skills to enact relationally aggressive behaviors. Nevertheless, there is compelling evidence that relational forms of bullying are potentially problematic across the life course. More research is needed to understand factors that exacerbate and ameliorate their effects.

REFERENCES

Archer, J. (2004). Sex differences in aggression in real world settings: A meta-analytic review. *Review of General Psychology, 8,* 291–322.

Bailey, C., & Ostrov, J. (2008). Differentiating forms and functions of aggression in emerging adults: Associations with hostile attribution biases and normative beliefs. *Journal of Youth and Adolescence, 37,* 713–722. doi:10.1007/s10964-007-9211-5

Banny, A. M., Heilbron, N., Ames, A., & Prinstein, M. J. (2011). Relational benefits of relational aggression: Adaptive and maladaptive associations with adolescent friendship quality. *Developmental Psychology, 47,* 1153–1166. doi:10.1037/a0022546

Bjorkqvist, K., Lagerspetz, K.M.J., & Kaukiainen, A. (1992). Do females manipulate and males fight? Developmental trends in regard to direct and indirect aggression. *Aggressive Behavior, 18,* 117–127.

Bradshaw, C. P., Waasdorp, T. E., & O'Brennan, L. M. (2013). A latent class approach to examining forms of peer victimization. *Journal of Educational Psychology, 105,* 839–849. doi:10.1037/a0032091

Buss, A. H. (1961). *The psychology of aggression.* New York: Wiley.

Cairns, R. B., Cairns, B. D., Neckerman, H. J., Ferguson, L. L., & Gariépy, J.-L. (1989). Growth and aggression: I. Childhood to early adolescence. *Developmental Psychology, 25,* 320–330.

Card, N. A., Stucky, B. D., Sawalani, G. M., & Little, T. D. (2008). Direct and indirect aggression during childhood and adolescence: A meta-analytic review of gender differences, intercorrelations, and relations to maladjustment. *Child Development, 79,* 1185–1229. doi:10.1111/j.1467-8624.2008.01184.x

Craig, W. M. (1998). The relationship among bullying, victimization, depression, anxiety, and aggression in elementary school children. *Personality and Individual Differences, 24,* 123–130.

Crick, N. R. (1995). Relational aggression: The role of intent attributions, feelings of distress, and provocation type. *Development and Psychopathology, 7,* 313–322. doi:10.1017/S0954579400006520

Crick, N. R., & Bigbee, M. A. (1998). Relational and overt forms of peer victimization: A multiinformant approach. *Journal of Consulting and Clinical Psychology, 66,* 337–347.

Crick, N. R., & Dodge, K. (1994). A review and reformulation of social information-processing mechanisms in children's social adjustment. *Psychological Bulletin, 115,* 74–101. doi:10.1037/0033-2909.115.1.74

Crick, N. R., & Grotpeter, J. K. (1995). Relational aggression, gender, and social-psychological adjustment. *Child Development, 66,* 710–722. doi:10.2307/1131945

Crick, N. R., Grotpeter, J. K., & Rockhill, C. (1999). Social information processing and children's loneliness. In K. Rotenberg & S. Hymel (Eds.), *Children's loneliness* (pp. 153–175). New York: Cambridge University Press.

Dahlen, E. R., Czar, K. A., Prather, E., & Dyess, C. (2013). Relational aggression and victimization in college students. *Journal of College Student Development, 54*(2), 140–154.

Galen, B. R., & Underwood, M. K. (1997). A developmental investigation of social aggression among children. *Developmental Psychology, 33,* 589–600.

Geiger, T. C., Zimmer-Gembeck, M., & Crick, N. R. (2004). The science of relational aggression: Can we guide intervention? In M. M. Moretti, C. L. Odgers, & M. A. Jackson (Eds.), *Females and aggression: Contributing factors and intervention principles* (pp. 27–40). New York: Kluwer Academic/Plenum Press.

Haines, B. A., Metalsky, G. I., Cardamone, A. L., & Joiner. T. (1999). Interpersonal and cognitive pathways into the origins of attributional style: A developmental perspective. In T. Joiner & J. C. Coyne (Eds.), *The interactional nature of depression: Advances in interpersonal approaches* (pp. 65–92). Washington, DC: American Psychological Association.

Hawley, P. H., & Vaughn, B. E. (2003). Aggression and adaptation: The bright side to bad behavior. Introduction to special volume. *Merrill-Palmer Quarterly, 49,* 239–244.

Hodges, E.V.E., Boivin, M., Vitaro, F., & Bukowski, W. M. (1999). The power of friendship: Protection against an escalating cycle of peer victimization. *Developmental Psychology, 35,* 94–101. doi:10.1037/ 0012-1649.33.6.1032

Kaukiainen, A., Björkqvist, K., Lagerspetz, K., Österman, K., Salmivalli, C., Rothberg, S., & Ahlbom, A. (1999). The relationships between social intelligence, empathy, and three types of aggression. *Aggressive Behavior, 25*(2), 81–89.

Klomek, A. B., Marrocco, F., Kleinman, M., Schonfeld, I. S., & Gould, M. S. (2007). Bullying, depression and suicidality in adolescents. *Journal of the American Academy of Child and Adolescent Psychiatry, 46,* 40–49.

LaFontana, K. M., & Cillessen, A.H.N. (2002). Children's perceptions of popular and unpopular peers: A multi-method assessment. *Developmental Psychology, 38,* 635–647.

Lagerspetz, K. M., Bjorkqvist, K., & Peltonen, T. (1988). Is indirect aggression typical of females? Gender differences in aggressiveness in 11- to 12-year-old children. *Aggressive Behavior, 14,* 403–414.

Lease, A. M., Kennedy, C. A., & Axelrod, J. L. (2002). Children's social constructions of popularity. *Social Development, 11,* 87–109.

Leff, S. S., & Crick, N. R. (2010). Interventions for relational aggression: Innovative programming and next steps in research and practice. *School Psychology Review, 39,* 504–507.

Leff, S. S., Waasdorp, T., & Crick, N. R. (2010). A review of existing relational aggression programs: Strengths, limitations, and future directions. *School Psychology Review, 39,* 508–535.

Prinstein, M. J., Boergers, J., & Vernberg, E. M. (2001). Overt and relational aggression in adolescents: Social–psychological adjustment of aggressors and victims. *Journal of Clinical Child Psychology, 30,* 479–491. doi:10.1207/S15374424JCCP3004_05

Rose, A. J., Swenson, L. P., & Carlson, W. (2004). Friendships of aggressive youth: Considering the influences of being disliked and of being perceived as popular. *Journal of Experimental Child Psychology, 88,* 25–45. doi:10.1016/j.jecp.2004.02.005

Rubin, K. H., & Rose-Krasnor, L. (1992). Interpersonal problem solving and social competence in children. In V. B. Van Hassett & M. Hersen (Eds.), *Handbook of social development: A lifespan perspective* (pp. 283–323). New York: Plenum Press.

Sacco, W. P. (1999). A social–cognitive model of interpersonal processes in depression. In T. Joiner & J. C. Coyne (Eds.), *The interactional nature of depression: Advances in interpersonal approaches* (pp. 329–362). Washington, DC: American Psychological Association.

Salmivalli, C., Kaukiainen, A., & Lagerspetz, K. (2000). Aggression and sociometric status among peers: Do gender and type of aggression matter? *Scandinavian Journal of Psychology, 41,* 17–24.

Schmeelk, K., Sylvers, P., & Lilienfeld, S. (2008). Trait correlates of relational aggression in a nonclinical sample: DSM-IV personality disorders and psychopathy. *Journal of Personality Disorders, 22*(3), 269–283. doi:10.1521/pedi.2008.22.3.269

Sutton, J., Smith, P. K., & Swettenham, J. (1999). Bullying and 'theory of mind': A critique of the 'social skills deficit' view of anti-social behaviour. *Social Development, 8,* 117–127.

Twenge, J., Catanese, K., & Baumeister, R. (2002). Social exclusion causes self-defeating behavior. *Journal of Personality and Social Psychology, 83,* 606–615.

Underwood, M. K. (2003). *Social aggression among females.* New York: Guilford Press.

Underwood, M. K., Galen, B. R., & Paquette, J. A. (2001). Top ten challenges for understanding gender and aggression in children: Why can't we all just get along? *Social Development, 10,* 248–266.

Vaughn, M. G., Fu, Q., Bender, K., DeLisi, M., Beaver, K. M., Perron, B. E., & Howard, M. O. (2010). Psychiatric correlates of bullying in the United States: Findings from a national sample. *Psychiatric Quarterly, 81*(3), 183–195. doi:10.1007/s11126-010-9128-0

Vitaro, F., Brendgen, M., & Barker, E. D. (2006). Subtypes of aggressive behaviors: A developmental perspective. *International Journal of Behavioral Development, 30*(1), 12–19. doi:10.1177/0165025406059968

Waasdorp, T. E., & Bradshaw, C. P. (2011). Examining student responses to frequent bullying: A latent class approach. *Journal of Educational Psychology, 103,* 336–352. doi:10.1037/a0022747

Werner, N. E., & Crick, N. R. (1999). Relational aggression and social-psychological adjustment in a college sample. *Journal of Abnormal Psychology, 108,* 615–623.

Xie, H., Swift, D. J., Cairns, B. D., & Cairns, R. B. (2002). Aggressive behaviors in social interaction and developmental adaptation: A narrative analysis of interpersonal conflicts during early adolescence. *Social Development, 11*(2), 205–224.

5

Bullying, Mental Health, and Suicide

Jeffrey Duong and Catherine P. Bradshaw

Highly publicized tragedies have led to the mounting recognition that bullying and suicide are serious public health issues. Meanwhile, there has also been a growing misconception that bullying and suicide are causally linked. Although many experts agree that bullying and suicide are strongly associated, it is equally important to acknowledge that the link between bullying and suicide is highly complex. To better understand this complexity, the role of mental health warrants consideration. In this chapter, we review the empirical research on bullying and suicide and highlight the important contributions of mental health. We also present evidence-based recommendations and guidelines on how mental health professionals may address bullying and suicide.

DEVELOPMENTAL CONSEQUENCES OF BULLYING AND SUICIDE OVER THE LIFE COURSE

Bullying and suicide represent major public health challenges that affect youth. Epidemiologic studies have reported that suicide is the fourth leading cause of death for those between ages five and 14, which spans childhood through early adolescence. Between adolescence and early adulthood (ages 15–24), however, suicide rises to become the second leading cause of death (Hoyert & Xu, 2012). The research estimates that 15.8 percent of all youth have seriously considered attempting suicide, 12.8 percent have made a plan about how they would attempt suicide, 7.8 percent have attempted suicide one or more times, and 2.4 percent have made a serious suicide attempt that required medical attention (Eaton et al., 2012). Given the high prevalence of suicidal behaviors among youth, it is imperative to identify and intervene in potential risk factors.

Research suggests that bullying often affects individuals earlier in life, prior to when suicidal behaviors are usually observed (Klomek et al., 2009). Bullying involvement tends to peak when children transition from elementary to middle school (Pellegrini & Bartini, 2000). Those who are involved in bullying are at increased risk for numerous physical and mental health problems. Victims of bullying often report psychosomatic complaints, such as headaches, backaches, or abdominal problems (Gini & Pozzoli, 2009). They also become less engaged in school, which can affect their academic performance (Juvonen, Wang, & Espinoza, 2011). Moreover, victimized youth typically exhibit depression, anxiety, and other mental health problems (Copeland, Wolke, Angold, & Costello, 2013). Perpetrators of bullying are at risk for a broad range of negative outcomes as well, including poor school adjustment, delinquency, and subsequent criminality and antisocial behavior (Ttofi & Farrington, 2011).

Childhood victimization is widely known to have long-term repercussions that last into adulthood (Klomek et al., 2013). For example, individuals who have been victimized frequently during childhood may become more likely to hold unfavorable cognitive appraisals of life experiences beyond bullying. Broad maladaptive appraisals of adverse life events may lead these individuals to become less likely to develop healthy and proactive responses to emerging challenges as adults (Hunter & Boyle, 2002). For instance, they may feel less control during interactions with others, which may lead to anxiety. Meanwhile, according to the hopelessness theory of depression, individuals are more likely to develop depressive disorders from attributing negative experiences to factors outside of their control (Abramson, Metalsky, & Alloy, 1989). Thus, victimized youth may learn to cope with conflicts by internalizing their emotions, which may lead to depression and suicide (Hunter & Boyle, 2002; Klomek et al., 2009).

Role of Mental Health in Bullying and Suicide

Considering the mental health implications of bullying involvement, it is not surprising that studies have consistently linked it to suicide (Copeland et al., 2013). Research has shown that youth involved in bullying may be three to five times more likely to engage in suicidal ideation or make suicide attempts compared with those who are not involved in bullying (Espelage & Holt, 2013). In evaluating these findings, however, it is important to be cognizant of the role of mental health (Arseneault, Bowes, & Shakoor, 2010). Bullying involvement may result in many negative mental health outcomes, which are strongly associated with youth suicide. Data from the National Violent Death Reporting System, for example, suggest that emotional concerns (for example, depressed mood or substance abuse) are common among suicide decedents (Karch, Logan, McDaniel, Floyd, & Vagi, 2013). It is therefore possible that suicide might not result directly from bullying. Instead, bullying may lead youth to develop mental health problems, which put them at greater risk for suicide.

Despite a robust association, a causal link between bullying and suicide has not yet been established in the extant research (Copeland et al., 2013). One common barrier is that most studies on the connection between bullying and suicide have been limited by their cross-sectional study design. Because cross-sectional research typically involves survey data collected at a single time point, it cannot demonstrate a temporal association between bullying and suicide. Recent longitudinal studies suggest that depression and suicidal behaviors may follow bullying experiences among youth, yet more studies are needed before establishing causality (Klomek et al., 2013). Another important consideration is that most bullied youth do not become suicidal (Suicide Prevention Resource Center [SPRC], 2011). Rather, mental health concerns, such as impulsivity, depression, or anxiety, may follow experiences of bullying among youth, putting them at risk for suicide (Klomek et al., 2009). Alternatively, those who already have a mental health condition may be affected more severely by bullying (Klomek et al., 2013). The risk for suicide might also be greater only among certain groups of frequently victimized individuals, such as sexual minority youth or children with disabilities (Birkett, Espelage, & Koenig, 2009; Duong & Bradshaw, 2014a; Rose, Espelage, Aragon, & Elliott, 2011). Moreover, bully–victims often are at greatest risk for mental health disorders and suicidal behaviors (Espelage & Holt, 2013; Kim & Leventhal, 2008). The evidence clearly shows that the association between bullying and suicide is highly complex, and it will be necessary to appreciate the role of mental health to address these concerns effectively.

Overlapping Risk and Protective Factors between Bullying and Suicide

Studies have shown that bullying and suicide share several overlapping risk and protective factors. For example, mental health plays an important role in both youth bullying and suicide. Specifically, youth with internalizing problems (for example, depression and anxiety) are at greater risk for bullying and suicide (Qin, Agerbo, & Mortensen, 2002; SPRC, 2011). Children with a family history of mental illness are also more likely to be bullied and engage in suicidal behavior (Qin et al., 2002; SPRC, 2011). Like those at risk for suicide, bullied youth have often experienced maltreatment and domestic violence at home as well (Baldry, 2003; Shields & Cicchetti, 2001). Childhood externalizing problems may also predispose youth to bullying and suicide. For instance, youth displaying aggressive and impulsive behavior during early childhood may experience peer rejection, resulting in social isolation and a greater likelihood of bullying involvement and suicidal behavior later in life (Snyder et al., 2003).

Conversely, studies have identified certain individual or environmental characteristics that may protect youth from bullying and suicide. Protective characteristics in youth include enhanced social competencies and skills, such as self-awareness and management, relationship skills, social awareness, and responsible decision making (Greenberg et al., 2003). Developing these skills can reduce both aggressive behaviors (for example, bullying) and internalizing problems in youth (Riggs, Greenberg, Kusché, & Pentz, 2006). In addition to individual characteristics, environmental factors such as social connectedness between youth and their family members, peers, and adults in school may decrease the likelihood that these youth will engage in harmful behaviors, including bullying and suicide (Bradshaw & Guerra, 2008; Duong & Bradshaw, 2014a; Resnick, Ireland, & Borowsky, 2004).

Comprehensive Public Health Approaches in Bullying and Suicide Prevention

The broad range of overlapping risk and protective factors for bullying and suicide necessitates comprehensive strategies to address these concerns. To that end, we present action-oriented guidelines on how mental health providers may address bullying and suicide. These empirically supported recommendations have been discussed in other publications (Duong & Bradshaw, 2014b; SPRC, 2011), and we elaborate on these integrative public health strategies in this section.

Start Prevention Early. Mental health practitioners can support early bullying and suicide prevention efforts in a variety of ways. Specifically, providers may help schools to carry out bullying assessments to aid in the monitoring and early identification of emerging problems. Early assessments allow school leaders to evaluate the magnitude of bullying in their schools, which will guide the implementation and modification of intervention activities. Early prevention should involve encouraging youth to report bullying situations to adults. When adults become aware of bullying situations, it is important for them to intervene immediately by separating those involved. Clearly stating that bullying is unacceptable is also crucial, as it may influence children's attitudes about aggressive behavior (O'Brennan, Bradshaw, & Sawyer, 2009). Early prevention also helps in identifying youth who may benefit from additional support services. For example, some youth may require more guidance in learning how to cope with adverse situations like bullying. Developing greater self-efficacy and assertiveness in children is particularly significant in enabling them to resolve peer conflicts in the future.

Integrate Bullying and Suicide Prevention Efforts. Currently, there exist multiple prevention programs aiming to address a range of risk behaviors among youth, including bullying and suicide (Gottfredson & Gottfredson, 2001). Given their overlapping risk and protective factors, however, prevention efforts should use integrative, multitiered public health approaches that affect both bullying and suicide. Such strategies involve targeting the school environment through universal programs, identifying at-risk youth who might benefit from behavioral and mental health services in selective programs, and establishing intervention protocols indicated for youth already engaged in bullying and suicidal behaviors (Arseneault et al., 2010; Guerra & Bradshaw, 2008; O'Brennan et al., 2009; Zenere & Lazarus, 2009).

Promote Positive and Supportive School Climates. The school climate is a crucial context for mental health providers to address bullying and suicide. Researchers widely agree that promoting positive and supportive school climates is an effective strategy for prevention (Birkett et al., 2009; Duong & Bradshaw, 2014a). Respect, care, and inclusion are particularly important features of positive and supportive climates that allow students to form healthy connections with adults, which may reduce the prevalence of bullying and suicide (Blum, 2005; Gini, Pozzoli, Borghi, & Franzoni, 2008). Climates that empower students to contribute to the prevention of bullying and suicide are also vital, as students—compared with adults—often have more knowledge about bullying situations and who among their peers may be at risk for suicide (Bradshaw, Sawyer, & O'Brennan, 2007). Teaching students that getting help is not the same as "tattling" is also a key strategy to creating a safer environment.

Train Adults How to Identify and Respond to At-Risk Youth. Screening programs and gatekeeper training are central components of bullying and suicide prevention (Wyman et al., 2008). Focused efforts are needed to identify bullied youth who may be at increased risk for suicide (Espelage & Swearer, 2003). Adults should receive training on how to respond appropriately when encountering youth who might be struggling (Duong & Bradshaw, 2013; Wyman et al., 2008). Appropriate responses include listening to and focusing on the needs of youth and providing assurances to victims that bullying is not their fault and that everyone deserves to be treated with respect (Mynard, Joseph, & Alexander, 2000). Furthermore, encouraging adults to be persistent in engaging youth who are struggling with bullying and suicidal behavior is essential. Following up regularly with youth who have previously been involved in bullying is important in determining the need for additional mental health services to reduce suicide risk.

Guiding school leaders to develop policies and protocols for how staff should respond to students who are at risk for bullying and suicide is also essential. Protocols should highlight the need for both timely interventions and referrals to mental health or social services for at-risk youth (Greene, 2003; Kumpulainen, Räsänen, & Puura, 2001). To support the work of mental health providers, administrators must ensure that students can access their services. For more information on mental health supports in schools, see the Substance Abuse and Mental Health Services Administration's (2012) *Preventing Suicide: A Toolkit for High Schools.*

Target Youth Populations Vulnerable to Bullying and Suicide. Identifying and supporting youth vulnerable to bullying or suicide is crucial to prevention. Bullying experiences may differ for youth on the basis of their race, gender, and sexual orientation or whether they have a disability or mental illness. Many prevention efforts do not account for these potentially vulnerable groups. For instance, race-based harassment and cultural bias represent crucial issues for ethnic minority groups (Russell, Sinclair, Poteat, & Koenig, 2012). In addition, research suggests that girls may be at greater risk for psychological maladjustment when they are involved in bullying (Klomek et al., 2009). *Homophobic bullying*, defined as bullying related to an individual's perceived sexual orientation, is a major concern pertaining to sexual minority youth (Berlan, Corliss, Field, Goodman, & Austin, 2010; Poteat, O'Dwyer, & Mereish, 2012). In light of these considerations, prevention efforts should aim to reduce intolerance, celebrate diversity, and establish structured support systems (for example, gay–straight alliances) in schools. The Gay, Lesbian & Straight Education Network (2013) provides safe space kits that offer guidance on training staff to reduce biased language and promote supportive environments in schools (see http://www.glsen.org/safespace).

Use Strategies That Include Families, Schools, and Communities. Adopting an ecological perspective is essential to understanding and reducing both bullying and suicide. Factors contributing to these problems may span multiple contexts, including schools, families, and communities. Comprehensive strategies that involve intervening in multiple contexts can greatly reduce violent behaviors such as bullying or suicide. For example, family settings are a crucial context for intervention, and caregivers serve as particularly important stakeholders, as they play a substantial role in resolving bullying situations that involve their children (Waasdorp, Bradshaw, & Duong, 2011). Thus, teaching caregivers how to talk with their children about bullying, suicide, and mental health is essential. Specifically, raising awareness about potential mental health problems associated with bullying and addressing potential issues such as stigma will help caregivers better support their children (Sawyer, Bradshaw, & O'Brennan, 2008).

To bolster prevention and outreach efforts, community involvement is imperative (Lindstrom Johnson, Finigan, Bradshaw, Haynie, & Cheng, 2011). Mental health providers can provide their expertise on health education and communication efforts, such as social marketing campaigns, which may be used to inform other professional groups (for example, medical or law enforcement) about bullying and suicide issues (Srabstein et al., 2008). In 2010, the Centers for Disease Control and Prevention launched the Striving to Reduce Youth Violence Everywhere initiative. The program takes a comprehensive, coordinated, multisector public health approach to reduce youth violence. It works by empowering youth to resist violence, fostering relationships between adults and youth and offering guidance on how to cultivate safe and connected communities. By bolstering social connectedness and building violence-free families, schools, and communities, this initiative can potentially promote healthy youth development.

Keep Up with Technology. As technology continues to advance, the dynamics surrounding bullying and suicide may become increasingly complicated. Cyberbullying has emerged as a growing concern in recent years, linked in the media to high-profile suicides (Hinduja & Patchin, 2010). Research estimates that over one in 10 students have been cyberbullied in their lifetimes (Schneider, O'Donnell, Stueve, & Coulter, 2012; Wang,

Nansel, & Iannotti, 2011). Although it may be the least common form of bullying that youth experience, cyberbullying differs from traditional bullying in many salient ways. For instance, cyberbullying has the potential to occur in front of a larger audience (Bradshaw, Waasdorp, & O'Brennan, 2013). Moreover, by not seeing the impact of cyberbullying on their victims, perpetrators may feel less empathy and not realize the consequences of their actions (Hinduja & Patchin, 2010). Cyberbullying is also more challenging to avoid, as it is not confined to the school. Finally, it is more difficult to identify victims and perpetrators, which creates challenges for adequately monitoring and supervising youth (Ybarra, Diener-West, & Leaf, 2007).

Youth who are cyberbullied are at risk for experiencing negative outcomes similar to those resulting from traditional bullying, including depression, poor academic performance, behavior problems, and suicidal ideation (Hinduja & Patchin, 2010; Schneider et al., 2012; Sourander et al., 2010). Addressing electronic media is therefore necessary for intervening in bullying and suicide. To that end, mental health practitioners can educate the public on the complex nature of cyberbullying and the different types of electronic media through which it occurs (for example, text messaging, social networks, blogs, and Web forums). It is also through these various forms of media that youth may begin to show signs of suicide risk (SPRC, 2011). Fostering cooperation between educators, caregivers, and youth may yield effective policies and strategies to reduce cyberbullying. For example, youth may serve as key informants in identifying emerging popular media outlets where cyberbullying might happen, which allows family caregivers and school officials to intervene (Hertz & David-Ferdon, 2008).

Exercise Caution in Reporting Bullying-Related Suicides. When reporting instances of bullying-related suicide, it is essential to avoid overstating the link between bullying and suicide (SPRC, 2011). Recent longitudinal studies have shown that the association between bullying and suicide is complex and may be partially explained by underlying mental health conditions (Arseneault et al., 2010; Copeland et al., 2013; Klomek et al., 2013). Furthermore, research on social contagion suggests that reporting and publicizing details of suicides may lead to an "epidemic" or increased rates of suicide, particularly among younger individuals or persons with mental health concerns (for example, depression or anxiety) (Joiner, 1999; Romer, Jamieson, & Jamieson, 2006). Through a process of "disinhibition," at-risk individuals who are exposed to details of a suicide may perceive that it is normative or acceptable to commit suicide to escape problems such as bullying. These individuals may feel that they have permission to act out on their suicidal thoughts (Joiner, 1999; Romer et al., 2006). Thus, mental health providers play a fundamental role in urging caution in the media's reporting of bullying-related suicides. Practitioners may offer their experienced perspective in discourse about bullying and suicide and emphasize the significance of mental health. Media releases on this topic should highlight the sophisticated nuances surrounding bullying and suicide to encourage conversations about youth mental health. Finally, the media should be reminded to follow established guidelines in reporting bullying and suicides. (For more information, see http://www.stopbullying.gov/news/media/index.html.)

CONCLUSION

Bullying and suicide are important public health issues facing youth and have captured the attention of policymakers and the general public in recent years. Mental health practitioners are uniquely positioned to contribute to prevention efforts by guiding school policy development, implementing prevention programs, and working closely with youth, families, and communities. As studies have demonstrated, bullying and suicide may share some common risk and protective factors. Thus, programs using public health approaches are essential for addressing these concerns. In implementing prevention programs, mental health providers should be aware of the special populations of youth that might be particularly vulnerable to both bullying and suicide (for example, minority groups). Although the school environment is a central context for addressing bullying and suicide, it is important not to ignore the potential contributions of families, peer groups, and the broader community. It is essential to use integrative, comprehensive public health approaches to reduce bullying and suicide among youth and to improve their mental health.

REFERENCES

Abramson, L. Y., Metalsky, G. I., & Alloy, L. B. (1989). Hopelessness depression: A theory-based subtype of depression. *Psychological Review, 96*, 358–372.

Arseneault, L., Bowes, L., & Shakoor, S. (2010). Bullying victimization in youths and mental health problems: 'Much ado about nothing'? *Psychological Medicine, 40*, 717–729.

Baldry, A. C. (2003). Bullying in schools and exposure to domestic violence. *Child Abuse & Neglect, 27*, 713–732.

Berlan, E., Corliss, H., Field, A., Goodman, E., & Austin, S. (2010). Sexual orientation and bullying among adolescents in the Growing Up Today Study. *Journal of Adolescent Health, 46*(4), 1–6.

Birkett, M., Espelage, D. L., & Koenig, B. (2009). LGB and questioning students in schools: The moderating effects of homophobic bullying and school climate on negative outcomes. *Journal of Youth and Adolescence, 38*, 989–1000.

Blum, R. W. (2005). A case for school connectedness. *Educational Leadership, 62*(7), 16–20.

Bradshaw, C. P., & Guerra, N. G. (2008). Future directions for research on core competencies. In N. G. Guerra & C. P. Bradshaw (Eds.), *Core competencies to prevent problem behaviors and promote positive youth development: New directions for child and adolescent development, 122*, 89–92.

Bradshaw, C. P., Sawyer, A. L., & O'Brennan, L. M. (2007). Bullying and peer victimization at school: Perceptual differences between students and school staff. *School Psychology Review, 36*(3), 361–382.

Bradshaw, C. P., Waasdorp, T. E., & O'Brennan, L. M. (2013). A latent class approach to examining forms of peer victimization. *Journal of Educational Psychology, 105*, 839–849.

Copeland, W. E., Wolke, D., Angold, A., & Costello, J. (2013). Adult psychiatric outcomes of bullying and being bullied by peers in childhood and adolescence. *JAMA Psychiatry, 70*, 419–426.

Duong, J., & Bradshaw, C. P. (2013). Using the extended parallel process model to examine teachers' likelihood of intervening in bullying. *Journal of School Health, 83*, 422–429.

Duong, J., & Bradshaw, C. (2014a). Associations between bullying and engaging in aggressive and suicidal behaviors among sexual minority youth: The moderating role of connectedness. *Journal of School Health, 84*, 636–645.

Duong, J., & Bradshaw, C. P. (2014b). Bullying and suicide prevention: Taking a balanced approach that is scientifically informed. In P. B. Goldblum, D. Espelage, J. Chu, & B. Bongar (Eds.), *The challenge of youth suicide and bullying* (pp. 19–27). Oxford, England: Oxford University Press.

Eaton, D. K., Kann, L., Kinchen, S., Shanklin, S., Flint, K. H., Hawkins, J., et al. (2012). Youth risk behavior surveillance: United States, 2011. *Morbidity and Mortality Weekly Report, 61*(4), 1–162.

Espelage, D. L., & Holt, M. K. (2013). Suicidal ideation and school bullying experiences after controlling for depression and delinquency. *Journal of Adolescent Health, 53*(1), S27–S31.

Espelage, D. L., & Swearer, S. M. (2003). Research on school bullying and victimization: What have we learned and where do we go from here? *School Psychology Review, 32*, 365–383.

Gay, Lesbian & Straight Education Network. (2013). *The Safe Space Kit: Guide to being an ally to LGBT students.* New York: Author.

Gini, G., & Pozzoli, T. (2009). Association between bullying and psychosomatic problems: A meta-analysis. *Pediatrics, 123*, 1059–1065.

Gini, G., Pozzoli, T., Borghi, F., & Franzoni, L. (2008). The role of bystanders in students' perception of bullying and sense of safety. *Journal of School Psychology, 46*, 617–638.

Gottfredson, G. D., & Gottfredson, D. C. (2001). What schools do to prevent problem behavior and promote safe environments. *Journal of Educational and Psychological Consultation, 12*, 313–344.

Greenberg, M. T., Weissberg, R. P., O'Brien, M. U., Zins, J. E., Fredericks, L., Resnik, H., & Elias, M. J. (2003). Enhancing school-based prevention and youth development through coordinated social, emotional, and academic learning. *American Psychologist, 58*, 466–474.

Greene, M. B. (2003). Counseling and climate change as treatment modalities for bullying in school. *International Journal for the Advancement of Counselling, 25*, 293–302.

Guerra, N. G., & Bradshaw, C. P. (2008). Linking the prevention of problem behaviors and positive youth development: Core competences for positive youth development. *New Directions for Child and Adolescent Development, 122*, 1–17.

Hertz, M. F., & David-Ferdon, C. (2008). *Electronic media and youth violence: A CDC issue brief for educators and caregivers.* Atlanta, GA: Centers for Disease Control and Prevention.

Hinduja, S., & Patchin, J. W. (2010). Bullying, cyberbullying, and suicide. *Archives of Suicide Research, 14*(3), 206–221.

Hoyert, D. L., & Xu, J. (2012). Deaths: Preliminary data for 2011. *National Vital Statistics Reports, 61*(6). Retrieved from http://www.cdc.gov/nchs/data/nvsr61/nvsr61_06.pdf

Hunter, S. C., & Boyle, J. M. (2002). Perceptions of control in the victims of school bullying: The importance of early intervention. *Educational Research, 44*, 323–336.

Joiner, T. E. (1999). The clustering and contagion of suicide. *Current Directions in Psychological Science, 8*(3), 89–92.

Juvonen, J., Wang, Y., & Espinoza, G. (2011). Bullying experiences and compromised academic performance across middle school grades. *Journal of Early Adolescence, 31*, 152–173.

Karch, D. L., Logan, J., McDaniel, D. D., Floyd, C. F., & Vagi, K. J. (2013). Precipitating circumstances of suicide among youth aged 10–17 years by sex: Data from the National Violent Death Reporting System, 16 states, 2005–2008. *Journal of Adolescent Health, 53*(1), S51–S53.

Kim, Y. S., & Leventhal, B. (2008). Bullying and suicide. A review. *International Journal of Adolescent Medicine and Health, 20*(2), 133–154.

Klomek, A. B., Kleinman, M., Altschuler, E., Marrocco, F., Amakawa, L., & Gould, M. S. (2013). Suicidal adolescents' experiences with bullying perpetration and victimization during high school as risk factors for later depression and suicidality. *Journal of Adolescent Health, 53*(1), S37–S42.

Klomek, A. B., Sourander, A., Niemelä, S., Kumpulainen, K., Piha, J., Tamminen, T., et al. (2009). Childhood bullying behaviors as a risk for suicide attempts and completed suicides: A population-based birth cohort study. *Journal of the American Academy of Child & Adolescent Psychiatry, 48*(3), 254–261.

Kumpulainen, K., Räsänen, E., & Puura, K. (2001). Psychiatric disorders and the use of mental health services among children involved in bullying. *Aggressive Behavior, 27*(2), 102–110.

Lindstrom Johnson, S. R., Finigan, N. M., Bradshaw, C. P., Haynie, D. L., & Cheng, T. L. (2011). Examining the link between neighborhood context and parental messages to their adolescent children about violence. *Journal of Adolescent Health, 49*(1), 58–63.

Mynard, H., Joseph, S., & Alexander, J. (2000). Peer-victimisation and posttraumatic stress in adolescents. *Personality and Individual Differences, 29*, 815–821.

O'Brennan, L. M., Bradshaw, C. P., & Sawyer, A. L. (2009). Examining developmental differences in the social-emotional problems among frequent bullies, victims, and bully/victims. *Psychology in the Schools, 46*(2), 100–115.

Pellegrini, A. D., & Bartini, M. (2000). A longitudinal study of bullying, victimization, and peer affiliation during the transition from primary school to middle school. *American Educational Research Journal, 37*, 699–725.

Poteat, V. P., O'Dwyer, L. M., & Mereish, E. H. (2012). Changes in how students use and are called homophobic epithets over time: Patterns predicted by gender, bullying, and victimization status. *Journal of Educational Psychology, 104*, 393–406.

Qin, P., Agerbo, E., & Mortensen, P. B. (2002). Suicide risk in relation to family history of completed suicide and psychiatric disorders: A nested case-control study based on longitudinal registers. *Lancet, 360*(9340), 1126–1130.

Resnick, M., Ireland, M., & Borowsky, I. (2004). Youth violence perpetration: What protects? What predicts? Findings from the National Longitudinal Study of Adolescent Health. *Journal of Adolescent Health, 35*, 424.e1–424.e10.

Riggs, N. R., Greenberg, M. T., Kusché, C. A., & Pentz, M. A. (2006). The mediational role of neurocognition in the behavioral outcomes of a social-emotional prevention program in elementary school students: Effects of the PATHS curriculum. *Prevention Science, 7*(1), 91–102.

Romer, D., Jamieson, P. E., & Jamieson, K. H. (2006). Are news reports of suicide contagious? A stringent test in six U.S. cities. *Journal of Communication, 56*(2), 253–270.

Rose, C. A., Espelage, D. L., Aragon, S. R., & Elliott, J. (2011). Bullying and victimization among students in special education and general education curricula. *Exceptionality Education International, 21*(2), 2–14.

Russell, S. T., Sinclair, K. O., Poteat, V. P., & Koenig, B. W. (2012). Adolescent health and harassment based on discriminatory bias. *American Journal of Public Health, 102*, 493–495.

Sawyer, A. L., Bradshaw, C. P., & O'Brennan, L. M. (2008). Examining ethnic, gender, and developmental differences in the way children report being a victim of "bullying" on self-report measures. *Journal of Adolescent Health, 43*, 106–114.

Schneider, S. K., O'Donnell, L., Stueve, A., & Coulter, R. (2012). Cyberbullying, school bullying, and psychological distress: A regional census of high school students. *American Journal of Public Health, 102*, 171–177.

Shields, A., & Cicchetti, D. (2001). Parental maltreatment and emotion dysregulation as risk factors for bullying and victimization in middle childhood. *Journal of Clinical Child Psychology, 30*, 349–363.

Snyder, J., Booker, E., Patrick, M. R., Snyder, A. Z., Schrepferman, L., & Stoolmiller, M. (2003). Observed peer victimization during elementary school: Continuity, growth, and relation to risk for child antisocial and depressive behavior. *Child Development, 74*, 1881–1898.

Sourander, A., Brunstein Klomek, A., Ikonen, M., Lindroos, J., Luntamo, T., Koskelainen, M., et al. (2010). Psychosocial risk factors associated with cyberbullying among adolescents: A population-based study. *Archives of General Psychiatry, 67*, 720–728.

Srabstein, J., Joshi, P., Due, P., Wright, J., Leventhal, B., Merrick, J., et al. (2008). Prevention of public health risks linked to bullying: A need for a whole community approach. *International Journal of Adolescent Medicine and Health, 20*(2), 185–200.

Substance Abuse and Mental Health Services Administration. (2012). *Preventing suicide: A toolkit for high schools* (HHS Publication No. SMA-12-4669). Rockville, MD: Center for Mental Health Services, Substance Abuse and Mental Health Services Administration.

Suicide Prevention Resource Center. (2011). *Issue brief: Suicide and bullying.* Newton, MA: Author.

Ttofi, M. M., & Farrington, D. P. (2011). Effectiveness of school-based programs to reduce bullying: A systematic and meta-analytic review. *Journal of Experimental Criminology, 7*(1), 27–56.

Waasdorp, T. E., Bradshaw, C. P., & Duong, J. (2011). The link between parents' perceptions of the school and their responses to school bullying: Variation by child characteristics and the forms of victimization. *Journal of Educational Psychology, 103*(2), 324–335.

Wang, J., Nansel, T., & Iannotti, R. (2011). Cyber bullying and traditional bullying: Differential association with depression. *Journal of Adolescent Health, 48*(4), 415–417.

Wyman, P. A., Brown, C. H., Inman, J., Cross, W., Schmeelk-Cone, K., Guo, J., & Pena, J. B. (2008). Randomized trial of a gatekeeper program for suicide prevention: 1-year impact on secondary school staff. *Journal of Consulting and Clinical Psychology, 76*, 104–115.

Ybarra, M. L., Diener-West, M., & Leaf, P. J. (2007). Examining the overlap in Internet harassment and school bullying: Implications for school intervention. *Journal of Adolescent Health, 41*, S42–S50.

Zenere, F. J., & Lazarus, P. J. (2009). The sustained reduction of youth suicidal behavior in an urban, multicultural school district. *School Psychology Review, 38*(2), 189–199.

6

Cyberbullying: Risk Factors and Consequences across the Life Course

Tracy E. Waasdorp, Zephyr Horowitz-Johnson, and
Stephen S. Leff

Researchers estimate that approximately 95 percent of teenagers use the Internet, 78 percent have cell phones, and 81 percent use social networking sites (Rainie, 2014), whereas 87 percent of adults use the Internet and 90 percent have cell phones (Pew Research Center, 2014b). These numbers continue to grow each year. Given the pervasive use of technology, it is not surprising that individuals use these technologies as a way in which to harm others. In fact, 40 percent of Internet users have experienced aggressive behaviors online, with those between the ages of 18 and 29 most likely to report having experienced it (Pew Research Center, 2014a). These aggressive behaviors have been called cyberbullying, electronic bullying, Internet bullying, or cyber aggression. For this chapter, the term *cyberbullying* will be used.

Given the growing importance of electronic media in today's social interactions, it is critical to understand the scope and impact of cyberbullying. The goal of this chapter is to provide a comprehensive review of the research on cyberbullying and the strengths, challenges, and next steps for inquiry in this important field. Taking a life course developmental perspective, we highlight the complexity of cyberbullying across different developmental periods.

The authors wish to acknowledge support from the Violence Prevention Initiative at the Children's Hospital of Philadelphia and a grant from the Institute of Educational Sciences in the Department of Education (R305AI30175).

TRADITIONAL BULLYING AND CYBERBULLYING

As described in chapter 1, traditional *bullying* is defined as intentionally aggressive behavior that occurs repeatedly against a victim, where there is an "observed or perceived" power imbalance, whether it be physical, verbal, or relational in nature (Gladden, Vivolo-Kantor, Hamburger, & Lumpkin, 2014). Given that *cyberbullying* is defined as bullying behavior that occurs through electronic media, similar criteria to physical or relational bullying must be met (for example, Gladden et al., 2014). However, there are distinctions in the experience of cyberbullying versus traditional bullying that affect the criteria commonly used to define bullying. For example, a single incident of cyber aggression is often repeatedly experienced by the victim without the incident actually recurring. This could include an e-mail or text being forwarded to multiple people or posted online and subsequently viewed by many. As this can occur at any time of day or night, repetition can be implied even in a one-time event. The power differential in cyberbullying is uniquely shaped by the ability to be anonymous (Dempsey, Sulkowski, Dempsey, & Storch, 2011) and the potential for technological skill to outweigh physical or social power typical of traditional bullying (Law, Shapka, Hymel, Olson, & Waterhouse, 2012).

Overlap of Traditional and Cyber Forms of Bullying

The notion that cyberbullying is a new form of bullying has received considerable attention in the literature. Some researchers argue that cyberbullying has resulted in a new subgroup of perpetrators and victims. Others contend that it is not a new form of bullying but rather a new medium for youth to electronically display traditional bullying behaviors such as teasing, name-calling, or rumor spreading. A recent study of high school–age youth (mean age = 15.9 years) found that 75 percent of those that reported being a victim of bullying were not bullied via electronic means. However, of those that were cyberbullied, the majority experienced at least one other traditional (in-person) form of bullying, with just 4.6 percent experiencing only cyberbullying (Waasdorp & Bradshaw, 2015). A recent meta-analysis of 131 studies of cyberbullying indicates that those youth who use traditional bullying are likely to be cyberbullies and those who are traditional victims are also likely to be cyber victims (Kowalski, Giumetti, Schroeder, & Lattanner, 2014). A review of the cyberbullying literature (Mehari, Farrell, & Le, 2014) and discussions (Olweus, 2012; Patchin & Hinduja, 2012) suggests that there is little empirical evidence to support the contention that cyberbullying is a separate form of bullying; rather those involved in traditional bullying are predominantly the same individuals who would be involved in cyberbullying (as perpetrators or victims). Though the individuals involved in traditional and cyberbullying situations may overlap, cyberbullying is undoubtedly a unique experience for bully and victim alike, given the nature of the "cyber world" (for example, ability to be anonymous, inability to delete, 24/7 access).

Definition of Cyberbullying

As with any new research area, there are issues surrounding how to define and measure cyberbullying and the comparability of studies using disparate definitions (for example, Kowalski et al., 2014). In its broadest sense, cyberbullying involves the use of electronic devices to harm others. Beyond that, additional criteria that vary across studies make it difficult to present a cohesive view of cyberbullying (for example, Kowalski et al., 2014; Mehari et al., 2014). Most cyberbullying researchers adapt Olweus's (1993) definition of bullying, marked by repeated aggression against a more vulnerable target. However, what constitutes repetition or an imbalance of power is inconsistent in the instruments used to assess cyberbullying. As a result, prevalence rates vary greatly depending on which definition is used, with some studies reporting as low as 5 percent and others reporting as high as 72 percent (see Patchin & Hinduja, 2012, for a review). Some prior studies have required multiple behaviors to be present before designating a series of actions as being cyberbullying, whereas other studies have required only one cyberbullying behavior to make this distinction (see, for example, Juvonen & Gross, 2008; Riebel, Jager, & Fischer, 2009).

Even if the range of prevalence rates across studies can be explained in part by differences among populations (for example, American versus German, 10-year-olds versus 10- to 21-year-olds, female versus male), it is clear that the varying definitions of cyberbullying make comparisons across studies challenging. Complementing the notion that cyberbullying is not a new form of bullying, recent definitions maintain that cyberbullying is actually the context in which bullying occurs, as opposed to a distinct form of bullying (Gladden et al., 2014; Mehari et al., 2014). The Centers for Disease Control and Prevention (CDC) recently defined *cyberbullying* as

> behaviors that use technology including but not limited to phones, email, chat rooms, instant messaging, and online posts [but] is not considered conceptually distinct from bullying that occurs in-person. . . . It involves primarily verbal (for example, threatening or harassing electronic communications) and relational aggression (for example, spreading rumors electronically). (Gladden et al., 2014, p. 25)

The CDC cautions that as technology continues to change at such a rapid pace, the specific ways in which youth and adults can electronically bully will change accordingly. In addition, as electronic media are increasingly integrated into everyday life, use of cyberspace to bully is also likely to increase across the life course (Piotrowski, 2012). Currently, much of the research on cyberbullying is on youth in middle and high school, with few longitudinal studies (Kowalski et al., 2014) or studies of individuals above age 25 (Piotrowski, 2012). Although the definition of cyberbullying should be consistent across the life course, the specific manifestations of behaviors may change. Accordingly, the next section reviews correlates of cyberbullying as it appears in childhood through adulthood.

CYBERBULLYING IN CHILDHOOD

The youngest age reported in published cyberbullying research was six years (Kowalski et al., 2014; Patchin & Hinduja, 2012); however, no specific details regarding this age group and their experiences were given (Hinduja & Patchin, 2007). In the United Kingdom, children as young as seven years were included in one study to examine the emergence of cyberbullying (Monks, Robinson, & Worlidge, 2012), but results combined youth age seven years with youth age eight and nine years in the same results. In that study, Monks and colleagues (2012) found that there were no differences in reports of cyberbullying perpetration between younger (seven to nine years) and older (10–11 years) youth, although the older youth were victimized by more distinct types of cyberbullying (for example, texts, videos, phone calls, chat room, instant messenger, and Web sites versus just texts). Many researchers suggest that there is a peak in cyberbullying in middle school (usually around sixth grade or ages 10–11), yet there are too few studies actually examine cyberbullying in elementary school to draw definitive conclusions. At the same time, the use of technology (for example, computers, tablets, cell phones) among young children is steadily increasing. For example, one study found that over a two-year period (2011–2013), technology access increased from 52 percent to 75 percent in children under age eight (Rideout, 2013), with the amount of time spent per day on these devices tripling. Compared with those under the age of five, those between the ages of five and eight were more likely to use technology to interact with others (Rideout, 2013). These children have access and skills to interact electronically with peers, and therefore, the possibility of involvement in cyberbullying at this age might increase.

During childhood, direct verbal teasing (for example, typing mean or teasing comments) or direct relationally aggressive behaviors (for example, threatening to uninvite someone to a party to hurt or manipulate) will be more common. Research on adolescents suggests that increased time spent online maximizes the likelihood of cyberbullying (for example, Werner, Bumpus, & Rock, 2010). It is therefore likely that younger children who have access to interactive electronic media would be at an increased risk for cyberbullying. It is unclear whether the intent to harm would be the same among those in middle to late childhood—young children may engage in these behaviors without realizing the impact on others. Therefore, it is important for researchers, practitioners, and schools to assess and monitor cyberbullying among younger children.

CYBERBULLYING IN ADOLESCENCE

Cyberbullying is prevalent among middle and high school–age youth, with most studies reporting between 10 and 40 percent of adolescents experiencing cyberbullying (Kowalski et al., 2014; Patchin & Hinduja, 2012). A current debate surrounds whether the rate of cyberbullying is increasing during adolescence. On the one hand, with increased access to electronic modalities, decreases in the cost associated with accessing the Internet and sending text messages, and rapid changes to electronic devices (for example, smartphones and iPads versus laptops or desktop computers), some researchers argue that there has been an increase in prevalence (see, for example, Jones, Mitchell, & Finkelhor, 2013). Approximately 10 years ago, most incidents of cyberbullying occurred via e-mails or posting on blogs. With limited access to computers (Smith, 2014) and higher costs of owning a cell phone and using text messaging, those from a lower socioeconomic group most likely had fewer experiences with cyberbullying. Therefore, the rates of cyberbullying among youth with lower incomes may have increased over the past few years. Others suggest that increases in rates of cyberbullying can be attributed to growing use by adolescents of social networking sites (for example, Facebook, Twitter) to interact with peers, and this most often occurs on their cell phones (Jones et al., 2013). On the other hand, Olweus (2012, 2013) has argued that based on several large-scale longitudinal studies, there is little evidence that prevalence rates are actually increasing. Nevertheless, the accessibility of cell phones and amount of time that adolescents use electronic media to interact with peers is undoubtedly increasing (Rideout, 2013), likely resulting in a higher likelihood for involvement in cyberbullying.

Correlates of Cyberbullying in Adolescence

Because research on cyberbullying is still in its infancy, most of the research on risks, consequences, or protective factors is cross-sectional. Therefore, the direction of the associations is generally undetermined (Livingstone & Smith, 2014). That being said, studies suggest that when compared with more traditional forms of victimization, cyberbullying may have a stronger negative impact because of the possibility of widespread dissemination of the harmful content combined with the difficulty of completely deleting this content (for example, Suzuki, Asaga, Sourander, Hoven, & Mandell, 2012). Furthermore, being a cyber victim is associated with low self-esteem and high levels of reported stress, anxiety, and depression (for example, Tokunaga, 2010). This association remains strong even after controlling for traditional victimization at school (Fredstrom, Adams, & Gilman, 2011). Research has shown that adolescent victims of cyberbullying are eight times more likely than other adolescents to carry a weapon to school over a 30-day period (for example, Fredstrom et al., 2011) and are also more likely to exhibit suicidal behaviors (Kowalski et al., 2014). This could be due to the additive effect of experiencing cyberbullying. For example, the endorsement of cyber victimization on a measure may be an indicator of an overall high level of victimization. Thus, the respondent is experiencing many forms of bullying and having poorer outcomes (Waasdorp & Bradshaw, 2011, 2015).

In a four-year longitudinal study following youth ages 14–15 years, Hemphill and Heerde (2014) mirrored the traditional bullying literature by confirming that involvement in cyberbullying (as perpetrator or victim) can predict later involvement with cyberbullying, which suggests a continuity of involvement over time. Moreover, being a cyberbully was related to being affiliated with antisocial peers, increased family conflict, and academic failure in early adolescence (Hemphill & Heerde, 2014). Similar to studies of traditional bullying (Waasdorp & Bradshaw, 2011), this research showed that being a cyberbully and cyber victim (that is, bully–victim) during early adolescence results in the poorest outcomes in late adolescence (Hemphill & Heerde, 2014).

Is Sexting Cyberbullying?

An important shift between childhood and adolescence is the increased significance of peer relationships and the formation of romantic relationships (Meece & Laird, 2006). With the majority of teenagers involved in a romantic relationship by mid adolescence (Collins, 2003), it is not surprising that a recent study of cyberbullied high school students found that the content of the cyberbullying messages was most often related to friendships (31 percent) and romantic relationships. This included dating partners, sexual behaviors, and sexuality (36.1, 31, and 21.1 percent, respectively) (Waasdorp & Bradshaw, 2015). Given that the use of electronic devices to interact is central to adolescence, it is not surprising that normative sexual exploration in adolescence also occurs via text messages, e-mails, and posts. *Sexting* is defined as taking and sending nude, nearly nude, or sexually suggestive pictures electronically (for example, Mitchell, Finkelhor, Jones, & Wolak, 2011). It is typically studied in late adolescence when sexual exploration is increasing (Gordon-Messer, Bauermeister, Grodzinski, & Zimmerman, 2013).

Sexting, by definition, is not bullying; however, these sensitive pictures can be used to cyberbully. Although the popular media may sensationalize sexting, and schools fear that it is a widespread problem (Vandebosch, Simulioniene, Marczak, Vermeulen, & Bonetti, 2013), research data suggest otherwise. Approximately 7.1 percent of adolescents (ages 10–17) reported engaging in sexting (Ybarra & Mitchell, 2014), and only 1 percent of those involved sexually explicit images (that is, naked breasts, genitals, or bottoms; Mitchell et al., 2011). Most sexts are sent by teenagers within the context of a romantic relationship, but few of these images are forwarded or posted (Mitchell et al., 2011) and thus do not meet the definition of cyberbullying. However, if the sexual image is redistributed to others with the intent to harm, it would constitute cyberbullying. This experience can be extremely emotionally taxing given the nature of the photo as well as the possibility that the individual breaking this confidence was once a romantic and trusted partner (Collins, 2003). A notable finding is that sexting is significantly higher among adolescents who pay their own cell phone bills (17 percent) compared with those who do not pay for their cell phones (3 percent; Lenhardt, 2009), suggesting that with the autonomy that is acquired throughout adolescence, the likelihood of experiencing sexting increases.

CYBERBULLYING IN YOUNG ADULTHOOD AND BEYOND

During young adulthood, autonomy increases; access to cell phones and other social media outlets often is not restricted by parents to the same extent as during adolescence (Bennett et al., 2011). With decreased parental monitoring and increased access, chances for involvement in cyberbullying are higher (Kowalski, Giumetti, Schroeder, & Reese, 2012; Lenhardt, 2009). Studies of college-age youth involvement in cyberbullying as a witness, victim, or perpetrator have found prevalence rates that range from 60 percent in the past month (Cunningham et al., 2015) to 92 percent cyberbullied in the past year (Bennett et al., 2011). Furthermore, prevalence rates of sexting appear to be higher for college-age youth (around 15–28 percent) as compared with adolescents (Temple et al., 2014). Although the prevalence rates vary because of definitional and related issues, cyberbullying is an issue facing many college-age and young adults, with those ages 18–29 more likely than all other age groups to report experiencing aggressive behaviors online (Pew Research Center, 2014a).

Studies vary regarding gender differences in the prevalence rates of cyberbullying in young adulthood. Some research indicates no gender differences (MacDonald & Roberts-Pittman, 2010), whereas later studies suggest that male youth are more likely to be perpetrators (for example, Cunningham et al., 2015; Schenk & Fremouw, 2012) as well as victims and bully–victims (Bennett et al., 2011). Others report that female youth are more likely to be victims (for example, Dilmaç, 2009) and perpetrators (Schnurr, Mahatmya, & Basche, 2013). In light of these discrepancies, additional studies are needed to ascertain whether there are gender differences at this life stage. Nevertheless, as with relational aggression (see chapter 4), studies show that female youth find cyberbullying more distressing than male youth do (Bennett et al., 2011). It is important to note that both male and female youth report anticipated distress if cyberbullying is perpetrated by a romantic partner rather than a friend (Bennett et al., 2011). When comparing those in college with those in graduate school, Gibb and Devereux (2014) found that reports of cyberbullying were lower for graduate students, yet reports remained consistent across the college-age sample, suggesting that rates may decrease across the progression to adulthood.

As for correlates and risks related to cyberbullying in young adulthood, studies mirror what is found among adolescent youth. For example, cyberbullies and victims were more likely than uninvolved youth to have contemplated, planned, or attempted suicide, and they reported more psychological difficulties such as anxiety, paranoia, and depression (Schenk & Fremouw, 2012).

Unfortunately, there is a dearth of studies examining cyberbullying that specifically occurs among young adults in the workplace (Hall & Lewis, 2014). A study by West, Foster, Levin, Edmison, and Robibero (2014) suggested that workplace cyberbullying is viewed similarly to what is found in college- and school-age youth; however, additional studies are necessary to examine the prevalence and impact of cyberbullying in the workplace.

FUTURE RESEARCH AND PRACTICE

Despite great interest in cyberbullying and a proliferation of studies over the past decade, there are a number of important areas for future research on definitions, measures, and preventative intervention development.

Universal Definitions and Measures

A uniform definition of cyberbullying is needed (Kowalski et al., 2014), and that definition should be consistent across the life span. Without a standardized definition, as discussed above, it is extremely difficult to assess true prevalence rates or to accurately identify those in need of support or intervention. In the traditional bullying literature, it is important to differentiate between conflicts and bullying; however, given the numerous definitions and measures of cyberbullying, it is not clear what differentiates these behaviors in a cyberbullying experience. For example, bullying situations that are private (for example, an e-mail sent privately) are not as distressing as those that are public (for example, harmful posts or pictures viewed by many), and it may be more distressing when the perpetrator is anonymous versus when the perpetrator is known (Sticca & Perren, 2013). Moreover, youth may send countless texts or pictures that can be perceived as harmful to an outsider (for example, researchers, parents), yet to the youth it is a more normative experience not viewed as especially harmful. Furthermore, although with traditional bullying it is important to focus on the frequency (for example, two or more times a month; Olweus, 1993), for cyberbullying it is the number of individuals who view the harmful e-mail, text, or post that will likely affect the individual's response (Williford et al., 2013).

Current criteria used to measure bullying may not be relevant or specific enough to measure cyberbullying (Bauman, Underwood, & Card, 2013). Bauman and colleagues (2013) suggested using the term *cyber-aggression* because of the unique manifestations (that is, challenges to the traditional criteria of intention, repeated behaviors, and power differential) of aggression via electronic media (Bauman et al., 2013) that are still understudied. They define *cyber-aggression* as an "intentional behavior aimed at harming another person or persons through computers, cell phones and other electronic devices, and perceived as aversive by the victim" (Bauman et al., 2013, p. 43). By defining it this way, they have taken out the power differential and the repeated behaviors from the definition, allowing it to be asked in separate questions (for example, how often it occurred and how harmful it was perceived). In doing so, researchers can continue to examine the details surrounding cyber behaviors to better differentiate normative cyber conflict from cyberbullying. With the recent CDC definition depicting cyberbullying as a medium through which youth verbally and relationally bully, it is likely that a standardized measure would reflect this (Gladden et al., 2014; Mehari et al., 2014) by asking about each form separately with the option of indicating that it occurred electronically.

Prevention and Intervention Development

A growing number of state policies encouraging the use of evidence-based prevention programming in schools directly address cyberbullying (Stuart-Cassel, Bell, & Springer, 2011). Although there are very few randomized studies providing evidence for prevention programs that reduce cyberbullying (Mishna, Cook, Saini, Wu, & MacFadden, 2011), one study, on the KiVa program in Finland, reported a reduction in cyberbullying (Williford et al., 2013). KiVa is a universal antibullying program that uses classroom-based lessons, targeted adult intervention, and peer support for victimized youth. The program addresses both traditional bullying and cyberbullying with a strong focus on the different roles of bystanders who witness bullying. It does not have specific curricula and has only limited measures of cyberbullying, including two items assessing cyberbullying and cyber victimization. Despite this, the program showed that those in KiVa schools had lower frequencies of cyberbullying compared with those in control schools (Williford et al., 2013). This program likely affects cyberbullying by incorporating bystanders and intervening in the classroom and beyond (for example, on school grounds, via parents, and at home), methods that have proven important in reducing traditional forms of bullying (Cross & Walker, 2013; Williford et al., 2013).

It is important for youth to recognize the importance of being a positive bystander, especially when witnessing cyberbullying. When a disparaging picture or comment is posted on a social networking site, it is the bystanders' witnessing of the post and their response, such as being passive (that is, doing nothing) or assistive (for example, "liking" the post or reposting), that makes the experience more harmful (Barlińska, Szuster, & Winiewski, 2013; Sticca & Perren, 2013). However, if the bystanders are active (for example, reporting the post and getting it removed, publicly posting a statement that supports the victim), this can make the experience much less distressing for the victim.

There are increased levels of traditional bullying in contexts with less adult supervision (for example, Zumbrunn, Doll, Dooley, LeClair, & Wimmer, 2013). In the cyber realm, there are few, if any, adults supervising. Taken with the fact that adults supervise even less as children grow, adults are probably less likely to know about cyberbullying than they are traditional bullying. In addition, because youth are less likely to tell an adult when they are cyberbullied (Waasdorp & Bradshaw, 2015), online bystanders will play a critical role in stemming cyberbullying (Cross & Walker, 2013). In some research, middle and high school youth report not confiding in a parent for a number of reasons including embarrassment, concerns that the parent will make the problem worse, or fear the parent will restrict the use of the technology by which they were bullied (for example, Kowalski, Limber, & Agatston, 2012). Among college-age youth and young adults, programming that targets the bystanders of cyberbullying will also likely be important. A recent study of university undergraduates found that students feel that cyberbullying occurring through nonuniversity, student-run sites should not be monitored by the university (Rowe, 2014). Furthermore, workplace organizations have been reluctant and unprepared to effectively deal with cyberbullying (Hall & Lewis, 2014; Piotrowski, 2012), unless it is thought to legally constitute sexual or cyber harassment or stalking. Therefore, prevention and intervention of cyberbullying among young adults may be more difficult at the organizational level than among school-age youth. Currently, however, there is virtually no research on how best to intervene with college-age youth or in the workplace, making this an extremely important area for future research.

Recent reviews of bullying prevention and intervention programs indicate that they are effective at reducing traditional bullying when they are implemented well (Bradshaw, 2015); these same programs may also reduce cyberbullying. It is important for programs to include curriculum specific to cyberbullying and a valid measure of cyberbullying (for example, more than two recurrences, clear definitions). As electronic media are increasingly incorporated into most day-to-day interactions, it is safe to assume that aggression through electronic devices will remain a concern for youth, parents, and schools and other institutions. With the research on cyberbullying lagging behind the desire for schools and other institutions to intervene, at the very least raising awareness about what constitutes cyberbullying, who it affects, and how to increase positive bystander responses (by both adults and youth) will be beneficial.

REFERENCES

Barlińska, J., Szuster, A., & Winiewski, M. (2013). Cyberbullying among adolescent bystanders: Role of the communication medium, form of violence, and empathy. *Journal of Community & Applied Social Psychology, 23*(1), 37–51. doi:10.1002/casp.2137

Bauman, S., Underwood, M. K., & Card, N. A. (2013). Definitions: Another perspective and a proposal for beginning with cyberaggression. In S. Bauman, D. Cross, & J. Walker (Eds.), *Principles of cyberbullying research: Definitions, measures, and methodology* (pp. 41–45). New York: Routledge.

Bennett, D. C., Guran, E. L., Ramos, M. C., & Margolin, G. (2011). College students' electronic victimization in friendships and dating relationships: Anticipated distress and associations with risky behaviors. *Violence and Victims, 26*, 410–429. doi:10.1891/0886-6708.26.4.410

Bradshaw, C. P. (2015). Translating research to practice in bullying prevention. *American Psychologist, 70*, 322–332. doi:10.1037/a0039114

Collins, W. A. (2003). More than myth: The developmental significance of romantic relationships during adolescence. *Journal of Research on Adolescence, 13*(1), 1–24.

Cross, D., & Walker, J. (2013). Using research to inform cyberbullying prevention and intervention. In S. Bauman, D. Cross, & J. Walker (Eds.), *Principles of cyberbullying research: Definitions, measures, and methodology* (pp. 274–293). New York: Routledge.

Cunningham, C. E., Chen, Y., Vaillancourt, T., Rimas, H., Deal, K., Cunningham, L. J., & Ratcliffe, J. (2015). Modeling the anti-cyberbullying preferences of university students: Adaptive choice-based conjoint analysis. *Aggressive Behavior, 41*, 369–385. doi:10.1002/ab.21560

Dempsey, A. G., Sulkowski, M. L., Dempsey, J., & Storch, E. A. (2011). Has cyber technology produced a new group of peer aggressors? *Cyberpsychology, Behavior and Social Networking, 14*(5), 297–302. doi:10.1089/cyber.2010.0108

Dilmaç, B. (2009). Psychological needs as a predictor of cyber bullying: A preliminary report on college students. *Kuram ve Uygulamada Eğitim Bilimleri* [Educational Sciences: Theory & Practice], *9*, 1307–1325.

Fredstrom, B. K., Adams, R. E., & Gilman, R. (2011). Electronic and school-based victimization: Unique contexts for adjustment difficulties during adolescence. *Journal of Youth and Adolescence, 40*, 405–415. doi:10.1007/s10964-010-9569-7

Gibb, Z. G., & Devereux, P. G. (2014). Who does that anyway? Predictors and personality correlates of cyberbullying in college. *Computers in Human Behavior, 38*, 8–16. doi:10.1016/j.chb.2014.05.009

Gladden, R. M., Vivolo-Kantor, A. M., Hamburger, M. E., & Lumpkin, C. D. (2014). *Bullying surveillance among youths: Uniform definitions for public health and recommended data elements, version 1.0.* Atlanta, GA: National Center for Injury Prevention and Control, Centers for Disease Control and Prevention, and U.S. Department of Education.

Gordon-Messer, D., Bauermeister, J. A., Grodzinski, A., & Zimmerman, M. (2013). Sexting among young adults. *Journal of Adolescent Health, 52*, 301–306.

Hall, R., & Lewis, S. (2014). Managing workplace bullying and social media policy: Implications for employee engagement. *Academy of Business Research Journal, 1*, 128–138.

Hemphill, S. A., & Heerde, J. A. (2014). Adolescent predictors of young adult cyberbullying perpetration and victimization among Australian youth. *Journal of Adolescent Health, 55*, 580–587. doi:10.1016/j.jadohealth.2014.04.014

Hinduja, S., & Patchin, J. W. (2007). Offline consequences of online victimization: School violence and delinquency. *Journal of School Violence, 6*(3), 89–112.

Jones, L. M., Mitchell, K. J., & Finkelhor, D. (2013). Online harassment in context: Trends from three youth Internet safety surveys (2000, 2005, 2010). *Psychology of Violence, 3*(1), 53–69.

Juvonen, J., & Gross, E. F. (2008). Extending the school grounds?—Bullying experiences in cyberspace. *Journal of School Health, 78*, 496–505. doi:10.1111/j.1746-1561.2008.00335.x

Kowalski, R. M., Giumetti, G. W., Schroeder, A. N., & Lattanner, M. R. (2014). Bullying in the digital age: A critical review and meta-analysis of cyberbullying research among youth. *Psychological Bulletin, 140*, 1073–1137.

Kowalski, R. M., Giumetti, G. W., Schroeder, A. N., & Reese, H. (2012). Cyberbullying among college students: Evidence from multiple domains of college life. In C. Wankel & L. Wankel (Eds.), *Misbehavior online in higher education* (pp. 293–321). Bingley, West Yorkshire, England: Emerald.

Kowalski, R. M., Limber, S. P., & Agatston, P. W. (2012). *Cyberbullying: Bullying in the digital age.* Malden, MA: Wiley-Blackwell.

Law, D. M., Shapka, J. D., Hymel, S., Olson, B. F., & Waterhouse, T. (2012). The changing face of bullying: An empirical comparison between traditional and Internet bullying and victimization. *Computers in Human Behavior, 28*(1), 226–232. doi:10.1016/j.chb.2011.09.004

Lenhardt, A. (2009). *Teens and sexting.* Washington, DC: Pew Research Center. Retrieved from http://www.pewinternet.org/2009/12/15/teens-and-sexting/

Livingstone, S., & Smith, P. K. (2014). Annual research review: Harms experienced by child users of online and mobile technologies: The nature, prevalence and management of sexual and aggressive risks in the digital age. *Journal of Child Psychology & Psychiatry, 55*, 635–654. doi:10.1111/jcpp.12197

MacDonald, C. D., & Roberts-Pittman, B. (2010). Cyberbullying among college students: Prevalence and demographic differences. *Procedia–Social and Behavioral Sciences, 9*, 2003–2009. doi:10.1016/j.sbspro.2010.12.436

Meece, D., & Laird, R. D. (2006). The importance of peers. In F. A. Villarruel & T. Luster (Eds.), *The crisis in youth mental health: Critical issues and effective programs, Vol. 2: Disorders in adolescence* (pp. 283–311). Westport, CT: Praeger Publishers/Greenwood Publishing Group.

Mehari, K. R., Farrell, A. D., & Le, A.-T.H. (2014). Cyberbullying among adolescents: Measures in search of a construct. *Psychology of Violence, 4*, 399–415. doi:10.1037/a0037521.supp

Mishna, F., Cook, C., Saini, M., Wu, M. J., & MacFadden, R. (2011). Interventions to prevent and reduce cyber abuse of youth: A systematic review. *Research on Social Work Practice, 21*(1), 5–14. doi:10.1177/1049731509351988

Mitchell, K. J., Finkelhor, D., Jones, L. M., & Wolak, J. (2011). Prevalence and characteristics of youth sexting: A national study. *Pediatrics, 129*, 1–8. doi:10.1542/peds.2011-1730

Monks, C. P., Robinson, S., & Worlidge, P. (2012). The emergence of cyberbullying: A survey of primary school pupils' perceptions and experiences. *School Psychology International, 33*, 477–491.

Olweus, D. (1993). *Bullying at school.* Oxford, England: Blackwell.

Olweus, D. (2012). Cyberbullying: An overrated phenomenon? *European Journal of Developmental Psychology, 9*, 520–538. doi:10.1080/17405629.2012.682358

Olweus, D. (2013). School bullying: Development and some important challenges. *Annual Review of Clinical Psychology, 9*, 751–780. doi:10.1146/annurev-clinpsy-050212-185516

Patchin, J. W., & Hinduja, S. (2012). Cyberbullying: An update and synthesis of the research. In J. W. Patchin & S. Hinduja (Eds.), *Cyberbullying prevention and response: Expert perspectives* (pp. 13–35). New York: Routledge.

Pew Research Center. (2014a). *Online harassment.* Retrieved from http://www.pewinternet .org/files/2014/10/PI_OnlineHarassment_102214_1.pdf

Pew Research Center. (2014b). *Pew research Internet project.* Retrieved from http://www .pewinternet.org/fact-sheets/mobile-technology-fact-sheet/

Piotrowski, C. (2012). From workplace bullying to cyberbullying: The enigma of e-harassment in modern organizations. *Organization Development Journal, 30*(4), 44–53.

Rainie, L. (2014). *13 thing to know about teens and technology.* Chicago: Pew Internet Project. Retrieved from http://www.pewinternet.org/files/2014/07/How-teens-do-research_ ACT-college-planners_pdf.pdf

Rideout, V. (2013). Zero to eight: Children's media use in America 2013. Retrieved from https://www.commonsensemedia.org/sites/default/files/research/zero-to- eight-2013.pdf

Riebel, J., Jager, R. S., & Fischer, U. C. (2009). Cyberbullying in Germany: An exploration of prevalence, overlapping with real life bullying and coping strategies. *Psychology Science Quarterly, 51,* 298–314.

Rowe, J. (2014). Student use of social media: When should the university intervene? *Journal of Higher Education Policy & Management, 36,* 241–256. doi:10.1080/01587919.2014.899054

Schenk, A. M., & Fremouw, W. J. (2012). Prevalence, psychological impact, and coping of cyberbully victims among college students. *Journal of School Violence, 11*(1), 21–37. doi:10.1080/15388220.2011.630310

Schnurr, M. P., Mahatmya, D., & Basche, R. A., III. (2013). The role of dominance, cyber aggression perpetration, and gender on emerging adults' perpetration of intimate part- ner violence. *Psychology of Violence, 3*(1), 70–83. doi:10.1037/a0030601

Smith, A. (2014). *African Americans and techology use: A demographic portrait.* Retrieved from http://www.pewinternet.org/files/2014/01/African-Americans-and-Technology-Use.pdf

Sticca, F., & Perren, S. (2013). Is cyberbullying worse than traditional bullying? Examining the differential roles of medium, publicity, and anonymity for the perceived severity of bullying. *Journal of Youth and Adolescence, 42,* 739–750. doi:10.1007/s10964-012-9867-3

Stuart-Cassel, V., Bell, A., & Springer, J. F. (2011). *Analysis of state bullying laws and policies.* Retrieved from http://www.ed.gov/about/offices/list/opepd/ppss/index.html

Suzuki, K., Asaga, R., Sourander, A., Hoven, C. W., & Mandell, D. (2012). Cyberbullying and adolescent mental health. *International Journal of Adolescent Medicine and Health, 24*(1), 27–35.

Temple, J. R., Le, V. D., van den Berg, P., Ling, Y., Paul, J. A., & Temple, B. W. (2014). Brief report: Teen sexting and psychosocial health. *Journal of Adolescence, 37*(1), 33–36.

Tokunaga, R. S. (2010). Following you home from school: A critical review and synthesis of research on cyberbullying victimization. *Computers in Human Behavior, 26*(3), 277–287. doi:10.1016/j.chb.2009.11.014

Vandebosch, H., Simulioniene, R., Marczak, M., Vermeulen, A., & Bonetti, L. (2013). The role of the media. In P. K. Smith & G. Steffgen (Eds.), *Cyberbullying through the new media: Findings from an international network* (pp. 99–118). New York: Psychology Press.

Waasdorp, T. E., & Bradshaw, C. P. (2011). Examining student responses to frequent bully- ing: A latent class approach. *Journal of Educational Psychology, 103,* 336–352. doi:10.1037/ a0022747

Waasdorp, T. E., & Bradshaw, C. P. (2015). The overlap between cyberbullying and traditional bullying. *Journal of Adolescent Health, 56,* 483–488. doi:10.1016/j.jadohealth.2014.12.002

Werner, N. E., Bumpus, M. F., & Rock, D. (2010). Involvement in Internet aggression during early adolescence. *Journal of Youth and Adolescence, 39,* 607–619. doi:10.1007/ s10964-009-9419-7

West, B., Foster, M., Levin, A., Edmison, J., & Robibero, D. (2014). Cyberbullying at work: In search of effective guidance. *Laws, 3,* 598–617.

Williford, A., Elledge, L. C., Boulton, A. J., DePaolis, K. J., Little, T. D., & Salmivalli, C. (2013). Effects of the kiva antibullying program on cyberbullying and cybervictimization frequency among Finnish youth. *Journal of Clinical Child and Adolescent Psychology, 42,* 820–833. doi:10.1080/15374416.2013.787623

Ybarra, M. L., & Mitchell, K. J. (2014). "Sexting" and its relation to sexual activity and sexual risk behavior in a national survey of adolescents. *Journal of Adolescent Health, 55,* 757–764. doi:10.1016/j.jadohealth.2014.07.012

Zumbrunn, S., Doll, B., Dooley, K., LeClair, C., & Wimmer, C. (2013). Assessing student perceptions of positive and negative social interactions in specific school settings. *International Journal of School & Educational Psychology, 1*(2), 82–93. doi:10.1080/21683603.2013.803001

Part III

Bullying among Youth: Cultural and Contextual Considerations

7

Developmental Model of Youth Bullying, Sexual Harassment, and Dating Violence Perpetration

Dorothy L. Espelage

Youth aggression, bullying, sexual harassment, and dating violence are widespread public health problems with negative consequences for victims (Basile et al., 2006; Gruber & Fineran, 2008; Nansel et al., 2001; Tjaden & Thoennes, 2006). Even though it is known that teenage dating and sexual harassment start early in life (Borowsky, Hogan, & Ireland, 1997) and that bullying also occurs and peaks in youth (Espelage, 2012), little research has examined the co-occurrence of and relations among these three types of aggression with a developmental lens. Although some conceptual and empirical literature suggests that they may share some developmental correlates (Basile, Espelage, Rivers, McMahon, & Simon, 2009; DeSouza & Ribeiro, 2005; Pellegrini, 2001; Pepler et al., 2006), very few studies have examined these phenomena in tandem (for an exception, see S. Miller et al., 2013, discussed later). In this chapter, I define these constructs. Next, I propose and provide empirical support for a developmental model of the longitudinal associations among bullying, sexual violence, and teenage dating violence perpetration across early to late adolescence.

AGGRESSION AND BULLYING: DEFINITIONS AND PREVALENCE

Bullying has been conceptualized as repeated attempts of physical, verbal (for example, threats, insults), relational (for example, social exclusion), or cyber aggression (for example, e-mail, texting) that involve abuse of power (Olweus, Limber, & Mahalic, 1999; Ybarra,

Espelage, & Mitchell, 2014). More recently, the Department of Education and the Centers for Disease Control and Prevention (CDC) released the following research definition:

> Bullying is any unwanted aggressive behavior(s) by another youth or group of youths who are not siblings or current dating partners that involves an observed or perceived power imbalance and is repeated multiple times or is highly likely to be repeated. Bullying may inflict harm or distress on the targeted youth including physical, psychological, social, or educational harm. (Gladden, Vivolo-Kantor, Hamburger, & Lumpkin, 2014, p. 7)

These behaviors include verbal and physical aggression that ranges in severity from making threats, spreading rumors, or excluding an individual to physical attacks causing injury and can occur face-to-face or through technology (for example, cell phones, computers). This definition does not include sexual harassment, which is a form of sex discrimination and is prohibited in schools by Title IX (U.S. Department of Education, Office for Civil Rights, 2001). Worldwide incidence rates for bullying among school-age youth range from 10 to 30 percent, and there is a notable increase during the middle school years (Cook, Williams, Guerra, Kim, & Sadek, 2010).

SEXUAL HARASSMENT AND VIOLENCE: DEFINITION AND PREVALENCE

Sexual violence is nonconsensual completed or attempted penetration (vaginal, oral, or anal), unwanted touching (for example, groping or fondling), or noncontact acts, such as exposing oneself, or verbal sexual harassment, committed by any perpetrator (Basile & Saltzman, 2002). *Sexual harassment* in school settings is defined as unwanted sexual conduct and can include unwelcome verbal, nonverbal, and physical behaviors that interfere with an individual's right to receive an equal education (American Association of University Women [AAUW], 2011). Sexual harassment is a common experience for youth; 56 percent of girls and 40 percent of boys in seventh through 12th grade experienced sexual harassment during the 2010–2011 school year (AAUW, 2011); this can also include being called "gay."

TEENAGE DATING VIOLENCE: DEFINITIONS AND PREVALENCE

The CDC (2014) defines *dating violence* as a type of intimate partner violence. It occurs between two people in a close relationship. The nature of dating violence can be physical, emotional, or sexual. Physical dating violence includes physically violent acts, such as slapping or punching a partner, whereas verbal dating violence includes name-calling and denigrating comments. Emotional and psychological abuse includes behaviors such as manipulation and verbal battering (for example, swearing, derogatory comments). Dating violence affects numerous adolescents each year, with prevalence rates ranging from 9 to 62 percent; discrepancies are based in part on variations in measurement approaches and samples (Holt & Espelage, 2005; Howard & Wang, 2003).

DEVELOPMENTAL MODEL OF BULLYING, SEXUAL HARASSMENT, AND DATING VIOLENCE

Research has demonstrated that youth problem behaviors tend to be interrelated and share common risk and protective factors (Donovan, Jessor, & Costa, 1991). The evidence indicates that this finding appears to hold true for adolescent dating violence as well (Howard, Wang, & Yan, 2007). The belief that it is acceptable to use violence is strongly associated with inflicting violence against a dating partner (Malik, Sorenson, & Aneshensel, 1997; O'Keefe, 1997). Boys who are aggressive, involved in fights, or carry guns are more likely to engage in sexual harassment (Howard et al., 2007; Pellegrini, 2001). Early antisocial behavior and aggression have been shown to predict later use of violence against dating partners in three longitudinal studies (Capaldi & Clark, 1998; Lavoie et al., 2002), and a study by Brendgen, Vitaro, Tremblay, and Lavoie (2001) showed aggression perpetrated by young adolescent boys was associated with later dating violence perpetration at ages 16 or 17 years.

Some research does suggest that efforts to address dating violence could be informed by the overlap among dating violence, bullying perpetration, and sexual harassment. However, very little is known regarding shared factors that determine resemblance, divergence, or desistance in pathways between early risk factors and trajectories for dating violence through late adolescence. I propose a developmental model that examines how bullying perpetration in early adolescence emerges from family conflict or abuse and how it is associated with later sexual harassment and teenage dating violence perpetration through anger and alcohol and drug use (see Figure 7.1).

Family Abuse and Conflict

Coercive exchanges between parents and children in the home often co-occur with the abusive and conflictual family dynamics linked to bullying. Cross-sectional investigations in the United States and other countries have found significant associations between exposure to physical violence in the home and bullying (Espelage, Low, & De La Rue, 2012; Holt, Kantor, & Finkelhor, 2009). Several longitudinal studies have also established this association (Bauer et al., 2006; Bolger & Patterson, 2001; Bowes et al., 2009). In a recent

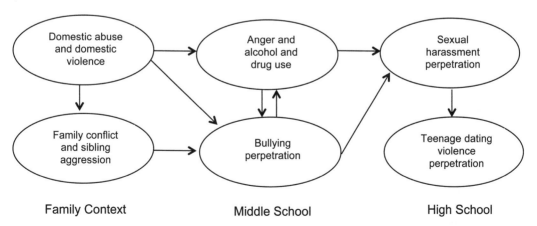

Figure 7.1: Developmental Model of Bullying, Sexual Harassment, and Dating Violence

longitudinal study, there was strong evidence linking family conflict and sibling aggression to bully perpetration. Thus, my coauthors and I hypothesized that these associations would emerge in this larger longitudinal path analysis (Espelage, Low, Rao, Hong, & Little, 2013).

Alcohol and Drug Use

The proposed model in Figure 7.1 includes longitudinal associations between family variables and alcohol and drug use, which is associated with bullying, sexual harassment, and violence perpetration, and teenage dating violence perpetration. A number of theoretical perspectives and longitudinal research findings substantiate that youth living in a home with widespread family conflict and violence are at a heightened risk of associating with deviant peers and engaging in antisocial behavior, including early alcohol and drug initiation. Several theories can facilitate our understanding of why children's early experiences with family violence can impair their ability to form satisfying friendships and peer relationships (Dodge, Pettit, & Bates, 1994; Ehrensaft, 2008; Fergusson & Horwood, 1999; Herrenkohl, Huang, Tajima, & Whitney, 2003; Margolin & Gordis, 2000; Tyler, Hoyt, Whitbeck, & Cauce, 2003). Child development researchers (for example, Cicchetti, Lynch, Shonk, & Manly, 1992) posit that children who are exposed to or experience family violence in early life are unlikely to form secure attachment relationships with caregivers. As a consequence, these children will learn to behave in ways that increase their risk of developing relationships with peers who engage in deviant activities, such as alcohol and drug use.

Social learning theorists also argue that children who are exposed to or experience family violence will have difficulty forming positive peer relationships, as they learn aggressive and coercive behaviors modeled by adults (Gelles & Straus, 1979). Schwartz and Protor (2000) found that children who experience family violence have difficulties regulating their emotion, making it difficult to socialize with conventional peer groups. These youth become "loners" or turn to deviant peer groups for social support (Bender, 2010). Moreover, they frequently run away from home, which makes them more susceptible to deviant peer affiliation. Tyler and colleagues (2003) investigated the impact of childhood sexual abuse on later sexual victimization among 372 homeless youth in Seattle. The authors reported that sexually abused youth who run away from home end up turning to deviant peers. In addition, family violence–involved youth are frequently placed in a residential care or group home settings through the child welfare system, which increases their exposure to deviant peer influence (Bender, 2010; Dishion, McCord, & Poulin, 1999; Ryan, Marshall, Herz, & Hernandez, 2008).

Anger and Hostility

Anger and hostility have consistently emerged as important correlates of both bullying and sexual violence perpetration. In several studies of bullying behavior (for example, name-calling, teasing, threatening), anger was the strongest predictor of bullying cross-sectionally and longitudinally (Basile et al., 2009; Espelage, Bosworth, & Simon, 2000; Low & Espelage, 2014).

Bully Involvement and Sexual Harassment Perpetration. The few studies that have investigated bullying and sexual harassment suggest that students who sexually harass their peers often also have a history of bullying their peers. For example, Pepler, Craig, Connolly, and Henderson (2002) found that sexual harassment perpetration in students in grades five through eight was associated with increased rates of bullying. Similarly,

Pellegrini (2001) found that boys who were aggressive were also likely to engage in sexual harassment. Similarly, students who reported experiencing sexual harassment victimization were more likely to report dating violence victimization than those students who had not experienced sexual harassment (Connolly, McMaster, Craig, & Pepler, 1997). Pepler and colleagues (2006) found a positive association between sexual harassment perpetration and bullying perpetration among students. In this cross-sectional study of 961 middle school students (grades six through eight) and 935 high school students (grades nine through 12), sexual harassment perpetration was more prevalent among students who bullied others than among those who did not.

Bullying Involvement, Sexual Harassment Perpetration, and Teenage Dating Violence. Some research does suggest that efforts to address dating violence could be informed by the overlap among dating violence, bullying perpetration, and sexual harassment. Students who reported bullying their peers also reported more violence in their dating relationships (both physical and social) than nonbullies (Connolly, Pepler, Craig, & Taradash, 2000). More recently, S. Miller and colleagues (2013) demonstrated how dating violence, bullying, and sexual harassment often co-occur, highlighting the need to recognize the interrelated natures of these behaviors. A latent class analysis was conducted with approximately 800 seventh-grade students and the intersections between dating violence, bullying, and sexual harassment. The study ultimately revealed five classes of behaviors. In fact, none of the five classes identified in their study consisted solely of dating violence, with three of the five classes including multiple behaviors. Two of the classes identified show distinct gender differences. There were considerably more boys in the class of students who reported bullying perpetration and victimization and sexual harassment victimization (S. Miller et al., 2013). Alternatively, more girls were in the class that reported perpetration and victimization for both bullying and sexual harassment.

EMPIRICAL SUPPORT FOR THE DEVELOPMENTAL MODEL AND RECOMMENDATIONS

The proposed model in Figure 7.1 was tested in a five-and-half-year longitudinal study of a large sample of youth who were followed from middle school through high school. Results indicated that the model was a good fit for both boys and girls; however, exposure to domestic violence and abuse dropped out of the model. In contrast, family conflict predicted bullying in middle school, which was also associated with anger during middle school. By high school, bullying perpetration was associated with alcohol and drug use, which was associated with sexual harassment and teenage dating violence perpetration (Espelage, Low, Anderson, & De La Rue, 2014). These results suggest that bullying perpetration is an important mechanism linking family violence and sexual harassment and violence and teenage dating violence perpetration. That is, bullying perpetration served as an indirect mechanism between family conflict and sibling aggression and later sexual harassment and violence and teenage dating violence perpetration for girls. For boys, bullying mediated the association between sibling aggression (not family conflict) and these later high school outcomes. The connection between familial violence and conflict and aggression at school is not surprising, given the intergenerational transmission of aggression and the importance of the parent microsystem in the social-ecological model (Reid, Patterson, & Snyder, 2002; Slomkowski, Rende, Conger, Simons, & Conger, 2001). Taken together, the findings from this study support the social information learning framework in understanding the relations among family violence and bullying in early adolescence. Youth need to have the opportunity to learn nonviolent ways of managing conflicts with peers and dating partners. In addition, family-level interventions should address corresponding and often overlapping forms of family conflict and aggression. Anger management strategies should be used to teach alternatives to bullying and other forms of aggression.

Certainly, teenage dating violence prevention efforts should align with the recommendations of Tharp (2012), who argued that the next generation of prevention should target individual-level and relationship-level factors. Indeed, few dating violence programs explicitly address family violence. Although some programs do work to help young people identify abusive behaviors across multiple domains (for example, woman abuse, child abuse, sexual harassment, racism) (Wolfe et al., 2003), few (if any) programs explicitly address the violence young people may have experienced in their families and how this serves to influence behaviors with peers or partners.

In the study testing this model, bully perpetration showed relatively little change during middle school and declined at the two high school waves, which is consistent with many research studies that have shown that bullying peaks during middle school (Nansel et al., 2001; Robers, Kemp, & Truman, 2013). Thus, generic bully prevention programs in high schools are not likely salient for this age group and do not support the decreasing trend of bullying over time. Of note, a recent meta-analysis indicates that bully prevention programs appear to be most efficacious up until seventh grade, but efficacy in eighth grade drops to zero (Yeager, Fong, Lee, & Espelage, 2015). Furthermore, there was a seeming reversal in efficacy through the high school years, such that programs, if anything, cause harm. Yeager and colleagues (2015) cautioned against transporting programs developed with children and young adolescents to older adolescents until more thought is given to the unique ways in which violence prevention messages are received by adolescents who are emerging adults.

Links between sexual harassment and bullying suggest that youth who engage in one type of aggression (that is, bullying) may be more likely to engage in the other (that is, sexual harassment; Espelage et al., 2012) and that bullying perpetration may lead to sexual harassment perpetration (S. Miller et al., 2013). In a longitudinal study of the middle school youth in this current sample, Espelage and colleagues (2012) found that bullying perpetration and homophobic teasing perpetration among a sample of fifth to seventh graders were related to perpetration of sexual harassment six months later (Espelage et al., 2012). Taken together, it is important to address gender-based language early in middle school to prevent sexual harassment prior to the onset of dating (E. Miller, 2012). Finally, the findings suggest that alcohol and drug use plays an important role in the development of sexual harassment and dating violence perpetration in high school, which is consistent with studies conducted with dating college students (Moore, Elkins, McNulty, Kivisto, & Handsel, 2011). Alcohol and drug prevention programs may have an impact on reducing the connection between bullying and subsequent forms of gender-based and relationship-based aggression.

SUMMARY

Despite considerable growth in prevention programming, our ability to have a positive impact on bullying and sexual and teenage dating violence is negligible at best (for review, see De La Rue, Polanin, Espelage, & Pigott, 2016; Espelage & Horne, 2008; Yeager et al., 2015). Specifying how interventions can be applied and optimized to work at peak efficacy and efficiency is an important next step in prevention science. This study suggests that bully prevention should occur before and during middle school, and gender-based content and relationship skills should be incorporated before high school. Interventions should focus on multiple forms of aggression and violence, rather than continuing the inefficient use of single prevention approaches for each form of aggression or violence (Hamby & Grych, 2013).

REFERENCES

American Association of University Women. (2011). *Crossing the line: Sexual harassment at school*. Washington DC: Author. Retrieved from http://www.aauw.org/resource/crossing-the-line-sexual-harassment-at-school-executive-summary/

Basile, K. C., Black, M. C., Simon, T. R., Arias, I., Brener, N. D., & Saltzman, L. E. (2006). The association between self-reported lifetime history of forced sexual intercourse and recent health-risk behaviors: Findings from the 2003 National Youth Risk Behavior Survey. *Journal of Adolescent Health, 39*(5), e1–e7.

Basile, K. C., Espelage, D. L., Rivers, I., McMahon, P. M., & Simon, T. R. (2009). The theoretical and empirical links between bullying behavior and sexual violence perpetration. *Aggressive and Violent Behavior, 14*, 336–347.

Basile, K. C., & Saltzman, L. E. (2002). Sexual violence surveillance: Uniform definitions and recommended data elements (version 1.0). Atlanta: Centers for Disease Control and Prevention, National Center for Injury Prevention and Control. Retrieved from http://www.cdc.gov/ncipc/pub-res/sv_surveillance/sv.htm

Bauer, N. S., Herrenkohl, T. I., Lozano, P., Rivara, F. P., Hill, K. G., & Hawkins, J. D. (2006). Childhood bullying involvement and exposure to intimate partner violence. *Pediatrics, 118*, e235–e242.

Bender, K. (2010). Why do some maltreated youth become juvenile offenders? A call for further investigation and adaptation of youth services. *Children and Youth Services Review, 32*, 466–473.

Bolger, K. E., & Patterson, C. J. (2001). Developmental pathways from child maltreatment to peer rejection. *Child Development, 72*, 549–568.

Borowsky, I. W., Hogan, M., & Ireland, M. (1997). Adolescent sexual aggression: Risk and protective factors. *Pediatrics, 100*, 1–8.

Bowes, L., Arseneault, L., Maughan, B., Taylor, A., Caspi, A., & Moffitt, T. E. (2009). School, neighborhood, and family factors are associated with children's bullying involvement: A nationally representative longitudinal study. *Journal of the American Academy of Child & Adolescent Psychiatry, 48*, 545–553.

Brendgen, M., Vitaro, F., Tremblay, R. E., & Lavoie, F. (2001). Reactive and proactive aggression: Predictions to physical violence in different contexts and moderating effects of parental monitoring and caregiving behavior. *Journal of Abnormal Child Psychology, 29*, 293–304. doi:10.1023/A:1010305828208

Capaldi, D. M., & Clark, S. (1998). Prospective family predictors of aggression toward female partners for at-risk young men. *Developmental Psychology, 34*(6), 1175–1188.

Centers for Disease Control and Prevention. (2014). *Understanding teen dating violence* [Fact sheet]. Retrieved from http://www.cdc.gov/violenceprevention/pdf/teen-dating-violence-factsheet-a.pdf

Cicchetti, D., Lynch, M., Shonk, S., & Manly, J. T. (1992). An organizational perspective on peer relationships in maltreated children. In R. Parke & G. Ladd (Eds.), *Family-peer relationships: Modes of linkage* (pp. 345–383). Hillsdale, NJ: Erlbaum.

Connolly, J. A., McMaster, L., Craig, W., & Pepler, D. (1997). Dating, puberty, & sexualized aggression in early adolescence. Presented at the annual meeting of the Association for the Advancement of Behavior Therapy, Miami, FL.

Connolly, J., Pepler, D., Craig, W., & Taradash, A. (2000). Dating experiences of bullies in early adolescence. *Child Maltreatment, 5*(4), 299–310.

Cook, C. R., Williams, K. R., Guerra, N. G., Kim, T. E., & Sadek, S. (2010). Predictors of bullying and victimization in childhood and adolescence: A meta-analytic investigation. *School Psychology Quarterly, 25,* 65–83.

De La Rue, L., Polanin, J. R., Espelage, D. L., & Pigott, T. D. (2016). Meta-analysis of school-based interventions aimed to prevent or reduce teen dating and sexual violence. *Review of Educational Research.* Advance online publication. doi:10.3102/0034654316632061

DeSouza, E. R., & Ribeiro, J. (2005). Bullying and sexual harassment among Brazilian high school developmental issues. *Merrill-Palmer Quarterly, 43,* 87–106.

Dishion, T., McCord, J., & Poulin, F. (1999). When interventions harm: Peer groups and problem behavior. *American Psychologist, 54,* 755–764.

Dodge, K. A., Pettit, G. S., & Bates, J. E. (1994). Effects of physical maltreatment on the development of peer relations. *Development and Psychopathology, 6,* 43–55.

Donovan, J. E., Jessor, R., & Costa, F. M. (1991). Adolescent health behavior and conventionality-unconventionality: An extension of problem-behavior therapy. *Health Psychology, 10*(1), 52–61.

Ehrensaft, M. K. (2008). Intimate partner violence: Persistence of myths and implications for intervention. *Children and Youth Services Review, 30*(3), 276–286.

Espelage, D. L. (2012). Bullying prevention: A research dialogue with Dorothy Espelage. *Prevention Researcher, 19*(3), 17–19.

Espelage, D. L., Bosworth, K., & Simon, T. R. (2000). Examining the social context of bullying behaviors in early adolescence. *Journal of Counseling and Development, 78,* 326–333.

Espelage, D. L., & Horne, A. (2008). School violence and bullying prevention: From research based explanations to empirically based solutions. In S. Brown & R. Lent (Eds.), *Handbook of counseling psychology* (4th ed., pp. 588–598). Hoboken, NJ: Wiley.

Espelage, D. L, Low, S. K., Anderson, C., & De La Rue, L. (2014). *Bullying, sexual and dating violence trajectories from early to late adolescence.* Retrieved from https://www.ncjrs.gov/pdffiles1/nij/grants/246830.pdf

Espelage, D. L., Low, S., & De La Rue, L. (2012). Relations between peer victimization subtypes, family violence, and psychological outcomes during early adolescence. *Psychology of Violence, 2*(4), 313–324.

Espelage, D. L., Low, S., Rao, M. A., Hong, J. S., & Little, T. (2013). Family violence, bullying, fighting, and substance use among adolescents: A longitudinal transactional model. *Journal of Research on Adolescence, 24,* 337–349.

Fergusson, D. M., & Horwood, L. J. (1999). Prospective childhood predictors of deviant peer affiliation in adolescence. *Journal of Child Psychology and Psychiatry, 40,* 581–592.

Gelles, R., & Straus, M. (1979). Determinants of violence in the family: Toward a theoretical integration. In W. Burr, R. Hill, F. Nye, & I. Reiss (Eds.), *Contemporary theories about the family* (pp. 549–581). New York: Free Press.

Gladden, R. M., Vivolo-Kantor, A. M., Hamburger, M. E., & Lumpkin, C. D. (2014). *Bullying surveillance among youths: Uniform definitions for public health and recommended data elements* (version 1.0). Atlanta: National Center for Injury Prevention and Control, Centers for Disease Control and Prevention, and U.S. Department of Education.

Gruber, J. E., & Fineran, S. (2008). Comparing the impact of bullying and sexual harassment victimization on the mental and physical health of adolescents. *Sex Roles, 59*, 1–13.

Hamby, S. L., & Grych, J. H. (2013). *The web of violence: Exploring connections among different forms of interpersonal violence and abuse.* New York: Springer.

Herrenkohl, T. I., Huang, B., Tajima, E. A., & Whitney, S. D. (2003). Examining the link between child abuse and youth violence: An analysis of mediating mechanisms. *Journal of Interpersonal Violence, 18*, 1189–1208.

Holt, M. K., & Espelage, D. L. (2005). Peer victimization among adolescents: A preliminary perspective on the co-occurrence of sexual harassment, dating violence, and bullying victimization. In K. A. Kendall-Tackett & M. Giacomoni (Eds.), *Child victimization: Maltreatment, bullying and dating violence, prevention and intervention* (pp. 13–16). Kingston, NJ: Civic Research Institute.

Holt, M. K., Kantor, G. K., & Finkelhor, D. (2009). Parent/child concordance about bullying involvement and family characteristics related to bullying and peer victimization. *Journal of School Violence, 8*, 42–63.

Howard, D. E., & Wang, M. Q. (2003). Risk profiles of U.S. adolescent girls who were victims of dating violence. *Adolescence, 38*, 1–14.

Howard, D. E., Wang, M. Q., & Yan, F. (2007). Psychosocial factors associated with reports of physical dating violence among U.S. adolescent females. *Adolescence, 42*, 311–324.

Lavoie, F., Hebert, M., Tremblay, R., Vitaro, F., Vezina, L., & McDuff, P. (2002). History of family dysfunction and perpetration of dating violence by adolescent boys: A longitudinal study. *Journal of Adolescent Health, 30*, 375–383.

Low, S., & Espelage, D. L. (2014). Conduits from community violence exposure to bullying and victimization: Contributions of parental monitoring, impulsivity and deviancy. *Journal of Counseling Psychology, 61*(2), 221–231.

Malik, S., Sorenson, S. B., & Aneshensel, C. S. (1997). Community and dating violence among adolescents: Perpetration and victimization. *Journal of Adolescent Health, 21*(5), 291–302.

Margolin, G., & Gordis, E. B. (2000). The effects of family and community violence on children. *Annual Review of Psychology, 51*, 445–479.

Miller, E. (2012). Coaching boys into men: A cluster-randomized controlled trial of dating violence prevention program. *Journal of Adolescent Health, 51*, 431–438.

Miller, S., Williams, J., Cutbush, S., Gibbs, D., Clinton-Sherrod, M., & Jones, S. (2013). Dating violence, bullying, and sexual harassment: Longitudinal profiles and transitions over time. *Journal of Youth and Adolescence, 42*, 607–618.

Moore, T. M., Elkins, S. R., McNulty, J. K., Kivisto, A. J., & Handsel, V. A. (2011). Alcohol use and intimate partner violence perpetration among college students: Assessing the temporal association using electronic diary technology. *Psychology of Violence, 1*, 315–328.

Nansel, T. R., Overpeck, M., Pilla, R. S., Ruan, W. J., Simmons-Morton, B., & Scheidt, P. (2001). Bullying behavior among U.S. youth: Prevalence and association with psychosocial adjustment. *JAMA, 285*, 2094–2100.

O'Keefe, M. (1997). Predictors of dating violence among high school students. *Journal of Interpersonal Violence, 12*, 546–568.

Olweus, D., Limber, S., & Mahalic, S. F. (1999). *Bullying prevention program.* Boulder: Center for the Study and Prevention of Violence, Institute of Behavioral Science, University of Colorado at Boulder.

Pelligrini, A. D. (2001). A longitudinal study of heterosexual relationships, aggression, and sexual harassment during the transition from primary school through middle school. *Applied Developmental Psychology, 22*, 119–133.

Pepler, D. J., Craig, W. M., Connolly, J., & Henderson, K. (2002). Aggression and substance use in early adolescence: My friends made me do it. In C. Werkle & A. M. Wall (Eds.), *The violence and addiction equation: Theoretical and clinical issues in substance abuse and relationship violence*. Philadelphia: Brunner/Mazel.

Pepler, D. J., Craig, W. M., Connolly, J. A., Yuile, A., McMaster, L., & Depeng, J. (2006). A developmental perspective on bullying. *Aggressive Behavior, 32*, 376–384.

Reid, J. B., Patterson, G. R., & Snyder, J. J. (Eds.). (2002). *Antisocial behavior in children and adolescents: A developmental analysis and a model for intervention*. Washington, DC: American Psychological Association.

Robers, S., Kemp, J., & Truman, J. (2013). *Indicators of school crime and safety: 2012* (NCES 2013-036/NCJ 241446). Washington, DC: U.S. Department of Education and U.S. Department of Justice.

Ryan, J. P., Marshall, J. M., Herz, D., & Hernandez, P. M. (2008). Juvenile delinquency in child welfare: Investigating group home effects. *Children and Youth Services Review, 30*, 1088–1099.

Schwartz, D., & Protor, L. (2000). Community violence exposure and children's social adjustment in the school peer group: The mediating roles of emotion regulation and social cognition. *Journal of Consulting and Clinical Psychology, 68*, 670–683.

Slomkowski, C., Rende, R., Conger, K. J., Simons, R. L., & Conger, R. D. (2001). Sisters, brothers, and delinquency: Evaluating social influence during early and middle adolescence. *Child Development, 72*, 271–283.

Tharp, A. (2012). Dating matters: The next generation of teen dating violence prevention. *Prevention of Science, 13*, 398–401.

Tjaden, P., & Thoennes, N. (2006). *Extent, nature, and consequences of rape victimization: Findings from the national violence against women survey* (NCJ 210346). Washington, DC: U.S. Department of Justice, National Institute of Justice.

Tyler, K. A., Hoyt, D. R., Whitbeck, L. B., & Cauce, A. M. (2003). The impact of childhood sexual abuse on later sexual victimization among runaway youth. *Journal of Research on Adolescence, 11*, 151–176.

U.S. Department of Education, Office of Civil Rights. (2001). *Revised sexual harassment guidance: Harassment of students by school employees, other students, or third parties: Title IX*. Retrieved from http://www2.ed.gov/about/offices/list/ocr/docs/shguide.html

Wolfe, D. A., Wekerle, C., Scott, K., Straatman, A., Grasley, C., & Reitzel-Jaffe, D. (2003). Dating violence prevention with at-risk youth: A controlled outcome evaluation. *Journal of Consulting and Clinical Psychology, 71*, 279–291.

Ybarra, M., Espelage, D. L., & Mitchell, K. J. (2014). Differentiating youth who are bullied from other victims of peer-aggression: The importance of differential power and repetition. *Journal of Adolescent Health, 55*, 293–300.

Yeager, D. S., Fong, C. J., Lee, H. Y., & Espelage, D. L. (2015). Declines in efficacy of anti-bullying programs among older adolescents: A developmental theory and a three-level meta-analysis. *Journal of Applied Developmental Psychology, 37*, 36–51.

8

Bullying among Sexual Minority Youth

Jeffrey Duong and Catherine P. Bradshaw

Since the mid-2000s, there has been tremendous growth in research on the challenges faced by youth identifying as lesbian, gay, bisexual, transgender, or queer (LGBTQ). The nature of these various challenges may be mental, physical, or social. In recent years, research has shown that bullying and victimization represent key public health concerns confronting today's sexual minority youth. In this chapter, we describe the magnitude of bullying as a public health problem affecting sexual minority youth. Furthermore, we summarize the implications of bullying involvement among LGBTQ youth by using Meyer's (2003) minority stress model as the guiding framework. Last, we highlight potential approaches to support sexual minority youth involved in bullying and recommend strategies for prevention.

BULLYING AND VICTIMIZATION AMONG SEXUAL MINORITY YOUTH

Research has estimated that nearly 30 percent of sexual minority youth have experienced bullying in school or online in the past year (Duong & Bradshaw, 2014). More specifically, over 10 percent of youth identifying as lesbian, gay, or bisexual have experienced both school and cyberbullying (Duong & Bradshaw, 2014). In addition to bullying, sexual minority youth often report other forms of victimization that lead them to feel unsafe or unwelcome at schools. Homophobic bullying, described as bullying that targets nonheterosexual students or those perceived to be nonheterosexual, warrants particular attention (Rivers, 2011). Surveys of LGBTQ youth between the ages of 13 and 18 have found that 85 percent of respondents were verbally harassed in the past year (Kosciw, Greytak, Palmer, & Boesen, 2014). Meanwhile, 65 percent reported hearing homophobic remarks (for example, "fag" or "dyke") either frequently or often at their school (Kosciw et al., 2014). Together, these experiences create unsafe and unwelcoming environments for LGBTQ students, which may increase their risk for poor mental health outcomes.

MINORITY STRESS MODEL FOR BULLYING INVOLVEMENT IN LGBTQ YOUTH

According to the minority stress model (Meyer, 2003), social stressors (for example, bullying and victimization) rooted in stigma and prejudice against one's minority status (for example, gender and sexual identity or expression) can affect these individuals' mental health. This model also posits a variety of processes through which stress can affect the physical, social, and emotional health of minorities. Furthermore, it suggests that stressors may have more serious impacts on sexual minority youth compared with heterosexual youth. Thus, the minority stress model provides a useful framework for organizing our understanding of how bullying and victimization can have an array of negative impacts on sexual minority youth.

Consistent with the minority stress model (Meyer, 2003), studies have shown that bullying among sexual minority youth often leads to psychological distress, depression, anxiety, posttraumatic stress, and substance abuse problems (D'Augelli, Pilkington, & Hershberger, 2002; Espelage, Aragon, Birkett, & Koenig, 2008). LGBTQ youth experiencing greater levels of victimization often have lower grades in school compared with those who have been harassed less often (Murdock & Bolch, 2005). Victimization may also have lasting impacts. For instance, frequently harassed LGBTQ youth report being less likely to plan to attend college (Kosciw et al., 2014). Furthermore, research suggests that bullying may socially and emotionally affect sexual minority youth more severely than their non–sexual minority peers (Birkett, Espelage, & Koenig, 2009).

APPROACHES TO ADDRESSING BULLYING AMONG SEXUAL MINORITY YOUTH

Create Safe and Supportive Environments for Students

Helping schools to create safe and supportive environments is crucial for LGBTQ youth (Goodenow, Szalacha, & Westheimer, 2006). Sexual minority youth often report that their school does not have the necessary resources and supports in place for LGBTQ students. For instance, only 50 percent of LGBTQ youth report having a gay–straight alliance (GSA) at their school (Hansen, 2007; Kosciw et al., 2014; Walls, Kane, & Wisneski, 2010). Such organizations or clubs are crucial in bullying prevention efforts in schools as they help to cultivate an inclusive environment. Specifically, these groups provide a forum for intergroup interactions and promote dialogue for students across campus (Griffin, Lee, Waugh, & Beyer, 2004). Studies have shown that students attending schools with GSAs report lower rates of harassment and higher levels of perceived safety, demonstrating that these benefits reach both sexual minority and heterosexual youth (Goodenow et al., 2006; Szalacha, 2003). The Gay, Lesbian & Straight Education Network provides safe space kits containing educational materials that can be used to help promote supportive environments in schools (see http://www.glsen.org/safespace).

Establish Clear Antibullying Policies

Comprehensive nondiscrimination and antibullying policies that specifically address sexual orientation and gender identity and expression play a central role in protecting LGBTQ youth (Russell, Kosciw, Horn, & Saewyc, 2010). In surveys of sexual minority youth, however, only 10.1 percent of respondents reported attending a school with such policies (Kosciw et al., 2014). In 2010, the U.S. Department of Education's Office for Civil Rights distributed a "Dear Colleague" letter to schools to remind them of their obligation to protect students from bullying and discriminatory harassment on the basis of race, color, national origin, disability, and sex. The letter noted that students who experience homophobic bullying may also be potential victims of sexual discrimination, which is prohibited under Title IX of the Education Amendments of 1972. Federal laws require schools to investigate instances of sexual discrimination and to take immediate action to prevent its recurrence. Students and families may file complaints of discrimination to report schools failing to comply with these regulations. Thus, staff members need to receive training on how to respond accordingly to the bullying of LGBTQ youth, as it may relate to discriminatory harassment.

Train Teachers and Staff on Preventing and Intervening in Bullying and Advocating for LGBTQ Youth

Teachers, staff, and other adults in school are pivotal to protecting LGBTQ youth from bullying. Identifying as LGBTQ and experiencing bullying are isolating experiences. Therefore, it is critical for school personnel to intervene in bullying proactively. When adults in school fail to intervene in bullying or harassment, students may believe that these behaviors are acceptable (Aboud & Miller, 2007). Teacher and staff training will be necessary to provide adults with the skills needed to foster respectful, caring, and inclusive environments in schools (Duong & Bradshaw, 2014). To help sexual minority youth feel more supported, it is also essential to train adults to be allies who openly discourage homophobic bullying and harassment (Rivers, 2011). To that end, schools and teachers should adopt classroom policies that explicitly combat homophobia and derogatory name-calling, including terms such as "gay," "homo," "tranny," and "fag." Adults must also stop homophobic bullying and harassment as they occur and remind students about the importance of being respectful to others. Adults also need to send clear messages to students about how derogatory name-calling is both unacceptable and hurtful. Through training, adults may learn how to teach students alternative ways to express their feelings without offending others (for example, saying "I don't like this assignment" versus "This assignment is so gay"). For some adults in school, using these strategies may be new or uncomfortable and decrease their willingness to intervene (Duong & Bradshaw, 2013). Therefore, extra opportunities to practice intervention strategies will also be fundamental to training endeavors.

Educate Students about Bullying and Diversity

Making resources more widely available to all students represents another important bullying prevention strategy. Such resources may include information about LGBTQ issues and lists of community-based organizations offering assistance to sexual minority youth. For sexual minority youth, these resources provide guidance on how they might be able to navigate difficult social interactions with their peers. Meanwhile, studies have shown that intolerance for those who are different plays a central role in creating hostile school climates (Swearer, Turner, Givens, & Pollack, 2008). To combat these sentiments, making information about LGBTQ issues more accessible to all students regardless of their sexual orientation will allow them to learn about concerns affecting youth from different backgrounds. Indeed, research suggests that promoting inclusion and bolstering students' knowledge about LGBTQ issues may reduce homophobic bullying (Poteat, Espelage, & Koenig, 2009). It may also enhance students' perceptions of safety and acceptance in their schools (Szalacha, 2003). For example, sexual minority youth with greater access to support resources may feel that adults at school care about them and that teachers treat students fairly. One potential educational resource about diversity and issues affecting sexual minorities is the *Talking About* series, published by GLAAD (see http://www.glaad.org/publications/talkingabout).

Provide Guidance to Families with Sexual Minority Youth

Families play an important role in the well-being of sexual minority youth. For example, rejection by families at home leads to poor health outcomes among sexual minority youth (Ryan, Huebner, Diaz, & Sanchez, 2009). Thus, it is important to strengthen the bonds between sexual minority youth and their families. Reorienting families to be more accepting may yield protective benefits for their sexual minority loved ones, such as greater self-esteem and perceived support (Ryan, Russell, Huebner, Diaz, & Sanchez, 2010; Shilo & Savaya, 2011). To that end, guidance efforts might include educating caregivers about the ways in which they can support their sexual minority children. When caregivers first discover that their child is gay, uncertainty and concern are common reactions. Caregivers may also worry that their child may be victimized for his or her sexual identity. In hopes of protecting their child, caregivers may try to suppress how their child expresses his or her gender or sexual identity (Ryan, 2009). Such responses may instead have adverse impacts on LGBTQ youth, making them more vulnerable to the negative consequences of experiences such as homophobic bullying (Espelage et al., 2008). In contrast, talking openly with their child about his or her gender and sexual identity, continuing to show affection and support despite personal concerns or attitudes, and fostering acceptance among other individuals in the child's life (for example, extended family, peers, and community members) are all important ways in which caregivers can help their child (Ryan, 2009). In addition, providing anticipatory guidance to caregivers will empower them to access a range of services for their families when further support is needed (Ryan, 2009).

Support Bullied and Victimized Sexual Minority Youth

Research suggests that youth on average "come out" to others around age 16. In recent years, however, they have started to come out at increasingly younger ages (Floyd & Bakeman, 2006). Meanwhile, studies have shown that bullying tends to peak as youth transition from elementary to middle school (Pellegrini & Long, 2002). Thus, there is increasing overlap between the times that LGBTQ youth are learning about their sexual identity and when bullying behaviors peak among children and adolescents. As bullying often makes youth feel isolated, it may be even more difficult for those who are just starting to come out or are already feeling confused or distressed about their identity (Goodenow et al., 2006; Ryan & Futterman, 1998). To help children and adolescents through this period, fostering positive identity formation will be a crucial strategy to reduce their risk for mental health concerns (Ryan & Futterman, 1998). Moreover, the scientific literature on youth resiliency suggests that simply targeting risk factors for bullying and addressing mental health concerns as they occur in sexual minority youth do not necessarily lead to healthy development (Russell, 2005). Rather, bolstering social-emotional competence (for example, self-confidence and coping skills) among sexual minority youth must also be considered, as this may buffer them from the consequences of bullying (Hershberger & D'Augelli, 2000). In working with sexual minority youth, it is also important to recognize that some may need individualized attention and could benefit from interventions that incorporate gay affirmative practice (Crisp & McCave, 2007; Ryan, 2009). Providing personalized guidance to at-risk sexual minority youth may better prepare them to avoid negative health outcomes later in life. Examples of practices to support LGBTQ youth include the following (adapted from Ryan, 2009):

1. Talk with the child about his or her LGBTQ identity.
2. Express affection when the child tells you or when you learn that your child is LGBTQ.
3. Support the child's LGBTQ identity even though you may feel uncomfortable.
4. Advocate for the child when he or she is mistreated because of his or her LGBTQ identity.
5. Encourage family members to respect the LGBTQ child.
6. Bring the child to LGBTQ organizations or events.
7. Connect the child with an LGBTQ adult role model to show him or her options for the future.
8. Work to make your faith community supportive of LGBTQ members or find a supportive faith community that welcomes the family and LGBTQ child.
9. Welcome the child's LGBTQ friends and partner to events and activities.
10. Support the child's gender expression.
11. Believe the child can have a happy future as an LGBTQ adult.
12. Talk with the child about his or her LGBTQ identity.
13. Express affection when the child tells you or when you learn that the child is LGBTQ.

CONCLUSION

Although shifting societal norms have helped to decrease the stigma associated with identifying as lesbian, gay, bisexual, transgender, or queer, sexual minority youth continue to be at risk for bullying and harassment. There is compelling evidence that LGBTQ youth are more likely than their heterosexual peers to be bullied and report negative outcomes (Duong & Bradshaw, 2014). However, several studies have shed light on the protective effects of fostering supportive relationships between sexual minority youth and their family, peers, teachers, and other adults whom they consider to be important in their lives. In schools, creating a safe and supportive environment through GSAs and teacher training may have buffering effects for LGBTQ youth (Kosciw et al., 2014). At home, caregivers may support their LGBTQ youth by showing greater acceptance of their gender and sexual identity (Ryan, 2009). With increased awareness of the social and emotional challenges that LGBTQ youth face, particularly when exposed to high rates of bullying, it is imperative to recognize the need for prevention and intervention programs that help schools and families to celebrate and promote diversity.

REFERENCES

Aboud, F., & Miller, L. (2007). Promoting peer intervention in name-calling. *South African Journal of Psychology, 37*, 803–819.

Birkett, M., Espelage, D. L., & Koenig, B. (2009). LGB and questioning students in schools: The moderating effects of homophobic bullying and school climate on negative outcomes. *Journal of Youth and Adolescence, 38*, 989–1000.

Crisp, C., & McCave, E. L. (2007). Gay affirmative practice: A model for social work practice with gay, lesbian, and bisexual youth. *Child and Adolescent Social Work Journal, 24*, 403–421.

D'Augelli, A. R., Pilkington, N. W., & Hershberger, S. L. (2002). Incidence and mental health impact of sexual orientation victimization of lesbian, gay, and bisexual youths in high school. *School Psychology Quarterly, 17*(2), 148–167.

Duong, J., & Bradshaw, C. P. (2013). Using the extended parallel process model to examine teachers' likelihood of intervening in bullying. *Journal of School Health, 83*, 422–429.

Duong, J., & Bradshaw, C. (2014). Associations between bullying and engaging in aggressive and suicidal behaviors among sexual minority youth: The moderating role of connectedness. *Journal of School Health, 84*, 636–645.

Espelage, D. L., Aragon, S. R., Birkett, M., & Koenig, B. W. (2008). Homophobic teasing, psychological outcomes, and sexual orientation among high school students: What influence do parents and schools have? *School Psychology Review, 37*(2), 202–216.

Floyd, F. J., & Bakeman, R. (2006). Coming-out across the life course: Implications of age and historical context. *Archives of Sexual Behavior, 35*, 287–296.

Goodenow, C., Szalacha, L., & Westheimer, K. (2006). School support groups, other school factors, and the safety of sexual minority adolescents. *Psychology in the Schools, 43*, 573–589.

Griffin, P., Lee, C., Waugh, J., & Beyer, C. (2004). Describing roles that gay-straight alliances play in schools: From individual support to school change. *Journal of Gay & Lesbian Issues in Education, 1*(3), 7–22.

Hansen, A. L. (2007). School-based support for GLBT students: A review of three levels of research. *Psychology in the Schools, 44*, 839–848.

Hershberger, S. L., & D'Augelli, A. R. (2000). Issues in counseling lesbian, gay, and bisexual adolescents. In R. M. Perez, K. A. DeBord, & K. J. Bieschke (Eds.), *Handbook of counseling and psychotherapy with lesbian, gay, and bisexual clients* (pp. 225–247). Washington, DC: American Psychological Association.

Kosciw, J. G., Greytak, E. A., Palmer, N. A., & Boesen, M. J. (2014). *The 2013 National School Climate Survey: The experiences of lesbian, gay, bisexual and transgender youth in our nation's schools.* New York: Gay, Lesbian & Straight Education Network.

Meyer, I. H. (2003). Prejudice, social stress, and mental health in lesbian, gay, and bisexual populations: Conceptual issues and research evidence. *Psychological Bulletin, 129*, 674–697.

Murdock, T. B., & Bolch, M. B. (2005). Risk and protective factors for poor school adjustment in lesbian, gay, and bisexual (LGB) high school youth: Variable and person-centered analyses. *Psychology in the Schools, 42*(2), 159–172.

Pellegrini, A. D., & Long, J. D. (2002). A longitudinal study of bullying, dominance, and victimization during the transition from primary school through secondary school. *British Journal of Developmental Psychology, 20*, 259–280.

Poteat, V. P., Espelage, D. L., & Koenig, B. W. (2009). Willingness to remain friends and attend school with lesbian and gay peers: Relational expressions of prejudice among heterosexual youth. *Journal of Youth and Adolescence, 38*, 952–962.

Rivers, I. (2011). *Homophobic bullying: Research and theoretical perspectives*. New York: Oxford University Press.

Russell, S. T. (2005). Beyond risk: Resilience in the lives of sexual minority youth. *Journal of Gay & Lesbian Issues in Education, 2*(3), 5–18.

Russell, S. T., Kosciw, J., Horn, S., & Saewyc, E. (2010). Safe schools policy for LGBTQ students. *Social Policy Report, 24*(4), 3–17.

Ryan, C. (2009). *Supportive families, healthy children: Helping families with lesbian, gay, bisexual, & transgender children*. San Francisco: Marian Wright Edelman Institute, San Francisco State University.

Ryan, C., & Futterman, D. (1998). *Lesbian and gay youth: Care and counseling*. Philadelphia: Hanley & Belfus.

Ryan, C., Huebner, D., Diaz, R. M., & Sanchez, J. (2009). Family rejection as a predictor of negative health outcomes in white and Latino lesbian, gay, and bisexual young adults. *Pediatrics, 123*(1), 346–352.

Ryan, C., Russell, S. T., Huebner, D., Diaz, R., & Sanchez, J. (2010). Family acceptance in adolescence and the health of LGBTQ young adults. *Journal of Child and Adolescent Psychiatric Nursing, 23*(4), 205–213.

Shilo, G., & Savaya, R. (2011). Effects of family and friend support on LGB youths' mental health and sexual orientation milestones. *Family Relations, 60*, 318–330.

Swearer, S. M., Turner, R. K., Givens, J. E., & Pollack, W. S. (2008). "You're so gay!" Do different forms of bullying matter for adolescent males? *School Psychology Review, 37*, 160–173.

Szalacha, L. A. (2003). Safer sexual diversity climates: Lessons learned from an evaluation of Massachusetts safe schools program for gay and lesbian students. *American Journal of Education, 110*(1), 58–88.

U.S. Department of Education. (2010, October 26). *Dear colleague letter: Harassment and bullying*. Washington, DC: Office for Civil Rights, U.S. Department of Education.

Walls, N. E., Kane, S. B., & Wisneski, H. (2010). Gay-straight alliances and school experiences of sexual minority youth. *Youth & Society, 41*, 307–332.

9

Bullying and Cultural Considerations

Joanna Lee Williams and Saida B. Hussain

The U.S. population is becoming increasingly diverse with respect to racial and ethnic group membership. It is projected that by 2020, over half of all children under age 18 will be people of color (Colby & Ortman, 2015). Consequently there is a critical need to understand the role of race and ethnicity in bullying and victimization. This chapter aims to develop this understanding by examining four relevant topics: (a) whether the prevalence of bullying involvement, either as a bully, a victim, or both, varies across racial and ethnic groups; (b) developmental factors in childhood and adolescence that can further our understanding of race- or ethnicity-related bullying involvement; (c) the frequency and impact of racial–ethnic bullying, which refers to bullying directed toward a person's racial, ethnic, or cultural background (McKenney, Pepler, Craig, & Connolly, 2006; Scherr & Larson, 2010); and (d) intervention approaches that may be effective in preventing and reducing racial–ethnic bullying. Notably, our review focuses primarily on childhood and adolescence, which are developmental periods in which bullying is most often studied and also when bullying is most likely to increase in prevalence (StopBullying.gov, 2014).

DIFFERENTIAL BULLYING INVOLVEMENT ACROSS RACIAL–ETHNIC GROUPS

Before reviewing the findings on racial–ethnic group differences in bullying involvement, it is important to acknowledge that racial–ethnic group membership in and of itself cannot be considered a causal factor with respect to bullying behavior; in other words, people do not engage in bullying because they are a member of a particular group. However, it is still important to consider why racial–ethnic group membership may appear to be related to bullying. For instance, factors such as economic segregation (for example, low-income families clustered together in the same neighborhood), which is highly correlated with racial–ethnic segregation, contribute to the existence of underresourced schools and communities where there are high levels of antisocial behavior, including bullying. When members of particular racial–ethnic groups (for example, African Americans) are over-represented in these communities, this can contribute to the perception that they are more likely to be involved in bullying behavior. Moreover, for members of the black community in particular, pervasive stereotypes of men as aggressive and "hypermasculine" and women as loud and angry (Morris, 2007; Stevenson, 2003) can also contribute to the perception of an increased involvement in bullying.

Although factors like segregation and stereotypes may contribute to bullying, research findings on differential involvement in bullying across racial–ethnic groups vary quite considerably. This suggests that no simple conclusions can be drawn at the intergroup level. For instance, in one study using a nationally representative sample of 11- to 14-year-old U.S. teenagers, African American and Asian American youth were less likely to be bullies compared with white youth (Barboza et al., 2009). However, similar studies have found no differences in bullying involvement across racial–ethnic groups (Spriggs, Iannotti, Nansel, & Haynie, 2007), or they have found that black youth were more likely than white youth to be involved in bullying (Wang, Iannotti, & Nansel, 2009). In a large sample of youth from 20 middle schools, Goldweber, Waasdorp, and Bradshaw (2013) reported that African American youth were more likely to be represented in the categories of "victim" or "bully–victim" as opposed to the category of "low involvement" in bullying, whereas Lovegrove, Henry, and Slater (2012) found that African American youth were more likely to be labeled a bully and less likely to be a victim compared with their peers. Other studies focused specifically on victimization have found that Asian American and immigrant youth are more likely to be victimized relative to their peers, particularly because of their ethnic group membership (Bucchianeri, Eisenberg, & Neumark-Sztainer, 2013; Sulkowski, Bauman, Wright, Nixon, & Davis, 2014).

SCHOOL CONTEXT

In trying to understand bullying and victimization in relation to racial–ethnic group membership, it is important to consider the role of context. For example, some studies have shown that the level of ethnic diversity in a school setting makes a difference for youth bullying behavior. In a large-scale study of Los Angeles middle schools, Graham and colleagues found that in more diverse schools and classrooms, students reported lower levels of vulnerability and victimization, more cross-ethnic friendships, and higher levels of positive adjustment (Graham, Bellmore, Nishina, & Juvonen, 2009). Greater school diversity and increased presence of same-race peers have also been linked to lower levels of victimization, greater school attachment, and stability in feelings of belonging at the high school level (Benner & Graham, 2009; Felix & You, 2011). Examinations of school climate reveal that perceived school multiculturalism (for example, the school values of racial harmony and cross-race interaction) and inclusive norms predict lower levels of interpersonal violence (Le & Johansen, 2011). Conversely, schools with highly structured academic hierarchies (for example, tracking or ability grouping) are believed to promote within-school ethnic segregation, as youth of color are frequently overrepresented in lower academic tracks, limiting cross-ethnic interactions (Hamm, Brown & Heck, 2005; Moody, 2001). Although little research has examined links between academic tracking and bullying, the existence of academic hierarchies in diverse schools is related to disproportionate disciplinary sanctions for black, Latino, and American Indian youth (Gregory, Skiba, & Noguera, 2010). Taken together, it is clear that the school ethnic context, students' perceptions of school climate, and institutionalized hierarchies are all factors that can contribute to differential involvement in bullying and victimization across racial–ethnic groups.

DEVELOPMENTAL TRENDS IN INCLUSION AND EXCLUSION

Normative Behaviors in Childhood

Biased bullying behavior observed in school-age children should be distinguished from normative patterns of social inclusion and exclusion that are frequently displayed by young children. Research shows that as early as three months old, babies can show visual preferences for people from their own racial group (Kelly et al., 2005). During toddlerhood, children learn about features associated with different social categories (for example, gender). Preschool-age children often show preferential biases for people from their own social group, in addition to negative evaluations toward people from other groups (Bigler & Liben, 2006). These explicit biases are normative and influenced both by children's cognitive abilities and by the socialization messages they are exposed to in family, school, and other settings (Aboud, 2008; Bigler & Liben, 2006; Patterson & Bigler, 2006). In addition to displays of explicit bias, increasing evidence suggests that as early as age six, children can also hold implicit biases (that is, unconscious and automatic biases toward or against particular groups of people) (Baron & Banaji, 2006). Moreover, by about age 10, most children can infer another person's stereotypical belief and understand that broadly held stereotypes about different groups exist. Children from historically stigmatized groups (for example, black and Latino youth) are often aware of this at earlier ages relative to their peers (McKown & Weinstein, 2003).

Although one's ability to control the expression of explicit bias increases with age and experience, implicit biases can be harder to consciously control and can be present even in a person who consciously expresses an inclusive, low-biased attitude toward others. Automatic preferences toward one's in-group and negative attitudes toward out-group members can vary depending on personal and contextual features as well. For instance, cross-group friendships and other forms of salient, frequent contact between members of different groups have been associated with lower levels of implicit bias in school-age children and adolescents (Turner, Hewstone, & Voci, 2007). Although we know from a developmental perspective that displays of explicit bias and implicitly biased attitudes can be considered normative, what is not known is whether and how these biases might translate into explicit bullying behavior. As Killen and Rutland (2011) stated,

> Implicit associations formed early in life may establish the potential for biases, but whether these biases turn into prejudices . . . is dependent on how children learn to reason about and judge issues of morality and group identity in everyday encounters. (p. 57)

Issues of group identity become even more meaningful as children transition into adolescence.

Social Identity and Belonging in Adolescence

In early adolescence, peer groups tend to be characterized by greater pressure to conform to group norms compared with earlier and later periods of development (Gavin & Furman, 1989). One reason for this might be related to normative developmental processes in judgment and decision making; specifically, adolescents tend to use stereotype-based information when making judgments that involve social group membership (Albert & Steinberg, 2011), which can manifest as rigid norms around what it means to be an in-group member. In the social setting of adolescent peer groups, ethnicity-related norms can create boundaries around inclusion and exclusion and influence youth's beliefs about diversity and intergroup contact. Indeed, several studies have shown that racially segregated peer groups are the norm for most youth, especially in early and middle adolescence (Hamm et al., 2005; Moody, 2001). Ethnically segregated peer groups may emphasize in-group norms and reject out-group norms to maintain group boundaries (Abrams & Rutland, 2008), which could manifest as lower levels of tolerance for difference. This is in keeping with the recent finding that, over time, black youth in segregated groups were less likely to choose cross-ethnic friends, and white youth in segregated groups reported greater dislike for cross-ethnic peers (Wilson & Rodkin, 2013). Thus, the combination of increasing needs for social belonging and the accompanying process of developing a deeper understanding of the meaning of one's racial–ethnic group membership often contributes to an increased emphasis on group boundaries in early adolescence. Taken together, these normative developmental factors have the potential to contribute to an increased prevalence of racial–ethnic bullying during this developmental period.

PREVALENCE AND IMPACT OF RACIAL–ETHNIC BULLYING

Racial–ethnic bullying, or bullying behavior that is directed toward a person's racial, ethnic, or cultural group membership, has been considered as part of a small but growing area of research on biased-based bullying (Rosenthal et al., 2013; Russell, Sinclair, Poteat, & Koenig, 2012). This review distinguishes between research on racial–ethnic bullying and the much larger field of research on racial–ethnic discrimination, though there are potential areas of overlap between the two fields (Fox & Stallworth, 2005; Melander, Sittner Hartshorn, & Whitbeck, 2013; Rosenthal et al., 2013). For instance, recent evidence suggests that youth who experience racial discrimination are more likely to be nominated as victims of overt and relational victimization compared with their peers (Seaton, Neblett, Cole, & Prinstein, 2013); however, an in-depth review of the discrimination literature is beyond the scope of this chapter. Specifically, this chapter drew from studies that have operationalized bullying in a way that recognizes the power differential between the bully (or bullies) and victim(s); bullying is also characterized as being intentional and typically recurs over an extended period of time (Olweus, 1993).

Recent studies of racial–ethnic bullying have found prevalence rates ranging from 17 percent (Russell et al., 2012) to 35 percent (Bucchianeri et al., 2013). According to the National Crime Victimization Survey's School Crime Supplement (U.S. Department of Justice, 2011), which asks about bullying behavior in schools, 9 percent of youth ages 12–18 reported experiencing some form of biased bullying (for example, targeting of their race, religion, or sexual orientation). Among this group, about half were called hate-related words because of their race, and 31 percent because of their ethnicity; however, these experiences varied across racial–ethnic groups. For example, being targeted because of race was extremely high among Asian American youth (88 percent) but less prevalent for white youth (43 percent), and two-thirds of black and Hawaiian/Pacific Islander youth who were targets of hate-related words reported that this was due to race. Finally, the presence of hate-related words or symbols in school was reported by almost 30 percent of students, suggesting that these kinds of negative slurs are still prevalent in U.S. schools.

Although the impact of racial–ethnic bullying has not been studied in-depth, existing research suggests that it can be more detrimental than general bullying. For instance, Russell and colleagues (2012) found that youth who experienced race-based bullying had higher odds of substance use, depression, suicidal ideation and attempts, truancy, and multiple forms of victimization compared with youth who experienced non-race-based bullying. Racial–ethnic bullying is also associated with greater emotional symptoms (for example, worrying, unhappiness) among black and Latino youth; it is important to note that these negative emotions can subsequently contribute to negative physical health outcomes like high blood pressure, body mass index, and poor self-rated health (Rosenthal et al., 2013). Scherr and Larson (2010) suggested that when one is bullied because of a social identity like race, ethnicity, or immigrant status, it may be more detrimental than nonbiased bullying because it targets an individual's personal characteristics as well as his or her group identity, customs, and beliefs. Cultural group membership is often a source of pride and collective esteem. Being bullied because of this may instead turn it into a source of embarrassment, especially in the absence of a context that supports diversity and appreciates difference.

RACIAL–ETHNIC BULLYING IN ADULTHOOD

Currently, there are very few studies of racial–ethnic bullying among adults, and most existing studies focus on workplace bullying and harassment. In the context of the workplace, existing power structures (that is, supervisor–supervisee relationships) can factor into bullying behavior, and regular contact between employees creates an opportunity for bullying to be sustained over time. In a study of full-time employees, reports of general bullying were similar across racial groups. However, black, Latino, and Asian American employees reported higher levels of racial–ethnic bullying compared with white employees, and for black employees compared with their white peers there was a stronger association between racial–ethnic bullying and emotional strain. In addition, racial–ethnic bullying was more likely to be attributed to supervisors rather than coworkers, and victims of this kind of bullying had little confidence in their organization's ability to intervene (Fox & Stallworth, 2005). Raver and Nishii (2010) also found that ethnic harassment was higher among ethnic minority employees compared with white employees and that experiences of ethnic harassment were associated with low job commitment and high turnover intentions. The limited work in this area thus far suggests that ethnic minority adults experience more workplace racial–ethnic bullying and harassment compared with white adults (Berdahl & Moore, 2006) and that experiencing racial–ethnic bullying can create emotional strain and decrease job satisfaction. More research is needed to document the prevalence and impact of workplace racial–ethnic bullying and to identify and intervene in the contextual factors that may facilitate it.

INTERVENTIONS TO REDUCE RACIAL–ETHNIC BULLYING

There are two primary areas of research that can inform intervention strategies for racial–ethnic bullying. The first comes from studies of effective bullying intervention programs that are not geared toward a particular kind of bullying. The second draws from studies of prejudice reduction programs designed to promote intergroup contact and appreciation of differences. General school-based bullying interventions are discussed in more detail in several other chapters in this volume. What seems to emerge most clearly from studies of these programs is that approaches need to address multiple levels of the school context (for example, classroom, school climate; Whitted & Dupper, 2005) and should extend beyond the school setting to actively include parents. This is in keeping with research showing that more inclusive school settings are related to greater student happiness and less interpersonal violence (Le & Johansen, 2011). When students feel connected to school and perceive their teachers as caring and trustworthy, they are less likely to engage in problem behavior (Freiberg & Lapointe, 2006). There is also emerging evidence in support of "threat assessment" approaches in which schools work on intervening in bullying behavior before it escalates, use flexible problem-solving approaches in lieu of zero-tolerance policies, and respond to individual threats (including bullying behavior) in a tailored manner that takes into account the student and his or her history and the nature of the event (Cornell, Shin, Ciolfi, & Sancken, 2013). This kind of approach is believed to foster a safe and supportive school climate and is also associated with a reduction in racial disparities in school suspensions (Cornell et al., 2013). It is important to note that research on effective bullying interventions has not examined whether they are effective for all types of bullying, so although these practices are likely to be beneficial to students and schools in general, it is unclear if and how they might affect racial–ethnic bullying.

PREJUDICE REDUCTION PROGRAMS

A second kind of approach that may be useful for targeting racial–ethnic bullying is one that emphasizes prejudice reduction. Typically, prejudice reduction programs are based on principles of intergroup contact theory (Allport, 1954), which specifies that reductions in prejudice are mostly likely to occur when groups are given equal status, when they are working toward a set of common goals, when there is intergroup cooperation, and when there is institutional support. This theory has found support in research. Studies show that intergroup contact seems to be effective in reducing prejudice as a result of increases in empathy and perspective taking and decreases in anxiety about interacting with people from other groups (Dessel, 2010; Dessel & Rogge, 2008; Pettigrew & Tropp, 2008). An evaluation of the "Mix It Up" program, which facilitates cross-racial social connections among high school students through structured dialogues and lunchtime interactions, revealed that the majority of educators felt it increased students' respect and willingness to cross social boundaries. Over half believed that the program led to a reduction of school conflict. Students reported that the program increased their understanding of school climate, social boundaries, and the role of cliques in perpetuating conflict (Nagda, McCoy, & Barrett, 2006).

Although there is some evidence that interracial dialogue interventions can foster prejudice reduction, which may subsequently decrease the likelihood of racial–ethnic bullying, there are some important limitations in this area. First, most research on these programs is nonexperimental, meaning that the intervention was conducted without randomly assigning participants to the intervention or to a control group (Paluck & Green, 2009). In the absence of an experimental design, it is difficult to determine whether the intervention itself played a direct role in any observed changes or if there were some other factors that contributed to the change instead. In addition, the bulk of intergroup dialogue programs in the United States have been implemented with college students (Dessel & Rogge, 2008) despite the fact that racial–ethnic bullying may not occur as frequently among this age group as it does among children and younger adolescents.

There are a number of laboratory-based experimental studies of prejudice reduction approaches (see Paluck & Green, 2009, for a review); however, the conditions in these experiments are typically contrived and it is not clear whether any observed benefits would translate into real-world settings (Bigler & Hughes, 2010). Based on the few field-based, "real-world" experimental studies of prejudice reduction programs, there is some evidence that cooperative learning techniques and reading and media programs in schools appear to facilitate perspective taking, empathy, positive peer relationships, and cross-racial interactions (Cameron, Rutland, Brown, & Douch, 2006); moreover, these approaches have been successfully implemented in elementary, middle, and high schools. Thus, as with the effective bullying interventions described above, it appears that prejudice reduction interventions may be most successful when they foster a climate that promotes inclusiveness and belonging, shared norms about tolerance and diversity, and individual increases in perspective taking and empathy. However, as with the current state of the evidence on general bullying interventions, we still do not know whether fostering prejudice reduction would have a direct impact on racial–ethnic bullying. An important area for future work would be to integrate findings from effective bullying and prejudice reduction programs to design interventions that could have a greater potential for targeting racial–ethnic bullying, particularly in contexts (schools, workplace, and so forth) where this kind of bullying has been identified as problematic.

CONCLUSIONS AND IMPLICATIONS

The current body of knowledge on the role of race–ethnicity in bullying suggests that patterns of involvement in bullying and victimization across racial–ethnic groups vary across samples. Some studies point toward higher levels of bullying and victimization among black and Asian American youth, and other studies find no group differences. What does emerge more consistently is the higher prevalence of experiencing racial–ethnic bullying for ethnic minority youth and adults compared with their white peers; and importantly, these experiences are associated with more detrimental psychological, physical, and behavioral outcomes relative to non-racial–ethnic bullying (Russell et al., 2012). In childhood and adolescence, cognitive, social, and contextual factors all contribute to increases in in-group preferences, out-group exclusion and biases, and racial–ethnic segregation, which may facilitate the likelihood of negative cross-group interactions; however, it is unclear whether these normative aspects of development contribute directly to racial–ethnic bullying. Finally, although there have been no direct studies of interventions to target racial–ethnic bullying, findings from research on general bullying interventions as well as on interventions designed to promote intergroup contact and reduce prejudice can be useful for considering approaches that have the potential to be effective.

Several recommendations emerge from these findings. First, practitioners should be knowledgeable about developmental factors that may contribute to negative cross-racial interactions and racial–ethnic bullying. In early childhood, in-group favoritism and out-group bias is normative; however, it can still be beneficial to explicitly teach children about intergroup biases (Bigler & Wright, 2014). Moreover, intergroup biases can be affected, either positively or negatively, by environmental influences, so it is important to consider the kinds of cues that might enhance or attenuate stereotypes (Patterson & Bigler, 2006). In adolescence, normative processes of identity development, a tendency to apply stereotypes to social information, and an increased focus on belonging all have the potential to increase the likelihood of racial–ethnic bullying. In secondary schools, it is critical to create a school climate that promotes inclusiveness and acceptance of differences. Classroom norms around intolerance of bullying need to be made explicit. In addition, attempts should be made to proactively include parents in the process of educating youth about racial–ethnic bullying. Intergroup dialogue activities may be beneficial in fostering open communication and increasing empathy between students from different racial–ethnic backgrounds (Dessel, 2010); additional benefits may be accrued if these activities result in increased cross-group friendships (Feddes, Noack, & Rutland, 2009). Finally, any attempt to intervene with students who perpetrate racial–ethnic bullying should take the student's individual history and developmental status into account and should be tailored and flexible rather than using a "one-size-fits-all" approach (Cornell et al., 2013).

Less is known about the prevalence and impact of racial–ethnic bullying in adulthood; however, studies of workplace bullying suggest that employers need to pay attention to supervisor–employee power dynamics that might facilitate bullying. In addition, all employees should be made aware of the role of implicit biases that may unintentionally contribute to perceived differential treatment of employees of color in particular. Workplace policies should also be explicit about intolerance of racial–ethnic bullying and should clearly communicate how these instances will be handled so that victims have a sense of confidence in their organization's ability to intervene. Finally, whether in a K–12 or workplace setting, practitioners should be aware of the racial–ethnic diversity of the environment as well as the balance of power and status across groups, as these all have the potential to increase the likelihood of racial–ethnic bullying and may also factor into differential involvement in bullying and victimization across groups.

Although the landscape of racial–ethnic relations has changed dramatically over the past century, racial–ethnic bullying remains an important social justice issue; indeed, severe bullying based on one's racial or ethnic group is protected against under the Civil Rights Act of 1964 (StopBullying.gov, 2016). Unfortunately, the field of research on the role of race–ethnicity in bullying is still in its infancy and there is a great deal of work that needs to be done in this area. Directions for future investigation might include an examination of the effectiveness of cultural competency training as a way of fostering more inclusive environments (Colorado Trust, 2008) or an assessment of national initiatives to reduce bullying in particular cultural communities, like the "Stand Up, Stand Strong" campaign for American Indian and Alaska Native Youth organized by the Indian Health Service (http://www.ihs.gov). Given the rapid demographic changes currently taking place in the United States, it is critical to acknowledge the ways in which race and ethnicity can factor into bullying and victimization and to continue increasing our understanding of effective practices for promoting tolerance and inclusion.

REFERENCES

Aboud, F. E. (2008). A social-cognitive developmental theory of prejudice. In S. M. Quintana & C. McKown (Eds.), *Handbook of race, racism, and the developing child* (pp. 55–71). Hoboken, NJ: Wiley.

Abrams, D., & Rutland, A. (2008). The development of subjective group dynamics. In S. R. Levy & M. Killen (Eds.), *Intergroup relations: An integrative developmental and social psychological perspective* (pp. 47–65). Oxford, England: Oxford University Press.

Albert, D., & Steinberg, L. (2011). Judgment and decision making in adolescence. *Journal of Research on Adolescence, 21*(1), 211–224.

Allport, G. W. (1954). *The nature of prejudice.* Cambridge, MA: Addison-Wesley.

Barboza, G. E., Schiamberg, L. B., Oehmke, J., Korzeniewski, S. J., Post, L. A., & Heraux, C. G. (2009). Individual characteristics and the multiple contexts of adolescent bullying: An ecological perspective. *Journal of Youth and Adolescence, 38*(1), 101–121.

Baron, A. S., & Banaji, M. R. (2006). The development of implicit attitudes evidence of race evaluations from ages 6 and 10 and adulthood. *Psychological Science, 17*(1), 53–58.

Benner, A., & Graham, S. (2009). The transition to high school as a developmental process among multi-ethnic youth. *Child Development, 80,* 356–376.

Berdahl, J. L., & Moore, C. (2006). Workplace harassment: Double jeopardy for minority women. *Journal of Applied Psychology, 91*(2), 426–436.

Bigler, R. S., & Hughes, J. M. (2010). Reasons for skepticism about the efficacy of simulated social contact interventions. *American Psychologist, 65,* 132–133.

Bigler, R. S., & Liben, L. S. (2006). A developmental intergroup theory of social stereotypes and prejudice. In R. V. Kail (Ed.), *Advances in child development and behavior* (Vol. 34, pp. 39–89). San Diego: Elsevier.

Bigler, R. S., & Wright, Y. F. (2014). Reading, writing, arithmetic, and racism? Risks and benefits to teaching children about intergroup biases. *Child Development Perspectives, 8*(1), 18–23.

Bucchianeri, M. M., Eisenberg, M. E., & Neumark-Sztainer, D. (2013). Weightism, racism, classism, and sexism: Shared forms of harassment in adolescents. *Journal of Adolescent Health, 53*(1), 47–53.

Cameron, L., Rutland, A., Brown, R., & Douch, R. (2006). Changing children's intergroup attitudes toward refugees: Testing different models of extended contact. *Child Development, 77,* 1208–1219.

Colby, S. L., & Ortman, J. L. (2015, March). *Projections of the size and composition of the U.S. population: 2014 to 2060* (Current Population Reports, P25-1143). Washington, DC: U.S. Census Bureau. Retrieved from http://www.census.gov

Colorado Trust. (2008). *Bullying prevention resource guide: Best practices in bullying prevention and intervention.* Retrieved from http://www.bullyingprevention.org/repository//Best%20Practices%20PDFs/BP-Prevention.Intervention.pdf

Cornell, D., Shin, C., Ciolfi, A., & Sancken, K. (2013, December). *Prevention v. punishment: Threat assessment, school suspensions, and racial disparities.* Charlottesville, VA: Legal Aid Justice Center and University of Virginia Curry School of Education.

Dessel, A. (2010). Prejudice in schools: Promotion of an inclusive culture and climate. *Education and Urban Society, 42,* 407–429.

Dessel, A., & Rogge, M. E. (2008). Evaluation of intergroup dialogue: A review of the empirical literature. *Conflict Resolution Quarterly, 26*(2), 199–238.

Feddes, A. R., Noack, P., & Rutland, A. (2009). Direct and extended friendship effects on minority and majority children's interethnic attitudes: A longitudinal study. *Child Development, 80,* 377–390.

Felix, E. D., & You, S. (2011). Peer victimization within the ethnic context of high school. *Journal of Community Psychology, 39,* 860–875.

Fox, S., & Stallworth, L. E. (2005). Racial/ethnic bullying: Exploring links between bullying and racism in the US workplace. *Journal of Vocational Behavior, 66,* 438–456.

Freiberg, H. J., & Lapointe, J. M. (2006). Research-based programs for preventing and solving discipline problems. In C. M. Evertson & C. S. Weinstein (Eds.), *Handbook of classroom management* (pp. 735–786). Mahwah, NJ: Lawrence Erlbaum.

Gavin, L. A., & Furman, W. (1989). Age differences in adolescents' perceptions of their peer groups. *Developmental Psychology, 25*, 827–834.

Goldweber, A., Waasdorp, T. E., & Bradshaw, C. P. (2013). Examining associations between race, urbanicity, and patterns of bullying involvement. *Journal of Youth and Adolescence, 42*(2), 206–219.

Graham, S., Bellmore, A., Nishina, A., & Juvonen, J. (2009). "It must be me": Ethnic diversity and attributions for peer victimization in middle school. *Journal of Youth and Adolescence, 38*, 487–499.

Gregory, A., Skiba, R. J., & Noguera, P. A. (2010). The achievement gap and the discipline gap: Two sides of the same coin? *Educational Researcher, 39*(1), 59–68.

Hamm, J., Brown, B., & Heck, D. (2005). Bridging the ethnic divide: Student and school characteristics in African American, Asian-descent, Latino, and white adolescents' cross-ethnic friend nominations. *Journal of Research on Adolescence, 15*, 21–46.

Kelly, D. J., Quinn, P. C., Slater, A. M., Lee, K., Gibson, A., Smith, M., et al. (2005). Three-month-olds, but not newborns, prefer own-race faces. *Developmental Science, 8*(6), F31–F36.

Killen, M., & Rutland, A. (2011). *Children and social exclusion: Morality, prejudice, and group identity.* Chichester, West Sussex, England: Wiley.

Le, T. N., & Johansen, S. (2011). The relationship between school multiculturalism and interpersonal violence: An exploratory study. *Journal of School Health, 81*, 688–695.

Lovegrove, P. J., Henry, K. L., & Slater, M. D. (2012). Examination of the predictors of latent class typologies of bullying involvement among middle school students. *Journal of School Violence, 11*(1), 75–93.

McKenney, K. S., Pepler, D., Craig, W., & Connolly, J. (2006). Peer victimization and psychosocial adjustment: The experiences of Canadian immigrant youth. *Electronic Journal of Research in Educational Psychology, 9*, 239–264.

McKown, C., & Weinstein, R. S. (2003). The development and consequences of stereotype consciousness in middle childhood. *Child Development, 74*, 498–515.

Melander, L. A., Sittner Hartshorn, K. J., & Whitbeck, L. B. (2013). Correlates of bullying behaviors among a sample of North American indigenous adolescents. *Journal of Adolescence, 36*, 675–684.

Moody, J. (2001). Race, school integration, and friendship segregation in America. *American Journal of Sociology, 107*, 679–716.

Morris, E. W. (2007). "Ladies" or "loudies"? Perceptions and experiences of black girls in classrooms. *Youth & Society, 38*, 490–515.

Nagda, B.R.A., McCoy, M. L., & Barrett, M. H. (2006). Mix it up: Crossing social boundaries as a pathway to youth civic engagement. *National Civic Review, 95*(1), 47–56.

Olweus, D. (1993). *Bullying at school: What we know and what we can do.* Cambridge, MA: Blackwell.

Paluck, E. L., & Green, D. P. (2009). Prejudice reduction: What works? A review and assessment of research and practice. *Annual Review of Psychology, 60*, 339–367.

Patterson, M. M., & Bigler, R. S. (2006). Preschool children's attention to environmental messages about groups: Social categorization and the origins of intergroup bias. *Child Development, 77*, 847–860.

Pettigrew, T. F., & Tropp, L. R. (2008). How does intergroup contact reduce prejudice? Meta-analytic tests of three mediators. *European Journal of Social Psychology, 38*, 922–934.

Raver, J. L., & Nishii, L. H. (2010). Once, twice, or three times as harmful? Ethnic harassment, gender harassment, and generalized workplace harassment. *Journal of Applied
Psychology, 95*, 236–254.

Rosenthal, L., Earnshaw, V. A., Carroll-Scott, A., Henderson, K. E., Peters, S. M., McCaslin,
C., & Ickovics, J. R. (2013). Weight- and race-based bullying: Health associations among
urban adolescents. *Journal of Health Psychology, 20*, 401–412.

Russell, S. T., Sinclair, K. O., Poteat, V. P., & Koenig, B. W. (2012). Adolescent health and
harassment based on discriminatory bias. *American Journal of Public Health, 102*, 493–495.

Scherr, T. G., & Larson, J. (2010). Bullying dynamics associated with race, ethnicity, and
immigration status. In S. R. Jimerson, S. M. Swearer, & D. L. Espelage (Eds.), *Handbook
of bullying in schools: An international perspective* (pp. 223–234). New York: Routledge.

Seaton, E. K., Neblett, E. W., Jr., Cole, D. J., & Prinstein, M. J. (2013). Perceived discrimination and peer victimization among African American and Latino youth. *Journal of Youth
and Adolescence, 42*, 342–350.

Spriggs, A. L., Iannotti, R. J., Nansel, T. R., & Haynie, D. L. (2007). Adolescent bullying
involvement and perceived family, peer and school relations: Commonalities and differences across race/ethnicity. *Journal of Adolescent Health, 41*, 283–293.

Stevenson, H. C. (Ed.). (2003). *Playing with anger: Teaching coping skills to African American
boys through athletics and culture.* Westport, CT: Praeger.

StopBullying.gov. (2016). *Facts about bullying.* Retrieved from http://www.stopbullying.gov

Sulkowski, M. L., Bauman, S., Wright, S., Nixon, C., & Davis, S. (2014). Peer victimization in
youth from immigrant and non-immigrant US families. *School Psychology International,
35*, 649–669.

Turner, R. N., Hewstone, M., & Voci, A. (2007). Reducing explicit and implicit outgroup
prejudice via direct and extended contact: The mediating role of self-disclosure and
intergroup anxiety. *Journal of Personality and Social Psychology, 93*, 369–388.

U.S. Department of Justice, Office of Justice Programs, Bureau of Justice Statistics. (2011).
National Crime Victimization Survey: School crime supplement, 2011 [Data file and code
book]. Retrieved from http://www.icpsr.umich.edu

Wang, J., Iannotti, R. J., & Nansel, T. R. (2009). School bullying among adolescents in the
United States: Physical, verbal, relational, and cyber. *Journal of Adolescent Health, 45*,
368–375.

Whitted, K. S., & Dupper, D. R. (2005). Best practices for preventing or reducing bullying
in schools. *Children & Schools, 27*, 167–175.

Wilson, T. M., & Rodkin, P. C. (2013). Children's cross-ethnic relationships in elementary
schools: Concurrent and prospective associations between ethnic segregation and social
status. *Child Development, 84*, 1081–1097.

10

Bullying among Youth with Disabilities

Chad A. Rose

Over the past four decades, students with disabilities have been guaranteed the right to a free and appropriate public education (FAPE), and the passing of the Education of All Handicapped Children Act of 1975 (P.L. 94-142) has served as the foundation for providing individualized supports to all students with disabilities. This landmark legislation was in reaction to the over one million students with disabilities who either were entirely excluded from the public educational system or received limited access to education (U.S. Department of Education, 2010). According to the U.S. Department of Education (2010), in 1970, "U.S. schools educated only one in five children with disabilities, and many states had laws excluding certain students from school, including children who were deaf, blind, emotionally disturbed, or mentally retarded [henceforth referred to as intellectual disability]" (p. 3). Since 1975, this landmark legislation has been reauthorized several times, including the Individuals with Disabilities Education Improvement Act (IDEA; 2004), resulting in, but not limited to, the individualization of educational programming, access to the least restrictive environment, access to the general curriculum, improved academic skills, increased graduation rates, and improved postsecondary outcomes for individuals with disabilities (U.S. Department of Education, 2010). Although it cannot be disputed that the U.S. educational system has made notable advancements in the education of school-age youth with disabilities, a strong emphasis has been placed on academic achievement, with much less focus on social and emotional development, including bullying involvement.

Unfortunately, social and emotional development is at the crux of many pervasive issues facing youth with disabilities. For example, students with disabilities are disproportionately involved within the bullying dynamic both as victims and perpetrators (see Rose, Monda-Amaya, & Espelage, 2011, for review). Although findings on prevalence rates are inconsistent as a result of measurement and definitional disparities (Rose, Simpson, &

Moss, 2015), evidence suggests that students with disabilities are victimized up to 1.5 times more often than students without disabilities (Blake, Lund, Zhou, Kwok, & Benz, 2012). For many youth with and without disabilities, victimization begins in preschool (Son, Parish, & Peterson, 2012) and continues through adolescence (Blake et al., 2012; Rose & Gage, 2016). This is especially disconcerting for individuals with disabilities because bullying involvement has been associated with detrimental short- and long-term outcomes (Swearer, Espelage, Vaillancourt, & Hymel, 2010), where individuals with disabilities report increased psychological distress and more emotional and physical harm than their peers without disabilities (Hartley, Bauman, Nixon, & Davis, 2015). Therefore, not only are students with disabilities overrepresented within the bullying dynamic, they are often less resilient when exposed to prolonged victimization.

Given these outcomes and disproportionate representation, the purpose of this chapter is to (a) detail state and federal legislative and policy issues related to bullying involvement among students with disabilities, (b) describe risk and protective factors associated with overrepresentation, and (c) provide recommendations for intervention efforts designed to reduce the prevalence of bullying among this population of students.

BULLYING INVOLVEMENT AND LEGISLATIVE EFFORTS

In 2011, President Barack Obama acknowledged the pervasiveness of bullying among school-age youth by holding the White House Conference on Bully Prevention. This conference initiated a national conversation on bullying prevention, and two important products emerged. First, the federal government launched stopbullying.gov, which is a comprehensive Web site designed to provide parents, educators, school-age youth, researchers, educational stakeholders, and community members with resources regarding bullying and bully prevention. Second, the Obama administration commissioned the nation's leaders in bully prevention to write a series of briefing manuscripts (briefs) that detail the complexity of the bullying dynamic. In these briefs, which provide a foundational understanding of the current state of bullying among the nation's youth, two subgroups of individuals were specifically highlighted as at risk for escalated bullying involvement: youth who are lesbian, gay, bisexual, transgender, or questioning (Espelage, 2011) and students with disabilities (Young, Ne'eman, & Gelser, 2011).

Unfortunately, even with increased national attention, a federal definition of bullying does not exist, and bully prevention legislation is primarily a state-initiated mandate (Yell, Katsiyannis, Rose, & Houchins, 2016). As of 2015, all 50 states have adopted antibullying legislation (http://www.bullypolice.org; Maag & Katsiyannis, 2012), many of which rely on the traditional definition of bullying (that is, imbalance of power, intent to cause harm, repeated acts of aggression; Olweus, 1993). Thirteen of the states' policies include language that specifically prohibits bullying among youth with disabilities (that is, California, Idaho, Illinois, Iowa, Maine, Massachusetts, New Hampshire, New Mexico, New York, Oklahoma, Texas, Vermont, Virginia; http://www.bullypolice.org). For example, Massachusetts, which has one of the most comprehensive bully prevention policies, encourages individualized education program (IEP) team members to include within the IEP skill development designed to avoid bullying for youth identified as at risk for escalated victimization (Mass. Gen. Laws, 2010 71B § 3). This legislative mandate recognizes the social nature of bullying. It also illustrates the skill development function of the IEP by suggesting that it can be used to acquire the prosocial skills necessary to avoid prolonged victimization.

Whereas Massachusetts specifically identifies the IEP as a tool for reducing bullying involvement, the other 12 states defer to federal harassment legislation (that is, the Rehabilitation Act of 1973, the Americans with Disabilities Act of 1990 [ADA]; see http://www.bullypolice.org). This deferment is likely in response to the U.S. Department of Education's Office of Civil Rights (OCR) and Office of Special Education and Rehabilitative Services (OSERS), who have issued a series of *Dear Colleague Letters* (2000, 2010, 2013, 2014) designed to provide guidance to educational professionals regarding the bullying involvement among individuals with disabilities that specifically states that "disability" is a protected class under federal harassment laws. Federal law has interpreted the differences between bullying (a broad class of aggressive behaviors) and harassment (aggression for which an individual has legal protection) as immaterial (Norlin, 2012). Consequently, disability-based harassment, which is harassment that is directly tied to the disability or disability characteristics (for example, mimicking the speech of someone with a speech or language impairment, placing obstacles in the path of an individual in a wheelchair, imitating the stereotypic behaviors of an individual with autism spectrum disorders), may be a violation of Section 504 of the Rehabilitation Act of 1973 (29 U.S.C. § 794) and Title II of the Americans with Disabilities Act of 1990 (ADA; 42 U.S.C. § 12131 et seq.). The precedent of what constitutes disability-based harassment was established via the Supreme Court through *Davis v. Monroe County Board of Education* (1999), which was a sexual harassment case (Yell et al., 2016). In this case, the U.S. Supreme Court established the following guidance:

1. Did the conduct represent harassment?
2. Was the harassment due to a legally protected attribute?
3. Was the harassment severe, persistent, and/or pervasive, where it limited or denied participation in typical educational activities or created a hostile environment?
4. Was the school or district notified of the harassment or should they have reasonably known about the harassment?
5. Did the school or district take the appropriate actions to respond to the harassment once notified?

The Davis case has been applied to disability-based harassment because it is grounded in Title IX of the Education Amendments of 1972, which prohibits gender-based harassment, and also parallels the civil rights afforded to individuals with disabilities through ADA and the Rehabilitation Act. Therefore, if disability-based harassment is suspected or reported, on the basis of the aforementioned guidance, schools should take action to resolve potential civil rights violations.

In addition to potential civil rights violations, OSERS's 2013 *Dear Colleague Letter* suggested that bullying of any type that involves youth with disabilities may violate the legal provisions of IDEA (2004) of FAPE and least restrictive environment (LRE), which is "a location where students with disabilities can receive an education and related services while still being educated in the regular classroom to the greatest extent possible" (Marx et al., 2014, p. 45). More specifically, OSERS cautioned against educational environment modification as a protective measure without convening an IEP team meeting, as this change may violate FAPE or LRE. Therefore, if an individual with a disability is involved in bullying, the IEP team should convene to determine whether the student's needs have changed as a result of bullying and derive an IEP that provides meaningful educational benefit (U.S. Department of Education, OSERS, 2013; Yell et al., 2016).

WHY ARE STUDENTS WITH DISABILITIES DISPROPORTIONATELY INVOLVED IN BULLYING?

The increased legislative and federal attention has led scholars to investigate the disproportionate representation of students with disabilities within the bullying dynamic. As previously stated, in a national sample of American youth, Blake and colleagues (2012) found that individuals with disabilities were up to 1.5 times more likely to experience victimization than their peers without disabilities. In addition, Rose, Espelage, and Monda-Amaya (2009) determined that students with disabilities reported higher levels of bully perpetration, whereas Farmer and colleagues (2012) suggested that individuals with disabilities disproportionately represent bully–victims (that is, students who experience victimization and engage in bully perpetration) when compared with their peers without disabilities. In a recent longitudinal study of youth in grades three through 12, Rose and Gage (2016) determined that students with disabilities reported higher rates of bullying and victimization over time when compared with their peers without disabilities and that the disparities of involvement persist regardless of grade level. On the basis of these foundational studies, it is necessary to evaluate the disproportionate representation of individuals with disabilities within the bullying dynamic though a multifaceted lens, including disability identification, special education services, and prosocial skill deficits.

Bullying as a Function of Disability Status

Much of the special education bullying literature is derived from disability identification. Rose and colleagues (2011) and McLaughlin, Byers, and Vaughn (2010) found that much of the early literature in bullying either dichotomized disability status or established arbitrary subgroups (for example, observable disability, nonobservable disability). To extend these foundational studies, scholars have begun to recognize that disability status is based on diagnostic criteria, and the rudimentary identification of a disability may over- or underrepresent specific subgroups of individuals with disabilities. For example, Rose, Simpson, and Moss (2015) determined that 14.5 percent of youth without disabilities experience high levels of victimization, whereas 35.3 percent of students with emotional and behavioral disorders, 33.9 percent of youth with autism spectrum disorders, 24.3 percent of youth with intellectual disabilities, 20.8 percent of youth with other health impairments, and 19.0 percent of individuals with specific learning disabilities report high levels of victimization. Conversely, 13.5 percent of youth without disabilities engage in high levels of bully perpetration, whereas 24.1 percent of youth with intellectual disabilities, 19.4 percent of individuals with autism spectrum disorders, 16.9 percent of youth with other health impairments, 15.3 percent of individuals with emotional and behavioral disorders, and 14.4 percent of youth with specific learning disabilities engage in high levels of bully perpetration. Overall, these prevalence rates suggest that students with specific disabilities are overrepresented within the bullying dynamic.

Learning Disabilities. Because special education eligibility is based on specific diagnostic criteria that are designed to identify a continuum of disabilities (Overton, 2009), it is conceivable that victimization rates may vary on the basis of disability identification (Rose & Espelage, 2012). Specific learning disabilities represent the largest subpopulation of students with disabilities (Aud et al., 2012), where identification of a learning disability represents a broad continuum of deficits, including discrepancies in listening, thinking, speaking, reading, writing, spelling, or mathematics (IDEA, 2004). The variability of classes associated with learning disability identification, including mechanisms for assessment (for example, discrepancy formula, response to intervention), may lead to inconsistencies in empirical findings related to bullying involvement (McKenzie, 2009; Rose, Espelage, Monda-Amaya, Shogren, & Aragon, 2015). For example, Bear, Mantz, Glutting, Yang, and Boyer (2015) found that students with learning disabilities were 1.3 times more likely to "sometimes" experience general and physical victimization than their peers without disabilities, and Twyman and colleagues (2010) suggested that students with learning disabilities were 5.7 times more likely than their peers without disabilities to engage in bully perpetration. Conversely, Rose, Espelage, and colleagues (2015) determined that victimization and perpetration rates were invariant between the two subgroups. Given these discrepant findings and the broad definition of specific learning disability, it is conceivable that the basic identification of a learning disability is not a primary risk factor for bullying involvement (that is, victimization, perpetration). Rather, risk may increase as a function of the learning disability coupled with other individual and environmental factors, such as prosocial skill deficits and restrictive educational placements (Rose, Simpson, & Moss, 2015).

Behavioral-Oriented Disabilities. Several disability classifications are grounded in the manifestation of internalizing or externalizing behavioral deficits, including emotional and behavioral disorders, other health impairments (including attention-deficit/hyperactivity disorder), and autism spectrum disorders. Although these disabilities are categorically different, it is plausible that these subgroups of students with behavioral-oriented disabilities are disproportionately represented within the bullying dynamic. For example, Blake and colleagues (2012) determined that students with other health impairments in elementary school experience higher levels of victimization than their peers without disabilities, and Bear and colleagues (2015) suggested that students with other health impairments experience higher levels of verbal, physical, and social victimization. Similarly, youth with autism spectrum disorders have been identified as frequent victims of bullying (Symes & Humphrey, 2010; Twyman et al., 2010; Zablotsky, Bradshaw, Anderson, & Law, 2013), especially through social exclusion or relational aggression (Bear et al., 2015; Symes & Humphrey, 2010). Although Asperger's syndrome has been subsumed under the umbrella of autism spectrum disorders in the fifth edition of the *Diagnostic and Statistical Manual of Mental Disorders* (American Psychiatric Association, 2013) and can be considered high-functioning autism, it should be noted that as much as 94 percent of youth with Asperger's experience victimization (Little, 2002). Zablotsky, Bradshaw, Anderson, and Law (2012) argued that students with Asperger's are at greater risk of victimization than students identified with other topographies on the autism spectrum. Finally, students with emotional and behavioral disorders are disproportionately represented as both victims (Bear et al., 2015; Blake et al., 2012) and perpetrators (Rose & Espelage, 2012; Swearer, Wang, Maag, Siebecker, & Frerichs, 2012). Although these behavioral-oriented disabilities maintain independent diagnostic criteria and require different educational, behavioral, and functional supports, empirical evidence suggests that these particular subgroups of students are at escalated risk for bullying involvement. However, the parallels in prevalence rates between these subgroups of students suggest that bullying involvement extends beyond primary disability classification and may be more accurately explained through common or tangentially related characteristics or skill deficits.

Intellectual Disabilities. Recently, scholars have suggested that students with intellectual disabilities experience higher rates of victimization than do other subgroups of students with disabilities (Christensen, Fraynt, Neece, & Baker, 2012; Sterzing, Shattuck,

Narendorf, Wagner, & Cooper, 2012). As previously stated, Rose, Simpson, and Moss (2015) reported that approximately 24 percent of youth with intellectual disabilities report bully perpetration and victimization. Given the similar rates of response, they also explored the reciprocity between perpetration and victimization and determined that approximately 58 percent of these youth are classified as bully–victims. Unfortunately, there are notable limitations to examining the involvement of students with more significant disabilities, as traditional self-report measures do not account for intellectual functioning and may not be appropriate for assessing the experiences of this population of students (Schroeder, Cappadocia, Bebke, Pepler, & Weiss, 2014). However, because students with intellectual disabilities are often placed in restrictive educational environments, their educational experiences are fundamentally different than those of students who are educated in more inclusive environments (Rose, Simpson, & Moss, 2015).

Bullying as a Function of Special Education Services

The experiences of students with disabilities extend beyond the initial identification of their disability status. Their unique needs can lead to a variety of educational, behavioral, and functional supports. Therefore, it is conceivable that a relationship exists between disability classification, independent need, and restrictiveness of educational placement. More specifically, IDEA (2004) requires schools to offer a continuum of special education services tailored to the needs of individual students. Therefore, as needs (or severity of the disability) increase, the restrictiveness of the services increases. This is an important distinction for evaluating bullying involvement. Restrictive placements provide fundamentally different experiences for students with disabilities than they would have in more inclusive settings. For example, Zablotsky and colleagues (2013) argued that students with autism spectrum disorders who were in a fully inclusive classroom and received educational services alongside their peers without disabilities experienced significantly higher levels of victimization than those in more restrictive settings. Given the current push for increased inclusive services for all students, these findings are disconcerting. However, they may point to skill deficits (for example, social skills, communication skills) that could place these students at escalated risk for victimization from their peers without disabilities. At the basic level, students with disabilities, even in inclusive environments, receive some level of special education services as a function of their IEP, which may deviate from the socially accepted norms of their peer group. In addition, students with disabilities in inclusive environments may appear dependent on adult support or have notably weaker social skills, which may place them at greater risk for victimization (Rose et al., 2011).

In contrast, Rose and colleagues (2009) reported that increased restrictiveness of placement is associated with higher levels of perpetration and victimization when compared with students without disabilities or students with disabilities in more inclusive settings. More specifically, when students received a majority of their education in restrictive settings, they tended to engage in higher levels of perpetration and experience higher levels of victimization than their peers in more inclusive settings. Unfortunately, the reciprocity of these behaviors was not examined. This is an important distinction because bullying is connected to an individual's social environment (Espelage et al., 2013), and students in more restrictive educational environments are, by default, bound to more restrictive social environments. For example, students with emotional and behavioral disorders are typically identified as frequent victims (Blake et al., 2012) and perpetrators (Rose & Espelage, 2012), engage in behaviors that necessitate school-level discipline (for example, office referrals;

Swearer et al., 2012), and are likely to be placed in restrictive environments (Maggin, Wehby, Partin, Robertson, & Oliver, 2011). Although these restrictive placements are designed to provide intensive supports (Maggin et al., 2011), it is also plausible that reciprocity exists in the bully–victim interactions between students in restrictive placements, where the roles are fluid on the basis of time and context (Rose, Simpson, & Moss, 2015), yet may be confined to a specific environment. For example, the perpetration and victimization may be occurring within the restrictive environment, between the same students, but not generalizing to students outside the restrictive placement.

Bullying as a Function of Skill Deficits

Unfortunately, disability identification and restrictiveness of placement oversimplifies the bullying involvement of students with disabilities. The crux of the problem is not whom or where but why. For example, Rose and Espelage (2012) argued that bullying involvement is grounded not in disability identification but rather in the characteristics associated with a specific disability. Although these constructs are interrelated, it is an important distinction because the disproportionate representation may be rooted in skill deficits, where special education services can be provided to support and address these deficits. More specifically, the IEP is designed as a vehicle to support a student's unique needs and provide meaningful educational benefit (Yell, 2012), including behavioral and functional skills.

In separate reviews, Rose and colleagues (2011) and McLaughlin and colleagues (2010) identified social and communication skill deficits as the most pervasive predictors of bullying involvement for students with disabilities. It is conceivable that social and communication skill deficits are more germane to bullying involvement among students with disabilities because bullying has been identified as a social construct that is grounded in complex interactions between an individual and the systems that surround the individual (Hong & Espelage, 2012). For example, an identification of autism spectrum disorder is grounded in social and communication skill deficits (American Psychiatric Association, 2013), where students with autism often experience higher levels of victimization (Little, 2002, Zablotsky et al., 2012, 2013) and peer rejection (Symes & Humphrey, 2010; Twyman et al., 2010) when compared with students without disabilities. Conversely, students with emotional and behavioral disorders are often identified as perpetrators of bullying (Rose & Espelage, 2012; Swearer et al., 2012) and often possess low prosocial skills (Swearer et al., 2012) when compared with their peers without disabilities. However, the aggressive behaviors and low prosocial skills may be a manifestation of their disability (IDEA, 2004). Students may be engaging in aggressive behaviors as a means of communication (Rose & Espelage, 2012). Most important, by differentiating between disability label and disability characteristics, skill deficits can be identified and supported through the IEP.

CONCLUSIONS AND IMPLICATIONS

Students with disabilities have been identified as disproportionately represented within the bullying dynamic. By prohibiting disability-based harassment and bullying, federal legislation establishes the precedence for supporting the social and emotional needs of this population of students. Social and communication skills deficits are two of the most pervasive predictors of bullying involvement for individuals with disabilities (McLaughlin et al., 2010; Rose et al., 2011). However, predictive and protective factors extend beyond the disability classification and include special education supports, restrictiveness of environment, and skill development.

Promising interventions for reducing bullying among school-age youth includes tiered systems of supports, social and emotional learning, and direct social and communication skill instruction. For example, Bradshaw (2013) argued that Positive Behavioral Interventions and Supports (PBIS) could serve as a systemwide framework for reducing bullying involvement among all students by incorporating a tiered approach for social and emotional skill development that includes universal supports (tier 1), selective group supports (tier 2), and intensive or targeted supports (tier 3). To support this argument, Waasdorp, Bradshaw, and Leaf (2012) conducted a four-year randomized controlled effectiveness trial of PBIS and demonstrated that students who were in PBIS schools, which included approximately 13 percent students with disabilities, reported significantly less bullying and peer rejection over time. Although the Special Education Status × PBIS interaction was not significant, the scholars argued that the overall finding was "promising because it suggests that the main effects are rather robust for all children within schools" (Waasdorp et al., 2012, p. 154; see chapter 15 for additional information on PBIS).

Within the framework of PBIS, schools could incorporate direct Social and Emotional Learning (SEL) programming to address characteristics that may place students at greater risk for bullying involvement. More specifically, the foundation of SEL programming is grounded in five central competencies: (a) self-awareness, (b) social awareness, (c) self-management, (d) relationship skills, and (e) responsible decision making (Collaborative for Academic, Social, and Emotional Learning, 2003). These skills are directly and tangentially related to social and communication skills, and the SEL framework can be used in tandem with PBIS, where skills can be taught within the same tiered structure, based on the individual needs of students. In a three-year randomized clinical trial, Espelage, Rose, and Polanin (2015) implemented an SEL program and demonstrated that students with disabilities who received SEL programming engaged in less bullying behaviors over time when compared with students with disabilities who did not receive SEL programming.

Although these systemwide approaches have demonstrated effectiveness in addressing bullying among school-age youth, PBIS suggests that targeted interventions may still be necessary for skill development. At the foundational level, students should be provided with opportunities to learn, practice, and validate their social and communication skills among their same-age peers (Llewellyn, 2000). For example, Ross and Horner (2009) implemented a protocol for bully prevention that was grounded in behavioral understanding (that is, recognizing bullying behaviors) and verbal (that is, saying "stop") and nonverbal (that is, stop hand motion, walking away) communication that functionally reduced physical and verbal aggression for selected target students. Consequently, students who have social and communication skill deficits may require direct instruction where teachers establish opportunities to increase social skills (that is, social behaviors) and social competence (that is, evaluations of social behaviors in a specific context; Gresham, Sugai, & Horner, 2001) through assessment and reinforcement procedures that support the nature of the deficit (Rose & Monda-Amaya, 2012). Social skills deficits may include acquisition deficits (for example, students have not learned the skill), performance deficits (for example, they are not sufficiently motivated to use the skill), or fluency deficits (for example, they show unskillful performance; Gresham et al., 2001). Therefore, to support social and communication skills as a vehicle for reduced bullying involvement, skills should be taught, modeled in context, and reinforced.

REFERENCES

American Psychiatric Association. (2013). *Diagnostic and statistical manual of mental disorders* (5th ed.). Arlington, VA: Author.

Americans with Disabilities Act of 1990, 42 U.S.C. 12131 et seq.

Aud, S., Hussar, W., Johnson, F., Kena, G., Roth, E., Manning, E., et al. (2012). *The condition of education 2012*. Washington, DC: U.S. Department of Education.

Bear, G. G., Mantz, L. S., Glutting, J. J., Yang, C., & Boyer, D. E. (2015). Differences in bullying victimization between students with and without disabilities. *School Psychology Review, 44*, 98–116.

Blake, J. J., Lund, E. M., Zhou, Q., Kwok, O., & Benz, M. R. (2012). National prevalence rates of bully victimization among students with disabilities in the United States. *School Psychology Quarterly, 27*, 210–222. doi:10.1037/spq0000008

Bradshaw, C. P. (2013). Preventing bullying through positive behavioral interventions and supports (PBIS): A multitiered approach to prevention and integration. *Theory into Practice, 52*, 288–295. doi:1080/00405841.2013.829732

Christensen, L. L., Fraynt, R. J., Neece, C. L., & Baker, B. L. (2012). Bullying and adolescents with intellectual disability. *Journal of Mental Health Research in Intellectual Disabilities, 5*, 49–65. doi:10.1080/19315864.2011.637660

Collaborative for Academic, Social, and Emotional Learning. (2003). *Safe and sound: An educational leader's guide to evidence-based social and emotional (SEL) programs*. Chicago: Author.

Davis v. Monroe County Board of Education, 526 U.S. 629 (1999).

Education Amendments of 1972, 20 U.S.C. § 1681 et seq.

Education of All Handicapped Children Act of 1975, 20 U.S.C. §§ 1401–1411.

Espelage, D. L. (2011). Bullying & the lesbian, gay, bisexual, transgender, questioning (LGBTQ) community. *White House Conference on Bully Prevention Briefing Paper* (pp. 65–72). Washington, DC: U.S. Department of Health and Human Services.

Espelage, D. L., Astor, R. A., Cornell, D., Lester, J., Mayer, M. J., Poteat, V. P., & Tynes, B. (2013). *Prevention of bullying in schools, colleges, and universities*. Washington, DC: American Educational Research Association.

Espelage, D. L., Rose, C. A., & Polanin, J. R. (2015). Social-emotional learning program to reduce bullying, fighting, and victimization among middle school students with disabilities. *Remedial and Special Education, 36*, 299–311. doi:10.1177/0741932514564564

Farmer, T. W., Petrin, R., Brooks, D. S., Hamm, J. V., Lambert, K., & Gravelle, M. (2012). Bullying involvement and the school adjustment of rural students with and without disabilities. *Journal of Emotional and Behavioral Disorders, 20*, 19–37. doi:10.1177/1063426610392039

Gresham, F. M., Sugai, G., & Horner, R. H. (2001). Interpreting outcomes of social skills training for students with high-incidence disabilities. *Exceptional Children, 67*, 331–344.

Hartley, M. T., Bauman, S., Nixon, C. L., & Davis, S. (2015). Comparative study of bullying victimization among students in gender and special education. *Exceptional Children, 81*, 176–193. doi:10.1177/0014402914551741

Hong, J. S., & Espelage, D. L. (2012). A review of research on bullying and peer victimization in school: An ecological system analysis. *Aggressive and Violent Behavior, 17*, 311–322. doi:10.1016/j.avb.2012.03.003

Individuals with Disabilities Education Improvement Act, P. L. 108-446, 118 Stat. 2647 (2004).

Little, L. (2002). Middle-class mothers' perceptions of peer and sibling victimization among children with Asperger's syndrome and nonverbal learning disorders. *Issues in Comprehensive Pediatric Nursing, 25,* 43–57. doi:10.1080/014608602753504847

Llewellyn, A. (2000). Perceptions of mainstreaming: A systems approach. *Developmental Medicine & Child Neurology, 42,* 106–115. doi:10.1017/S0012162200000219

Maag, J. W., & Katsiyannis, A. (2012). Bullying and students with disabilities: Legal and practice considerations. *Behavioral Disorders, 37*(2), 78–86.

Maggin, D. M., Wehby, J. H., Partin, M., Robertson, R., & Oliver, R. M. (2011). A comparison of the instructional context for students with behavioral issues enrolled in self-contained and general education classroom. *Behavioral Disorders, 36,* 84–99.

Marx, T. A., Hart, J. L., Nelson, L., Love, J., Baxter, C. M., Gartin, B., & Shaefer Whitby, P. J. (2014). Guiding IEP teams on meeting the least restrictive environment mandate. *Intervention in School and Clinic, 50,* 45–50. doi:10.1177/1053451214532345

Mass. Gen. Laws, An Act Relative to Bullying in Schools, Ch. 71B § 3 (2010).

McKenzie, R. G. (2009). Elevating instruction for secondary-school students with learning disabilities by demystifying the highly qualified subject matter requirement. *Learning Disabilities Research & Practice, 24,* 143–150.

McLaughlin, C., Byers, R., & Vaughn, R. P. (2010). *Responding to bullying among children with special educational needs and/or disabilities.* London: Anti-Bullying Alliance.

Norlin, J. W. (2012). *Disability-based bullying and harassment in the schools: Legal requirements for identifying, investigating, and responding.* Palm Beach, FL: LRP Publications.

Olweus, D. (1993). *Bullying at school: What we know and what we can do.* Oxford: Blackwell.

Overton, T. (2009). *Assessing learners with special needs: An applied approach* (6th ed.). Upper Saddle River, NJ: Merrill Pearson.

Rehabilitation Act of 1973, 19 U.S.C. § 794.

Rose, C. A., & Espelage, D. L. (2012). Risk and protective factors associated with the bullying involvement of students with emotional and behavioral disorders. *Behavioral Disorders, 37*(3), 133–148.

Rose, C. A., Espelage, D. L., & Monda-Amaya, L. E. (2009). Bullying and victimization rates among students in general and special education: A comparative analysis. *Educational Psychology, 29,* 761–776.

Rose, C. A., Espelage, D. L., Monda-Amaya, L. E., Shogren, K. A., & Aragon, S. R. (2015). Bullying and middle school students with and without specific learning disabilities: An examination of social-ecological predictors. *Journal of Learning Disabilities, 48,* 239–254. doi:10.1177/0022219413496279

Rose, C. A., & Gage, N. A. (2016). Exploring the involvement in bullying among individuals with and without disabilities over time. *Exceptional Children.* Advance online publication. doi:10.1177/0014402916667587

Rose, C. A., & Monda-Amaya, L. E. (2012). Bullying and victimization among students with disabilities: Effective strategies for classroom teachers. *Intervention in School and Clinic, 48,* 99–107. doi:10.1177/1053451211430119

Rose, C. A., Monda-Amaya, L. E., & Espelage, D. L. (2011). Bullying perpetration and victimization in special education: A review of the literature. *Remedial and Special Education, 32,* 114–130.

Rose, C. A., Simpson, C. G., & Moss, A. (2015). The bullying dynamic: Prevalence of involvement among a large-scale sample of middle and high school youth with and without disabilities. *Psychology in the Schools, 52,* 515–531. doi:10.1002/pits.21840.

Ross, S. W., & Horner, R. H. (2009). Bully prevention in positive behavior support. *Journal of Applied Behavior Analysis, 42,* 747–759. doi:10.1901/jaba.2009.42-747

Schroeder, J. H., Cappadocia, M. C., Bebke, J. M., Pepler, D. J., & Weiss, J. A. (2014). Shedding light on a pervasive problem: A review of research on bullying experiences among children with autism spectrum disorders. *Journal of Autism and Developmental Disorders, 44*, 1520–1534. doi:10.1007/s10803-013-2011-8

Son, E., Parish, S. L., & Peterson, N. A. (2012). National prevalence of peer victimization among young children with disabilities in the United States. *Children and Youth Services Review, 34*, 1540–1545.

Sterzing, P. R, Shattuck, P. T., Narendorf, S. C., Wagner, M., & Cooper, B. P. (2012). Bullying involvement and autism spectrum disorders: Prevalence and correlates of bullying involvement among adolescents with an autism spectrum disorder. *Archives of Pediatric and Adolescent Medicine, 166*, 1058–1064.

Swearer, S. M., Espelage, D. L., Vaillancourt, T., & Hymel, S. (2010). What can be done about school bullying? Linking research to educational practice. *Educational Researcher, 39*, 38–47. doi:10.3102/0013189X09357622

Swearer, S. M., Wang, C., Maag, J. W., Siebecker, A. B., & Frerichs, L. J. (2012). Understanding the bullying dynamic among students in special and general education. *Journal of School Psychology, 50*, 503–520. doi:10.1016/j.jsp.2012.04.001

Symes, W., & Humphrey, N. (2010). Peer-group indicators of social inclusion among pupils with autistic spectrum disorders (ASD) in mainstream secondary schools: A comparative study. *School Psychology International, 31*, 478–494. doi:10.1177/0143034310382496

Twyman, K. A., Saylor, C. F., Saia, D., Macias, M. M., Taylor, L. A., & Spratt, E. (2010). Bullying and ostracism experiences in children with special health care needs. *Journal of Developmental & Behavioral Pediatrics, 31*, 1–8.

U.S. Department of Education. (2010). *History: Twenty-five years of progress in educating children with disabilities through IDEA.* Washington, DC: Author.

U.S. Department of Education, Office for Civil Rights. (2010). *Dear colleague letter.* Washington, DC: Author.

U.S. Department of Education, Office for Civil Rights. (2014). *Dear colleague letter.* Washington, DC: Author.

U.S. Department of Education, Office of Special Education and Rehabilitative Services. (2013). *Dear colleague letter.* Washington, DC: Author.

U.S. Department of Education, Office of Special Education and Rehabilitative Services, & Office for Civil Rights. (2000). *Dear colleague letter.* Washington, DC: Author.

Waasdorp, T. E., Bradshaw, C. P., & Leaf, P. J. (2012). The impact of schoolwide positive behavioral interventions and supports on bullying and peer rejection. *Archives of Pediatrics & Adolescent Medicine, 166*, 149–156.

Yell, M. L. (2012). *The law and special education* (3rd ed.). Boston, MA: Pearson.

Yell, M., Katsiyannis, A., Rose, C. A., & Houchins, D. (2016). Bullying and harassment of students with disabilities in schools: Legal considerations and policy formation. *Remedial and Special Education, 37*(5), 274–284. doi:10.1177/0741932515614967

Young, D., Ne'eman, A., & Gelser, S. (2011). Bullying and students with disabilities. *White House Conference on Bully Prevention Briefing Paper* (pp. 73–82). Washington, DC: U.S. Department of Health and Human Services.

Zablotsky, B., Bradshaw, C. P., Anderson, C. M., & Law, P. (2012). Involvement in bullying among children with autism spectrum disorders: Parents' perspectives on the influence of school factors. *Behavioral Disorders, JAMA Pediatrics, 37*, 179–191.

Zablotsky, B., Bradshaw, C. P., Anderson, C. M., & Law, P. (2013). Risk factors for bullying among children with autism spectrum disorders. *Autism, 18*, 419–427. doi:10.1177/1362361313477920

Part IV

Bullying among and by Adults

11

Bullying and Prevention of Bullying on College Campuses

Elizabeth Bistrong, Hillary K. Morin, and Catherine P. Bradshaw

The topic of bullying often is associated with younger students. However, students in higher education, be they at the undergraduate or graduate level, are not immune to these behaviors. As students entering college learn to navigate their new and likely wider social networks on campus, they continue to be at risk for experiencing physical, relational, and cyber forms of bullying. In addition, as students continue through their college experience, they may be exposed to related behavioral and relationship concerns, such as sexual harassment or hazing (Paludi, 2008). Research suggests that bullying is a widespread issue on college campuses, with 60 percent of college students witnessing a student bully another student and about 25 percent of college students self-identifying as victims of bullying (Chapell et al., 2004; Pontzer, 2010). In addition, 36 percent to 55 percent of college students have participated in at least one incident of hazing (Allan & Madden, 2013; Campo, Poulos, & Sipple, 2005); the rates of cyberbullying victimization among college students range from 1 to 11 percent (Kraft & Wang, 2010; Schenk & Fremouw, 2012; Smith & Yoon, 2013). However, the rates of sexual harassment among peers on university campuses in a given year are considerably higher, ranging from 20 to 80 percent (Dziech, 2003; Paludi, Nydegger, Desouza, Nydegger & Dicker, 2006). Given that involvement in bullying and related behavior problems can negatively affect the psychological well-being of children and adolescents, it is important to understand the role of bullying at the college level as well as its associated risk factors and psychosocial correlates. The current chapter focuses on bullying prevention on college campuses. We apply a slightly broader conceptualization of bullying to include harassment and hazing, as well as more traditional forms of bullying, such as relational victimization and cyberbullying. After mapping out these core dimensions of bullying on college campuses, we explore the unique context of the college campus and relevant risk factors, and then conclude by highlighting what is known about prevention on college campuses.

UNIQUENESS OF THE UNIVERSITY CAMPUS

The social environment on a college campus lends itself to bullying. Thousands of young adults with different backgrounds and values come together to interact in a variety of academic, work, and social environments. This intersection of often diverse groups of students creates social conditions that may contribute to bullying, hazing, and harassment. Students are exposed to heterogeneous peers in their dormitories, within classrooms, and in their extracurricular activities. College students' behaviors are not subject to the rules and parental restrictions that are commonplace in primary and secondary school; they have considerable autonomy and less accountability for their daily routines and whereabouts, which creates more opportunity for engagement in problematic behavior and lowers the possibility of detecting concerning impacts. Attending college typically occurs during the developmental phase often referred to as emerging adulthood (Arnett, 2000). During this time, there is still considerable identity formation and increased freedom to explore sexual behaviors and romantic relationships and to experiment with substance use (Eccles, Templeton, Barber, & Stone, 2003). College also creates an environment of broader social networks, novel peer interactions, and changes in the balance of power among students (Paludi, 2008). With over 21 million young adults attending colleges in the United States, it is important to determine the impact of bullying incidents on campus (U.S. Department of Education, 2014).

DEVELOPMENTAL CONTINUITY IN THE EXPERIENCE OF BULLYING

Developmental research suggests there is continuity between bully and victim status across childhood and adolescence and into college (Chapell et al., 2006; Isaacs, Hodges, & Salmivalli, 2008). For example, among those who identify as bullies or victims at the college level, many have had similar experiences during primary and secondary school. Longitudinal studies of children and adolescents indicate that there is a moderate to strong relationship between being peer nominated as a bully or a victim across different time points. One such study found that a child's status as a bully or victim at age eight was positively correlated with his or her status at age 16 as well as in college (Sourander, Helstelä, Helenius, & Piha, 2000). In addition, half of the college students who identified as bully–victims had also been bully–victims in high school and elementary school (Chapell et al., 2006). Similar trends have been found for perpetrators of bullying in college, with about half of college bullies reporting having bullied others in high school and elementary school (Chapell et al., 2006). Studies of victims of bullying in college have found high rates of prior victimization in secondary school (Bauman & Newman, 2013; Chapell et al., 2006; Isaacs et al., 2008). Taken together, these data provide evidence of a relatively high level of continuity in the experience of bullying across grade school, through high school, and into college.

RISK FACTORS, CORRELATES, AND CONSEQUENCES OF DIFFERENT FORMS OF BULLYING AMONG COLLEGE-AGE YOUTH

Next we consider some different forms of victimization that college-age youth experience, including physical or verbal bullying, cyberbullying, relational aggression, hazing, and harassment. We focus on various risk factors, correlates, and consequences of involvement in these different forms of bullying among college-age youth. Although we have attempted to isolate one form of bullying from the others, it is important to note that there is often considerable overlap in the various forms of victimization.

Traditional Bullying

We first consider research on the occurrence and risk factors for traditional forms of bullying on college campuses, including unwanted aggressive behaviors that are typically repeated over time and often occur in the context of a perceived power imbalance (Olweus, 1993). There is a large and growing body of literature showing that lesbian, gay, bisexual, transgender, and queer (LGBTQ) university students report higher levels of involvement in traditional bullying than their heterosexual peers (Wensley & Campbell, 2012). Specifically, nonheterosexual women were more likely to report being both perpetrators and victims of traditional bullying, whereas nonheterosexual men experienced higher levels only of traditional victimization (Wensley & Campbell, 2012). Graduate medical students report high levels of bullying experiences as well, with 8 percent of medical students personally experiencing bullying and a further 14 percent of medical trainees witnessing bullying (General Medical Council, 2014). As in studies of younger school-age children, college men report being more physically aggressive or threatening than their female peers (Storch, Bagner, Geffken, & Baumeister, 2004). There is also some evidence that international college students experience higher rates of bullying (Lavikainen, 2010). Together, these studies suggest that some of the same risk factors for bullying in adolescence (for example, LGBTQ status, being "different") are also risk factors in college-age youth; however, the rates of sexually relevant victimization and harassment are typically higher among college-age youth.

There are several negative psychosocial outcomes of college students involved in traditional bullying. Overt forms of bullying (for example, physically damaging actions or threats of such actions) is predictive of alcohol use among college-age men, whereas physical bullying or threats of physical harm were uniquely predictive of social anxiety, loneliness, and depressive symptoms among college-age women (Storch et al., 2004). Women who are physically aggressive may experience a more negative psychosocial impact because of societal gender norms that suggest it is not acceptable for a woman to be openly aggressive. Research also suggests that women who engage in gender non-normative forms of aggression, such as women being physically aggressive, experience higher rates of adjustment problems compared with those who engage in gender normative aggression (Crick, 1997). Among college students, a history of being bullied has also been linked with high levels of stress and avoidant coping strategies (for example, avoiding social situations or physical sensations, withdrawing; Newman, Holden, & Delville, 2011).

Cyberbullying

Cyberbullying involves aggressive acts that are intentionally and repeatedly carried out in an electronic context, such as via text messages, social media, or blogs (Kowalski, Limber, & Agatston, 2012). Research suggests that college students who were cyberbullied in high school are at greater risk for victimization during college (Kraft & Wang, 2010). University students who maintain a high profile on campus, such as athletes or members of the student government, are often targets for cyber victimization. For example, college students who are involved in Greek life, through participation in sororities and fraternities, are at an increased risk of being both a cyberbully and a cyber victim (Baldesare, Bauman, Goldman, & Robie, 2012). When compared with their heterosexual peers, LGBTQ students experienced more frequent unwanted online contact and experienced more anonymous cyberbullying (Bauman & Baldasare, 2015). However, other research suggests that their experiences with cyberbullying are comparable to those of heterosexual peers (Wensley & Campbell, 2012).

The research on gender as a predictor of cyberbullying and cyber victimization is mixed among college students. For example, one study of college students found that women were over four times more likely to be victims of cyberbullying (15.5 percent and 3.6 percent, respectively; Zalaquett & Chatters, 2014). Other studies have found that men report more cyberbullying behaviors than women do (Dilmac, 2009; Kokkinos, Antoniadou, & Markos, 2014). In contrast, some studies have found no significant gender differences in reported cyberbullying behaviors (for example, MacDonald & Roberts-Pittman, 2010). Ethnicity may also be a risk factor for being cyberbullied in college, as Asian Americans report experiencing cyberbullying four times more frequently than African Americans, Hispanic Americans, or European Americans (Zalaquett & Chatters, 2014).

Victims of cyberbullying experience a wide range of psychosocial outcomes. College students who were victims of cyberbullying scored higher on depression, anxiety, phobic anxiety, and paranoia (Schenk & Fremouw, 2012). In addition, college student victims of cyberbullying report trouble concentrating and feeling stressed, sad, hurt, angry, and frustrated as a result of their victimization. College student cyber victims also tend to endorse more suicidal ideation and planning or attempts than do youth who have not had such experiences (Schenk & Fremouw, 2012). Another study of 613 college students found that 19 percent ($n = 115$) were cyber victimized. The college cyber victims reported a wide range of negative correlates: 45 percent felt angry, 41 percent felt sad, 32 percent felt stressed, and 9 percent reported a loss in productivity, whereas only 6 percent of victims reported no effects (Zalaquett & Chatters, 2014). Cyber victimization was not found to be associated with risky behaviors over and above those associated with other forms of victimization, with the exception of alcohol use among women (Bennett, Guran, Ramos, & Margolin, 2011).

It is not just the victims of cyberbullying but also the perpetrators of cyberbullying who experience distress and negative psychosocial outcomes. Studies suggest that cyberbullies and cyberbully–victims (that is, those who are both perpetrators and victims) experience higher levels of depression, interpersonal sensitivity, paranoia, phobic anxiety, hostility, and psychoticism than do college students who are not involved in cyberbullying. Cyberbullies also endorsed more suicidal thoughts and tendencies than their peers who did not report involvement in cyberbullying (Schenk, Fremouw, & Keelan, 2013). College cyberbullies and cyberbully–victims were also more aggressive than individuals in the control group. There is significant overlap in the negative psychosocial outcomes of those involved in cyberbullying as perpetrators or victims. The numerous negative outcomes indicate that both college student victims and perpetrators of cyberbullying are at increased risk of experiencing a range of negative psychosocial adjustment problems, although given the study designs it is difficult to infer causality. (See chapter 6 for more on cyberbullying.)

Relational Aggression

Relational aggression includes behaviors used to damage or threaten to damage peer relationships and social standing through exclusion, withdrawal of friendship, or gossip and rumor spreading (Crick, 1995). Although often thought to be a more traditionally "female form" of bullying, the research on gender differences in relational aggression at the college level has been somewhat mixed. For example, some studies have suggested that men report more relational aggression than their female peers, whereas other studies suggest similar rates of relational aggression among men and women (Dahlen, Czar, Prather, & Dyess, 2013; Loudin, Loukas, & Robinson, 2003). Given these varied findings, gender cannot decisively be considered a risk factor for relational aggression among college students.

You and Bellmore (2014) studied relationally aggressive behaviors in college students and identified the variables that intervened in college students' participation in this type of bullying. They found that college students' beliefs about relational aggression and whether this behavior is acceptable affected their likelihood to engage in relational aggression. When students believed that relational aggression was acceptable, they participated in greater assisting and reinforcing behaviors and defended other students to a lesser degree (You & Bellmore, 2014). Moreover, college students with more exposure to relational aggression within their peer group may begin to view this behavior less negatively. Similarly, Chapell and colleagues found that college students were more likely to engage in relational aggression after witnessing this behavior by other peers (Chapell et al., 2004; You & Bellmore, 2014).

Levels of social anxiety and empathy are also important to consider when examining relationally aggressive behavior among college students. Understanding how others might feel when harm is directed at them is an important factor when identifying students who may be at an increased risk of bullying others. There is some research to suggest that college students with less effective perspective-taking skills are more likely than their peers to use relationally aggressive behaviors (Loudin et al., 2003). Similarly, male undergraduate students who have low levels of empathetic concern for others may display more relational aggression than their peers with high levels of empathetic concern. College students who report greater fear of negative evaluation (for example, "I usually worry about what kind of impression I will make") also experience higher levels of relational aggression (Loudin et al., 2003). These individual differences in social anxiety and empathic concern may contribute to the risk of being relationally aggressive. Given the cross-sectional nature of this research, it is important to note that the directionality of these associations is unclear; however, these findings do suggest an association between relational aggression and reduced empathy.

Research suggests that relationally aggressive behavior among college students is associated with higher levels of peer rejection, antisocial personality features, borderline personality features, and lower levels of prosocial behavior. Relational aggression in women also appears to be associated with a higher rate of bulimic symptoms (Werner & Crick, 1999). Relational aggression is also uniquely predictive of social anxiety, loneliness, depressive symptoms, and alcohol and drug problems among women; however, relational aggression was not predictive of any of the study's psychosocial adjustment factors for men (Storch et al., 2004). Taken together, these negative psychosocial outcomes related to engaging in relational aggression in college suggest that relational aggression is associated with maladjustment among college-age youth, and the effects appear to be exacerbated among women.

Hazing

Hazing is a related concern on college campuses. *Hazing* is defined as "an activity that a high-status member orders other members to engage in or suggests that they engage in that in some way humbles a newcomer who lacks the power to resist, because he or she wants to gain admission into a group" (Nuwer, 2001, p. xxv). It often consists of degrading, abusing, or endangering behaviors (Allan & Madden, 2008). Involvement in campus clubs, teams, and organizations increases the risk for experiencing hazing, with one study finding that 55 percent of students experienced hazing related to their involvement in a campus group (Allan & Madden, 2013). Sadly, hazing is becoming an increasingly normalized and expected part of campus culture, with 69 percent of students reporting that they are aware of hazing occurring in campus groups other than their own. Approximately 70 percent of varsity athletes and social fraternity and sorority members report that they experienced hazing (Allan & Madden, 2013). Students involved in activities and clubs outside of athletics and Greek organizations also experience hazing, with approximately 20–60 percent reporting experiences of hazing associated with their campus organization (Allan & Madden, 2013). Male students, group leaders, and upperclassman students are at an increased risk of participating in hazing (Alfred University & Hoover, 1999; Paludi, 2008).

Hazing has numerous negative psychosocial correlates. Victims of hazing have a decreased sense of well-being, a compromised sense of control over their lives, and a lowered ability to cope. Victims of hazing report emotional symptoms such as exhaustion, depression, anxiety, retraumatization, and humiliation. Victims of hazing also report experiencing physical symptoms such as stress-induced illness, injuries, or medical emergencies, and some hazing has resulted in the victim's death (Cornell University, n.d.; Paludi, 2008). The perpetrators of hazing report discomfort, guilt, and conflict arising from their actions as hazers. If caught, perpetrators of hazing also face disciplinary consequences.

Although controversial, studies have examined the varied benefits identified by both victims and perpetrators of college-based hazing. Victims of hazing cite an enhanced sense of accomplishment, increased self-discipline, and improved coping skills as benefits of engaging in hazing rituals. Perpetrators of hazing report that their involvement in hazing is associated with pride in continuing group traditions, bonding with fellow members, and diminished anger regarding their own hazing experiences (Cornell University, n.d.; Paludi, 2008). Although the perceived relationship and bonding benefits of engaging in hazing rarely outweigh the psychological and physical costs, better understanding these perceived benefits can help clarify why these behaviors continue to occur on college campuses.

Allan and Madden (2008) conducted one of the most extensive national studies of hazing to date. They surveyed 11,482 students across 53 college campuses nationwide; they also conducted over 300 personal interviews (Allan & Madden, 2008). One important finding from this study was in regard to the behaviors of bystanders, who knew these acts were occurring. Although hazing behaviors are typically characterized by secrecy, many hazing behaviors are seen by the public via postings on social media or because they are conducted in a public place, discussed with peers or family, and accepted by athletic coaches (Allan & Madden, 2008). Moreover, students reported minimal exposure to antihazing prevention or interventions. Related research by Campo et al. (2005) suggests that friendships outside of the organization where the student was hazed helped the student disengage from the organization and therefore the hazing. Having a strong friendship with the perpetrator of the hazing was a factor that enabled students to intervene and attempt to stop the behavior. The way students perceived their friend's attitudes toward hazing significantly predicted whether the friend engaged in hazing (Campo et al., 2005).

Sexual Harassment

The American Association of University Women states that "Sexual harassment is unwanted and unwelcome sexual behavior which interferes with your life. Sexual harassment is not behaviors that you like or want (for example, wanted kissing, touching, or flirting)" (Hill &

Silva, 2005, p. 5). On college campuses, these behaviors may include shouting obscenities as a woman walks by a residence hall or fraternity building or being intentionally brushed up against at a party in a sexual way. Several research teams have examined unique predictors of sexual harassment among college students. These predictors include being a woman of color, being a woman in a male-dominant major (for example, engineering), being a lesbian, being economically disadvantaged, being physically or emotionally disabled, being a residential life advisor, being socially isolated, and attending a small college or taking courses in a small academic department (for example, DeFour, David, Diaz & Thompkins, 2003; Dziech, 2003). Sexual harassment at a university occurs not only among students but also by professors and staff; such behaviors may include sexually inappropriate comments or coercing students into a sexual relationship by threatening their academic standing (for example, grades, scholarships, letters of recommendation; Dziech, 2003; Paludi, 2008).

Studies of college students who are victims of sexual harassment reveal a wide variety of negative outcomes. These include decreased class attendance, decreased satisfaction with their studies, damage to interpersonal relationships, and altered career goals (Lundberg-Love & Marmion, 2003; Paludi, 2008). Other social-emotional correlates include experiencing fear, guilt, anger, anxiety, depression, powerlessness, and decreased self-esteem. Victims of sexual harassment also may withdraw from social settings and develop a fear of rape, of crime in general, and of meeting new people (Dziech, 2003; Paludi, 2008).

PROGRAMS AND STRATEGIES TO PREVENT BULLYING AND RELATED CONCERNS ON COLLEGE CAMPUSES

Few studies have empirically tested preventive interventions to address bullying on college campuses, as the vast majority of bullying prevention research is implemented in elementary and secondary school contexts. As a result, the following bullying prevention strategies are largely based on higher education adaptations of what works in high school settings, or generally accepted "best practice," rather than rigorous research conducted on college and university campuses. As noted below, this is a context where there is a great need for additional bullying-related research and prevention programming.

Bullying prevention can be implemented in various contexts on the college campus. For example, including information about cyberbullying, harassment, and hazing in new student orientations may be timely and helpful in prevention of such behaviors, as this sets the stage and expectations early on for all students about the safety of the campus environment and specific consequences of bullying behaviors on campus (Zalaquett & Chatters, 2014). The classroom itself also provides a venue for educating students about bullying and related forms of victimization through inclusion of an antibullying curriculum in introductory courses (for example, required freshman-year psychology course) for first-year college students (Zalaquett & Chatters, 2014). This approach not only targets students at the universal level early in their college experience but also provides a more extended opportunity to engage students in prevention. Campus counseling centers also provide rich opportunities for implementation of bullying prevention targeting college students, including open workshops for the entire student body and group and individual sessions for youth at greater risk to foster nonharmful communication between bullies and victims (Zalaquett & Chatters, 2014). The promotion of more face-to-face communication through group sessions may increase empathy and reduce the likelihood that hurtful things will be said. Similarly, implementing trust-building and perspective-taking activities in such group sessions can improve the way students communicate with one another (Loudin et al., 2003; Storch et al., 2004). Providing students with a platform to communicate openly with one another in a safe space may also promote greater tolerance of diverse perspectives and reduce rates of victimization. Such campus centers also often facilitate peer-to-peer counseling, which (in combination with an appropriate bullying curriculum) could serve to help address bullying bystander behaviors on campus. Finally, to address cyberbullying on campus, a number of universities and colleges have developed online policies and procedures (for example, anonymous reporting) to create a more civil online experience for college students (Loudin et al., 2003; Storch et al., 2004).

Although there is a growing body of research documenting the potential impacts of youth bystander-focused prevention programming (Polanin, Espelage, & Pigott, 2013), there has been limited empirical investigation into the impacts of these programs in college settings. Nonetheless, the extant research suggests that bystander intervention may be a viable and promising approach for preventing sexual harrassment and relational aggression in college samples (You & Bellmore, 2014).

Common approaches to college hazing prevention include participation in group community service, provision of information of antihazing policies during orientation, identification of locations to report suspected hazing, clear no-hazing messages by coaches and advisors, written copies of antihazing policies given to new students, no-hazing contracts, and hazing prevention workshops presented by adults or peers (Allan, 2009; Allan & Madden, 2012). Although there are many approaches to hazing prevention, there has been limited research on the effectiveness of these strategies. It is important that we understand what hazing prevention options work to actually prevent this behavior. Not only are hazing behaviors physically and psychologically damaging, they are also widely accepted among hazing victims.

POLICY CONSIDERATIONS

One clear challenge in policy and prevention is that most colleges and universities lack a salient definition of bullying that is consistent on a national level or grounded in empirical work. Moreover, within a university, there are many different organizations and departments that often use different definitions and procedures for addressing bullying or have a vested interest in different or specific forms of bullying behavior. Without a clear definition within and across universities, consequences and enforcement of rules becomes difficult. In fact, there appear to be inconsistencies in the implementation of policies and the related repercussions. Nevertheless, policy is an important aspect of bullying and peer victimization prevention on college campuses. In the following sections, we discuss a few specific policies in greater depth and provide recommendations for improving current practice.

Many universities have policies on specific behaviors that fall under the umbrella term of bullying, such as hazing or sexual harassment, but traditional bullying policies are rare. Although policies for students that explicitly refer to bullying are rare, there are some examples, such as the antibullying policy at Eastern Washington University. The purpose of the policy is to set "university standards for managing incidents of bullying" (Eastern Washington University, 2010). The policy establishes procedures for handling violations and is applicable for all university personnel, students, or others who participate in any business with the university at any on- or off-campus university-related event. Furthermore, the policy explicitly defines bullying, gives examples and an in-depth explanation of exactly what behaviors are not tolerated, and entails a complaints and sanctions process. Confidentiality is guaranteed in this process, it is made clear where to report any incident, and any victim may print out a form to turn in a formal complaint to the appropriate office.

Historical events and tragedies have also had an impact on antibullying policies on college campuses. The Tyler Clementi Higher Education Anti-Harassment Act of 2011 is one such example, which was enacted after Tyler Clementi, an 18-year-old Rutgers University freshman, committed suicide when his roommate streamed private video footage (that is, a video of Tyler and another male student engaging in sexual activity) without Tyler's permission. A subsequent federal bill was passed in 2014, which requires that any college receiving federal student aid funding has an antiharassment policy. Specifically, this legislation

> prohibits harassment of enrolled students by other students, faculty, and staff based on actual or perceived race, color, national origin, sex, disability, sexual orientation, gender identity or religion and requires colleges to distribute their anti-harassment policy to all students and employees, including prospective students and employees upon request. It also explicitly prohibits behavior often referred to as cyber bullying. (Human Rights Campaign, n.d.)

Hazing Policies

Hazing policies differ by state. Only six states in the United States do not have antihazing laws, and many universities have their own policies. Accordingly, there is a lack of consistency across higher education institutions. Florida State University, for example, gives students a clear definition of hazing, providing students with context and consequences. To begin, they define *hazing* in the context of a code of conduct for students as "any group or individual action or activity that endangers the mental or physical health or safety or which may demean, disgrace, or degrade any person, regardless of location, intent or consent of participant(s)" (Florida State University, n.d.). The university Web site discusses Florida's laws on hazing and lists specific behaviors that violate them. Many colleges and universities have similarly clear hazing policies. Moreover, many university Web sites, such as Auburn University, provide a link to Allan and Madden's (2008, 2012) National Hazing Study. However, some universities lack specific hazing policies but rather address hazing under other policies, such as alcohol consumption (Minnesota State University, n.d.). Given the lack of nationally consistent antihazing policies in higher education settings, it is important that each university make its policies as clear and easily accessible to students as possible. Moreover, universities should consider findings by Allan and Madden's (2008, 2012) study to help determine best practice in enacting policy that will resonate with a student body.

Sexual Harassment Policies

Most colleges in the United States have sexual harassment policies in place, but students' awareness and perception of these policies is instrumental in the prevention of this type of behavior. Approximately 79 percent of college students are aware of their college's policy, 60 percent of students report that their college distributed written materials regarding sexual harassment policy, and 55 percent of students are aware of the mandated university official to contact regarding an incident of sexual harassment (Hill & Silva, 2005). Students at larger colleges and universities were more likely to be aware of sexual harassment policy (Hill & Silva, 2005). For example, the Pennsylvania State University (n.d.) policy (entitled Policy AD85) begins by defining *sexual harassment* as "unwelcome sexual advances, requests for sexual favors, and other verbal or physical conduct of a sexual nature that is unwanted, inappropriate, or unconsented to. Any type of sexual harassment is prohibited at the university." The policy also provides examples and defines types of sexual harassment, including misconduct, stalking, dating violence, and retaliation. The policy goes even further by discussing consensual relationships where power differentials, such as between a student and teacher, are considered. It also provides victims with instructions and actions to take in the face of sexual harassment. Although it is promising to see that most colleges and universities in the United States have a sexual harassment policy (Hill & Silva, 2005), the implementation and enforcement of these policies is inconsistent nationally.

CONCLUSIONS AND FUTURE RESEARCH DIRECTIONS

The prevalence and negative outcomes associated with bullying are well documented among children and adolescents (Swearer, Espelage, Vaillancourt, & Hymel, 2010); however, there has been considerably less focus on bullying and its prevention at the college level. The available research on university-based bullying demonstrates that bullying behavior is common on college campuses and continues to be associated with a range of negative psychosocial correlates. Additional research is needed to better understand the risk factors and consequences of bullying among college-attending students, as well as among emerging adults who are not attending college. Furthermore, much of the available work has focused on students at four-year colleges, despite the growing population of students attending community, junior, and online higher education institutions. These emerging adults have largely been overlooked in the literature. Moreover, many of the available studies are limited to a single university or sampling strategies that preclude generalizability of findings to this population as a whole.

A related challenge for the field is inconsistency in terminology and definitions used to characterize bullying on college campuses. Although we have used "bullying" as a broad umbrella term in this chapter, relatively few college students would likely characterize their hazing or harassment experiences as bullying. Even the relational aggression and cyberbullying experienced may be considered something other than bullying by students. Regardless of the terminology used, it is clear that college campuses are not immune to bullying.

Although many colleges and universities do have policies (for example, on hazing and sexual harassment) that may be helpful in deterring unwanted and harmful bullying behaviors, there is a lack of rigorous and systematic work on prevention and intervention on the college campus. Furthermore, there is insufficient research to determine whether these practices are actually having an impact on rates of victimization or buffering the social-emotional effects for victims. Additional research is needed to systemically and rigorously test higher education bullying interventions to determine their efficacy. It is critical that researchers, educators, and policymakers collaborate to implement novel and developmentally appropriate intervention and prevention efforts to address the complexities of bullying on college campuses.

REFERENCES

Alfred University & Hoover, N. C. (1999). *Initiation rites and athletics: A national survey of NCAA sports teams: Final report*. Alfred, NY: Alfred University.

Allan, E. J. (2009). *Hazing in view: College students at risk: Initial findings from the national study of student hazing*. Collingdale, PA: Diane Publishing.

Allan, E. J., & Madden M. (2008). *Hazing in view: College students at risk: Initial findings from the National Study of Student Hazing*. Retrieved from http://www.stophazing .org/wp-content/uploads/2014/06/hazing_in_view_web1.pdf

Allan, E. J., & Madden, M. (2012). The nature and extent of college student hazing. *International Journal of Adolescent Medicine and Health, 24*, 83–90. doi:10.1515/ijamh.2012.012

Allan, E. J., & Madden, M. (2013). The nature and extent of college student hazing. In J. C. Srabstein & J. Merrick (Eds.), *Bullying: A public health concern* (pp. 103–117). Hauppauge, NY: Nova Science Publishers.

Arnett, J. J. (2000). Emerging adulthood: A theory of development from the late teens through the twenties. *American Psychologist, 55*, 469–480.

Baldesare, A., Bauman, S., Goldman, L., & Robie, A. (2012). Cyberbullying? Voices of college students. In C. Wankel & L. Wankel (Eds.), *Misbehavior in online education* (pp. 127–156). Bingley, West Yorkshire, England: Emerald.

Bauman, S., & Baldasare, A. (2015). Cyber aggression among college students: Demographic differences, predictors of distress, and the role of the university. *Journal of College Student Development, 56*, 317–330.

Bauman, S., & Newman, M. L. (2013). Testing assumptions about cyberbullying: Perceived distress associated with acts of conventional and cyber bullying. *Psychology of Violence, 3*, 27–38.

Bennett, D. C., Guran, E. L., Ramos, M. C., & Margolin, G. (2011). College students' electronic victimization in friendships and dating relationships: Anticipated distress and associations with risky behaviors. *Violence and Victims, 26*, 410–429.

Campo, S., Poulos, G., & Sipple, J. W. (2005). Prevalence and profiling: Hazing among college students and points of intervention. *American Journal of Health Behavior, 29*(2), 137–149.

Chapell, M., Casey, D., De la Cruz, C., Ferrell, J., Forman, J., Lipkin, R., et al. (2004). Bullying in college by students and teachers. *Adolescence, 39*, 53–64.

Chapell, M. S., Hasselman, S. L., Kitchin, T., Lomon, S. N., MacIver, K. W., & Sarullo, P. L. (2006). Bullying in elementary school, high school, and college. *Adolescence, 41*, 633–648.

Cornell University. (n.d.). *Hazing: Arguments for & against*. Retrieved from http://www .hazing.cornell.edu/cms/hazing/issues/arguments.cfm

Crick, N. R. (1995). Relational aggression: The role of intent attributions, feelings of distress, and provocation type. *Development and Psychopathology, 7*, 313–322. doi:10.1017/ S0954579400006520

Crick, N. R. (1997). Engagement in gender normative versus nonnormative forms of aggression: Links to social–psychological adjustment. *Developmental Psychology, 33*, 610–617.

Dahlen, E. R., Czar, K. A., Prather, E., & Dyess, C. (2013). Relational aggression and victimization in college students. *Journal of College Student Development, 54*(2), 140–154. doi:10.1353/csd.2013.0021

DeFour, D. C., David, G., Diaz, F. J., & Thompkins, S. (2003). The interface of race, sex, sexual orientation, and ethnicity in understanding sexual harassment. In M. Paludi & C. A. Paludi, Jr. (Eds.), *Academic and workplace sexual harassment: A handbook of cultural, social science, management, and legal perspectives* (pp. 31–45). Westport, CT: Praeger.

Dilmac, B. (2009). Psychological needs as a predictor of cyberbullying: A preliminary report on college students. *Educational Sciences: Theory and Practice, 9,* 1307–1325.

Dziech, B. (2003). Sexual harassment on college campuses. In M. Paludi & C. A. Paludi, Jr. (Eds.), *Academic and workplace sexual harassment: A handbook of cultural, social science, management, and legal perspectives* (pp. 147–171). Westport, CT: Praeger.

Eastern Washington University. (2010). *Bullying prevention and response: Standards of conduct.* Retrieved from http://cfweb.ewu.edu/policy/PolicyFiles/EWU_901_04.pdf

Eccles, J., Templeton, J., Barber, B., & Stone, M. (2003). Adolescence and emerging adulthood: The critical passage ways to adulthood. In M. H. Bornstein, L. Davidson, C. L. M. Keyes, & K. A. Moore (Eds.), *Well-being: Positive development across the life course. Crosscurrents in contemporary psychology* (pp. 383–406). Mahwah, NJ: Lawrence Erlbaum.

Florida State University. (n.d.) *Hazing: Florida law and university policy.* Retrieved from http://hazing.fsu.edu

General Medical Council. (2014). *National training survey 2014: Bullying and undermining.* Retrieved from http://www.gmcuk.org/NTS_bullying_and_undermining_report_2014_FINAL.pdf_58648010.pdf

Hill, C., & Silva, E. (2005). *Drawing the line: Sexual harassment on campus.* Washington, DC: American Association of University Women Educational Foundation.

Human Rights Campaign. (n.d.). *Tyler Clementi Higher Education Anti-Harassment Act.* Retrieved from http://www.hrc.org/resources/entry/tyler-clementi-higher-education-anti-harassment-act

Isaacs, J., Hodges, E., & Salmivalli, C. (2008). Long-term consequences of victimization: A follow-up from adolescence to young adulthood. *European Journal of Developmental Science, 2,* 387–397.

Kokkinos, C. M., Antoniadou, N., & Markos, A. (2014). Cyber-bullying: An investigation of the psychological profile of university student participants. *Journal of Applied Developmental Psychology, 35*(3), 204–214. doi:10.1016/j.appdev.2014.04.001

Kowalski, R. M., Limber, S. E., & Agatston, P. W. (2012). *Cyberbullying: Bullying in the digital age* (2nd ed.). Malden, MA: Wiley-Blackwell.

Kraft, E. M., & Wang, J. (2010). An exploratory study of the cyberbullying and cyberstalking experiences and factors related to victimization of students at a public liberal arts college. *International Journal of Technoethics, 1,* 74–91.

Lavikainen, E. (2010). *Opinskelijan ammattikorkeakoulu 2010: Tutkimus ammattikorkeakouluopiskelijoiden koulutuspoluista, koulutuksen laadusta ja opiskelukyvystä* [Student's university of applied sciences 2010: Research on the study tracks, views on the quality of education, and own ability to study of students in the universities of applied sciences]. Helsinki, Finland: Opiskelijarajärjestöjen tutkimussäätiö Otus.

Loudin, J. L., Loukas, A., & Robinson, S. (2003). Relational aggression in college students: Examining the roles of social anxiety and empathy. *Aggressive Behavior, 29,* 430–439.

Lundberg-Love, P., & Marmion, S. (2003). Sexual harassment in the private sector. In M. Paludi & C. A. Paludi, Jr. (Eds.), *Academic and workplace sexual harassment: A handbook of cultural, social science, management, and legal perspectives* (pp. 77–101). Westport, CT: Praeger.

MacDonald, C. D., & Roberts-Pittman, B. (2010). Cyberbullying among college students: Prevalence and demographic differences. *Procedia–Social and Behavioral Sciences, 9,* 2003–2009.

Minnesota State University. (n.d.). *University policies: Statement of student responsibilities.* Retrieved from http://www.mnsu.edu/students/basicstuff/policies.html

Newman, M. L., Holden, G. W., & Delville, Y. (2011). Coping with the stress of being bullied: Consequences of coping strategies among college students. *Social Psychological and Personality Science, 2*(2), 205–211. doi:10.1177/1948550610386388

Nuwer, H. (2001). *Wrongs of passage: Fraternities, sororities, hazing and binge drinking.* Bloomington: Indiana University Press.

Olweus, D. (1993). *Bullying at school.* Oxford, England: Blackwell.

Paludi, M. (Ed.). (2008). *Understanding and preventing campus violence.* Westport, CT: Praeger.

Paludi, M., Nydegger, R., Desouza, E., Nydegger, L., & Dicker, K. A. (2006). International perspectives on sexual harassment of college students: The sounds of silence. In F. L. Denmark, H. H. Krauss, E. Halpern, & J. A. Sechzer (Eds.), *Annals of the New York Academy of Sciences* (pp. 103–120). Malden, MA: Blackwell.

Pennsylvania State University. (n.d.). *Policy AD85: Discrimination, harassment, sexual harassment and related inappropriate conduct.* Retrieved from https://guru.psu.edu/policies/ad85.html

Polanin, J. R., Espelage, D. L., & Pigott, T. D. (2013). A meta-analysis of school-based bullying prevention programs' effects on bystander intervention behavior. *School Psychology Review, 41*(1), 47–65.

Pontzer, D. (2010). A theoretical test of bullying behavior: Parenting, personality, and the bully/victim relationship. *Journal of Family Violence, 25,* 259–273.

Schenk, A. M., & Fremouw, W. J. (2012). Prevalence, psychological impact, and coping of cyberbully victims among college students. *Journal of School Violence, 11,* 21–37. doi:10.1080/15388220.2011.630310

Schenk, A. M., Fremouw, W. J., & Keelan, C. M. (2013). Characteristics of college cyberbullies. *Computers in Human Behavior, 29,* 2320–2327.

Smith, J. A., & Yoon, J. (2013). Cyberbullying presence, extent, & forms in a midwestern post-secondary institution. *Information Systems Education Journal, 11,* 52–78.

Sourander, A., Helstelä, I., Helenius, H., & Piha, J. (2000). Persistence of bullying from childhood to adolescence: A longitudinal 8-year follow-up study. *Abuse and Neglect, 24,* 873–881.

Storch, E. A., Bagner, D. M., Geffken, G. R., & Baumeister, A. L. (2004). Association between overt and relational aggression and psychosocial adjustment in undergraduate college students. *Violence & Victims, 19,* 689–700. doi:10.1891/vivi.19.6.689.66342

Swearer, S. M., Espelage, D. L., Vaillancourt, T., & Hymel, S. (2010). What can be done about school bullying? Linking research to educational practice. *Educational Researcher, 1,* 38–47.

U.S. Department of Education. (2014). National Center for Education Statistics, Common Core of Data (CCD), Integrated Postsecondary Education Data System (IPEDS), Fall Enrollment Survey (IPEDS-EF:90-99); and IPEDS Spring 2001 through Spring 2013, enrollment component. Washington, DC: Author.

Wensley, K., & Campbell, M. (2012). Heterosexual and nonheterosexual young university students' involvement in traditional and cyber forms of bullying. *Cyberpsychology Behavior and Social Networking, 15,* 649–654.

Werner, N. E., & Crick, N. R. (1999). Relational aggression and social-psychological adjustment in a college sample. *Journal of Abnormal Psychology, 108,* 615–623. doi:10.1037/0021-843X.108.4.615

You, J., & Bellmore, A. (2014). College students' behavioral reactions upon witnessing relational peer aggression. *Aggressive Behavior, 40,* 397–408. doi:10.1002/ab.21542

Zalaquett, C. P., & Chatters, S. J. (2014). Cyberbullying in college. *SAGE Open, 4*(1), 2158244014526721.

12

Bullying in the Workplace

Catherine P. Bradshaw, Hillary K. Morin, Elizabeth Bistrong, and Katherine Figiel-Miller

Workplace bullying is a phenomenon experienced worldwide. However, there has been relatively limited systematic research on the topic, particularly when compared with the amount of work on bullying among school-age youth. Heinz Leymann (1990) is often credited as the first to identify the construct of workplace bullying, which he adapted from the literature on bullying among youth. *Workplace bullying* has many definitions, such as "negative workplace behavior including such behaviors as being humiliated or ridiculed, being ignored or excluded, being shouted at, receiving hints that you should quit your job, receiving persistent criticism, and excessive monitoring of your work" (Simons, 2008, p. E49). From a legal perspective, some state bills have been proposed that address "abusive work environments," defining them as "a workplace where an employee is subjected to abusive conduct so severe that it causes physical or psychological harm"; abusive conduct is considered to be "conduct of an employer or employee in the workplace, with malice, that a reasonable person would find hostile, offensive, and unrelated to an employer's legitimate business interests" (Martucci & Sinatra, 2009, p. 78). The current chapter explores the topic of bullying within the workplace, with a particular interest in adults working in schools.

WHAT IS WORKPLACE BULLYING?

Despite slightly different emphases, workplace bullying definitions tend to include four conditions or characteristics (Lutgen-Sandvik, Tracy, & Alberts, 2007). For an interaction to be considered workplace bullying, it must have intensity (perpetrator's actions are

This work was supported in part through a contract with the National Education Association (NEA). The thoughts and opinions expressed in this document are those of the authors and not of the NEA. The authors would also like to acknowledge Joanne Morris of the NEA for her comments and feedback on a draft of this chapter.

perceived by the target as harmful), repetition (occurring at least twice weekly), duration (ongoing for a minimum of six months), and power disparity (the target feels that it is difficult or impossible to defend him- or herself). We see several similarities between these dimensions and the core features of bullying outlined in the Olweus (1993) and Centers for Disease Control and Prevention definition (Gladden, Vivolo-Kantor, Hamburger, & Lumpkin, 2014). From a legal perspective, workplace bullying requires testimony of a medical or psychological professional that there has been harm (for example, emotional, psychological, physical, financial) caused as a result of the abuse (Namie, 2012). Although many scholars and legal professionals have embraced the term "bullying" when discussing adults in the workplace, other researchers have questioned the appropriateness of the term. In fact, there is considerable variation in the extent to which adults use the word "bullying" to describe their experience. Regardless, the word "bullying" is commonly used in the research to describe incidents at work in which workers are ridiculed or humiliated, are prevented from access to information necessary for their jobs, are physically threatened, are pressured or coerced to miss entitlements like vacation time, are ignored, are treated in an angry or hostile manner, or receive insinuations that they should quit (Lutgen-Sandvik et al., 2007). The gap between worker self-labeling of bullying and researcher identification of bullying makes it challenging to determine true prevalence estimates of workplace bullying.

Workplace bullying can take several different forms. One study examined the most common forms of workplace bullying experienced. From a list of 40 workplace bullying behaviors, the following behaviors are the five most commonly experienced: (a) information is withheld, which affects one's performance; (b) one's decisions, procedures, and judgment are questioned; (c) tasks are set with unreasonable or impossible targets or deadlines; (d) attempts are made to belittle and undermine one's work; and (e) recognition, acknowledgment, and praise are withheld (Riley, Duncan, & Edwards, 2009).

HOW DOES WORKPLACE BULLYING DIFFER FROM HARASSMENT?

In the exploration of workplace bullying and workplace bullying prevention, it is useful to examine workplace harassment, a construct closely related to workplace bullying. Workplace harassment is distinct because of its long history of legislation, which establishes protections for employees and liability for employers. Discriminatory harassment is conceptually different from bullying because harassment harms an individual for being a member of a protected class, such as race–ethnicity or gender, whereas bullying may have nothing to do with a person's group membership (Martucci & Sinatra, 2009). Unlike bullying, harassment can occur without singling out a particular target, without repeated acts, and without specific intent to harm; rather, harassment is defined by creating a hostile environment for individuals of a particular group known as a protected class (Ali, 2010). Because of a variety of factors such as severity, legal differences, and targeting protected groups, workplace harassment is clearly distinct from workplace bullying.

HOW COMMON IS WORKPLACE BULLYING?

Given the measurement and definitional challenges noted above, it is difficult to estimate the prevalence of workplace bullying (Namie & Namie, 2009). In 2006, the International Labour Organization reported that workplace bullying was at epidemic proportions in

15 European Union countries. However, studies suggest that workplace bullying is slightly more common in the United States than in Europe, which might be attributable to greater workplace inequality in the United States (Lutgen-Sandvik et al., 2007). The Workforce Bullying Institute, a U.S.-based national nonprofit, commissioned a survey of workplace bullying prevalence using a sample of 2,092 U.S. adults, which was weighted to be representative of the population by region, political party, age, race, gender, education, and religion (Zogby International, 2010). This study defined *workplace bullying* simply as "repeated mistreatment at work, including sabotage by others that prevented work from getting done, verbal abuse, threatening conduct, intimidation, or humiliation" (p. 5). It found that 35 percent of workers had experienced workplace bullying and another 15 percent had witnessed it—thereby, fully half of the American labor force reported direct exposure to workplace bullying. Namie and Namie (2009) estimated that the prevalence of workplace bullying is at least 13 percent at any time, whereas the lifetime prevalence rate for workplace bullying is closer to 30 percent.

WORKPLACE BULLYING OF EDUCATORS

In trying to understand the prevalence of workplace bullying among educators, we draw on several different studies from the United States and abroad (for a review see Bradshaw & Figiel, 2012). For example, the National Education Association (NEA) Bullying Survey was conducted in spring 2010 to examine a variety of issues related to bullying and school connectedness (Bradshaw, Waasdorp, & O'Brennan, 2011; Bradshaw, Waasdorp, O'Brennan, & Gulemetova, 2013). The survey was completed by 5,056 NEA members, of whom 82.1 percent (n = 4,165) were professionals/teachers and 17.9 percent were education support professionals (ESPs; n = 905). The findings indicated that approximately 18 percent of teachers and 13.7 percent of ESPs reported that they were bullied in the workplace by someone else at the school where they currently work. In addition, educators who work in urban environments were 36 percent more likely to report that they were bullied in the workplace than those in suburban or rural environments.

Workplace Bullying by Principals and Other Staff

Research suggests that principals or other authority figures are responsible for approximately 25 percent of cases of workplace bullying against teachers and ESPs (Ontario Secondary School Teachers Federation [OSSTF], 2005). The power imbalance due to job position (such as a principal toward a teacher) appears to be a major factor in workplace bullying behavior (Riley et al., 2009). Coworkers were named as responsible for 19 percent of workplace bullying offenses against teachers in an Ontario study; however, it is anticipated that this rate is much higher within the United States (OSSTF, 2005).

Workplace Bullying of Adults by Students

Revisiting the definition of workplace bullying, we recall that it has four major characteristics: frequency, intensity, duration, and power imbalance. At first glance, the idea that school staff are at a power disadvantage to students may be illogical, given that a classroom or other school environment is clearly established with the adult as the assumed authority figure. However, students have been identified as a major source of workplace bullying experienced by teachers, with 36 percent of cases in Ontario (OSSTF, 2005) and 29–30 percent of cases in the U.S. sample indicating a student as the perpetrator (Bradshaw et al., 2011). In addition, a study in Ireland found that 28 percent of students admitted to workplace bullying of teachers (James et al., 2008). Workplace bullying behaviors by students against teachers typically involve insubordination and disruptive classroom behaviors, some of which can cause the teacher physical harm as well as emotional damage (James et al., 2008). Although behavior management can be challenging for educators, it can be improved with experience, professional development, and mentoring (Bradshaw, Waasdorp, & O'Brennan, 2010; Bradshaw et al., 2011).

WHAT FACTORS CONTRIBUTE TO WORKPLACE BULLYING?

Role of Context

There is a growing body of research exploring possible factors that contribute to workplace bullying. Historically speaking, workplace bullying may be a natural result of the capitalist system in which some workers have little status outside being used by an employer for their labor (Beale & Hoel, 2011). In modern workplaces, managers balance the tendency to view workers as valuable solely for their labor with the idea that the organization benefits from long-term relationships with and investment in the skills of their employees. This tension can give rise to power struggles between bosses and employees.

Other factors, such as inappropriate coping with job stress, can also contribute to workplace bullying (Baillien, Neyens, De Witte, & De Cuyper, 2009). Some aggressors appear to take out their stress on others, whereas targets may have maladaptive coping strategies that facilitate others taking advantage of them through acts of workplace bullying. Several characteristics of the work environment can lead to job stress, including being overworked, lack of role clarity, and low job autonomy (Agervold, 2009; Baillien et al., 2009; Strandmark & Hallberg, 2007). Characteristics of the organizational culture have also been identified that relate to workplace bullying. One such characteristic is a culture of gossip and teasing (Baillien et al., 2009). Disorder or chaos is another way of characterizing the quality of an organization in which the organization lacks (a) transparency—that is, expectations, rewards, and punishments clearly visible to employees; (b) accountability or clear role divisions; and (c) capacity to motivate employees (Hodson, Roscigno, & Lopez, 2006). A chaotic environment such as this might give rise to bullying because workers are under stress or simply because the unpredictable environment leads workers to vie for order and power. In addition, styles of leadership in an organization have often been associated with workplace bullying

Several theories of workplace bullying suggest that it comes about as a result of system-induced status struggles beyond the control of a given employee or employer. Simons (2008) characterized bullying and conflict in the workplace using a theoretical framework of oppressed groups. For example, because nurses are trained in a system of care largely subordinated to another system (that is, medicine), they are an oppressed group; this oppression gives rise to struggling among themselves, which serves as a precursor to workplace bullying. Traditional gender differences in nurses relative to doctors and administrators also reinforce this power differential and may contribute to power struggles within a medical and health-related workplace.

Self-determination theory posits that all individuals have three psychological needs in order to function at their highest potential and satisfy general well-being: autonomy, competence, and relatedness (Deci & Ryan, 2008). Previous studies and writing on workplace bullying have revealed that need for satisfaction, a proponent of self-determination theory, is salient in regards to employee functioning and well-being in the workplace (Deci & Ryan, 2008). A study by Trépanier, Fernet, and Austin (2015) used self-determination theory to study workplace bullying as it related to poor employee functioning. Findings revealed that employees' fundamental psychological needs were derailed upon recurrent and prolonged exposure to hostile behaviors in the workplace (Trépanier et al., 2015). Overall findings and implications from this empirical study indicated that workplace bullying should be addressed and resolved with haste, as prolonged workplace bullying will likely take a toll on the psychological energy, work-task dedication, and turnover intention of employees (Trépanier et al., 2015). These theories seem disheartening because they imply that workplace bullying is inherently a part of our contemporary system of labor; however, they also reflect the pervasive nature of workplace bullying.

Focus on School Context

With regard to schools more specifically, data from the U.S. *Indicators of National School Crime and Safety* show a number of risk factors for educator victimization, including school location, instructional level, and teacher gender, experience, and education (Robers, Zhang, Truman, & Snyder, 2011). As noted above, teachers are more likely to be threatened in urban schools than in rural or suburban schools (Casteel, Peek-Asa, & Limbos, 2007; Espelage et al., 2013; Robers et al., 2011); likewise, schools with inadequate resources and poor building safety tend to have more teachers targeted (Gerberich et al., 2011). The experience of workplace violence has also been shown to differ by instructional level, as middle school educators generally report more threats and incidents of violence than high school teachers, who, in turn, are more at risk than elementary school teachers (Robers et al., 2011). The findings linking victimization and teacher characteristics like age, teaching experience, and education have been inconsistent. For example, one study of teachers in Los Angeles found that schools with more highly educated and more experienced teachers had higher rates of violence against teachers (Casteel et al., 2007). However, Gerberich et al. (2011) reported that teachers who were younger and unmarried were more likely to face physical and nonphysical workplace violence than their colleagues. Teachers of special education and speech pathology appear to be especially at risk of experiencing violence and victimization at school (Gerberich et al., 2011). Male teachers were more likely to be threatened or assaulted than female teachers (Espelage et al., 2013; Robers et al., 2011).

A Virginia study of 280 high schools found that aspects of the school climate were related to teacher victimization (Gregory, Cornell, & Fan, 2012). Specifically, teacher victimization was less common in high schools with greater clarity of the school rules, as perceived by students and staff. Similarly, teacher victimization was lower in schools where the teachers reported that students were more comfortable seeking help for their problems. Finally, threats and violence against teachers vary by region.

WHAT ARE SOME OF THE EFFECTS OF WORKPLACE BULLYING?

A meta-analysis of 66 empirical studies by Nielsen and Einarsen (2012) focused on some of the problematic correlates and outcomes of bullying in the workplace. Their findings revealed that symptoms of posttraumatic stress, mental health problems, and absenteeism were common among individuals who experienced workplace bullying (Nielsen & Einarsen, 2012). Furthermore, victims of workplace bullying were more likely to have an intention to leave the job, lower job satisfaction, and lower organizational commitment (Lutgen-Sandvik et al., 2007). Bond, Tuckey, and Dollard (2010) found that, over time, workplace bullying led to symptoms of posttraumatic stress disorder, particularly in workplaces with low *psychosocial safety climate*, which was defined as "freedom from psychological harm at work" (Law, Dollard, Tuckey, & Dormann, 2011, p. 1783; see also Bond et al., 2010). With regard to educators more specifically, the OSSTF (2005) report found that 10 percent of bullied educators missed time from work as a direct result of the experience; 53 percent experienced physical and emotional consequences, including loss of sleep, loss of appetite, anxiety, depression, compromised self-confidence, and increased substance use; and 34 percent of targets sought psychological treatment for their workplace bullying-related problems (also see Gerberich et al., 2011). Educators who are bullied at work often become isolated from their colleagues as well as from their work, questioning their competence and suffering in their performance (de Wet, 2010). Compared with nonabused educators, they tend to be in poorer health, have less job satisfaction, and report that their jobs are more stressful (de Wet, 2010; Gerberich et al., 2011).

Educators who experienced violence by students were more likely to experience negative affect and decreased job satisfaction (Dzuka & Dalbert, 2007). Teachers who were the targets of violence by their students had a 61 percent chance of experiencing physical consequences and an 84 percent chance of suffering emotional consequences (Wilson, Douglas, & Lyon, 2010). Violence experienced by a teacher was a significant predictor of compromised teaching performance (Wilson et al., 2010). Witnesses of workplace bullying also have more negative perceptions of their workplace and are less productive than those who do not experience or witness workplace bullying (Lutgen-Sandvik et al., 2007). Actual workplace violence predicts teachers' negative outcomes, but also the fear of experiencing workplace violence has been shown to negatively affect teaching and cause emotional distress (Wilson et al., 2010). Teachers who fear the threat of workplace violence have been found to be less motivated in their jobs than their colleagues (Vettenberg, 2002). Furthermore, the psychological aspects of workplace mistreatment may create more problems than violence itself. Educators who experience nonphysical workplace bullying have lower job satisfaction, higher stress levels, and lower overall health than those who experience physical workplace violence (Gerberich et al., 2011).

Taken together, research suggests that workplace bullying is a significant social stressor that has a negative impact on the workplace (Nielsen & Einarsen, 2012). There appears to be a cyclical relationship between workplace bullying and mental outcomes, where stressor–strain and strain–stressor associations with these factors suggested a mutually reinforcing relationship (Nielsen & Einarsen, 2012). Therefore, it is critical to address the threats, fear, and psychological mistreatment experienced by employees, as they are possibly even more damaging than physical violence.

WHAT ARE SOME POTENTIAL SOLUTIONS TO WORKPLACE BULLYING?

Organizational psychologists highlight potential solutions for workplace bullying, including addressing demographic risks (Gerberich et al., 2011; Robers et al., 2011), assessing legal and policy protections (American Federation of Teachers, 2006), and improving the organizational culture (Baillien et al., 2009; Hodson et al., 2006). Buy-in by leadership, supervisors, and administrators in the workplace is also important for workplace bullying prevention efforts (Cleary, Hunt, Walter, & Robertson, 2009). In addition to the prevention strategies coming from organizational psychology, there is a large body of research on the beneficial impacts of strategies that foster connectedness and relationships among employees. There is a clear need for more professional development and policies focused on preventing workplace bullying, beyond those that are focused more specifically on harassment (NEA, 2000). Efforts to address power differentials, promote equity, enhance communication, and improve the climate and culture of the workplace also seem central to reducing rates of workplace bullying. Employers should increase awareness of workplace bullying and its consequences and consistently implement disciplinary approaches when it does occur. There is also a great need for confidential work-based supports for both adults who bully and those who are targeted, so that employees can seek help and assistance without the stigma or fear of retaliation. These activities need to be backed up by policies, reporting systems, and professional development trainings, many of which are led by human resource departments and strongly supported by supervisors and the leadership.

CONCLUSIONS AND IMPLICATIONS

The purpose of this chapter was to summarize the research on workplace bullying and provide recommendations for addressing and preventing workplace bullying. The available research on workplace bullying suggests that it is a widespread problem in the United States and around the world. Workplace bullying can increase the likelihood that employees will experience a range of psychological and physical problems, including anxiety, sleep loss, and other symptoms of posttraumatic stress as a result of the victimization (Gerberich et al., 2011). Workplace bullying also negatively affects the broader climate of the work environment and can lead to reduced productivity and staff turnover. Unfortunately, little has been done legally or otherwise to protect employees specifically from bullying in the workplace. There are, however, a number of policies and laws that protect workers from harassment. Although there is some overlap, acts of bullying often are not considered harassment unless they are related to a worker's status as a member of a protected class. Further research is needed to identify professional development models and policies for reducing rates of workplace bullying.

REFERENCES

Agervold, M. (2009). The significance of organizational factors for the incidence of bullying. *Scandinavian Journal of Psychology, 50*, 267–276. doi:10.1111/j.1467-9450.2009.00710.x

Ali, R. (2010). *Dear colleague letter: Harassment and bullying.* Washington, DC: U.S. Department of Education, Office for Civil Rights. Retrieved from http://www2.ed.gov/about/offices/list/ocr/letters/colleague-201010.pdf

American Federation of Teachers. (2006). *Sexual harassment: Unprofessional, unacceptable, unlawful! A resource guide.* Washington, DC: Author.

Baillien, E., Neyens, I., De Witte, H., & De Cuyper, N. (2009). A qualitative study on the development of workplace bullying: Towards a three way model. *Journal of Community & Applied Social Psychology, 19*(1), 1–16. doi:10.1002/casp.977

Beale, D., & Hoel, H. (2011). Workplace bullying and the employment relationship: Exploring questions of prevention, control and context. *Work Employment Society, 25,* 5–18. doi:10.1177/0950017010389228

Bond, S., Tuckey, M. R., & Dollard, M. F. (2010). Psychosocial safety climate, workforce bullying, and symptoms of posttraumatic stress. *Organizational Development Journal, 28*(1), 37–56.

Bradshaw, C., & Figiel, K. (2012). *Prevention and intervention for workplace bullying in schools* [Technical report prepared for the National Education Association]. Washington, DC: National Education Association.

Bradshaw, C. P., Waasdorp, T. E., & O'Brennan, L. M. (2010). *Whole-school approaches to bullying prevention: Engaging teachers and education support professionals in the prevention process.* Washington, DC: National Education Association.

Bradshaw, C. P., Waasdorp, T. E., & O'Brennan, L. M. (2011). *Teachers' and education support professionals' perspectives on bullying and prevention.* Washington, DC: National Education Association.

Bradshaw, C. P., Waasdorp, T. E., O'Brennan, L., & Gulemetova, M. (2013). Teachers' and education support professionals' perspectives on bullying and prevention: Findings from a National Education Association (NEA) survey. *School Psychology Review, 42,* 280–297.

Casteel, C., Peek-Asa, C., & Limbos, M. A. (2007). Predictors of nonfatal assault injury to public school teachers in Los Angeles City. *American Journal of Industrial Medicine, 50,* 932–939. doi:10.1002/ajim.20520

Cleary, M., Hunt, G. E., Walter, G., & Robertson, M. (2009). Dealing with bullying in the workplace: Toward zero tolerance. *Journal of Psychosocial Nursing, 47*(12), 34–41.

de Wet, C. (2010). The reasons for and the impact of principal-on-teacher bullying on the victims' private and professional lives. *Teaching and Teacher Education, 26,* 1450–1459. doi:10.1016/j.tate.2010.05.005

Deci, E. L., & Ryan, R. M. (2008). Self-determination theory: A macro theory of human motivation, development, and health. *Canadian Psychology/Psychologie Canadienne, 49,* 182–185.

Dzuka, J., & Dalbert, C. (2007). Student violence against teachers. *European Psychologist, 12,* 253–260. doi:10.1027/1016-9040.12.4.253

Espelage, D., Anderman, E. M., Brown, V. E., Jones, A., Lane, K. L., McMahon, S. D., et al. (2013). Understanding and preventing violence directed against teachers: Recommendations for a national research, practice, and policy agenda. *American Psychologist, 68,* 75–87. doi:10.1037/a0031307

Gerberich, S. G., Nachreiner, N. M., Ryan, A. D., Church, T. R., McGovern, P. M., Geisser, M. S., et al. (2011). Violence against educators. *Journal of Occupational and Environmental Medicine, 53,* 294–302. doi:10.1097/JOM.0b013e31820c3fa1

Gladden, R. M., Vivolo-Kantor, A. M., Hamburger, M. E., & Lumpkin, C. D. (2014). *Bullying surveillance among youths: Uniform definitions for public health and recommended data elements, Version 1.0.* Atlanta: Centers for Disease Control and Prevention.

Gregory, A., Cornell, D., & Fan, X. (2012). Teacher safety and authoritative school climate in high schools. *American Journal of Education, 118,* 401–425.

Hodson, R., Roscigno, V. J., & Lopez, S. H. (2006). Chaos and the abuse of power: Workplace bullying in organizational and interactional context. *Work and Occupations, 33,* 382–416. doi:10.1177/0730888406292885

International Labour Organization. (2006, June 14). *New forms of violence at work on the rise worldwide* [News release]. Geneva: International Labour Organization, United Nations.

James, D. J., Lawlor, M., Courtney, P., Flynn, A., Henry, B., & Murphy, N. (2008). Bullying behaviour in secondary schools: What roles do teachers play? *Child Abuse Review, 17*(3), 160–173. doi:10.1002/car.1025

Law, R., Dollard, M. F., Tuckey, M. R., & Dormann, C. (2011). Psychosocial safety climate as a lead indicator of workplace bullying and harassment, job resources, psychological health and employee engagement. *Accident Analysis & Prevention, 43*, 1782–1793.

Leymann, H. (1990). Mobbing and psychological terror at workplaces. *Violence and Victims, 5*, 119–126.

Lutgen-Sandvik, P., Tracy, S. J., & Alberts, J. K. (2007). Burned by bullying in the American workplace: Prevalence, perception, degree, and impact. *Journal of Management Studies, 44*, 837–861.

Martucci, W. C., & Sinatra, K. R. (2009). Antibullying legislation: A growing national trend in the new workplace. *Employment Relations Today, 35*(4), 77–83. doi:10.1002/ert.20227

Namie, G. (2012). *Healthy workplace bill: The solution.* Retrieved from http://www.healthyworkplacebill.org/bill.php

Namie, G., & Namie, R. (2009). U.S. workplace bullying: Some basic considerations and consultation interventions. *Consulting Psychology Journal: Practice and Research, 61*, 202–219. doi:10.1037/a0016670

National Education Association. (2000). *Anti-harassment policy and complaint procedures.* Washington, DC: Author.

Nielsen, M. B., & Einarsen, S. (2012). Outcomes of exposure to workplace bullying: A meta-analytic review. *Work & Stress, 26*, 309–332.

Olweus, D. (1993). *Bullying at school.* Oxford, England: Blackwell.

Ontario Secondary School Teachers Federation. (2005). *Bullying in the workplace survey.* Toronto: Author.

Riley, D., Duncan, D. J., & Edwards, J. (2009). *Investigation of staff bullying in Australian schools: Executive summary.* Australian Catholic University and University of New England. Retrieved from http://www.schoolbullies.org.au/InvestigationOfStaffBullying_ExecSummary.pdf

Robers, S., Zhang, J., Truman, J., & Snyder, T. D. (2011). *Indicators of school crime and safety: 2011.* Washington, DC: Institute of Education Sciences, National Center for Educational Statistics.

Simons, S. (2008). Workplace bullying experinced by Massachusetts registered nurses and the relationship to intention to leave the organization. *Advances in Nursing Science, 31*(2), E48–E59.

Strandmark, K. M., & Hallberg, L. R. (2007). The origin of workplace bullying: Experiences from the perspective of bully victims in the public service sector. *Journal of Nursing Management, 15*, 332–341.

Trépanier, S.-G., Fernet, C., & Austin, S. (2015). A longitudinal investigation of workplace bullying, basic need satisfaction, and employee functioning. *Journal of Occupational Health Psychology, 20*(1), 105–116.

Vettenburg, N. (2002). Unsafe feelings among teachers. *Journal of School Violence, 1*, 33–49.

Wilson, C. M., Douglas, K. S., & Lyon, D. R. (2010). Violence against teachers: Prevalence and consequences. *Journal of Interpersonal Violence, 26*, 2353–2371. doi:10.1177/0886260510383027

Zogby International. (2010). *The WBI U.S. Workplace Bullying Survey.* Bellingham, WA: Workplace Bullying Institute.

13

Bullying of Children by Adults: The Undiscussables

Stuart W. Twemlow, Peter Fonagy, and Chloe Campbell

Bullying is a significant concern for youth, and unfortunately, sometimes adults act as perpetrators. Although this taboo topic is rarely addressed in the literature or in professional development, this critical yet "undiscussable" issue needs to be more directly addressed in schoolwide prevention programming and in the research. We define *adult bullying* in this chapter as the use of power to punish, manipulate, or disparage a student beyond the point most would consider reasonable disciplinary procedure. We define *undiscussable* as an issue that is extremely difficult to articulate and confront. This may trigger tremendous anxiety among group members, which could halt progress the group might make in dealing with it. Everyone tends to know about the problem, yet no one wants to be responsible for having to tackle it. An undiscussable may be rooted in a wide spectrum of school policies and quite possibly extend into many levels of the school's hierarchy. It is vital that the nature of these undiscussables and how they might be broached are considered when selecting and implementing a program. For example, implementing a program in the hope of eliminating schoolyard bullying without addressing the question of whether teachers may also be bullying students will, at best, have short-term, limited impact. In the current chapter, we explore this complex issue, starting with a focus on teachers who bully and then considering other adults, such as administrators, coaches, and parents, who may use their power to have a negative impact on children.

BULLYING BY TEACHERS

Exposure to bullying dynamics is widely reported by teachers. This includes perpetrating or observing bullying and being victimized by students, students' parents, or school

This research was supported by the Child and Family Programs of the Menninger Foundation, Topeka, Kansas; and the Baylor College of Medicine, Houston, Texas.

administrators. Teachers are often working under pressure in environments of high emotional arousal. In one study we conducted, 116 elementary school teachers responded to an anonymous questionnaire about their perceptions of teachers who bully students in their broad school experience. The surprising results indicated that over 40 percent of teachers openly reported bullying students themselves. However, we must emphasize that, overall, our work has found that teachers who bully represent a minority in a challenging profession. As a group "bullying teachers," compared with nonbullying teachers, tend to have experienced more bullying when they were children and adolescents and had worked with and observed more teachers who bullied over the past three years (Twemlow, Fonagy, Sacco, & Brethour, 2006). The reasons teachers listed for their bullying behavior included lack of administrative support, lack of training in how to discipline effectively, fear of being hurt by a student, and resentment toward more academic students (Twemlow et al., 2006).

We have also found that there are two different categories of bullying teacher: the sadistic bullying type and the bully–victim type. The first type tends to use their position of power to bully, shame, and humiliate their students. The behavior of the second type of teacher is characterized by a pattern of provoking victimization by students and then reacting in an inappropriate and coercive fashion. Many of these bully–victim teachers appear burned out and are unable to generate the energy necessary to change the power dynamics within their classroom or the larger school environment. This group is more likely to be amenable to retraining and to be responsive to an improved school climate than the sadistic bullying group. As we were interested to learn, the questionnaire was experienced by some of the participating teachers as a wakeup call, highlighting some of their key concerns and showing them that they were not alone in both their frustrations and behavior patterns.

In a study of 214 teachers in elementary, middle, and high schools, we found a similar profile to the bullying teacher among those working in schools with the highest suspension rates (that is, schools with greater behavioral problems). We found that such schools tend to have more teachers who reported that they themselves had bullied students, had experienced bullying when they were students, and had seen more bullying teachers in their school. The implication of this is that teachers who bully their students have a role in creating a climate in which student bullying in general is a problem (Twemlow & Fonagy, 2005). A recent study has clarified the extent to which a supportive school climate is associated with positive help-seeking attitudes among students for bullying and threats of violence (Eliot, Cornell, Gregory, & Fan, 2010). It is perhaps unsurprising that students who feel that their teachers will overlook bullying and take no action to stop it will not feel inclined to report it (Unnever & Cornell, 2004). Given the difficulties that students often feel about reporting bullying, creating an environment that encourages students to feel that they can seek help is critical in tackling a bullying climate (Oliver & Candappa, 2007). Furthermore, the intersecting, intergenerational relationship between teachers who have experienced bullying in their personal history and the emergence of a school environment in which students are more likely to bully other students or teachers indicates the self-generating nature of a bullying system and the vital importance of systemic interventions in inhibiting the cycle of bullying behavior. Of the many interventions that now exist to deal with bullying in schools, evidence suggests that the most effective, evidence-based interventions share the characteristic of being based on the whole school (Shetgiri, Espelage, & Carroll, 2015).

We have conducted extensive studies on teachers bullying students and have found this to be an understandably delicate issue (Twemlow et al., 2006; Twemlow & Sacco, 2008). Teaching is a highly pressurized as well as a noble profession. Supporting teachers requires honest engagement with the reality that certain conditions may make coercive behavior more likely. Teacher demoralization and low morale are major problems in the U.S. school system (Haynes, 2014). However, this does not need to be the case: it is essential to support teachers in good practice so they can continue to access the moral rewards that often motivated them to enter the profession. This requires a systemic approach rather than one that blames individual teachers and their personal vulnerability to burnout (Santoro, 2011). Such a systemic approach needs to confront the circumstances that may make it difficult for principals to take action against a bullying teacher (for example, a teacher's community connections, the role of labor groups). In some cases, teachers who report their concerns about a colleague complain of being ignored and even sidelined as a consequence (Twemlow & Sacco, 2008). Quite a number of school principals learn not to place vulnerable children with bullying teachers but do not confront the issue directly for fear of possible repercussions (Twemlow & Sacco, 2008). In the complex social system of a school, these considerations can allow a bullying-related issue to become undiscussable and feel intractable. Teachers bullying students is but one of a wide range of undiscussables that exist in every school or organization. We have begun our discussion of undiscussable topics with an analysis of teachers bullying students; we will now examine other potentially relevant undiscussables that negatively affect contemporary school climates and reduce the likelihood of successfully implementing positive changes.

ADMINISTRATOR BULLYING

Teachers work within a hierarchical system, led by administrators following policies set by elected or appointed school board members. It is not uncommon for schools to be forced into accepting arbitrary and politicized decisions as a matter of policy (Twemlow & Sacco, 2008). In too many cases, administrators assume a punishment surveillance model when responding to teachers. This results in a climate within the school in which the external disciplinary presence of the administrator is the primary way of relating to teachers on a day-to-day basis. This in turn creates a situation in which teachers are left on their own to control situations that occur in their classrooms or while supervising students in everyday school activities.

A study of the mistreatment of teachers by administrators found that 40 percent of the 172 teachers in the United States and Canada who were administered the Principal Mistreatment-Abuse Inventory had been a victim of principal mistreatment that lasted from one to three years, and 25 percent of the teachers were found to have experienced mistreatment that lasted more than three years (Blase, Blase, & Du, 2008). The administrator behaviors that were judged by teachers to cause the most harm and to be the most frequently experienced included unwillingness to support teachers in difficult interactions with parents and students, intimidation, favoritism, and failure to recognize and praise teachers' achievements in their work. Other commonly reported behaviors that caused significant distress to teachers were unfair criticism and reprimands, work overload, lying, micromanaging, inappropriate gossiping, and isolating tactics (Blase, 2009; Blase et al., 2008).

This research is congruent with our conceptualization of administrative bullying as taking two main forms. One common form of administrative bullying involves an administrator taking an abdicating bystander role. In this instance, administrators do very little to acknowledge the existence of problems, and they fail to protect teachers from unreasonable and aggressive parents and irrelevant or contradictory policies handed down from school boards. Teachers reported that it is such factors that drive burnout and push older teachers to consider early retirement (Twemlow & Sacco, 2008). This type of bullying administrator is primarily concerned with maintaining the illusion of a healthy school and will ignore issues that may be undermining teachers' abilities to control and maintain a positive school environment. This can result in teachers forming their own unhealthy and often-coercive subgroups. Some teachers are able to function independently of the larger support of their colleagues and peers. They simply survive by controlling their own classrooms and existing in a vacuum, but the result is a fragmented social climate rendered fertile for the growth of coercive activities by both students and teachers.

The second type of bullying administrator is a more sadistic individual who uses his or her power to make decisions that detrimentally affect the quality of life for both teachers and students. This type of administrator is likely to target specific teachers, engaging in a pattern of imposing humiliating tasks and disciplinary actions, and transferring responsibilities as a way of maintaining power and superiority. This type of administrator will appear to be strict and concerned with maintaining discipline in a rather controlled environment, but his or her dictatorial stance will alienate teachers. This dilemma represents a quintessential undiscussable. Some principals may indicate that they are interested in having an antiviolence program but will minimize its potential value by denying the resources necessary to complete the needed tasks for climate interventions, slowly undermining or devaluing the process. The school might try a number of different programs with promising outcomes, only to find that they are paying lip service to administrators who are simply creating an image for their own superiors. These schools will tend to rely more on expulsion and suspension as a way of dealing with student misbehavior. Authoritarian teachers who "talk a good game" will be supported and favored by this type of bully administrator (Twemlow & Sacco, 2008, 2012a, 2012b).

A school will struggle to implement any antiviolence program effectively unless it is able to deal with these management problems. Research by Blases suggested that 77 percent of the teachers questioned reported that administrator mistreatment had a detrimental impact on their performance by reducing motivation; diminishing their capacity to show care, patience, or tolerance of students; undermining their tendency to show creativity in the classroom; and increasing their propensity to fall back on rigid, outdated, and authoritarian teaching methods (Blase, 2009; Blase et al., 2008). Conversely, we conducted a controlled study where an antibullying program was initiated and embraced by the teachers and the principal, as well as by students. The net result was a significant increase in academic performance, especially on the part of bystander children, many of whom had initially said they hated their school (Fonagy, Twemlow, Vernberg, Sacco, & Little, 2005). In other words, when a school works together to eliminate coercive activities at all levels, children learn better because teachers are freer to focus on teaching well and responding creatively to their students' educational and emotional needs.

BULLYING COACHES

It is not uncommon for high schools to define themselves by the success of their ambitious athletic and competitive programs. Whatever the competitive extracurricular activity is, there is generally a coach of some sort who selects students to represent the school. The coach is entrusted to choose a team, train that team, and guide its members through the season. A small minority of coaches use this rather singular status within their school in an abusive manner. In one study of 803 young athletes from fifth through eighth grades, 7 percent of children reported that their coach encouraged them to cheat, 8 percent reported being encouraged to hurt an opponent, and over a third of youth reported their coaches yelling angrily at children for making mistakes (Shields, Bredemeier, LaVoi, & Power, 2005). Having been hit, kicked or slapped by their coach was reported by 4 percent of the children in the same study (Shields et al., 2005).

Coaches are placed in the position of having to get their team into an excited and competitive mind-set. In our work in schools, we have certainly observed a number of coaches being needlessly coercive in their selection and training approaches (Twemlow & Sacco, 2008). Even seemingly well-intentioned coaches often forget that the main point of extracurricular activities is to develop students as overall human beings rather than as robotic athletes or performers. In other words, it becomes more about the coach's success than about what is best for the team or its individual members. Bullying coaches often use exclusion and failure to motivate students in games or practices. If students complain to their parents or to the extracurricular director, they are frequently told to return to the coach and simply "work it out." If questioned or held accountable by concerned parents or administrators, coaches can respond by withholding playing time or participation opportunities. If a parent questions a coach's approach or decision during practice or a game, the athletic director or school administrator frequently supports the coach, maintaining the status quo under the guise of creating "tough" students able to participate in the competitive world they will encounter outside of school. Various techniques have recently been described as ways that coaches may normalize or justify their behavior, such as arguing that their techniques are common practice, minimizing the seriousness of an incident and blaming the victim, or threatening the victim with the consequences that might arise from raising a complaint (Swigonski, Enneking, & Hendrix, 2014).

When a school overvalues its extracurricular participation, the ability to question the wisdom of a coercive coach becomes increasingly difficult (Twemlow & Sacco, 2008). Bullying coaches can also act as abdicating bystanders if their athletes or scholars are engaged in bullying activities. For example, if a senior quarterback sexually abuses a freshman, the impact of this transgression may become minimized and misdirected. We have observed instances in which the victim is even blamed for seducing a popular athlete and making problems later (Twemlow & Sacco, 2008). The bullying coach can become an undiscussable that may be of concern to other teachers. Colleagues may see the negative impact of a bullying coach on their students, but they will be unable to address the issue because of the undiscussable nature of the problem and the idealized role of the coach in certain schools (Twemlow & Sacco, 2008).

NONTEACHING STAFF

Children may be exposed to bullying by nonteaching adults in school. Students often have few options to communicate about this to anyone. Often, teachers and administrators downplay the significance of this type of adult bullying because they lack awareness of the scale of its impact on children. Schools require a wide range of adults to maintain the school building, provide catering, and run extracurricular programs and activities. We have encountered numerous instances of secretaries and librarians acting in bullying ways toward the student body. Custodians, who have a large role to play in the maintenance of a school's physical appearance, frequently have contact with students during the conduct of their business. Maintenance workers are often protected because of their labor contracts and are not trained to the level of teachers and administrators in the skills necessary to interact with students in a safe and positive manner.

In a small private school we recently studied and consulted with, a custodian was found to have evaded the typical background check and had engaged in repeated patterns of sexual exploitation of children over a long period of time. This protected private school setting became the ideal cover for a corrupt and deeply troubled adult (Twemlow & Sacco, 2008). Because the school enjoyed a very high status in the community, the idea that an ancillary school staff member could have engaged in a systematically abusive and bullying process was not countenanced until it could no longer be ignored. When the events finally became known, they were minimized until the eruption of a criminal molestation case left the school with no option but to reevaluate itself and deal with its undiscussable problems.

Adult support personnel within a school can be a source of both tremendous inspiration and encouragement to the children, as well as a potential source of bullying. A recent study has found that students' perception that all school staff—teaching and nonteaching— are supportive is associated with students feeling more positive about the idea of seeking help for bullying and threats of violence (Eliot et al., 2010). The role played by all adults who have contact with children must be discussed seriously by team leaders seeking to change their school's climate. The possible impact of grouchy janitors, critical librarians, or mean-spirited lunch workers needs to be consistently addressed. There is clearly a need to include these adults in any discussion involving overall school climate. It has been convincingly argued that as research findings increasingly point to the value of regarding the school as an ecosystem, all staff within a school need to understand bullying and be able to recognize bullying behavior and intervene appropriately (Espelage, 2014).

PREJUDICE

The question of prejudice and stigma is extremely difficult to discuss as a matter of policy. In an elementary school intervention we led in Topeka, Kansas, we found that it was possible to reduce prejudice and the stigmatization of people of color as a by-product of addressing bullying (Twemlow & Sacco, 2008). Similarly, it has been found that homophobic prejudice and sexual harassment decline in schools where bullying in general is tackled (Rinehart & Espelage, 2016). Why? When bullying is seen as a social role shared by children and adults, it is easier to qualify the coercive behavior as bullying, rather than identify it as a type of racial prejudice or bias. Prejudice itself can be seen as a form of bullying in which victims are targeted because of some perceived characteristics, such as race, culture, social-economic status, fashion, choice of interest, way of speaking, or physical attractiveness. The pressure to be perceived as fair rather than biased is quite high in most schools, and this pressure may lead to the denial of bullying activity.

PARENT BULLYING

Occasionally parents can become overly involved in their children's schools, making unreasonable demands and criticizing various aspects of the way the schools are run. Another type of parent bullying involves parents who abdicate their responsibility, then react aggressively to any questioning of their feelings by the school. When abdicating bullying parents are contacted by the school about issues related to their children, they often will respond by bullying concerned teachers and administrators with threats and angry accusations and assertions that they are protecting the rights of their children.

A safe and creative school climate requires that parents take responsibility for their own levels of coercion and cooperation—or lack thereof—with the school. We have noticed an increasing divide or disconnect between the signals that children receive from their parents and from their schools. When the child is permitted to cause friction between the school and parents, parents are likely to engage in bullying behavior as a form of pseudo-protection or to demonstrate their involvement with their children. This is increasingly true with parents burdened by the excessive demands of employment necessary to support a family. The inconsistency of these signals from both parent and school creates the opportunity for a child to engage in increasing amounts of coercive behavior at school. When children believe that their bullying can be neutralized by the bullying of their parents, the child will feel emboldened to bully more at school (Twemlow, Fonagy, & Sacco, 2005b). A bullying parent will have power only when school administrators allow him or her to continue. If an administrator abdicates responsibility, then the bullying parent is unleashed on the teacher, who may become sandwiched between an abdicating bully principal and a sadistic bully parent. The result, once again, is that the situation becomes an undiscussable.

THE "PROBLEM" OF EXCELLENCE

Not all coercive school environments are violent. Many high-achieving and socially elite schools have extremely coercive bullying school environments without resulting in instances of physical violence on a regular basis or poor grades (Twemlow & Sacco, 2012a, 2012b). However, in the quest for excellence, there may be an unwitting commitment to a coercive style of encouraging competition among both teachers and students that builds an unhealthy school climate for all involved. There are remarkably few studies of bullying in affluent schools. We are in the fifth year of study of 12 affluent schools, primarily white, where malignant bullying occurs, even though grade point averages are often very high. All schools try to bring out the best in their students and want to set high academic standards. However, when this process is taken to an extreme, both teachers and students are dehumanized. Such pressures can naturally lead to the creation of an unhealthy school climate. For example, a case study in an elite U.S. private school found that both teachers and students considered the highly competitive and pressurized nature of the environment—often compounded by familial pressure to achieve a place at a top university—to play a role in creating a bullying culture (Stoudt, Kuriloff, Reichert, & Ravitch, 2010).

In our experience, private schools and affluent public schools suffer from a higher level of malignant social aggression than many of their public counterparts. There is a higher tolerance in these schools for children and teachers to behave in a mean-spirited fashion during their struggle to increase social status and academic reputation. These schools often seem clean, neat, and orderly with well-dressed, articulate students and teachers. When you pierce the first layer, however, it becomes clear that many of the children are quite unhappy and the teachers feel constantly devalued and pressured. The pursuit of excellence can become a form of coercion that is presented as admirable determination. It is not uncommon for communities to set their schools on pedestals and overvalue their abilities to score the highest levels measured by the state or the governing body. We are not suggesting that schools abandon their goals and aspirations for academic excellence, but when it comes at the expense of human beings, research suggests that it is necessary to approach these goals differently.

The pursuit of excellence is clearly, in this sense, an undiscussable. That striving for excellence can be problematic sounds paradoxical, but parents who value a school that focuses solely or unhealthily on academic excellence can allow coercion to grow within the school climate. Discussions that challenge the single-minded obsession with achievement are quickly seen as wishing to undermine academic success, and all too often the focus shifts away from the real problem: bullying and coercive behavior. In the pursuit of excellence, children are sometimes viewed as needing to model their parents' behavior rather than think for themselves. Both teachers and parents can underestimate the impact that the pressure to excel places on children. Children can become at risk for higher rates of dropping out, substance abuse, and even suicide. For example, in a small private school, a father unabashedly indicated that his son's B grade compelled him to inform his son that he had shamed their family. In addition, in a family session following a suicide attempt by a bright but very stressed out high school senior, we witnessed this student's parents angrily confront her about failure to follow house rules. In tears she pleaded that she had gotten 93 percent on a test. Her father said, "And it would have been 98 percent if you had done what you were told." These anecdotal accounts shed light on the effects that these high-achieving schools can have on students and their families.

SEXUAL EXPLOITATION OF CHILDREN BY TEACHERS

The problem of sexual exploitation of children by adults in positions of authority has become a major cause for concern over the past decade (Grayson, 2006). Obtaining definitive figures on the scale of the problem of sexual abuse by teachers is difficult. According to some estimates, two-thirds of both male and female respondents reported having been the target of unwanted sexual comments, jokes, gestures, or looks at school. In addition, about half of the students reported having been touched, pinched, or grabbed at some point by their teachers. Student-to-student sexual harassment was the most common problem, accounting for nearly 80 percent of the incidents, whereas harassment involving teachers, custodians, and coaches accounted for about 20 percent. One respondent noted that verbal harassment occurs mostly in the classroom, whereas physical contact, sexual or clearly defined sexual harassment, is more likely to occur outside of the classroom.

There are many subtle ways in which teachers may be verbally abusive to their students; these incidents are often difficult to prosecute. In fact, instances of both teacher bullying and teacher exploitation of students are grossly underreported because of the shame induced by such activities (Fekkes, Pijpers, & Verloove-Vanhorick, 2005; Twemlow & Sacco, 2012a, 2012b). A recent study showed how a school's overall commitment to preventing bullying was associated with lower levels of sexual harassment; in addition, a specific commitment to gender equity and an intolerance of sexual harassment within a school was associated with lower levels of homophobic name-calling as well as lower levels of harassment (Rinehart & Espelage, 2016). This is in keeping with our hypothesis that problematic behaviors can be meaningfully addressed only in the context of a systemic, schoolwide approach to bullying prevention and the development of a positive school climate.

A response pattern that could be used for teacher bullying as well as teacher sexual exploitation includes the following interventions:

- Implementing a code of conduct that details the exact boundaries for teachers in responding to students both verbally and physically;

- Establishing grievance procedures for harassment victims that can be distributed, understood, and adhered to by teachers, parents, administrators, and students;
- Protecting against false complaints and allegations. These recommendations include punishments for false allegations against a teacher by a student or parent;
- Impartially adhering to policies that involve a due-process procedure for all parties identified as bullies, victims, or bystanders; and
- Providing training to assist teachers in avoiding false allegations of any type of bullying.

CREATING A PEACEFUL SCHOOL ENVIRONMENT (CAPSLE): A SYSTEMS APPROACH

Before concluding, we briefly describe CAPSLE, a program developed to tackle bullying in schools, as an example of a whole-school intervention. CAPSLE is one of three bullying prevention strategies recently found by a large meta-analysis to be most effective (Ttofi & Farrington, 2011), the other two programs being the Olweus Bully Prevention Program and Finland's KiVa national antibullying program (Shetgiri et al., 2015). The CAPSLE approach draws on mentalizing theory, which emphasizes the capacity to be aware of and understand the thoughts, feelings, and beliefs that underpin all human behavior. Only if we are able to mentalize both ourselves and other people can we reflect, empathize, set boundaries, modulate stormy emotions and overreactions, and have a strong sense of agency. This same principle can be applied to social groups. The CAPSLE approach also acknowledges that dysfunctional social systems cause the collapse of mentalizing and result in the highly reactive, tense, and defensive interactions that can lead to violence. A school in which violence, aggression, and bullying are the norm is by definition a social environment that works to close down mentalizing in staff members and pupils.

The emphasis of CAPSLE, which differentiates it from the many other antibullying programs, is that it focuses on the whole school community and seeks to create a mentalizing climate and a group dynamic that can resist and limit the potency and currency carried by individual acts of violence or aggression (Twemlow, Fonagy, & Sacco, 2005a, 2005b). CAPSLE is made up of four components:

1. A "positive climate" campaign uses reflective classroom discussion by each class at the end of the school day, with children self-rating their perceived success in creating a shift in the language and thinking. In K–5, mentalizing games are used by teachers.
2. A classroom management plan develops the teachers' discipline skills by focusing on understanding and correcting problems at the root rather than punishing and criticizing only the behavior that is apparent. For example, a behavior problem in a single child is conceptualized as a problem for all the pupils in the class, who, often unwittingly, participate in bully, victim, or bystander roles. This approach reduces scapegoating, and insight into the meaning of the behavior becomes paramount.
3. A physical education program, derived from a combination of role-playing, relaxation, and self-defensive techniques, teaches children skills to deal with victimization and bystander behavior. This component of the program helps children

to protect themselves and others by using nonviolent physical and cognitive strategies. For example, enacting bully–victim–bystander roles provides pupils with the opportunity to role-play and work out alternative actions to fighting. Learning ways to physically defend oneself (for example, when grabbed, pushed, or punched), coupled with classroom discussion, teaches personal self-control as well as respect and helpfulness toward others.

4. Schools may put in place one or two support programs: peer mentorship or adult mentorship. These relationships provide additional containment and modeling to assist children in mastering the skills and language to deal with power struggles. For example, mentors instruct children in refereeing games, resolving playground disputes, and the importance of helping others.

In a cluster-randomized control trial involving nine elementary schools in a city in the United States (Fonagy et al., 2009), the CAPSLE program was found to substantially reduce aggression and improve classroom behavior. There was a reduction in children's experience of aggression and victimization. The program's effectiveness was also indicated by a reduction in the number of children nominated by their peers as being aggressive, victimized, or engaging in aggressive bystander behaviors. This was confirmed by behavioral observation of reduced disruptive and off-task classroom behavior in schools implementing CAPSLE. The program develops a schoolwide awareness of the omnipresence of power struggles and their effects on individuals' capacity to think about others' points of view. The study's findings suggested that empathic mentalizing increased in schools using the CAPSLE program. This is consistent with the view that the emotional and cognitive skills learned in handling interpersonal power struggles enhance both the emotional and the cognitive empathic aspects of mentalizing and self-agency (Baron-Cohen, 2005) and thus may reduce the likelihood of an individual resorting to physical aggression (Fonagy, 2003).

CAPSLE focuses on the power dynamics in the relationship between bullies, victims, and bystanders and emphasizes the role of bystanders in restoring mentalizing within this dynamic. Through the components of the program outlined above, bystanders are trained to act to encourage bullies, victims, and other bystanders to be aware of and move away from "pathological" roles. In a nonmentalizing environment, the witness to a power struggle—that is, the bystander, who could be a member of staff as well as a student—may experience sadistic feelings of pleasure in seeing another's difficulty or suffering. This is possible only when the witness feels distanced from the internal world of the other person and is then able use the victim to contain the unwanted (usually frightened) part of him- or herself. The CAPSLE intervention constitutes a deliberate attempt to scaffold the unbalanced, fluctuating, and emerging mentalizing capacities of children and young people and the highly pressurized teachers reacting to them. The goal of this intervention is to create a social environment in which more balanced mentalizing can be practiced and reinforced and its benefits experienced.

CAPSLE, in its whole-school approach, assumes that all members of a school community, including teachers and other adults in the school, play a role in bullying. It is therefore an approach that seeks to make teachers and other staff aware of the impact of their behavior and to reflect on their interactions with the students. However, to do this, the adults within a school community need to be supported, and the complex social, emotional, and political considerations involved in working in a school community need to be understood and articulated. We call this process discussing the undiscussables.

WHY DISCUSS THE UNDISCUSSABLES?

A school's ability to implement programs that improve the quality of a school requires that all subjects be openly discussed. This requires a systemic breadth of vision and avoiding the temptation to focus simplistically on one particular aspect of character development (such as empathy) or to fixate on single issues (such as achievement or an individual teacher). Failure to discuss the undiscussables will inhibit any program targeted to improve the school's climate. There is a strict relationship between what a program can do and what it is allowed to do. Sometimes the undiscussable is unchangeable; in such cases this needs to be accommodated and creative workarounds should be developed. The group should search for ways to make these problems addressable in practical ways that stress positive approaches rather than blaming, attacking, and finger-pointing. The challenge is to not become trapped in one issue. It must be made possible to explore undiscussables and try some alternatives designed to shift the current culture away from ignoring an undiscussable.

REFERENCES

Baron-Cohen, S. (2005). Autism. In B. Hopkins (Ed.), *Cambridge encyclopedia of child development* (pp. 398–401). Cambridge, England: Cambridge University Press.

Blase, J. (2009). School administrator mistreatment of teachers. In L. Saha & A. Dworkin (Eds.), *International handbook of research on teachers and teaching: Part one* (pp. 433–448). New York: Springer.

Blase, J., Blase, J., & Du, F. (2008). The mistreated teacher: A national study. *Journal of Educational Administration, 46*(3), 263–301.

Eliot, M., Cornell, D., Gregory, A., & Fan, X. (2010). Supportive school climate and student willingness to seek help for bullying and threats of violence. *Journal of School Psychology, 48*, 533–553.

Espelage, D. (2014). Ecological theory: Preventing youth bullying, aggression, and victimization. *Theory into Practice, 53*(4), 257–264.

Fekkes, M., Pijpers, F., & Verloove-Vanhorick, S. (2005). Bullying: Who does what, when and where? Involvement of children, teachers and parents in bullying behavior. *Health Education Research, 20*(1), 81–91.

Fonagy, P. (2003). Towards a developmental understanding of violence. *British Journal of Psychiatry, 183*, 190–192.

Fonagy, P., Twemlow, S. W., Vernberg, E. M., Nelson, J. M., Dill, E. J., Little, T. D., & Sargent, J. A. (2009). A cluster randomized controlled trial of child-focused psychiatric consultation and a school systems-focused intervention to reduce aggression. *Journal of Child Psychology and Psychiatry, 50*, 607–616.

Fonagy, P., Twemlow, S. W., Vernberg, E., Sacco, F. C., & Little, T. D. (2005). Creating a peaceful school learning environment: The impact of an antibullying program on educational attainment in elementary schools. *Medical Science Monitor, 11*(7), 317–325.

Grayson, J. (2006). Sexual abuse by educators and school staff. *Virginia Child Protection Newsletter, 76*, 1–6.

Haynes, M. (2014). *On the path to equity: Improving the effectiveness of beginning teachers.* Washington, DC: Alliance for Excellent Education.

Oliver, C., & Candappa, M. (2007). Bullying and the politics of telling. *Oxford Review of Education, 33*(1), 71–86.

Rinehart, S., & Espelage, D. (2016). A multilevel analysis of school climate, homophobic name-calling, and sexual harassment victimization/perpetration among middle school youth. *Psychology of Violence, 6,* 213–222.

Santoro, D. A. (2011). Good teaching in difficult times: Demoralization in the pursuit of good work. *American Journal of Education, 118*(1), 1–23.

Shetgiri, R., Espelage, D., & Carroll, L. (2015). *Practical strategies for clinical management of bullying.* New York: Springer.

Shields, D. L., Bredemeier, B. L., LaVoi, N. M., & Power, F. C. (2005). The sports behavior of youth, parents and coaches: The good, the bad, and the ugly. *Journal of Research in Character Education, 3*(1), 43–59.

Stoudt, B., Kuriloff, P., Reichert, M., & Ravitch, S. (2010). Educating for hegemony, researching for change: Collaborating with teachers and students to examine bullying at an elite private school. In A. Howard & R. Gaztambide-Fernandez (Eds.), *Educating elites: Class privilege and advantage* (pp. 31–53). Lanham, MD: Rowman & Littlefield.

Swigonski, N. L., Enneking, B. A., & Hendrix, K. (2014). Bullying behavior by athletic coaches. *Pediatrics, 133*(2), 273–275.

Ttofi, M., & Farrington, D. (2011). Effectiveness of school-based programs to reduce bullying: A systematic and meta-analytic review. *Journal of Experimental Criminology, 7*(11), 27–56.

Twemlow, S. W., & Fonagy, P. (2005). The prevalence of teachers who bully students in schools with differing levels of behavioral problems. *American Journal of Psychiatry, 162,* 2387–2389.

Twemlow, S. W., Fonagy, P., & Sacco, F. C. (2005a). A developmental approach to mentalizing communities: I. A model for social change. *Bulletin of the Menninger Clinic, 69*(4), 265–281.

Twemlow, S. W., Fonagy, P., & Sacco, F. C. (2005b). A developmental approach to mentalizing communities: II. The Peaceful Schools experiment. *Bulletin of the Menninger Clinic, 69*(4), 282–304.

Twemlow, S. W., Fonagy, P., Sacco, F. C., & Brethour, J. R. (2006). Teachers who bully students: A hidden trauma. *International Journal of Social Psychiatry, 52*(3), 187–198.

Twemlow, S. W., & Sacco, F. C. (2008). *Why school antibullying programs don't work.* Lanham, MD: Jason Aronson.

Twemlow, S. W., & Sacco, F. C. (2012a). Bullying is a process, not a person: Inviting the community into the school. In S. W. Twemlow & F. C. Sacco (Eds.), *Preventing bullying and school violence* (pp. 111–146). Arlington, VA: American Psychiatric Association.

Twemlow, S. W., & Sacco, F. C. (2012b). *Preventing bullying and school violence.* Arlington, VA: American Psychiatric Association.

Unnever, J., & Cornell, D. (2004). Middle school victims of bullying: Who reports being bullied? *Aggressive Behavior, 30,* 373–388.

Part V

Approaches to Prevention and Intervention

14

The Transactional Association between School Climate and Bullying

Lindsey O'Brennan and Catherine P. Bradshaw

There is a large body of research linking school climate with a range of positive outcomes for students, including reduced involvement in bullying, improved academic performance, enhanced student engagement, and increased likelihood of school completion (Bradshaw, Koth, Thornton, & Leaf, 2009; Cohen & Geier, 2010; Shochet, Dadds, Ham, & Montague, 2006; Thapa, Cohen, Guffey, & Higgins-D'Alessandro, 2013; Wang & Degol, 2015). Given the importance of school climate, it is not surprising that it is often an important target for school improvement efforts, including bullying prevention and intervention programs. The school climate research fits within Bronfenbrenner's social-ecological model as it highlights the relevance of context (that is, schools and classrooms) with regard to a child's development (Bronfenbrenner & Morris, 1998). The social-ecological framework has been applied to bullying in the school setting (see Espelage & Swearer, 2004), specifically the broad and lasting influence of the climate and culture of schools and the bidirectional influences between behavior and school context.

Although the interconnectedness of bullying and school climate is a growing research topic, the vast majority of work in this area has focused on student perceptions in K–12 settings. Additional research is needed to examine bullying in higher education settings in relation to both student and faculty perceptions of school climate. Furthermore, there is also increased attention to parent and staff perspectives of bullying and school climate, as well the potential use of observational tools in tandem with self-report and administrative records. This chapter summarizes the current research on school climate with particular

The writing of this chapter was supported in part through grants to Catherine P. Bradshaw from the U.S. Department of Education and the William T. Grant Foundation through the Maryland Safe and Supportive Schools initiative.

focus on bullying prevention. We review some common definitional and measurement issues related to school climate. We also consider various ways to measure school climate and provide concrete suggestions for improving school climate and reducing bullying through schoolwide programs and interventions and data-informed approaches.

DEFINING SCHOOL CLIMATE

There are several definitions of school climate, which often overlap with the related concept of school culture. For example, the National School Climate Council (2007) defines *school climate* as "norms, values, and expectations that support people feeling socially, emotionally and physically safe" (p. 4). School climate is a product of the interpersonal relationships between students, families, teachers, support staff, and administrators. Positive school climate is fostered through a shared vision of respect and engagement across the educational system (Thapa et al., 2013). Emphasis is also placed on the collective sense of safety and care for the school's physical environment. School culture is a related concept that refers to the "unwritten rules and expectations" among the school staff (Gruenert, 2008). For example, one might differentiate school climate as being the mood or attitude of the school, instead of the culture, which is the enduring personality of the school. Similarly, school climate may be based on perceptions, whereas culture may be based on values and beliefs (for more examples of the distinction, see Gruenert, 2008). Despite these somewhat subtle differences between culture and climate, many researchers and practitioners use these terms interchangeably.

Although there is no universally agreed upon set of core domains or features, the National School Climate Center identifies five elements of school climate: (a) safety (for example, rules and norms, physical security, social-emotional security); (b) teaching and learning (for example, support for learning, social and civic learning); (c) interpersonal relationships (for example, respect for diversity, social support from adults, social support from peers); (d) institutional environment (for example, school connectedness and engagement, physical surroundings); and (e) staff relationships (leadership, professional relationships). Similarly, the U.S. Department of Education (DOE) Safe and Supportive Schools model of school climate includes the three interrelated domains or features of student engagement (for example, relationships, respect for diversity, and school participation), safety (for example, social-emotional safety, physical safety, and substance use), and the school environment (for example, physical environment, academic environment, wellness, and disciplinary environment). The DOE Safe and Supportive Schools model was validated by researchers involved in Maryland's Safe and Supportive Schools (MDS3) project using data from over 25,000 high schoolers (Bradshaw, Waasdorp, Debnam, & Lindstrom Johnson, 2014). Their findings supported the hypothesized three-factor school climate model of safety, engagement, and environment, although some of the subscales shifted slightly. For example, they found that engagement can be further broken down into student connections to teachers and schools, as well as parent engagement with the school (see Figure 14.1). Likewise, perceptions of safety were further explored as related to specific forms of at-risk behaviors, including bullying, aggressive behaviors, and alcohol and drug use.

Other states, such as Vermont, have adapted the DOE model by breaking out a fourth dimension of teaching and learning (see http://education.vermont.gov/safe-schools/school-climate). There have also been some applications of this Safe and Supportive Schools framework in higher education settings. For example, the University of Virginia (2015)

Figure 14.1: U.S. Department of Education's Safe and Supportive Schools Model of School Climate

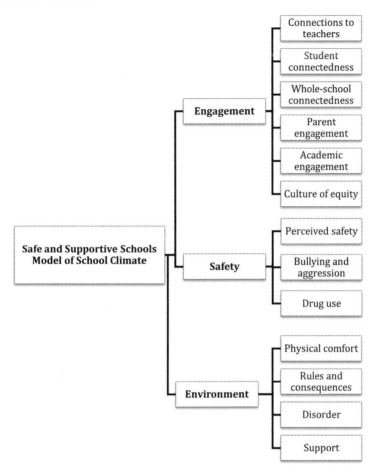

Adapted from C. P. Bradshaw, T. E. Waasdorp, K. Debnam, & S. Lindstrom Johnson (2014), Measuring school climate: A focus on safety, engagement, and the environment, *Journal of School Health, 84,* 593–604.

recently adapted this model to characterize the climate and culture of the university. In this adaptation, the university considered the importance of alumni involvement, in addition to parents. A committee of students, staff, and faculty further adapted the framework to include harassment, rather than bullying specifically (see full model in the report by the University of Virginia, 2015).

BENEFITS OF A POSITIVE SCHOOL CLIMATE

Regardless of how school climate is defined, a positive school climate is recognized as an important target for school reform and improving behavioral, academic, and mental health outcomes for students of all ages, as well as for the staff who work in these environments (Thapa et al., 2013; Thapa, Cohen, Higgins-D'Alessandro, & Guffy, 2012). Specifically, schools with positive climates tend to have fewer student discipline problems (Cohen & Geier, 2010), aggressive and violent behavior (Gregory et al., 2010), bullying (Bradshaw, Sawyer, & O'Brennan, 2009; Meyer-Adams & Conner, 2008), and harassment (Attar-Schwartz, 2009). In addition to reducing students' exposure to risk factors, school climate can promote positive youth development. Specifically, positive school climate has been related to higher student academic motivation and engagement (Eccles et al., 1993) as well as elevated psychological well-being (Ruus et al., 2007; Shochet et al., 2006). It is not surprising that schools promoting engaging learning environments tend to have fewer student absences (Gottfredson, Gottfredson, Payne, & Gottfredson, 2005) and improvements in academic achievement across grade levels (Brand, Felner, Shim, Seitsinger, & Dumas, 2003; Stewart, 2008).

A positive school climate also has benefits for teachers and educational staff. Research shows that when school staff feel supported by their administration, they report higher levels of commitment and more collegiality (Singh & Billingsley, 1998). Likewise, schools where staff openly communicate with one another feel supported by their peers and administration and establish strong student–educator relationships tend to have better student academic and behavioral outcomes (Brown & Medway, 2007). A favorable school climate has also been linked with greater staff efficacy and reduced burnout (Pas, Bradshaw, & Hershfeldt, 2012). Moreover, school climate efforts have the potential of increasing job satisfaction and teacher retention, which is a major concern given the high rate of turnover in the field of education (Boe, Cook, & Sunderland, 2008; Kaiser, 2011). Given the wide range of benefits linked to a positive school climate, a clear plan of action is needed to help educators regularly assess and enhance the current climate of their school.

CAUSE OR CONSEQUENCE?

Research has demonstrated a clear link between school climate and the behavior of students and staff within that setting. However, few studies have pieced apart the transactional nature of this relationship. An interesting and potentially novel aspect of the Safe and Supportive Schools model is that it includes perceptual data as well as behavioral indicators (Bradshaw et al., 2014; also see Figure 14.1). The inclusion of bullying, aggression, and substance use as facets of school climate is fairly innovative, as many may consider these to be outcomes or products of school climate. However, given the social-ecological model, which highlights the bidirectional nature of these transactional processes, it is reasonable to expect that the school climate will affect behavior and that the behavior may also affect the climate (see Figure 14.2).

One may anticipate that as rates of bullying increase within the school, the climate may deteriorate. This could be either a direct result of the increasing level of risk for harm or because of a shift in the perception that students feel connected to the school or safe on its property. Furthermore, students may become less bonded to the adults and generally feel less cared for; some may even sense that adults are tolerating the level of bullying or apathetic to this particular concern (Lindstrom Johnson, Waasdorp, Debnam, & Bradshaw, 2013). Bystander behavior is also likely to vary as a function of school climate. In schools with greater connection, students as well as staff are more likely to intervene and help out other students (Bradshaw, Waasdorp, O'Brennan, & Gulemetova, 2013; Lindstrom Johnson et al., 2013). We cannot assume that the influences run one way, either from climate to behavior or from behavior to climate. Rather, it is likely that

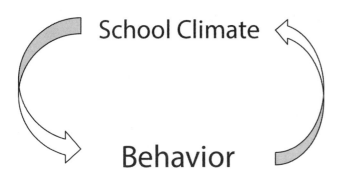

Figure 14.2: Transactional Influences of School Climate on Student and Adult Behavior

both play a role in this dynamic process, and thus the transactional process between behavior and school climate should be carefully considered. Therefore, it is reasonable to expect that efforts to reduce bullying and other forms of problem behavior may in turn improve relationships within the school, perceptions of safety, and engagement in the school community. Programs aiming merely to improve climate, such as through increased student engagement or connectedness, may also secondarily reduce bullying and discipline problems.

MEASURING SCHOOL CLIMATE

Surveys

Given the importance of positive school climate for students and staff, it is essential for schools to monitor school climate on a regular basis (Wang & Degol, 2015). The most common approach to measuring school climate is through self-report measures, which are often completed anonymously by students, parents, staff (for example, teachers, administrators, education support professionals), and possibly even alumni. The DOE's National Center on Safe Supportive Learning Environments has created an online compendium of research-based school climate measures, including surveys to be completed by students, parents, and teachers. One such measure included in the collection is the California Healthy Kids Survey, which measures school connectedness, opportunities for meaningful participation, and perceptions of safety across elementary, middle, and high school. Another such tool is the ED School Climate Surveys, an online school climate assessment system. The Comprehensive School Climate Inventory similarly measures the multiple elements through items on orderly school environment, parent and community involvement, collaboration within the school, and instructional practices. Other assessments, such as the Communities That Care Youth Survey, gather data on school, community, family, and peer risk and protective factors related to perceptions of school climate.

Observations

There have been relatively few observational tools developed that measure school climate. Measures of school engagement and student–educator interactions may tap into some aspects of classroom climate (Pianta, La Paro, & Hamre, 2008). One such tool, the Classroom Assessment Scoring System (CLASS; Pianta et al., 2008), gauges several dimensions of classroom-based school climate, including the quality of teacher–student interactions. The CLASS and CLASS—Secondary (for use in middle and high schools) are widely used and tap into aspects of school classroom interactions related to student engagement. The CLASS data are often used to inform the coaching of teachers related to instruction and behavior management.

Other non-classroom-based school climate observational tools have been created, such as those derived from the Crime Prevention through Environmental Design (CPTED; Crowe, 1991) model. Originally developed in the context of community-based violence and crime prevention, CPTED highlights the importance of context as a driver for adolescents' risk for involvement in substance use and violence. The School Assessment for Environmental Typology (SAfETy) is one such tool derived from the CPTED model that assesses eight indicators of school, physical, and social environment (that is, disorder, trash, graffiti and vandalism, appearance, illumination, surveillance, ownership, and positive behavioral expectations; Bradshaw, Milam, Furr-Holden, & Lindstrom Johnson, 2015). Data from 58 high schools provide preliminary evidence of the validity and reliability of SAfETy, which is also generally consistent with the three dimensions of the Safe and Supportive Schools model of school climate. Regardless of which instrument is used, data on school climate should be collected in multiple settings, such as within the classrooms, in nonclassroom settings (for example, hallways, cafeteria), and across school grounds to gain a holistic perspective of the school environment.

Administrative Data

Many schools lack the resources to collect observational and survey data but may have easy access to administrative data that could provide some insight into school climate. For example, data on student and staff attendance have been used in some studies as an indicator of engagement. Related indicators of student and staff turnover have also been linked with school climate data and may signal issues of instability within the school. Even parent attendance at teacher–parent meetings or schoolwide events may provide some insight into the climate, as it indicates parent engagement. Office discipline referral data, as well as suspensions, may also provide some indication of the overall levels of disruption occurring within the school. As noted above, there is some question regarding whether these administrative data are providing insight on climate or behaviors resulting from poor climate. Nevertheless, it is helpful to triangulate multiple sources of school climate data when identifying potential areas for improvement and monitoring the impact of prevention programming.

Factors to Consider When Assessing School Climate

When assessing school climate, educators and leaders should consider the following six key factors:

1. **Chose a reliable and valid assessment.** School climate has multiple features (for example, safety, interpersonal relationships, and physical environment); thus, survey instruments should reflect the multidimensional nature of the school's culture. Schools should aim for a survey that addresses the emotional (that is, student–teacher relationships), physical (that is, bullying, physical fights), and environmental (that is, adult supervision) aspects of school climate.

2. **Assess school climate annually.** School climate should be assessed on an annual basis; thus, surveys should be quick and easy to administer. A variety of data need to be used when making decisions about universal, selective, and targeted programs. These data include, but are not limited to, students, parent, and staff surveys; discipline data (for example, office discipline referrals, suspensions); schoolwide observational data; and school demographics (for example, enrollment, student mobility). Likewise, schools should plan to reassess the school climate, celebrate improvements, and plan for the next phase of school culture enhancements as part of their yearly evaluations.

3. **Survey across multiple perspectives.** Parents, students, and staff often differ in their perceptions of the school climate (Bradshaw, Sawyer, & O'Brennan, 2009; Waasdorp, Pas, O'Brennan, & Bradshaw, 2011). Although some may debate which perspective is more accurate, it is important to understand multiple perspectives on school climate, including areas of convergence and divergence. Thus, students, families, teachers, administrators, and educational support professionals across grade levels should be involved in the school climate assessment.

4. **Triangulate data sources.** As noted above, school climate surveys are more common than observational tools. However, there may be some benefit of triangulating multiple data sources, including observations, administrative data, and survey data. Furthermore, it is important to assess climate in classroom as well as nonclassroom settings and across the school grounds.

5. **Communicate findings.** An often overlooked but critical piece of the assessment process is delivering results back to the school community. Research indicates that prevention programs not only are more effective but are more likely to be sustained over time if the entire school community (students, staff, administrators) contributes to developing the program (Hirschstein & Frey, 2006; Rigby, 2007). For example, as part of the MDS3 project, "Youth Ambassadors" were recruited to attend monthly school climate meetings as part of their service learning hours. Likewise, education support professionals, such as bus drivers, cafeteria workers, and paraprofessionals, were encouraged to participate in both the monthly meetings and implementation of evidence-based programs.

6. **Take action.** After stakeholders are informed and engaged, planning must follow. School staff can use the data and knowledge of the current school climate to determine needed steps toward improvement that match their school's unique needs. These discussions can happen via schoolwide presentations, community discussions, Parent–Teacher Association meeting presentations, and classroom discussions. These will help gain buy-in for school climate and bullying initiatives and future planning.

MODELS FOR CREATING POSITIVE SCHOOL CLIMATES

Once a school has measured the school climate and recognizes that change is necessary, educators and school leaders need to consider ways to change the school norms, values, and expectations. Although there is no one-size-fits-all program, there are common features of evidence-based practices related to school climate enhancement. Integrated and multitiered models are often the most effective approaches (Greenberg, Domitrovich, & Bumbarger, 2001; O'Connell et al., 2009). Although the use of a single targeted program may change specific problem behaviors in the school (for example, bullying), there is growing interest in the use of multicomponent approaches that provide a continuum of programs and support services that target behavior problems and address the broader social ecology of the school.

One multitiered program is Positive Behavioral Interventions and Supports (PBIS; Sugai & Horner, 2006). PBIS is a three-tiered prevention strategy that focuses on the prevention of student behavior problems and promotes a positive, collaborative school environment. School staff work together to create a schoolwide program that clearly articulates positive behavioral expectations, recognizes when students meet those expectations, and encourages data-based decision making by staff and administrators. Schools implementing PBIS have documented significant decreases in discipline problems (for example, suspensions, office discipline referrals), bullying, aggressive behavior, and concentration problems; reduced need for counseling and special education services; as well as improved academic outcomes, emotion regulation, and prosocial behavior (Bradshaw, Mitchell, & Leaf, 2010; Horner et al., 2009; Waasdorp, Bradshaw, & Leaf, 2012). It is important to note that the effects of PBIS on school climate are experienced not only among students but also among school staff (Bradshaw, Koth, et al., 2009; Horner et al., 2009).

Another three-tiered evidence-based program designed to reduce and prevent bullying and improve school climate is the Olweus Bullying Prevention Program (Olweus et al., 2007). The program is implemented across all school contexts and includes schoolwide components, classroom activities (for example, class rules against bullying, class meetings), targeted interventions for individuals identified as bullies or victims, as well as activities aimed at increasing community involvement by parents, mental health workers, and others. Previous studies of the Olweus program have demonstrated significant reductions in students' reports of bullying and antisocial behaviors (for example, fighting, theft, and truancy), as well as improvements in schools' social climate (Limber, Nation, Tracy, Melton, & Flerx, 2004; Olweus, 2005).

Social and Emotional Learning (SEL; Collaborative for Academic, Social, and Emotional Learning [CASEL], 2015) is another framework for choosing programs aimed at developing social and emotional competencies in children. This framework is based on the understanding that learning is maximized in the context of supportive relationships and engaging educational settings. SEL programs are implemented schoolwide and can improve the sense of the school as a caring, supportive environment. For instance, the Caring School Community program and the Responsive Classroom are both SEL programs that have been shown to improve student and staff perceptions of the school climate and increase positive behavior and academic performance (CASEL, 2015; Durlak, Weissberg, Dymnicki, Taylor, & Schellinger, 2011).

SUMMARY AND CONCLUSIONS

The social-ecological framework tells us that poor school climate is associated with increased bullying and negative outcomes for students and staff. In contrast, positive, schoolwide approaches to student behavior management have been shown to improve school climate and consequently have the potential to reduce bullying. Schools are encouraged to use these proactive positive approaches as an alternative to punitive approaches to bullying prevention. Yet it is important to note that there is no one quick solution for improving school climate, as any prevention effort will need to be systemic and sustained. First and foremost, regular assessment of school climate is critical in any school improvement effort. With that said, schools and districts need to either adapt the federal definition of school climate or refine it based on their school community's unique needs. Multidisciplinary teams (including educators, school psychologists, counselors, educational support professionals, and principals) are needed to regularly review data on school climate and related indicators of student behavioral, academic, and mental health concerns, as well as develop plans for improving conditions for student learning.

School staff and leaders also need professional development and resources on the importance of school climate and effective ways of improving and sustaining a positive school climate. Given the multidimensional nature of school climate, many members of the school community may have difficulty understanding the importance of climate as it relates to the functioning of the school. As a consequence, pre-service and in-service training models are needed to increase awareness of the link between school climate, bullying, and student behavior. Last, schools are encouraged to partner with other community organizations and families to promote the broader message regarding the role of school climate in reducing bullying and improving outcomes for students.

REFERENCES

Attar-Schwartz, S. (2009). Peer sexual harassment victimization at school: The roles of student characteristics, cultural affiliation, and school factors. *American Journal of Orthopsychiatry, 79*, 407–420.

Boe, E. E., Cook, L. H., & Sunderland, R. J. (2008). Teacher turnover: Examining exit attrition, teaching area transfer, and school migration. *Exceptional Children, 75*, 7–31.

Bradshaw, C. P., Koth, C. W., Thornton, L. A., & Leaf, P. J. (2009). Altering school climate through school-wide Positive Behavioral Interventions and Supports: Findings from a group-randomized effectiveness trial. *Prevention Science, 10*, 100–115. doi:10.1007/s11121-008-0114-9

Bradshaw, C. P., Milam, A. J., Furr-Holden, C. D., & Lindstrom Johnson, S. (2015). The School Assessment for Environmental Typology (SAfETy): An observational measure of school environment. *American Journal of Community Psychology, 56*, 280–329. doi:10.1007/s10464-015-9743-x

Bradshaw, C. P, Mitchell, M. M., & Leaf, P. J. (2010). Examining the effects of school-wide Positive Behavioral Interventions and Supports on student outcomes: Results from a randomized controlled effectiveness trial in elementary schools. *Journal of Positive Behavior Interventions, 12*, 133–148.

Bradshaw, C. P., Sawyer, A. L., & O'Brennan, L. M. (2009). A social disorganization perspective on bullying-related attitudes and behaviors: The influence of school context. *American Journal of Community Psychology, 43*, 204–220.

Bradshaw, C. P., Waasdorp, T. E., Debnam, K. J., & Lindstrom Johnson, S. (2014). Measuring school climate: A focus on safety, engagement, and the environment. *Journal of School Health, 84*, 593–604. doi:10.1111/josh.12186

Bradshaw, C. P., Waasdorp, T. E., O'Brennan, L., & Gulemetova, M. (2013). Teachers' and education support professionals' perspectives on bullying and prevention: Findings from a National Education Association (NEA) survey. *School Psychology Review, 42*, 280–297.

Brand, S., Felner, R., Shim, M., Seitsinger, A., & Dumas, T. (2003). Middle school improvement and reform: Development of validation of a school-level assessment of climate, cultural pluralism and school safety. *Journal of Educational Psychology, 95*, 570–588.

Bronfenbrenner, U., & Morris, P. (1998). The ecology of developmental processes. In W. Damon (Ed.), *Handbook of child psychology: Vol. 1. Theoretical models of human development* (pp. 993–1028). New York: Wiley.

Brown, K. E., & Medway, F. J. (2007). School climate and teacher beliefs in a school effectively serving poor South Carolina (USA) African-American students: A case study. *Teaching and Teacher Education, 23*, 529–540.

Cohen, J., & Geier, V. K. (2010). *School climate research summary: January 2010.* Retrieved from https://www.schoolclimate.org/climate/documents/policy/sc-brief-v1.pdf

Collaborative for Academic, Social, and Emotional Learning. (2015). *CASEL guide: Effective social and emotional learning programs, preschool and elementary school edition.* Retrieved from http://casel.org/guide/

Crowe, T. D. (1991). *Crime prevention through environmental design: Applications of architectural design and space management concepts.* Louisville, KY: National Crime Prevention Institute.

Durlak, J. A., Weissberg, R. P., Dymnicki, A. B., Taylor, R. D., & Schellinger, K. B. (2011). The impact of enhancing students' social and emotional learning: A meta-analysis of school-based universal interventions. *Child Development, 82*(1), 405–432.

Eccles, J. S., Wigfield, A., Midgley, C., Reuman, D., MacIver, D., & Feldlaufer, H. (1993). Negative effects of traditional middle schools on students' motivation. *Elementary School Journal, 93*, 553–574.

Espelage, D. L., & Swearer, S. M. (Eds.). (2004). *Bullying in American schools: A social-ecological perspective on prevention and intervention.* Hillsdale, NJ: Lawrence Erlbaum.

Gottfredson, G. D., Gottfredson, D. C., Payne, A., & Gottfredson, N. C. (2005). School climate predictors of school disorder: Results from national delinquency prevention in school. *Journal of Research in Crime and Delinquency, 42*, 421–444.

Greenberg, M. T., Domitrovich, C., & Bumbarger, B. (2001). The prevention of mental disorders in school-aged children: Current state of the field. *Prevention and Treatment, 4*, 1–62.

Gregory, A., Cornell, D., Fan, X., Sheras, P., Shih, T., & Huang, F. (2010). Authoritative school discipline: High school practices associated with lower student bullying and victimization. *Journal of Educational Psychology, 102*, 483–496.

Gruenert, S. (2008, March–April). *School culture, school climate: They are not the same thing.* Alexandria, VA: National Association of Elementary School Principals. Retrieved from https://www.naesp.org/resources/2/Principal/2008/M-Ap56.pdf

Hirschstein, M. K., & Frey, K. S. (2006). Promoting behavior and beliefs that reduce bullying: The STEPS TO RESPECT program. In S. Jimerson & M. Furlong (Eds.), *The handbook of school violence and school safety: From research to practice* (pp. 309–324). Mahwah, NJ: Lawrence Erlbaum.

Horner, R. H., Sugai, G., Smolkowski, K., Eber, L., Nakasato, J., Todd, A. W., & Esperanza, J. (2009). A randomized, wait-list controlled effectiveness trial assessing school-wide Positive Behavior Support in elementary schools. *Journal of Positive Behavior Interventions, 11*, 133–144.

Kaiser, A. (2011). *Beginning teacher attrition and mobility: Results from the first through third waves of the 2007–08 Beginning Teacher Longitudinal Study* (NCES 2011-318). Washington, DC: National Center for Education Statistics, U.S. Department of Education. Retrieved from http://nces.ed.gov/pubsearch

Limber, S. P., Nation, M., Tracy, A. J., Melton, G. B., & Flerx, V. (2004). Implementation of the Olweus Bullying Prevention programme in the Southeastern United States. In P. K. Smith, D. Pepler, & K. Rigby (Eds.), *Bullying in schools: How successful can interventions be?* (pp. 55–79). New York: Cambridge University Press.

Lindstrom Johnson, S., Waasdorp, T. E., Debnam, K. J., & Bradshaw, C. P. (2013). The role of bystander perceptions and school climate in influencing victims' responses to bullying: To retaliate or seek support? *Journal of Criminology*, article ID 780460, 1–10. doi:10.1155/2013/780460

Meyer-Adams, N., & Conner, B. T. (2008). School violence: Bullying behaviors and the psychosocial school environment in middle schools. *Children & Schools, 30*, 211–221.

National School Climate Council. (2007). *The School Climate Challenge: Narrowing the gap between school climate research and school climate policy, practice guidelines and teacher education policy.* Retrieved from http://www.schoolclimate.org/climate/documents/policy/school-climate-challenge-web.pdf

O'Connell, M. E., Boat, T., Warner, K. E., & Committee on the Prevention of Mental Disorders and Substance Abuse Among Children, Youth and Young Adults: Research Advances and Promising Interventions; Institute of Medicine; National Research Council. (2009). *Preventing mental, emotional, and behavioral disorders among young people: Progress and possibilities.* Washington, DC: National Academies Press.

Olweus, D. (2005). A useful evaluation design, and effects of the Olweus Bullying Prevention Program. *Psychology, Crime & Law, 11*, 389–402.

Olweus, D., Limber, S. P., Flerx, V. C., Mullin, N., Riese, J., & Snyder, M. (2007). *Olweus Bullying Prevention Program: Schoolwide guide.* Center City, MN: Hazelden.

Pas, E. T., Bradshaw, C. P., & Hershfeldt, P. A. (2012). Teacher- and school-level predictors of teacher efficacy and burnout: Identifying potential areas of support. *Journal of School Psychology, 50*(1), 129–145. doi:10.1016/j.jsp.2011.07.003

Pianta, R., La Paro, K., & Hamre, B. (2008). *Classroom Assessment Scoring System (CLASS) Manual: Pre-K.* Baltimore: Brookes Publishing.

Rigby, K. (2007).*Children and bullying: How parents and educators can reduce bullying at school.* Malden, MA: Wiley-Blackwell.

Ruus, V., Veisson, M., Leino, M., Ots, L., Pallas, L., Sarv, E., & Veisson, A. (2007). Students' well-being, coping, academic success, and school climate. *Social Behavior & Personality: An International Journal, 35*, 919–936.

Shochet, I. M., Dadds, M. R., Ham, D., & Montague, R. (2006). School connectedness is an underemphasized parameter in adolescent mental health: Results of a community prediction study. *Journal of Clinical Child & Adolescent Psychology, 35*, 170–179.

Singh, K., & Billingsley, B. S. (1998). Professional support and its effects on teachers' commitment. *Journal of Educational Research, 91*, 229–239.

Stewart, E. B. (2008). School structural characteristics, student effort, peer associations, and parental involvement: The influence of school- and individual-level factors on academic achievement. *Education & Urban Society, 40*(2), 179–204.

Sugai, G., & Horner, R. (2006). A promising approach for expanding and sustaining school-wide positive behavior support. *School Psychology Review, 35*, 245–259.

Thapa, A., Cohen, J., Guffey, S., & Higgins-D'Alessandro, A. (2013). A review of school climate research. *Review of Educational Research, 83*, 357–385. doi:10.3102/0034654313483907

Thapa, A., Cohen, J., Higgins-D'Alessandro, A., & Guffy, S. (2012, August). *School climate research summary* (Issue Brief No. 3). Bronx, NY: National School Climate Center.

University of Virginia. (2015, May 1). *Culture working group report to the Ad Hoc Committee on University Climate and Culture.* Charlottesville, VA: University of Virginia. Retrieved from http://www.climateandculture.virginia.edu/presidents-update-and-working-group-reports

Waasdorp, T. E., Bradshaw, C. P., & Leaf, P. J. (2012). The impact of school-wide Positive Behavioral Interventions and Supports (SWPBIS) on bullying and peer rejection: A randomized controlled effectiveness trial. *Archives of Pediatrics and Adolescent Medicine*, *116*(2), 149–156. doi:10.1001/archpediatrics.2011.755

Waasdorp, T. E., Pas, E. L., O'Brennan, L. M., & Bradshaw, C. P. (2011). A multilevel perspective on the climate of bullying: Discrepancies among students, school staff, and parents. *Journal of School Violence, 10*, 115–132.

Wang, M.-T., & Degol, J. L. (2015). School climate: A review of the construct, measurement, and impact on student outcomes. *Educational Psychology Review, 28*, 315–352. doi:10.1007/s10648-015-9319-1

15

Integrating Bullying Prevention Efforts through Positive Behavioral Interventions and Supports

Catherine P. Bradshaw

The research on the efficacy of bullying prevention programs has been mixed, with some programs demonstrating significant effects on bullying but others producing only limited impacts (for a review, see Bradshaw, 2015; Merrell, Gueldner, Ross, & Isava, 2008; Smith, Schneider, Smith, & Ananiadou, 2004; Ttofi & Farrington, 2011). Schools need guidance on which programs to implement, as well as strategies for optimizing program impacts, enhancing implementation quality, and integrating their bullying prevention work with other climate improvement efforts within the school. This is particularly challenging given the multitude of program options available, relatively few of which have been systematically studied.

A multitiered system of support model, called Positive Behavioral Interventions and Supports (PBIS; Sugai & Horner, 2006), holds promise as a framework for addressing issues related to bullying, as well as more general concerns related to school climate and student discipline problems. Recent research documents the impacts of PBIS on a range of outcomes, including bullying (for example, Bradshaw, Waasdorp, & Leaf, 2012; Horner et al., 2009; Ross & Horner, 2009; Waasdorp, Bradshaw, & Leaf, 2012); however, it also serves as a general framework for integrating other existing programs. As a result, PBIS may be particularly helpful for guiding the selection, implementation, and integration of bullying prevention efforts within the broader context of other school-based initiatives aiming to improve conditions for learning (Bradshaw, Bottiani, Osher, & Sugai, 2014). The PBIS orientation toward bullying prevention is also consistent with the movement away from zero-tolerance policies, which have historically been used as a reactive approach for addressing issues related to student discipline and bullying (American Psychological Association, 2008;

The writing of this chapter was supported in part by grants from the U.S. Department of Education and the National Institute of Justice.

Boccanfuso & Kuhfeld, 2011). The current chapter describes the multitiered PBIS framework and how it can be used to address issues related to bullying and school climate. I highlight prior research on the effectiveness of the PBIS framework for addressing issues of discipline, bullying, and school climate and summarize complementary models, which can be integrated within the three-tiered framework. The overarching goal of this chapter is to illustrate the importance of integrating prevention programs within a multitiered system of supports framework.

PUBLIC HEALTH APPROACH TO PREVENTING BULLYING AND YOUTH VIOLENCE

One can conceptualize bullying as a public health concern (Vivolo, Holt, & Massetti, 2011) and apply the tiered public health prevention framework (Mrazek & Haggerty, 1994; O'Connell, Boat, & Warner, 2009) to school-based prevention programming. We see several parallels to this approach in education through response to intervention (Hawken, Vincent, & Schumann, 2008) and other multitiered system of supports models, such as PBIS (Ross & Horner, 2009; Walker et al., 1996; also see Espelage & Swearer, 2008; Swearer, Wang, Collins, Strawhun, & Fluke, 2014). These tiered approaches include a "universal" system of support, or a set of activities that affect all students within a defined community or school setting. In fact, most of the bullying prevention programs that have been evaluated have used a universal approach to prevention, whereby a set of activities (for example, lessons) or supports are put in place to benefit all individuals within a particular setting (for example, school). Yet, consistent with the public health approach, these universal programs could fit within a tiered framework. Layered onto this are "selective" (that is, targeted) and "indicated" (that is, tailored) approaches, which are used to meet the needs of individuals at greater risk for involvement in bullying or already displaying signs and symptoms of involvement, respectively (O'Connell et al., 2009). Therefore, more intensive preventive supports are layered onto that first universal tier, thereby targeting the subgroup of at-risk students. Similarly, the third level of support includes indicated interventions for youth already showing early signs of problem behaviors; these supports often include the family and community-based services.

POSITIVE BEHAVIORAL INTERVENTIONS AND SUPPORTS

Overview

One could consider PBIS to be like an "operating system" for a school, much like an operating system on a personal computer. Similarly, PBIS helps to organize the working environment and helps create a predictable structure for organizing information and implementing programs. PBIS refers to a schoolwide application of behavioral systems and interventions to change the climate and organizational structure of schools (Horner, Sugai, & Anderson, 2010). It has the flexibility to fit a variety of school cultures and contexts and can be implemented in any school level, type, or setting from preschool through high school. There are even elements of PBIS that could be used in both higher education settings and the workplace. The model is also being implemented in alternative learning environments, special education settings, juvenile justice settings, and day and inpatient treatment settings, to name just a few. As described above, PBIS applies a three-tiered, public health systemwide framework (Mrazek & Haggerty, 1994; O'Connell et al., 2009; Walker et al., 1996) for implementing a continuum of behavioral and academic programs and services in which universal (Tier 1, schoolwide), selective (Tier 2), and indicated (Tier 3) systems promote outcomes for students (see Figure 15.1). The universal elements of the model, typically referred to as schoolwide PBIS, are the most commonly implemented aspect of the three-tiered model. Currently, over 22,000 schools have participated in the implementation of the universal schoolwide elements of PBIS (http://www.pbis.org).

The tiered PBIS model focuses on the academic, behavioral, and environmental context in which behavior problems occur. Applying PBIS, schools establish a set of positively stated, schoolwide expectations for student behavior (for example, "Be respectful, responsible, and ready to learn"), which are developed by the school's PBIS team and taught to all students and staff. A schoolwide system is then developed to reward students who exhibit the expected positive behaviors, often through the use of tangible reinforcements, such as tickets, parties, prizes, or special privileges like an opportunity to have lunch with a favorite teacher or administrator. PBIS focuses on replacing discrete behaviors (for example, tardiness, attendance problems, fighting) that repeatedly divert staff time and contribute to chaotic learning environments with prosocial behaviors consistent with the behavioral expectations.

PBIS aims to change adult behavior and the way adults interact with students to promote consistency across school contexts. There is a strong emphasis on schoolwide implementation, which requires staff buy-in and is facilitated through a team-based process. Each PBIS school forms a PBIS team, which is composed of a teacher from each grade level, at least one administrator, and student support staff. The PBIS team is led by a PBIS team leader, who is often an administrator or experienced teacher. A coaching process is used at the school, district, and state level to promote high-fidelity implementation through

Figure 15.1: The Three-Tiered Framework

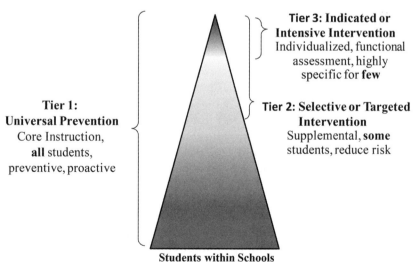

Tier 3: Indicated or Intensive Intervention
Individualized, functional assessment, highly specific for **few**

Tier 1: Universal Prevention
Core Instruction, **all** students, preventive, proactive

Tier 2: Selective or Targeted Intervention
Supplemental, **some** students, reduce risk

Students within Schools

Note: Schools can list different programs and strategies being used across the three tiers, which will enable the identification of strengths and gaps in tiered prevention programming. Figure adapted from material at PBIS.org.

ongoing progress monitoring. PBIS coaches can be either internal or external to the school and are typically school psychologists, guidance counselors, social workers, or other staff who have expertise in behavior management and functional behavioral assessment. A district and state-level support team is also formed to provide training and technical assistance related to PBIS (Sugai & Horner, 2006).

PBIS is a data-informed approach (Irvin et al., 2006; Sugai & Horner, 2006) that emphasizes the collection of multiple data elements on both desired and problem behaviors to monitor implementation quality and program outcomes. The school's PBIS team regularly reviews multiple data elements, such as office discipline referrals (for example, number of events per day, type of event, location and characteristics of problem behaviors), and develops interventions accordingly for the whole school, groups of students, or individual students. The data are also used to determine whether the behavioral interventions implemented for individual students or groups of students are producing the desired effects. In addition, data are used to monitor PBIS implementation fidelity, as several instruments have been created to assess the extent to which the critical features of PBIS are in place within a school (for example, Bradshaw, Debnam, Koth, & Leaf, 2009; Horner et al., 2004).

Empirical Support

Increasing evidence suggests that successful implementation of schoolwide or the universal (Tier 1) PBIS system is associated with sustainable changes in disciplinary practices and improved systems to promote positive behavior among students (Barrett, Bradshaw, & Lewis-Palmer, 2008; Bradshaw, Reinke, Brown, Bevans, & Leaf, 2008; Horner et al., 2009, 2010). Quality implementation of schoolwide PBIS has been linked with significant reductions in disruptive behaviors and improved social skill knowledge (Barrett et al., 2008; Horner et al., 2009). Several studies, including two randomized controlled trials of schoolwide PBIS in elementary schools, have shown that high-quality implementation of the model is associated with significant reductions in office discipline referrals and suspensions (Bradshaw, Mitchell, & Leaf, 2010; Horner et al., 2009) and other problem behavior, such as teacher ratings of classroom behavior problems, concentration problems, emotion regulation problems, and bullying perpetration and peer rejection (Bradshaw, Waasdorp, & Leaf, 2012; Waasdorp et al., 2012).

Significant improvements also have been documented on teachers' ratings of students' prosocial behavior (Bradshaw, Waasdorp, & Leaf, 2012), student reports of school climate (Horner et al., 2009), staff reports of the school's organizational health (for example, principal leadership, teacher affiliation, and academic emphasis) (Bradshaw, Koth, Bevans, Ialongo, & Leaf, 2008; Bradshaw, Koth, Thornton & Leaf, 2009), teacher self-efficacy, and academic achievement (Bradshaw et al., 2010; Horner et al., 2009). Improvements in the schools' organizational context achieved through PBIS may enhance the implementation quality of other more intensive preventive interventions (Bradshaw, Koth, et al., 2009) and reduce the need for more intensive school-based services (Bradshaw, Waasdorp, & Leaf, 2012). Research indicates that the impact of PBIS may vary as a function of the child's risk profile or the age at which she or he is first introduced to a PBIS environment (Bradshaw, Waasdorp, & Leaf, 2012, 2015; Waasdorp et al., 2012). Furthermore, in a randomized controlled trial of PBIS in which the universal, schoolwide PBIS model was contrasted with selective preventive interventions in combination with schoolwide PBIS, significant impacts were demonstrated on teacher efficacy, academic performance, and special education service use (Bradshaw, Pas, Goldweber, Rosenberg, & Leaf, 2012).

Although much of the systematic research on PBIS has been at the elementary level, a recent randomized trial of PBIS in 58 high schools demonstrated significant impacts on school climate and student behavior. In this trial, high schools used school climate data to guide the selection and implementation of other evidence-based bullying prevention and school climate promotion programs for integration across the three tiers. Preliminary findings from this high school trial indicate significant impacts on weapon carrying, being threatened or injured by a weapon, skipping school because of a fear for safety, marijuana use, and engagement (Bradshaw, Debnam, et al., 2014). It is interesting to note that schools with higher baseline rates of bullying generally implemented PBIS with greater fidelity. This suggests that schools with increased bullying may be particularly motivated to adopt PBIS (Bradshaw, Pas, Debnam, & Lindstrom Johnson, 2015). Taken together, these findings and others from prior studies suggest that PBIS is a promising approach for improving school climate and reducing behavior problems, including bullying (for a more comprehensive review, see Horner et al., 2010).

APPLYING PBIS AND THE TIERED FRAMEWORK TO BULLYING PREVENTION

Consistent with the social-ecological framework (Espelage & Swearer, 2004), schools should address the social environment and the broader culture and climate of bullying (Bradshaw & Waasdorp, 2009). Research documents the importance of schoolwide prevention efforts that provide positive behavior support, establish a common set of expectations for positive behavior across all school contexts, and involve all school staff in prevention activities (Ross & Horner, 2009). Effective supervision—especially in bullying "hot spots"—and clear antibullying policies are essential elements of a successful schoolwide prevention effort (Olweus, 1993). The ongoing data collection efforts through the PBIS framework can help identify where, when, and for whom behavior problems, like bullying, are occurring (Irvin et al., 2006). For example, the playground appears to be a particularly important context for increasing supervision to prevent bullying in elementary schools (Frey et al., 2005; Leff, Power, Costigan, & Manz, 2003; Ttofi & Farrington, 2011), but the classroom continues to be the context where most bullying occurs, merely because students spend more time in the classroom than in any other context (Bradshaw, Sawyer, & O'Brennan, 2007). Collecting data on bullying via anonymous student surveys can inform the supervision and intervention process. These data can identify potential areas for intensive training for school staff, which is an essential element of successful bullying prevention efforts (Ttofi & Farrington, 2011). Data are also critical for monitoring progress toward the goal of reducing bullying (Olweus, 1993). The high rates of bullying in the classroom also highlight the need for effective classroom management strategies as a universal approach for improving the conditions for learning. Yet teachers need additional training in both the detection and de-escalation of bullying behaviors. Coaching supports and intensive guided practice may be needed to address challenges related to both detection and intervention (Bradshaw, 2015).

Families also play a critical role in bullying prevention by promoting the disclosure of bullying incidents and by fostering coping skills in their children. Parents need training in how to talk with their children about bullying, how to communicate their concerns about bullying to the school, and how to get actively involved in school-based bullying prevention efforts (Waasdorp, Bradshaw, & Duong, 2011). There also are important bullying prevention activities that can occur at the community level. These can include awareness or social marketing campaigns that encourage all youth and adults—such as doctors, police officers, and storekeepers—to intervene when they see bullying and to become actively involved in school- and community-based prevention activities (Olweus, 1993; Olweus et al., 2007). Through the PBIS framework, parents can receive training on supporting the home–school connection and setting consistent expectations for positive behavior across settings (Ross & Horner, 2009).

In applying this framework to prevent bullying in schools, a tiered approach might include lessons on social-emotional skill development for all students—thus making it a universal program. In fact, research highlights the importance of providing class time to discuss bullying (Olweus, 1993) and the use of lessons to foster skills and competencies, effective communication, and strategies for responding to bullying (Ttofi & Farrington, 2011); such strategies can also have a positive impact on academic and other behavioral outcomes (Durlak, Weissberg, Dymnicki, Taylor, & Schellinger, 2011). Effective classroom management is also critical, as well-managed classrooms are rated as having a more favorable climate, being safer and more supportive, and having lower rates of bullying (Koth, Bradshaw, & Leaf, 2008). At the second tier, selective interventions may include social skills training for small groups of children at risk for becoming involved in bullying. Finally, an indicated preventive intervention (Tier 3) may include more intensive supports and programs tailored to meet the needs of students identified as a bully or victim and the needs of their families (Espelage & Swearer, 2008; Ross & Horner, 2009). Unfortunately, relatively few large-scale studies have been conducted examining the effects of multitiered programs on bullying, as much of the available research has aimed to address bullying at the universal level (Bradshaw, 2015). Nevertheless, several researchers have encouraged the use of a multitiered approach when aiming to prevent bullying and other forms of youth violence (for example, Bradshaw & Waasdorp, 2009; Espelage & Swearer, 2008; Olweus et al., 2007; Swearer et al., 2014; Vivolo et al., 2011; Waasdorp et al., 2012). For additional information regarding specific Tier 2 and 3 programs that can be used to address the issue of bullying, see chapter 17. Figure 15.1 may also serve as a tool that educators and school leaders can use to list the programs they are implementing across the three tiers. Completing the boxes by listing the different programs currently in place across these three tiers may illustrate both gaps as well as strengths in existing programming.

INTEGRATING PREVENTION EFFORTS THROUGH PBIS

It is important to consider how schools can integrate bullying prevention efforts with their other existing programs and supports. Research by Gottfredson and Gottfredson (2001) indicates that, on average, schools are using about 14 different strategies or programs to prevent violence and promote a safe learning environment. This influx of information can often be overwhelming for school staff to execute well, thereby leading to poor implementation fidelity. Therefore, schools are encouraged to integrate their prevention efforts so that there is a seamless system of support (Domitrovich et al., 2010), which is coordinated and monitored for high-fidelity implementation and includes all staff across all school contexts. Instead of adopting a different program to combat each new problem that emerges, it is recommended that schools develop a consistent and long-term prevention plan that addresses multiple student concerns through a set of well-integrated programs and services. Such efforts would address multiple competencies and skills to prevent bullying and help students cope and respond appropriately when bullying does occur. The three-tiered public health model provides a framework for connecting bullying prevention with other programs to address bullying within the broader set of behavioral and academic concerns (Walker et al., 1996).

PBIS provides a framework for the integration of programs and services. Students whose needs are not fully met by a universal bullying prevention program or a universal system of positive behavior support (Sugai & Horner, 2006) would require targeted or individually tailored preventive interventions based on systematic assessment of their needs (Debnam, Pas, & Bradshaw, 2012; Hawken et al., 2008; Sugai et al., 2000; Walker et al., 1996). Like other tiered prevention models, such as response to intervention, PBIS emphasizes data-based decision making, continuous progress monitoring, a continuum of evidence-based interventions, and monitoring of implementation fidelity (Hawken et al., 2008). Through review of data at the child, classroom, or school level, other more intensive evidence-based practices can be selected to meet the needs of the target population. The PBIS framework provides an opportunity for integration of programs to meet a range of student social and emotional learning needs. Other complementary evidence-based practices can be implemented and integrated through the use of the PBIS common language, logic, and structure. Integration of various programs through PBIS may also result in more sustainable changes in the school environment and optimize outcomes for the student (Domitrovich et al., 2010; Sugai & Horner, 2006).

PBIS also provides an enhanced organizational context, which may actually optimize implementation quality of other bullying prevention programs. As Han and Weiss (2005) noted, "sustainability is likely to occur only in the context of institutionalization of systemic changes in attitudes, expectations, support mechanisms, and infrastructure" (p. 667). Therefore, a multilevel, schoolwide discipline framework that has documented effects on promoting organizational climate and reducing problem behaviors across school settings (for example, Bradshaw, Koth, et al., 2009; Bradshaw et al., 2010) may provide the optimal context for enhancing the implementation quality and outcomes achieved by bullying prevention programs. The organizational framework offered by PBIS may help encourage sustained implementation of bullying prevention programs. For example, PBIS can provide a schoolwide context in which the skills can be taught, practiced, and reinforced throughout the day. Moreover, by improving schoolwide climate and behavior management practices across school settings, PBIS may enhance the implementation quality and effects of classroom-based bullying prevention efforts (Domitrovich et al., 2008, 2010). Furthermore, PBIS has been shown to increase the amount of instructional time available to teachers (Scott & Barrett, 2004), which makes it more likely that teachers will have the class time to administer classroom-based programs as intended.

IMPORTANT FACTORS TO CONSIDER WHEN IMPLEMENTING AND INTEGRATING PROGRAMS

There has been a movement toward the use of "packaged" evidence-based prevention programs over the past several years. The work by Ttofi and Farrington (2011) sheds some light on the most efficacious elements of multicomponent bullying prevention programs. However, schools should be cautious when implementing just a few components of a program, as they may not produce the same effects when implemented in isolation. The cost and related resource needs may also serve as barriers to implementing the more rigorously tested evidence-based prevention programs. Getting buy-in from all students and staff is critical to the success of any prevention effort, especially for multicomponent schoolwide models, which can be difficult to implement with high fidelity (Bradshaw, Koth et al., 2009; Durlak et al., 2011). Research highlights a number of contextual factors, like principal leadership, staff attitudes toward the program, and the availability of resources that affect implementation quality (Domitrovich et al., 2008). Therefore, considerable pre-implementation planning is needed to garner staff support and buy-in for the program and to integrate the new program with existing supports and services (Limber, 2004). The PBIS model also places great emphasis on obtaining staff buy-in and the role of principal leadership in supporting a successful launch of the framework within a school (Debnam et al., 2012).

Once implemented, the collection of fidelity and outcome data is critical to ensuring high-quality implementation, tracking progress toward outcomes, and promoting sustainability. Unfortunately, most programs lack valid and efficient tools for tracking implementation fidelity, and regular assessments of self-reports of bullying can be costly and burdensome for some schools. Many schools find it helpful to use the PBIS team to lead the implementation and help with the integration of programs and the program monitoring process (Limber, 2004). An implementation specialist or PBIS coach can also be helpful in ensuring high-quality implementation of bullying prevention programs. Changing school climate and the culture of bullying is difficult and requires sustained and intensive commitment from all students, staff, families, and the community. The development of an implementation infrastructure, at the school, district, and state level, is essential to scaling up the available research-based programs (for examples of statewide scale-up of PBIS, see Barrett et al., 2008; Bradshaw, Debnam, et al., 2014; Bradshaw & Pas, 2011; Bradshaw, Pas, Bloom, et al., 2012).

CONCLUSIONS AND RECOMMENDATIONS

The findings summarized in this chapter illustrate the potential utility of PBIS as a multitiered system of supports for addressing bullying, school climate, and other discipline problems. Although the focus here has been largely on behavior, it is also highly relevant for addressing academics. Various tiers within the model have been tested, both independently and in combination (see Horner et al., 2010), but the strength of the model is largely in the data, systems, and practices that are installed to optimize the organization of the school's initiatives, and efforts related to prevention and promotion. This proactive positive approach to discipline is likely to be more attractive to multiple stakeholders and more easily integrated with other existing initiatives. Additional professional development is needed for staff related to the implementation of classroom-based supports, as well as for student services staff related to the implementation of programs across the advanced tiers.

REFERENCES

American Psychological Association, Zero Tolerance Task Force. (2008). Are zero tolerance policies effective in the schools? An evidentiary review and recommendations. *American Psychologist, 63*, 852–862.

Barrett, S., Bradshaw, C. P., & Lewis-Palmer, T. (2008). Maryland state-wide PBIS initiative: Systems, evaluation, and next steps. *Journal of Positive Behavior Interventions, 10*, 105–114.

Boccanfuso, C., & Kuhfeld, M. (2011). *Multiple responses, promising results: Evidence-based, nonpunitive alternatives to zero tolerance* (Research-to-Results Brief, Publication #2011-09). Washington, DC: Child Trends.

Bradshaw, C. P. (2015). Translating research to practice in bullying prevention. *American Psychologist, 70*, 322–332.

Bradshaw, C. P., Bottiani, J., Osher, D., & Sugai, G. (2014). Integrating Positive Behavioral Interventions and Supports (PBIS) and social emotional learning. In M. D. Weist, N. A. Lever, C. P. Bradshaw, & J. Owens (Eds.), *Handbook of school mental health: Advancing practice and research* (2nd ed.). New York: Springer.

Bradshaw, C. P., Debnam, K. J., Koth, C., & Leaf, P. J. (2009). Preliminary validation of the Implementation Phases Inventory for assessing fidelity of school-wide Positive Behavior Supports. *Journal of Positive Behavior Interventions, 11*, 145–160.

Bradshaw, C. P., Debnam, K. J., Lindstrom Johnson, S., Pas, E., Hershfeldt, P., Alexander, A., et al. (2014). Maryland's evolving system of social, emotional, and behavioral interventions in public schools: The Maryland Safe and Supportive Schools Project. *Adolescent Psychiatry, 4*(3), 194–206.

Bradshaw, C. P., Koth, C. W., Bevans, K. B., Ialongo, N., & Leaf, P. J. (2008). The impact of school-wide Positive Behavioral Interventions and Supports (PBIS) on the organizational health of elementary schools. *School Psychology Quarterly, 23*, 462–473.

Bradshaw, C. P., Koth, C. W., Thornton, L. A., & Leaf, P. J. (2009). Altering school climate through school-wide Positive Behavioral Interventions and Supports: Findings from a group-randomized effectiveness trial. *Prevention Science, 10*, 100–115.

Bradshaw, C. P., Mitchell, M. M., & Leaf, P. J. (2010). Examining the effects of school-wide Positive Behavioral Interventions and Supports on student outcomes: Results from a randomized controlled effectiveness trial in elementary schools. *Journal of Positive Behavior Interventions, 12*, 133–148.

Bradshaw, C. P., & Pas, E. T. (2011). A state-wide scale-up of Positive Behavioral Interventions and Supports (PBIS): A description of the development of systems of support and analysis of adoption and implementation. *School Psychology Review, 40*, 530–548.

Bradshaw, C. P., Pas, E., Bloom, J., Barrett, S., Hershfeldt, P., Alexander, A., et al. (2012). A state-wide collaboration to promote safe and supportive schools: The PBIS Maryland Initiative. *Administration and Policy in Mental Health and Mental Health Services Research, 39*(4), 225–237.

Bradshaw, C. P., Pas, E., Debnam, K., & Lindstrom Johnson, S. (2015). A focus on implementation of Positive Behavioral Interventions and Supports (PBIS) in high schools: Associations with bullying and school disorder. *School Psychology Review, 44*, 480–498.

Bradshaw, C. P., Pas, E. T., Goldweber, A., Rosenberg, M., & Leaf, P. (2012). Integrating school-wide Positive Behavioral Interventions and Supports with tier 2 coaching to student support teams: The PBISplus Model. *Advances in School Mental Health Promotion, 5*(3), 177–193.

Bradshaw, C. P., Reinke, W. M., Brown, L. D., Bevans, K. B., & Leaf, P. J. (2008). Implementation of school-wide Positive Behavioral Interventions and Supports (PBIS) in elementary schools: Observations from a randomized trial. *Education & Treatment of Children, 31*, 1–26.

Bradshaw, C. P., Sawyer, A. L., & O'Brennan, L. M. (2007). Bullying and peer victimization at school: Perceptual differences between students and school staff. *School Psychology Review, 36*, 361–382.

Bradshaw, C. P., & Waasdorp, T. E. (2009). Measuring and changing a "culture of bullying." *School Psychology Review, 38*, 356–361.

Bradshaw, C. P., Waasdorp, T. E., & Leaf, P. J. (2012). Effects of school-wide Positive Behavioral Interventions and Supports on child behavior problems. *Pediatrics, 130,* e1136–e1145.

Bradshaw, C. P., Waasdorp, T. E., & Leaf, P. J. (2015). Examining variation in the impact of school-wide Positive Behavioral Interventions and Supports: Findings from a randomized controlled effectiveness trial. *Journal of Educational Psychology, 107,* 546–557.

Debnam, K. J., Pas, E., & Bradshaw, C. P. (2012). Secondary and tertiary support systems in schools implementing school-wide Positive Behavioral Interventions and Supports: A preliminary descriptive analysis. *Journal of Positive Behavior Interventions, 14,* 142–152.

Domitrovich, C. E., Bradshaw, C. P., Greenberg, M. T., Embry, D., Poduska, J., & Ialongo, N. S. (2010). Integrated preventive interventions: The theory and logic. *Psychology in the Schools, 47*(1), 71–88.

Domitrovich, C. E., Bradshaw, C. P., Poduska, J., Hoagwood, K., Buckley, J., Olin, S., et al. (2008). Maximizing the implementation quality of evidence-based preventive interventions in schools: A conceptual framework. *Advances in School Mental Health Promotion: Training and Practice, Research and Policy, 1*(3), 6–28.

Durlak, J. A., Weissberg, R. P., Dymnicki, A. B., Taylor, R. D., & Schellinger, K. B. (2011). The impact of enhancing students' social and emotional learning: A meta-analysis of school-based universal interventions. *Child Development, 82*(1), 405–432.

Espelage, D. L., & Swearer S. M. (2004). *Bullying in American schools: A social-ecological perspective on prevention and intervention.* Mahwah, NJ: Lawrence Erlbaum.

Espelage, D. L., & Swearer, S. M. (2008). Current perspectives on linking school bullying research to effective prevention strategies. In T. W. Miller (Ed.), *School violence and primary prevention* (pp. 335–353). Secaucus, NJ: Springer.

Frey, K. S., Hirschstein, M. K., Snell, J. L., Edstrom, L.V.S., MacKenzie, E. P., & Broderick, C. J. (2005). Reducing playground bullying and supporting beliefs: An experimental trial of the steps to respect program. *Developmental Psychology, 41,* 479–491.

Gottfredson, G. D., & Gottfredson, D. C. (2001). What schools do to prevent problem behavior and promote safe environments. *Journal of Educational and Psychological Consultation, 12,* 313–344.

Han, S. S., & Weiss, B. (2005). Sustainability of teacher implementation of school-based mental health programs. *Journal of Abnormal Child Psychology, 33,* 665–679.

Hawken, L. S., Vincent, C. G., & Schumann, J. (2008). Response to intervention for social behavior: Challenges and opportunities. *Journal of Emotional and Behavioral Disorders, 16,* 213–225.

Horner, R. H., Sugai, G., & Anderson, C. M. (2010). Examining the evidence base for school-wide positive behavior support. *Focus on Exceptional Children, 42*(8), 1–14.

Horner, R. H., Sugai, G., Smolkowski, K., Eber, L., Nakasato, J., Todd, A. W., & Esperanza, J. (2009). A randomized, wait-list controlled effectiveness trial assessing school-wide positive behavior support in elementary schools. *Journal of Positive Behavior Interventions, 11,* 133–144.

Horner, R. H., Todd, A. W., Lewis-Palmer, T., Irvin, L. K., Sugai, G., & Boland, J. B. (2004). The school-wide evaluation tool (SET): A research instrument for assessing school-wide positive behavior support. *Journal of Positive Behavior Interventions, 6,* 3–12.

Irvin, L. K., Horner, R. H., Ingram, K., Todd, A. W., Sugai, G., Sampson, N. K., & Boland, J. B. (2006). Using office discipline referral data for decision making about student behavior in elementary and middle schools: An empirical evaluation of validity. *Journal of Positive Behavior Interventions, 8*(1), 10–23.

Koth, C. W., Bradshaw, C. P., & Leaf, P. J. (2008). A multilevel study of predictors of student perceptions of school climate: The effect of classroom-level factors. *Journal of Educational Psychology, 100,* 96–104.

Leff, S., Power, T., Costigan, T., & Manz, P. (2003). Assessing the climate of the playground and lunchroom: Implications for bullying prevention programming. *School Psychology Review, 32,* 418–430.

Limber, S. P. (2004). Implementation of the Olweus Bullying Prevention Program: Lessons learned from the field. In D. Espelage & S. Swearer (Eds.), *Bullying in American schools: A social-ecological perspective on prevention and intervention* (pp. 351–363). Mahwah, NJ: Lawrence Erlbaum.

Merrell, K. W., Gueldner, B. A., Ross, S. W., & Isava, D. M. (2008). How effective are school bullying intervention programs? A meta-analysis of intervention research. *School Psychology Quarterly, 23,* 26–42.

Mrazek, P. J., & Haggerty, R. J. (1994). *Reducing risks for mental disorders: Frontiers for preventive intervention research.* Washington, DC: Institute of Medicine, National Academies Press.

O'Connell, M. E., Boat, T., & Warner, K. E. (2009). *Preventing mental, emotional, and behavioral disorders among young people: Progress and possibilities.* Washington, DC: Institute of Medicine, National Research Council, National Academies Press.

Olweus, D. (1993). *Bullying at school.* Oxford, England: Blackwell.

Olweus, D., Limber, S. P., Flerx, V. C., Mullin, N., Riese, J., & Snyder, M. (2007). *Olweus Bullying Prevention Program: Schoolwide guide.* Center City, MN: Hazelden.

Ross, S. W., & Horner, R. H. (2009). Bully prevention in positive behavior support. *Journal of Applied Behavior Analysis, 42,* 747–759.

Scott, T., & Barrett, S. (2004). Using staff and student time engaged in disciplinary procedures to evaluate the impact of school wide PBS. *Journal of Positive Behavior Intervention, 6*(1), 21–27.

Smith, J., Schneider, B., Smith, P., & Ananiadou, K. (2004). The effectiveness of whole-school antibullying programs: A synthesis of evaluation research. *School Psychology Review, 33,* 547–560.

Sugai, G., & Horner, R. (2006). A promising approach for expanding and sustaining schoolwide positive behavior support. *School Psychology Review, 35,* 245–259.

Sugai, G., Horner, R., Dunlap, G., Hieneman, M., Lewis, T. J., Nelson, C. M., et al. (2000). Applying positive behavior supports and functional behavioral assessment in schools. *Journal of Positive Behavior Interventions, 2,* 131–143.

Swearer, S., Wang, C., Collins, A., Strawhun, J., & Fluke, S. (2014). Bullying: A school mental health perspective. In M. D. Weist, N. A. Lever, C. P. Bradshaw, & J. Owens (Eds.). *Handbook of School Mental Health: Advancing Practice and Research* (2nd ed., pp. 341–354). New York: Springer.

Ttofi, M. M., & Farrington, D. P. (2011). Effectiveness of school-based programs to reduce bullying: A systematic and meta-analytic review. *Journal of Experimental Criminology, 7*(1), 27–56.

Vivolo, A. M., Holt, M. K., & Massetti, G. M. (2011). Individual and contextual factors for bullying and peer victimization: Implications for prevention. *Journal of School Violence, 10*(2), 201–212. doi:10.1080/15388220.2010.539169

Waasdorp, T. E., Bradshaw, C. P., & Duong, J. (2011). The link between parents' perceptions of the school and their responses to school bullying: Variation by child characteristics and the forms of victimization. *Journal of Educational Psychology, 103*(2), 324–335.

Waasdorp, T. E., Bradshaw, C. P., & Leaf, P. J. (2012). The impact of School-Wide Positive Behavioral Interventions and Supports (SWPBIS) on bullying and peer rejection: A randomized controlled effectiveness trial. *Archives of Pediatrics and Adolescent Medicine, 116*(2), 149–156.

Walker, H., Horner, R. H., Sugai, G., Bullis, M., Sprague, J., Bricker, D., & Kaufman, M. J. (1996). Integrated approaches to preventing antisocial behavior patterns among school-age children and youth. *Journal of Emotional and Behavioral Disorders, 4,* 194–209.

16

Lessons Learned from Scaling Up the Olweus Bullying Prevention Program

Susan P. Limber and Dan Olweus

Although bullying is an ancient phenomenon, systematic research on the nature and prevalence of bullying and efforts to systematically prevent and address bullying are fairly recent. The earliest studies on bullying were conducted in the 1970s in Scandinavia (Olweus, 1973, 1978), and although international interest grew slowly in the 1980s and early 1990s, it was not until the late 1990s and 2000s that attention to bullying exploded among researchers, policymakers, and the general public in the United States and in many other countries around the globe. The first systematic attempts to prevent bullying also can be traced to Scandinavia. In 1983, the Norwegian Ministry of Education initiated a national campaign against bullying in schools in response to public concerns fueled by the suicides of three severely bullied teenage boys. What later became known as the Olweus Bullying Prevention Program (OBPP) was developed, implemented, and evaluated within this context (Olweus, 1991; Olweus & Limber, 2010a). In the 30 years since its initial development, aspects of the OBPP naturally have been adapted to be responsive to different cultural and educational conditions, recent research, and technological advances; however, the principles of the OBPP and its core elements have remained intact. In this chapter, we provide an overview of the principles and core elements of the OBPP and briefly summarize research on its effectiveness (both in Scandinavia and initial studies in the United States). We then describe a recent large-scale effort in Pennsylvania to implement and evaluate the OBPP, summarize the effects of these efforts, and highlight some lessons learned in supporting these endeavors.

OVERVIEW OF THE OBPP

The OBPP is a comprehensive, school-based program designed to reduce the prevalence of existing bullying problems, prevent the development of new problems, and improve peer relations at the school (Olweus et al., 2007a, 2007b). Although the OBPP has been used with students from grades three to 12, the primary focus until recent years has been on elementary and middle school grades. Recognizing that risk factors for bullying others include a lack of parental warmth and involvement, supervision, and clear rules to govern children's behavior (Olweus, 1993), the OBPP was built on the following four principles. Adults in a school setting (and ideally at home) should (a) show warmth and positive interest in students; (b) set firm limits to unacceptable behavior; (c) use consistent, nonhostile, and developmentally appropriate consequences when rules for behavior are not followed; and (d) act as authorities and positive role models for children and youth. Components of the program are implemented at four levels: the schoolwide level, the classroom level, the individual level, and the community level (see Table 16.1). (For a detailed description of the program components, see Olweus & Limber, 2010b; Olweus et al., 2007.)

EFFECTIVENESS OF THE OBPP

The OBPP has been extensively evaluated in Norway through seven, mostly large-scale studies. In the initial evaluation, which involved 2,500 students in grades 5–8, Olweus and colleagues documented marked reductions in students' reports of being bullied (by 62 percent after 8 months and 64 percent after 20 months) and bullying others (reductions of 33 percent after 8 months and 53 percent after 20 months) and significant improvements in aspects of school climate, including improvements in students' satisfaction with school life and more positive social relationships (Olweus, 1991, 1994, 1997, 2005; Olweus & Limber, 2010a, 2010b). When key program elements were implemented with higher fidelity, there were more positive program outcomes (Olweus & Alsaker, 1991; Olweus & Kallestad, 2010). Six follow-up evaluations in Norway, involving more than 20,000 students from more than 150 schools, have revealed consistently positive program effects among students in grades 4–7 (Olweus & Limber, 2010b) and positive but less consistent and weaker program effects among students in grades 8–10 (Olweus & Limber, 2010a). Notably, a five-year follow-up study of students in 14 schools revealed that the program effects were sustained over time, as self-reports of being bullied decreased by 40 percent and self-reports of bullying others decreased 51 percent over five years (Olweus & Limber, 2010a).

A smaller number of studies have evaluated the OBPP in diverse settings in the United States, with somewhat mixed results. In a study of elementary and middle school students in six school districts in rural South Carolina, researchers found positive program effects on students' self-reports of bullying others, delinquency, vandalism, and school misbehavior but no program effects on students' reports of being bullied (Limber, Nation, Tracy, Melton, & Flerx, 2004). Bauer and colleagues (Bauer, Lozano, & Rivara, 2007) used a nonrandomized controlled study design to evaluate the OBPP with students in 10 middle schools in Washington state. Positive program effects were observed for relational and physical victimization among white students (but not for students of other races) and for all students' perceptions that peers actively intervened in bullying incidents. In a subsequent study, Black and Jackson (2007) evaluated the OBPP in six large public elementary and middle schools in Philadelphia with predominantly minority students (82 percent African

Table 16.1: Components of the Olweus Bullying Prevention Program

General Requirement
Generate awareness and involvement on the part of the adults in the school

School-Level Components
- Establish a Bullying Prevention Coordinating Committee.
- Conduct committee and staff trainings.
- Administer the Olweus Bullying Questionnaire schoolwide.
- Hold staff discussion group meetings.
- Introduce the school rules against bullying, using consistent, developmentally appropriate positive and negative consequences for behavior.
- Review and refine the school's supervisory system.
- Hold a school kick-off event to launch the program.
- Involve parents.

Classroom-Level Components
- Post and enforce schoolwide rules against bullying.
- Hold regular class meetings.
- Hold meetings with students' parents.

Individual-Level Components
- Supervise students' activities.
- Ensure that all staff intervene on the spot when bullying occurs.
- Hold meetings with students involved in bullying (typically separately).
- Hold meetings with parents of involved students.
- Develop individual intervention plans for involved students.

Community-Level Components
- Involve community members on the Bullying Prevention Coordinating Committee.
- Develop partnerships with community members to support your school's program.
- Help to spread antibullying messages and principles of best practice in the community.

Adapted from D. Olweus, S. P. Limber, V. Flerx, N. Mullin, J. Riese, & M. Snyder (2007), *Olweus Bullying Prevention Program: Schoolwide guide*, Center City, MN: Hazelden. Copyright © Hazelden Foundation. Reprinted by permission of Hazelden Foundation, Center City, MN.

American, 10 percent Latino) from predominantly low-income families. Over the course of four years, researchers found reductions in observations of bullying (using an observational measure of bullying incident density to identify incidents of physical, verbal, and emotional bullying during recess or lunch time) of 45 percent over four years.

Several meta-analyses and systematic reviews of school-based bullying prevention programs have been conducted (Baldry & Farrington, 2007; Farrington & Ttofi, 2009; Ferguson, San Miguel, Kilburn, & Sanchez, 2007; Merrell, Gueldner, Ross, & Isava, 2008; Polanin, Espelage, & Pigott, 2012; Smith, Schneider, Smith, & Ananiadou, 2004; Ttofi & Farrington, 2011; Vreeman & Carroll, 2007). Some of the reviews have been relatively pessimistic in their conclusions about the effectiveness of bullying prevention programs in schools (Ferguson et al., 2007; Merrell et al., 2008), although other reviewers have been much more optimistic (Farrington & Ttofi, 2009; Polanin et al., 2012; Ttofi & Farrington, 2011). The most comprehensive meta-analysis to date was conducted by Ttofi and Farrington (Farrington & Ttofi, 2009; Ttofi & Farrington, 2011), who analyzed 44 different studies and determined that school-based bullying prevention programs were effective in reducing bullying perpetration by an average of 20–23 percent and bullying victimization by an average of 17–20 percent. It should be noted that there was great variation among the programs in terms of methodological quality and success rate. In addition, the evaluations of all programs except the OBPP were first-time ("efficacy") studies. Ttofi and Farrington (2011) further assessed elements of bullying prevention programs that were positively related to decreases in rates of bullying, including a whole-school approach; teacher training; increased supervision on playgrounds; classroom rules about bullying; classroom management; and teacher meetings, training, and information. They noted that programs "inspired by the work of Dan Olweus worked best" (Ttofi & Farrington, 2011, pp. 41–42), but they also highlighted that in their review of studies, program effects were stronger in Norway compared with the United States and Canada.

Common Challenges

Although comprehensive bullying prevention programs hold much promise for reducing bullying within a school environment, educators seeking to implement schoolwide programs such as the OBPP face some common challenges: those related to staff resistance, a lack of readiness, a short-term focus, and fidelity of implementation (Limber, 2011). Below we consider these factors in greater detail.

Resistance on the Part of Administrators and Staff. Historically, one of the biggest barriers to the successful implementation of comprehensive bullying prevention efforts was resistance on the part of school administrators or staff in the United States. Fortunately, the numbers of vocal skeptics have likely been much reduced in recent years, as public attention to the issue has grown significantly and as laws in all 50 states now require schools to develop policies to address bullying (Federal Partners in Bullying Prevention, 2015; U.S. Department of Education, 2011). However, as Limber (2011) noted, despite these shifting attitudes, "it still is not uncommon to find at least a handful of staff or parents at any given school who believe that bullying is not a concern" (p. 299). Some adults underestimate the frequency of bullying, while others acknowledge its existence but seriously misjudge the social, emotional, and academic costs of bullying and the ability of children and youth to effectively address it without adult support. In our experience, such attitudes and misunderstandings may be changed with education. Data from surveys of students at one's own school have proved particularly compelling and have helped to persuade adults not only that bullying is prevalent but that it is an issue of concern for most students (Davis & Nixon, 2014; Limber, 2011).

Although it is not uncommon to have a handful of naysayers within a school, efforts to implement a comprehensive bullying prevention effort may fall flat if a majority of staff fail to view bullying as a serious issue or agree to address it. Olweus and colleagues (Olweus, 1993; Olweus et al., 2007a, 2007b) have emphasized two prerequisites to the successful implementation of the OBPP: (a) awareness from a majority of staff about problems related to bullying and (b) a commitment from a majority of staff to collaborate to prevent and address it. The attitudes and actions of building-level administrators are particularly important in this regard. As Limber noted, "it is difficult to change the climate of a school without the support of the school's natural leader" (Limber, 2011, p. 300).

Focus on Simple or Short-Term Approaches. With an increased focus on bullying and state legal requirements for nearly all U.S. schools to develop bullying policies, many administrators feel both a desire to address bullying and a pressure to do so in a manner that will take as little time as possible from instruction. Often this translates into administrators and their staff adopting a short-term or piecemeal approach to bullying prevention. Bullying may be the topic of a staff in-service training, a Parent–Teacher Association or Parent–Teacher Organization meeting, a schoolwide assembly, or lessons taught by individual teachers. Although each of these efforts may represent important initial steps in adoption of a comprehensive, long-term strategy, they likely will do little to significantly reduce bullying problems on their own (Federal Partners in Bullying Prevention, n.d.; Limber, 2011). Efforts to educate school leaders about effective (and ineffective) prevention efforts are critical.

Lack of Preparedness of School Staff to Implement and Sustain a Comprehensive Effort. Even where awareness and commitment exist to implement a comprehensive effort to address bullying, school administrators and staff may find themselves unready to do so if needed preparations are not taken. Readiness to implement a program has been shown to adversely affect program outcomes in many studies of organizational change (Goh, Cousins, & Elliott, 2006; Miao, Umemoto, Gonda, & Hishinuma, 2011), but it is a newer area of inquiry in the educational literature (Molnar-Main & Cecil, 2014). Molnar-Main and Cecil (2014) identified three categories of variables related to the readiness of a school to implement comprehensive prevention initiatives: (a) *organizational capacity*, which includes resources, structures, and organizational practices of the school (for example, availability of financial resources, space within the curricula to address key classroom-level interventions, time for necessary training of staff); (b) *implementer characteristics*, which include buy-in, commitment, and self-efficacy of faculty and staff (addressed above); and (c) *leadership factors*, which include such variables as leadership stability, an ethos of shared leadership and a commitment to ongoing improvement, encouragement of parental engagement, and a clear understanding on the part of school leaders of the program requirements. To help school personnel determine their readiness to implement the OBPP within U.S. schools, OBPP authors developed a readiness checklist, which assesses aspects of organizational capacity (whether time has been set aside for key program elements, including regular class meetings with students, training for the school team and all school staff; whether funding has been seeded for any material and training and consultation costs; and whether at least a three-year commitment exists to include the OBPP as part of schoolwide improvement efforts); implementer characteristics (for example, whether administrators and a majority of teaching staff have identified bullying prevention and creation of a safe school climate as a priority); and leadership factors (for example, whether school leaders have a thorough understanding of the program and believe it matches their needs).

Implementation with Fidelity. Another challenge experienced in the dissemination of the OBPP (as well as many other prevention efforts) relates to implementation of program components with fidelity (Limber, 2011; Olweus & Limber, 2010a). In light of the numerous stressors and competing demands for educators' attention, it is not surprising that some school personnel are inclined to embrace program elements that appear less demanding to implement and fail to give sufficient attention to those that may require more time, attention, and training (Limber, 2011; Olweus & Limber, 2010a). An example of one such key program element is holding classroom meetings to discuss bullying and related social issues. The OBPP recommends holding meetings on a weekly basis throughout the school year. These meetings provide opportunities for social and emotional learning, where students can freely express ideas and concerns about bullying and peer relations and learn important social skills. They also enable teachers to keep their fingers on the pulse of students' concerns and provide time and space for teachers and students to build a sense of caring and community within the classroom (Limber, 2011). Olweus (1993) has shown that classrooms that held regular classroom meetings had significantly greater reductions in reports of bullying than those that did not. Moreover, anecdotal reports suggest that OBPP class meetings are a good investment of educators' time. By setting aside 20–30 minutes each week to discuss bullying and peer relations within a classroom, teachers may spend less time dealing with related problems as they arise throughout the school week (Limber, 2011). To support schools' efforts to implement the OBPP with fidelity, OBPP authors developed several fidelity checklists, which teachers and leaders of OBPP teams complete twice per school year and which are regularly reviewed by OBPP coordinating teams to improve implementation (Olweus et al., 2007a, 2007b).

Large-Scale Implementation and Evaluation of the OBPP in Pennsylvania

Recognizing the opportunity to significantly reduce bullying among school-age children by implementing a research-based comprehensive bullying prevention program on a large scale, and cognizant of common challenges of such an undertaking, the Highmark Foundation launched a large-scale implementation of the OBPP in the Commonwealth of Pennsylvania in 2007. This effort was part of a five-year $100 million initiative focused on five critical child health issues: nutrition, physical activity, grieving, self-esteem, and bullying. The Highmark Foundation identified two key partners to implement the project and make the OBPP available to interested schools across the state over the course of three years: the Center for Safe Schools, which serves as a statewide resource on school safety and youth violence, and the Center for Health Promotion and Disease Prevention at the Windber Research Institute in Windber, PA (Masiello & Schroeder, 2014). The Highmark Healthy High Five bullying prevention initiative reached more than 200,000 students and 17,000 teachers in 29 counties across Pennsylvania (Masiello & Schroeder, 2014). We will briefly describe the efforts that were developed to support the initiative, and findings from the evaluation.

Support of the Large-Scale Effort. Early in the development of the initiative, an expert panel of state, national, and international leaders was created, which included leaders from the two state partners (the Center for Safe Schools and Windber Research Institute), the secretary of education in Pennsylvania, bullying prevention experts and researchers at Clemson University and the University of Bergen, and a representative from the Centers for Disease Control and Prevention. Panel members were convened semiannually throughout the project to discuss and provide critical input on issues relating to sustainability and support of the statewide endeavor.

Building awareness. The partners, funders, and expert panelists recognized the importance of raising awareness among educators about the problem of bullying and effective prevention efforts. A bullying prevention summit in 2007 marked the inaugural event of the Healthy High Five bullying prevention initiative, which convened more than 700 Pennsylvania educators, administrators, and members of the public. The gathering, which highlighted bullying as a public health crisis, featured talks by national experts on the nature, prevalence, and effects of bullying and effective school-based prevention (Masiello & Schroeder, 2014). Throughout the Healthy High Five initiative, ongoing continuing education opportunities (Bullying Prevention 101) were held for school-based professionals who were not currently involved in bullying prevention efforts in their buildings or districts and who wanted to gain basic information about bullying, effective prevention practices, and the OBPP in particular (Masiello, 2009).

Ensure schools are ready to implement the program. To ensure that interested school personnel were adequately prepared to implement the OBPP, both Pennsylvania partners worked with schools to assess their readiness prior to any schools receiving funding and training. For example, the Pennsylvania Center for Safe Schools included questions addressing site readiness on the grant application and, beginning in 2011, extended readiness support to schools that did not meet readiness criteria (Molnar-Main & Cecil, 2014). This support included a site visit from a certified OBPP trainer, who reviewed program elements with administrators, answered questions about implementation, and established criteria for the school to meet to be prepared to implement the OBPP (Molnar-Main & Cecil, 2014). As part of this visit, the administrator committed to implementing all program components with fidelity, identified staff to serve on the OBPP leadership team, and set key dates for trainings and data collection. Comparing schools that received a readiness site visit with those that did not, Molnar-Main and Cecil (2014) found that this pre-implementation support contributed to greater fidelity of implementation for some key program elements, including reading program materials, viewing and discussing program videos with students, enforcing negative consequences for students who bully, providing positive consequences for students who help bullied students, and investigating bullying incidents.

Build local expertise and facilitate peer sharing. Recognizing the importance of building local expertise to support the training, continuing education, and consultation needs of schools implementing the OBPP over time, the initiative offered a number of important educational and networking opportunities. Through Clemson University's OBPP Trainer Certification Course, approximately 65 individuals received five days of training and ongoing (at least monthly) consultation from Olweus Technical Assistance Consultants to become OBPP certified trainers. These individuals (typically district or building-level employees) in turn trained leadership teams at each school and assisted the leadership teams in training all school staff. Other optional educational resources and processes included regular online informational and coaching sessions for educators; periodic regional workshops of OBPP leadership teams; a school administrators' retreat focused on effective policy, planning, and intervention strategies; and periodic in-person gathering of the Pennsylvania network of OBPP trainers. These opportunities not only provided ongoing education on the implementation of the OBPP model and relevant research, but they also provided important opportunities for teachers, trainers, and administrators to network with each other to share successes and challenges. This enhanced the fidelity, positive effects, and sustainability of the program (Windber Research Institute, 2011).

Assess fidelity of implementation and provide ongoing feedback to schools. Although each school's bullying prevention efforts will have important, unique differences based on their strengths and needs, fidelity of implementation of core components of the OBPP is important for successful outcomes. In this large-scale implementation, OBPP trainer–consultants met with school administrators and members of the leadership team to review results from the Olweus Bullying Questionnaire and fidelity reports to identify areas where the school had challenges in implementing the program with fidelity. Schools received an individualized action plan outlining suggested steps to address challenges with implementation (Windber Research Institute, 2011).

Evaluation of the Large-Scale Effort. An evaluation of this large-scale effort was undertaken to address several key research questions, including whether there were changes in students' reports of being bullied and bullying others after implementing the OBPP; whether there would be changes in students' attitudes, bystander behaviors, and perceptions of peer and staff behaviors after implementing the OBPP; whether these effects would be stronger the longer the program was in effect; and whether other (for example, historical) reasons could be ruled out as likely explanations for our findings (Limber, Olweus, Breivik, & Wang, 2016). The study used a strong quasi-experimental research design (an "extended age cohort design"; Olweus, 2005), in which students of the same age were compared across three years. This design is particularly well suited for school-based interventions with consecutive grade cohorts of students and can often be used to advantage when it is not possible or practical to conduct a randomized controlled trial (Cook & Campbell, 1979; Olweus & Limber, 2010b). Participants included approximately 70,000 students (at baseline) in grades 3–11 who came from some 200 schools in Pennsylvania. These students represented three different consecutive cohorts of schools; this study examined long-term changes in students' reports that were assessed with a subsample of students from some 90 schools from two cohorts (including approximately 30,000 students at baseline assessment) (Limber et al., 2016).

Preliminary results of the evaluation indicated that after two years of implementation of the OBPP, there were clear and significant decreases in being bullied and bullying others for all grade levels, with a few exceptions (for example, 11th graders on both measures of being bullied and one of two measures of bullying others) (Limber et al., 2016). Year-by-year analyses of the smaller sample over three years showed significant reductions in being bullied and bullying others among students in grades 3–8 after just one year of program implementation and larger program effects over time. Among students in grades 9–11, reductions in being bullied and bullying others emerged after two years, rather than after one year of program implementation. These reductions were observed for both boys and girls, although there were slightly larger decreases for boys versus girls in grades 3–5.

The evaluation also revealed the following changes over time in students' reactions to bullying that they witnessed: increases in sympathy for bullied students, decreases in students' inclination to join in bullying, and increases in students' perceptions that peers are helping to put a stop to bullying. As Limber and colleagues (2016) noted, these findings "lend support for the notion that the OBPP is helping to shift student attitudes and behaviors about bullying and is contributing to a more positive and inclusive school climate" (p. 41). Finally, students in grades 3–5 were more likely after just one year of implementation of the OBPP to report that teachers and other adults in their school were counteracting bullying, and students of all ages reported more positive assessments of their own teacher's efforts to reduce bullying. Analyses revealed no significant differences among cohorts, thus suggesting that the changes over time were due to program effects, rather than historical effects, such as concurrent public information efforts to raise awareness about bullying.

CONCLUSIONS

The OBPP is built on the strong belief that bullying need not and should not be a common experience for children and youth in schools (Olweus & Limber, 2010a, 2010b). Research from Norway and the United States indicates that bullying can be significantly reduced by comprehensive school-based efforts that reduce opportunities and rewards for bullying others, provide support for social and emotional learning, and build a feeling of responsibility and community among students and adults. Findings from the wide-scale implementation of the OBPP in Pennsylvania, through Highmark's Healthy High Five initiative, indicate that efforts to scale up the OBPP were successful in reducing bullying perpetration and victimization among students in grades 3–10. The OBPP also improved aspects of the school climate, as evidenced by students' increasingly positive attitudes and behaviors as witnesses and perceptions of their teachers' efforts to counteract bullying. The success of this endeavor was, no doubt, enhanced by ensuring that key supports were in place, including early and ongoing efforts to raise awareness among educators and practitioners across the state about bullying and effective (and ineffective) bullying prevention strategies; activities to assess and ensure readiness of schools wishing to implement the OBPP; efforts to build local expertise in the OBPP and facilitate sharing of successes and challenges among peers; and tools and activities to encourage high fidelity of program implementation.

REFERENCES

Baldry, A. C., & Farrington, D. P. (2007). Effectiveness of programs to prevent school bullying. *Victims and Offenders, 2*, 183–204.

Bauer, N. S., Lozano, P., & Rivara, F. P. (2007). The effectiveness of the Olweus Bullying Prevention Program in public middle schools: A controlled trial. *Journal of Adolescent Health, 40*, 266–274.

Black, S. A., & Jackson, E. (2007). Using bullying incident density to evaluate the Olweus Bullying Prevention Programme. *School Psychology International, 28*, 623–638.

Cook, T. D., & Campbell, D. T. (1979). *Quasi-experimentation: Design & analysis issues for field settings.* Boston: Houghton Mifflin.

Davis, S., & Nixon, C. (2014). *Youth Voice Project: Student insights into bullying and peer mistreatment.* Champaign, IL: Research Press.

Farrington, D. P., & Ttofi, M. M. (2009). School-based programs to reduce bullying and victimization: A systematic review. *Campbell Systematic Reviews, 5*(6). Retrieved from https://www.campbellcollaboration.org/library/school-based-programs-to-reduce-bullying-and-victimization-a-systematic-review.html

Federal Partners in Bullying Prevention. (2015). *Policies and laws.* Retrieved from http://www.stopbullying.gov/laws/index.html

Federal Partners in Bullying Prevention. (n.d.). *Misdirections in bullying prevention and intervention.* Retrieved from http://www.stopbullying.gov/prevention/at-school/educate/misdirections-in-prevention.pdf

Ferguson, C. J., San Miguel, C., Kilburn, J. C., & Sanchez, P. (2007). The effectiveness of school-based anti-bullying programs: A meta-analytic review. *Criminal Justice Review, 32*, 401–414.

Goh, S. C., Cousins, J. B., & Elliott, C. (2006). Organizational learning capacity, evaluative inquiry and readiness for change in schools: Views and perceptions of educators. *Journal of Educational Change, 7*, 289–318.

Limber, S. P. (2011). Implementation of the Olweus Bullying Prevention Program in American schools: Lessons learned from the field. In D. L. Espelage & S. M. Swearer (Eds.), *Bullying in North American schools* (2nd ed.). New York: Routledge.

Limber, S. P., Nation, M., Tracy, A. J., Melton, G. B., & Flerx, V. (2004). Implementation of the Olweus Bullying Prevention Program in the southeastern United States. In P. K. Smith, D. Pepler, & K. Rigby (Eds.), *Bullying in schools: How successful can interventions be?* (pp. 55–79). Cambridge, England: Cambridge University Press.

Limber, S. P., Olweus, D., Breivik, K., & Wang, W. (2016). *Evaluation of the Olweus Bullying Prevention Program: A large scale study of students in grades 3–11.* Unpublished manuscript.

Masiello, M. G. (2009). *Bullying prevention: A statewide collaborative that works.* Retrieved from http://www.bullyingpreventioninstitute.org/LinkClick.aspx?fileticket=bwBwDQLRCao%3d&tabid=72

Masiello, M. G., & Schroeder, D. (2014). *A public health approach to bullying prevention.* Washington, DC: American Public Health Association Press.

Merrell, K. W., Gueldner, B. A., Ross, S. W., & Isava, D. M. (2008). How effective are school bullying intervention programs? A meta-analysis of intervention research. *School Psychology Quarterly, 23*, 26–42.

Miao, T. A., Umemoto, K., Gonda, D., & Hishinuma, E. S. (2011). Essential elements for community engagement in evidence-based youth violence prevention. *American Journal of Community Psychology, 48*, 120–132.

Molnar-Main, S., & Cecil, H. (2014). Readiness and bullying prevention. In M. G. Masiello & D. Schroeder (Eds.), *A public health approach to bullying prevention* (pp. 149–172). Washington, DC: American Public Health Association Press.

Olweus, D. (1973). Personality and aggression. In J. K. Cole & D. D. Jensen (Eds.), *Nebraska Symposium on Motivation 1972* (pp. 261–321). Lincoln: University of Nebraska Press.

Olweus, D. (1978). *Aggression in the schools: Bullies and whipping boys*. Washington, DC: Hemisphere.

Olweus, D. (1991). Bully/victim problems among schoolchildren: Basic facts and effects of a school based intervention program. In D. J. Pepler & K. H. Rubin (Eds.), *The development and treatment of childhood aggression* (pp. 411–448). Hillsdale, NJ: Lawrence Erlbaum.

Olweus, D. (1993). *Bullying at school: What we know and what we can do*. New York: Blackwell.

Olweus, D. (1994). Annotation. Bullying at school: Basic facts and effects of a school based intervention program. *Journal of Child Psychology and Psychiatry, 35*, 1171–1190.

Olweus, D. (1997). Bully/victim problems in school: Facts and intervention. *European Journal of Psychology of Education, 12*, 495–510.

Olweus, D. (2005). A useful evaluation design, and effects of the Olweus Bullying Prevention Program. *Psychology, Crime & Law, 11*, 389–402.

Olweus, D., & Alsaker, F. D. (1991). Assessing change in a cohort longitudinal study with hierarchical data. In D. Magnusson, L. R. Bergman, G. Rudinger, & B. Törestad (Eds.), *Problems and methods in longitudinal research* (pp. 107–132). New York: Cambridge University Press.

Olweus, D., & Kallestad, J. H. (2010). The Olweus Bullying Prevention Program: Effects of classroom components at different grade levels. In. K. Oseterman (Ed.), *Indirect and direct aggression* (pp. 113–131). New York: Peter Lang.

Olweus, D., & Limber, S. P. (2010a). Bullying in school: Evaluation and dissemination of the Olweus Bullying Prevention Program. *American Journal of Orthopsychiatry, 80*, 124–134.

Olweus, D., & Limber, S. P. (2010b). The Olweus Bullying Prevention Program: Implementation and evaluation over two decades. In S. R. Jimerson, S. M. Swearer, & D. L. Espelage (Eds.), *Handbook of bullying in schools: An international perspective* (pp. 377–401). New York: Routledge.

Olweus, D., Limber, S. P., Flerx, V., Mullin, N., Riese, J., & Snyder, M. (2007a). *Olweus Bullying Prevention Program: Schoolwide guide*. Center City, MN: Hazelden.

Olweus, D., Limber, S. P., Flerx, V., Mullin, N., Riese, J., & Snyder, M. (2007b). *Olweus Bullying Prevention Program: Teacher guide*. Center City, MN: Hazelden.

Polanin, J. R., Espelage, D. L., & Pigott, T. D. (2012). A meta-analysis of school-based bullying prevention programs' effects on bystander intervention behavior. *School Psychology Review, 41*, 47–65.

Smith, J. D., Schneider, B. H., Smith, P. K., & Ananiadou, K. (2004). The effectiveness of whole-school antibullying programs: A synthesis of evaluation research. *School Psychology Review, 33*, 547–560.

Ttofi, M. M. & Farrington, D. P. (2011). Effectiveness of school-based programs to reduce bullying: A systematic meta-analytic review. *Journal of Experimental Criminology, 7,* 27–56.

U.S. Department of Education. (2011). *Analysis of state bullying laws and policies.* Washington, DC: Author.

Vreeman, R. C., & Carroll, A. E. (2007). A systematic review of school-based interventions to prevent bullying. *Archives of Pediatrics and Adolescent Medicine, 161,* 78–88.

Windber Research Institute. (2011). *Bullying prevention: The impact on Pennsylvania school children.* Retrieved from http://www.bullyingpreventioninstitute.org/LinkClick .aspx?fileticket=JC-nNJDmrbE%3d&tabid=39

17

Prevention and Early Intervention Efforts for Targets of Bullying and Youth Who Bully

Amanda B. Nickerson, Danielle Guttman, and Erin Cook

Bullying is a significant concern for targets and youth who bully, yet we know little about the effectiveness of various prevention and intervention approaches to address the specific needs of youth who are directly affected by bullying. This chapter provides an overview of strategies that clinicians and practitioners might use to work with individuals who are targets of bullying and for those who bully others. We start by reviewing correlates and outcomes for targets and perpetrators of bullying. This is followed by a discussion of how to respond to bullying situations. We then describe approaches that address the specific areas of concern for individuals involved in bullying, including interventions for internalizing problems, peer relation difficulties, and increasing peer support.

CORRELATES AND OUTCOMES OF BULLYING VICTIMIZATION AND PERPETRATION

As reviewed throughout this handbook, targets of bullying may experience a wide range of concurrent and long-term problems. Ample research indicates that targets of bullying experience internalizing symptoms, such as anxiety, depression, loneliness, and withdrawal (Kochenderfer & Ladd, 1996; van Oort, Greaves-Lord, Ormel, Verhulst, & Huizink, 2011), and a greater likelihood of suicidal ideation and attempts than their peers (Karch, Logan, McDaniel, Floyd, & Vagi, 2013; Nickerson & Slater, 2009; Ttofi, Farrington, Lösel, & Loeber, 2011). For those targeted, peer victimization is also associated with characterological

The research projects summarized in this chapter were supported in part through grants from the National Institute of Mental Health, the Institute of Education Sciences, and the National Institute of Justice. The authors would like to thank Samantha Vanhout for comments on an earlier version of this chapter.

self-blame (that is, attributing the victimization to internal, stable, and uncontrollable factors) and low self-worth (Graham & Juvonen, 1998) that is contingent on what others think of them (Ghoul, Niwa, & Boxer, 2013). Students who perceive themselves to be victims of bullying have poorer psychosocial adjustment than students who do not view themselves as victims (Juvonen, Nishina, & Graham, 2000). In addition, self-worth is a protective factor for internalizing problems (Ghoul et al., 2013). Victims of bullying also tend to have pervasive social difficulties with their peers, such as rejection and lack of acceptance (Ivarsson, Broberg, Arvidsson, & Gillberg, 2005; Salmivalli, Lagerspetz, Björkqvist, Österman, & Kaukiainen, 1996). The lack of reciprocated friendships and corresponding loneliness can also lead to more peer victimization (Boulton, Trueman, Chau, Whitehand, & Amatya, 1999). Social support can be a protective factor (Nishina & Juvonen, 2005), and having a peer defend a bullied student is related to better psychosocial adjustment and social standing for the victim (Sainio, Veenstra, Huitsing, & Salmivalli, 2010).

Bullying perpetration is also associated with a wide range of concurrent and long-term problems. Youth who bully others may also engage in other high-risk behaviors, such as weapon carrying (Dukes, Stein, & Zane, 2010) or substance abuse (Kim, Catalano, Haggerty, & Abbott, 2011) and, over time, are more likely to sexually harass others (Espelage, Basile, & Hamburger, 2012) and engage in aggressive behavior toward their spouses (Kim et al., 2011). Bullying perpetration in early adolescence is associated with later violent crime (Lösel & Bender, 2011; Ttofi & Farrington, 2011). Bullying others is also associated with depression, suicidal ideation, and suicide attempts (Klomek, Marrocco, Kleinman, Schonfeld, & Gould, 2007; Nickerson & Slater, 2009). Students who bully others are also more likely to feel sad and unsafe in school compared with their uninvolved peers (Glew, Fan, Katon, Rivara, & Kernic, 2005).

RESPONSE TO BULLYING BEHAVIOR

When bullying occurs, it is critical to respond in a way that sends the message that it is unacceptable and that support will be provided to change the behavior. Therefore, adults should strive to identify bullying interactions at an early stage, meet individually with the student(s) engaging in the bullying to communicate that this behavior is unacceptable, and provide support to the target (Horne, Bartolomucci, & Newman-Carlson, 2003; Pepler & Craig, 2000).

An important component of effective interventions for bullying behavior is to apply consistent disciplinary consequences (Ttofi & Farrington, 2011). However, several forms of discipline can be counterproductive, such as the use of threats and zero-tolerance policies (American Psychological Association, Zero Tolerance Task Force, 2008; Nickerson, Cornell, Smith, & Furlong, 2013). In addition, traditional out-of-school suspensions tend to be disproportionately applied to students from low-income and ethnic and racial minority backgrounds (Gregory, Skiba, & Noguera, 2010; Shabazian, 2015) and are associated with loss of instructional time, academic difficulties, disengagement from school, and increased dropout risk (Gregory et al., 2010; Lee, Cornell, Gregory, & Fan, 2011).

As an alternative to traditional punitive approaches, Allen (2010b) implemented and evaluated a system using a continuum of responses to bullying incidents, including environmental modifications, family or student meetings, student support, and traditional discipline. In this system, a Social Emotional Learning Intervention Team (SELIT) coach met with students (perpetrators and bystanders) involved in bullying to communicate concern about the situation, gather additional information, and obtain suggestions for and commitment to making the problem better. Over a two-year evaluation period, this system resulted in decreased bullying and student aggression, reduced fear of being bullied, increased disclosure of victimization and empathy for victims, and increased staff knowledge of bullying and how to respond (Allen, 2010a). The SELIT approach draws on other nonpunitive consequence models, such as the No-Blame Approach (Support Group Method) and the Method of Shared Concern, which rely on the assumption that bullying is a group phenomenon (Rigby & Griffiths, 2011). The Method of Shared Concern and the Support Group Method focus on collective empathy for the victim, problem solving, and actions to resolve the situation (Garandeau, Poskiparta, & Salmivalli, 2014). The Method of Shared Concern begins with individual and group meetings with the perpetrator(s), whereas the Support Group Method interviews the victim first and then holds group and individual meetings.

Garandeau and colleagues (2014) assessed the effectiveness of confrontational approaches (for example, "Bullying behavior is wrong and should stop immediately") and nonconfrontational approaches (for example, share concern for victim, ask for suggestions for improvement) to bullying and found both to be effective, with victims reporting that bullying stopped in 78 percent of cases. The confrontational approach was more effective than the nonconfrontational approach in grades 7–9 and in cases of short-term victimization (for example, one month or less) but not in grades 1–6 or in cases of long-term victimization (Garandeau et al., 2014). This suggests that younger children who have less developed moral reasoning and perspective-taking skills may benefit from nonconfrontational strategies that raise awareness of the victim's suffering (Garandeau et al., 2014). In contrast, with aggressive adolescents who exhibit advanced moral competence (that is, know right from wrong) but have low levels of empathy and compassion (Gini, Pozzoli, & Hauser, 2011), a more confrontational approach may be necessary (Garandeau et al., 2014).

INDIVIDUALIZED INTERVENTIONS

Within a multitiered prevention model (see chapter 15 on multitiered frameworks), youth who exhibit problems, despite more universal prevention efforts, may need to be provided with more intensive and individualized supports to minimize the impact of difficulties and prevent the development of future problematic behaviors by focusing on the development of desirable behaviors and maximizing environmental supports (Miller, Nickerson, & Jimerson, 2014). Because youth may be involved in bullying for a variety of reasons, it is important to assess the contributing factors so that the intervention can match the student's needs (Swearer, Espelage, & Napolitano, 2009). For example, within a Positive Behavioral Intervention and Supports framework, behavior education programs consisting of daily check-ins, checkouts, and behavioral progress monitoring has been found to be effective (McCurdy, Kunsch, & Reibstein, 2007). Functional behavioral assessments can also be used to gather systematic information about behavior setting events, antecedents, and consequences (Watson & Steege, 2003). This can help determine the function of behavior, or why the student is behaving a particular way, to facilitate the development of an individualized behavior intervention plan (BIP) to identify appropriate replacement behaviors, teach alternative skills, change antecedents, and alter consequences in order to reduce problem behaviors (Goh & Bambara, 2012; Watson & Steege, 2003).

Another approach at the individualized level that uses assessment information is the Target Bullying Intervention Program (T-BIP; Swearer & Givens, 2006). The program offers an alternative to suspension and expulsion to assess and address the needs of youth who engage in ongoing or severe bullying (Swearer & Givens, 2006). T-BIP is an individual, three-hour single-session cognitive–behavioral intervention that includes (a) assessment, (b) psychoeducation, and (c) feedback (Strawhun, Fluke, & Peterson, 2013). The assessment seeks to identify the contributing factors to the bullying. It is followed by a PowerPoint psychoeducational presentation with activities from the Bully Busters program (Newman, Horne, & Bartolomucci, 2000) and an antibullying video (Strawhun et al., 2013). After the intervention, the therapist summarizes results and makes recommendations to share with the student's family (Strawhun et al., 2013). This approach is built on the assumption that the treatment of underlying conditions such as depression, anxiety, aggression, impulsivity, distorted thinking, and skill deficits can help reduce bullying behaviors (Swearer et al., 2009). Following the logic that treatment of underlying conditions help to reduce bullying behaviors, the interventions described below aim to treat the factors that contribute to bullying victimization and perpetration.

INTERVENTIONS FOR INTERNALIZING PROBLEMS

Because targets of bullying may experience anxiety and depressive symptoms, evidence-based treatment approaches for internalizing disorders may be appropriate to help these youth manage symptoms and increase coping skills. For example, Coping Cat is a manualized cognitive–behavioral group intervention that teaches children to recognize anxious emotions and thoughts and develop coping strategies for dealing with triggers; research has demonstrated this to be effective in reducing symptoms of anxiety in children (Albano & Kendall, 2002; van Starrenburg, Kuijpers, Hutschemaekers, & Engels, 2013). Similarly, cognitive–behavioral groups that include psychoeducation about depression and creating plans to reduce stress through strategies like engaging in pleasurable activities may be helpful for students who have depressive symptoms (Asarnow, Scott, & Mintz, 2002). For example, McElearney, Adamson, Shevlin, and Bunting (2013) found that the use of cognitive–behavioral strategies with targets of bullying in elementary and secondary school settings in Ireland resulted in significant decreases in reports of distress and problems related to peer relations.

Mindfulness interventions, which teach people to have an intentional, accepting focus on thoughts and emotions in the present, have begun to be used in school settings to target adolescents' emotional regulation (Metz et al., 2013) and stress management skills (Felver, Doerner, Jones, Kaye, & Merrell, 2013). Because targets of bullying may experience stress and problems with emotional regulation, these interventions may be applicable. A pilot study indicated that mindfulness reduced symptoms of depression in adolescents in an eight-week group intervention (Ames, Richardson, Payne, Smith, & Leigh, 2014). In particular, this may be a promising approach to manage depressive symptoms for students involved in bullying, although additional research is needed on this population.

Given that both targets and children who bully are at higher risk for suicide than noninvolved peers, students involved in bullying should be assessed for depression and suicidality (Espelage & Holt, 2013; Klomek et al., 2007). This assessment should be a standard part of the response to bullying, and any indication of depression or suicidal ideation should be documented with an intervention plan created and a referral made, if appropriate (Espelage & Holt, 2013). Because of the wide range of factors that contribute to suicidal thoughts and behaviors among youth, an accurate assessment considers all risk and protective factors for the individual child. For example, problem solving, coping skills, the availability of parent support, and connectedness to parents serve as protective factors for both violence perpetration and suicide (Nickerson & Slater, 2009). A thorough understanding of an individual's risk and protective factors is important for informing intervention.

INTERVENTIONS TO BUILD SPECIFIC SKILLS AND REDUCE AGGRESSION

Youth displaying bullying and other aggressive or externalizing behaviors may have relationship or social skill deficits that prevent them from behaving in more prosocial ways (Mytton, DiGuiseppi, Gough, Taylor, & Logan, 2007). Cognitive–behavioral therapy (CBT) programs and techniques can produce significant reductions in anger, aggression, and externalizing behaviors (McCart, Priester, Davies, & Azen, 2006; Sukhodolsky, Kassinove, & Gorman, 2004). For example, the Coping Power Program and the Anger Coping Program (Lochman & Wells, 2002) focus on the development of emotion recognition and awareness, social problem solving, perspective taking, anger management, and goal setting and have been shown to be effective in reducing externalizing behavior problems, aggression, and disruptive classroom behavior, as well as improving self-esteem and social competence (Lochman, 1992; Lochman, Powell, Boxmeyer, & Jimenez-Camargo, 2011). In addition, school-based interventions including behavioral approaches, counseling, and social competence training, especially those that were correctly implemented in a one-to-one format, have been found to result in significant reductions in aggressive behaviors (Wilson, Lipsey, & Derzon, 2003).

Anger is a significant predictor of bullying perpetration and other behavioral issues (Bosworth, Espelage, & Simon, 1999; Swearer et al., 2009). Anger management interventions help children identify triggers of the anger response, enable them to think about the situation differently, and provide the opportunity for students to learn and practice new responses and behaviors (Gansle, 2005). A meta-analysis completed by Gansle (2005) based on 20 peer-reviewed journal articles found significant evidence for the effectiveness of school-based interventions for reducing anger and associated problems.

Youth who bully others but who are also bullied tend to exhibit more reactive aggressive behavior, owing in part to their hostile attribution bias (Perren, Ettekal, & Ladd, 2013). This social information-processing deficit leads youth to selectively attend to hostile instead of neutral social cues and to interpret others' intent as threatening (Perren et al., 2013). Interventions that seek to change the maladaptive cognitions and teach conflict resolution, anger management, adaptive coping, empathy, and social problem-solving skills may be promising for countering bullying and promoting healthy relationships (DeRosier, 2004). For example, problem-solving skills training can be used to teach children how to identify alternative interpretations for others' behavior, increase awareness of the physiological signs of anger, improve social problem-solving skills, and cope with conflict (Lochman & Lenhart, 1993). Although not applied to bullying behavior specifically, problem-solving training has been shown to decrease disruptive and aggressive behavior and increase prosocial behavior (Bushman & Gimpel Peacock, 2010; Jaffe & D'Zurilla, 2003).

INTERVENTIONS FOR PEER RELATIONSHIP DIFFICULTIES

Some children targeted by bullying are also more socially withdrawn and rejected by their peer group. Interventions for socially withdrawn children typically include specific social skills instruction focused on making friends, increasing positive prosocial strategies, regulating anxiety, and being assertive (Bienert & Schneider, 1995; Gazelle & Ladd, 2002). More recently, group social skills training has been used for victims of bullying to increase assertiveness and coping skills (Hall, 2006) and to reinforce prosocial beliefs and behaviors (DeRosier, 2004). For example, the Social Skills Group Intervention was used for third graders who were bullied, with results indicating increased peer liking, improved self-worth, and decreased symptoms of social anxiety compared with children in the control group. It should be noted that other research has found that social skills training may increase feelings of self-worth but may not have an impact on victim status or observed social skills (Fox & Boulton, 2003).

Using a solution-focused brief therapy support group for young adolescent targets of bullying, Kvarme, Aabø, and Sæteren (2013) found that bullying incidents decreased and targets of bullying reported decreased safety concerns and more peer support both after the intervention and at the follow-up months later. Although this was an exploratory qualitative study, it lends support to the notion that enhancing peer support may be helpful to targets of bullying.

INTERVENTIONS FOR ENHANCING PEER SUPPORT

Training a small group of peer helpers through after-school clubs, buddying, and peer telephone listening services has been used in European countries to offer companionship to children suffering from distress, including bullying (Cowie & Wallace, 2000; Sharp & Cowie, 1998). These approaches can increase peer helpers' confidence, sense of responsibility, involvement, and communication; improve the overall school climate (Cowie, 1998; Naylor & Cowie, 1999); and increase the strength of victims to overcome the problem (Naylor & Cowie, 1999); but these methods have had limited success in reducing actual bullying rates (Menesini, Codecasa, Benelli, & Cowie, 2003; Naylor & Cowie, 1999). These interventions may be more helpful in empowering students to establish positive environments to prevent future instances of bullying (that is, prevention) rather than having an immediate effects on preexisting bullying behaviors. Mentoring by college students has also been used to support victims of bullying. In Elledge, Cavell, Ogle, and Newgent's (2010) study, 12 fourth- and fifth-grade victims of bullying were paired with college students as mentors who visited twice weekly during lunch during the spring term. Following the intervention, children reported fewer peer reports of victimization than peers who had not participated, and there were no instances of bullying related to having a mentor.

As part of KiVa, a bullying prevention and intervention program developed by Finnish researchers that focuses largely on increasing self-efficacy among bystanders (Williford et al., 2012), specially trained bully educators work with classroom teachers when bullying occurs. The bully team meets with the bully and target separately, and the victim identifies potential allies who are then invited to meet with staff and encouraged to support the victim in the classroom. Results of the program include reduced victimization, reduced symptoms of anxiety and depression, and increased positive peer perceptions (Williford et al., 2012).

INTERVENTIONS INVOLVING PARENTS

Parent trainings are associated with the reduction of bullying and are one of the most well-established interventions for children with aggressive problems (Ttofi & Farrington, 2009). Many parent training approaches are based on empirical work showing that disruptions in parental management practices lead to the development and maintenance of aggressive and antisocial behavior (Patterson, 1986). The Incredible Years Parent Program is an example of a parent training program that results in children exhibiting increased prosocial behaviors and improved socioemotional competence and a reduction in conduct problems (Menting, Orobio de Castroa, & Matthys, 2013; Posthumus, Raaijmakers, Maassen, van Engeland, & Matthys, 2012). In addition, immediate and long-term gains in parenting skills and interactions have been found (Posthumus et al., 2012).

Another CBT-based parent training program is the Coping Power Parent Program (Lochman et al., 2011). Typically used in conjunction with the youth-focused program described above, the parent sessions focus on improving the parent–child bond and helping parents to use positive parenting skills (Lochman et al., 2011). Additional parent skills may include stress management, building family communication and cohesion, and problem solving (Lochman et al., 2011).

For youth exhibiting more chronic externalizing behaviors, multisystemic therapy (MST) has also been used to empower caregivers to serve as change agents through the

Table 17.1: Possible Interventions for Bullying Victimization and Perpetration

Intervention	Examples of Interventions	
	Target	Perpetrator
Individualized interventions	CBT for anxiety or depression • Coping Cat program • Recognize emotions • Develop coping strategies • Engage in pleasurable activities Solution-focused group therapy • Addressing immediate safety concerns Social skills training • Group or individual • Developing friendships • Being assertive	Problem-solving skills training and clear nonpunitive consequences for behavior • Social Emotional Team Coach • No Blame Approach • Method of Shared Concern Promote prosocial behaviors • Functional behavioral assessment • Behavioral intervention plan Anger management training • Learn new responses and behaviors • Conflict resolution
Involving other students	Mentoring • Older students as role models Support from allies or peer helpers • Specific strategies	Coaching of perpetrator and bystanders to problem solve • KiVa program • Teacher involvement • Meet with all parties • Promote ally involvement
Parental involvement	Parent component of CBT interventions • Improving relationships with child • Parental support as a protective factor	Parent management training • Skill development • Appropriate discipline • Coping Power program • Incredible Years program Multisystemic interventions

Note: CBT = cognitive–behavioral therapy.

identification of factors that interfere with their ability to provide nurturance, monitoring, and discipline for their child (Henggeler, Schoenwald, Rowland, & Cunningham, 2002). Caregiver strengths and resources (for example, supportive extended family, social skills) are identified and expanded to facilitate implementation of interventions (Henggeler et al, 2002). MST has been found to be successful in not only reducing problem behaviors but also decreasing residential placement and rearrest rates for students with severe, chronic behavior problems (Henggeler, 2011; Henggeler et al., 2002).

CONCLUSION

Given the complexity of bullying victimization and perpetration, it is critical to understand the issues that are unique to the individual and the context in order to develop and implement interventions that have been shown through research to be effective. In this chapter, several contributors and outcomes of bullying were reviewed, and options for interventions based on these contributing factors were presented. Table 17.1 summarizes some options of interventions that may be considered at the individual, peer group, and family levels for bullying. Clearly, additional research is needed to document the impact of these programs on bullying behavior specifically and to investigate the extent to which they ameliorate the impact of bullying among targets.

REFERENCES

Albano, A. M., & Kendall, P. C. (2002). Cognitive behavioural therapy for children and adolescents with anxiety disorders: Clinical research advances. *International Review of Psychiatry, 14*, 129–134. doi:10.1080/09540260220132644

Allen, K. P. (2010a). A bullying intervention system in high school: A two-year school-wide follow-up. *Studies in Educational Evaluation, 36*, 83–92. doi:10.1016/j.stueduc.2011.01.002

Allen, K. P. (2010b). A bullying intervention system: Reducing risk and creating support for aggressive students. *Preventing School Failure, 54*, 199–209. doi:10.1080/10459880903496289

American Psychological Association, Zero Tolerance Task Force. (2008). Are zero tolerance policies effective in the schools? An evidentiary review and recommendations. *American Psychologist, 63*, 852–862. doi:10.1037/0003-066X.63.9.852

Ames, C. S., Richardson, J., Payne, S., Smith, P., & Leigh, E. (2014). Innovations in practice: Mindfulness based cognitive therapy for depression in adolescents. *Child and Adolescent Mental Health, 19*, 74–78. doi:10.1111/camh.12034

Asarnow, J. R., Scott, C. V., & Mintz, J. (2002). A combined cognitive–behavioral family education intervention for depression in children: A treatment development study. *Cognitive Therapy & Research, 26*, 221–229.

Bienert, H., & Schneider, B. H. (1995). Deficit-specific social skills training with peer-nominated aggressive-disruptive and sensitive-isolated preadolescents. *Journal of Clinical Child Psychology, 24*, 287–299.

Bosworth, K., Espelage, D. L., & Simon, T. R. (1999). Factors associated with bullying behavior in middle school students. *Journal of Early Adolescence, 19*, 341–362. doi:10.1177/0272431699019003003

Boulton, M. J., Trueman, M., Chau, C., Whitehead, C., & Amatya, K. (1999). Concurrent and longitudinal links between friendship and peer victimization: Implications for befriending interventions. *Journal of Adolescence, 22*, 461–466. doi:10.1006/jado.1999.0240

Bushman, B. B., & Gimpel Peacock, G. (2010) Does teaching problem-solving skills matter? An evaluation of problem-solving skills training for the treatment of social and behavioral problems in children. *Child and Family Behavior Therapy, 32*, 103–124. doi:10.1080/07317101003776449

Cowie, H. (1998). Perspectives of teachers and pupils on the experience of peer support against bullying. *Educational Research and Evaluation, 4*, 108–125.

Cowie, H., & Wallace, P. (2000). *Peer support in action: From bystanding to standing by.* London: Sage Publications.

DeRosier, M. S. (2004). Building relationships and combating bullying: Effectiveness of a school-based social skills group intervention. *Journal of Clinical Child & Adolescent Psychology, 33*, 196–201. doi:10.1207/S15374424JCCP3301_18

Dukes, R. L., Stein, J. A., & Zane, J. I. (2010). Gender differences in the relative impact of physical and relational bullying on adolescent injury and weapon carrying. *Journal of School Psychology, 48*, 511–532. doi:10.1016/j.jsp.2010.08.001

Elledge, L. C., Cavell, T. A., Ogle, N. T., & Newgent, R. A. (2010). School-based mentoring as selective prevention for bullied children: A preliminary test. *Journal of Primary Prevention, 31*, 171–187. doi:10.1007/s10935-010-0215-7

Espelage, D. L., Basile, K. C., & Hamburger, M. E. (2012). Bullying perpetration and subsequent sexual violence perpetration among middle school students. *Journal of Adolescent Health, 50*, 60–65. doi:10.1016/j.jadohealth.2011.07.015

Espelage, D. L., & Holt, M. K. (2013). Suicidal ideation and school bullying experiences after controlling for depression and delinquency. *Journal of Adolescent Health, 53*, S27–S31. doi:10.1016/j.jadohealth.2012.09.017

Felver, J. C., Doerner, E., Jones, J., Kaye, N. C., & Merrell, K. W. (2013). Mindfulness in school psychology: Applications for intervention and professional practice. *Psychology in the Schools, 50*, 531–547. doi:10.1002/pits.21695

Fox, C. L., & Boulton, M. J. (2003). Evaluating the effectiveness of a social skills training (SST) programme for victims of bullying. *Educational Research, 45*, 231–247. doi:10.1080/0013188032000137238

Gansle, K. A. (2005). The effectiveness of school-based anger interventions and programs: A meta-analysis. *Journal of School Psychology, 43*, 321–341. doi:10.1016/j.jsp.2005.07.002

Garandeau, C. F., Poskiparta, E., & Salmivalli, C. (2014). Tackling acute cases of school bullying in the KiVa anti-bullying program: A comparison of two approaches. *Journal of Abnormal Child Psychology, 42*, 981–991. doi:10.1007/s10802-014-9861-1

Gazelle, H., & Ladd, G. W. (2002). Interventions for children victimized by peers. In P. A. Schewe (Ed.), *Preventing violence in relationships: Interventions across the lifespan* (pp. 55–78). Washington, DC: American Psychological Association.

Ghoul, A., Niwa, E. Y., & Boxer, P. (2013). The role of contingent self-worth in the relation between victimization and internalizing problems in adolescents. *Journal of Adolescence, 36*, 457–464. doi:10.1016/j.adolescence.2013.01.007

Gini, G., Pozzoli, T., & Hauser, M. (2011). Bullies have enhanced moral competence to judge relative to victims, but lack moral compassion. *Personality and Individual Differences, 50*, 603–608. doi:10.1016/j.paid.2010.12.002

Glew, G. M., Fan, M., Katon, W. J., Rivara, F. P., & Kernic, M. A. (2005). Bullying, psychosocial adjustment, and academic performance in elementary school. *Archives of Pediatric and Adolescent Medicine, 159*, 1026–1031. doi:10.1001/archpedi.159.11.1026

Goh, A. E., & Bambara, L. M. (2012). Individualized positive behavior support in school settings: A meta-analysis. *Remedial and Special Education, 33,* 271–286. doi:10.1177/0741932510383990

Graham, S., & Juvonen, J. (1998). Self-blame and peer victimization in middle school: An attributional analysis. *Developmental Psychology, 34,* 587–599. doi:10.1037/0012-1649.34.3.587

Gregory, A., Skiba, R. J., & Noguera, P. A. (2010). The achievement gap and the discipline gap: Two sides of the same coin? *Educational Researcher, 39,* 59–68. doi:10.3102/0013189X09357621

Hall, K. (2006). Using problem-based learning with victims of bullying behavior. *Professional School Counseling, 9*(3), 231–237.

Henggeler, S. W. (2011). Efficacy studies to large-scale transport: The development and validation of multisystemic therapy programs. *Annual Review of Clinical Psychology, 7,* 351–381. doi:10.1146/annurev-clinpsy-032210-104615

Henggeler, S. W., Schoenwald, S. K., Rowland, M. D., & Cunningham, P. B. (2002). *Serious emotional disturbance in children and adolescents: Multisystemic therapy.* New York: Guilford Press.

Horne, A. M., Bartolomucci, C. L., & Newman-Carlson, D. (2003). *Bully busters: A teacher's manual for helping bullies, victims, and bystanders (grades K–5).* Champaign, IL: Research Press.

Ivarsson, T., Broberg, A. G., Arvidsson, T., & Gillberg, C. (2005). Bullying in adolescence: Psychiatric problems in victims and bullies as measured by the youth self-report (YSR) and the depression self-rating scale (DSRS). *Norwegian Journal of Psychiatry, 59,* 365–375. doi:10.1080/08039480500227816

Jaffe, W. B., & D'Zurilla, T. J. (2003). Adolescent problem solving, parent problem solving, and externalizing behavior in adolescents. *Behavior Therapy, 34,* 295–311. doi:10.1016/S0005-7894(03)80002-3

Juvonen, J., Nishina, A., & Graham, S. (2000). Peer harassment, psychological adjustment, and school functioning in early adolescence. *Journal of Educational Psychology, 2,* 349–359. doi:10.1037/0022-0663.92.2.349

Karch, D. L., Logan, J., McDaniel, D. D., Floyd, C. F., & Vagi, K. J. (2013). Precipitating circumstances of suicide among youth aged 10–17 years by sex: Data from the National Violent Death Reporting System, 16 States, 2005–2008. *Journal of Adolescent Health, 53,* S51–S53. doi:10.1016/j.jadohealth.2012.06.028

Kim, M. J., Catalano, R. F., Haggerty, K. P., & Abbott, R. D. (2011). Bullying at elementary school and problem behavior in young adulthood: A study of bullying, violence, and substance use from age 11 to age 21. *Criminal Behaviour and Mental Health, 21,* 136–144. doi:10.1002/cbm.804

Klomek, A. B., Marrocco, F., Kleinman, M., Schonfeld, I. S., & Gould, M. S. (2007). Bullying, depression, and suicidality in adolescents. *Journal of the American Academy of Child and Adolescent Psychiatry, 46,* 40–49. doi:10.1097/01.chi.0000242237.84925.18

Kochenderfer, B. J., & Ladd, G. W. (1996). Peer victimization: Cause or consequence of school maladjustment? *Child Development, 67,* 1305–1317. doi:10.1111/j.1467-8624.1996.tb01797.x

Kvarme, L. G., Aabø, L. S., & Sæteren, B. (2013). "I feel I mean something to someone": Solution-focused brief therapy support groups for bullied schoolchildren. *Educational Psychology in Practice, 29,* 416–431. doi:10.1080/02667363.2013.859569

Lee, T., Cornell, D., Gregory, A., & Fan, X. (2011). High suspension schools and dropout rates for black and white students. *Education and Treatment of Children, 34,* 167–192. doi:10.1353/etc.2011.0014

Lochman, J. E. (1992). Cognitive-behavioral interventions with aggressive boys: Three-year follow-up and preventive effects. *Journal of Consulting and Clinical Psychology, 60,* 426–432.

Lochman, J. E., & Lenhart, L. A. (1993). Anger coping intervention for aggressive children: Conceptual models and outcome effects. *Clinical Psychology Review, 13,* 785–805.

Lochman, J. E., Powell, N. P., Boxmeyer, C. L., & Jimenez-Camargo, L. (2011). Cognitive-behavioral therapy for externalizing disorders in children and adolescents. *Child and Adolescent Psychiatric Clinics of North America, 20,* 305–318. doi:10.1016/j.chc.2011.01.005

Lochman, J. E., & Wells, K. C. (2002). The Coping Power Program at the middle-school transition: Universal and indicated prevention effects. *Psychology of Addictive Behaviors, 16,* 40–54. doi:10.1037/0893-164X.16.4S.S40

Lösel, F., & Bender, D. (2011). Emotional and antisocial outcomes of bullying and victimization at school: A follow-up from childhood to adolescence. *Journal of Aggression, Conflict, and Peace Research, 3,* 89–96. doi:10.1108/17596591111132909

McCart, M. R., Priester, P. E., Davies, W. H., & Azen, R. (2006). Differential effectiveness of behavioral parent training and cognitive-behavioral therapy for antisocial youth: A meta-analysis. *Journal of Abnormal Child Psychology, 34,* 527–543. doi:10.1007/s10802-006-9031-1

McCurdy, B. L., Kunsch, C., & Reibstein, S. (2007). Secondary prevention in the urban school: Implementing the behavior education program. *Preventing School Failure: Alternative Education for Children and Youth, 51*(3), 12–19. doi:10.3200/PSFL.51.3.12-19

McElearney, A., Adamson, G., Shevlin, M., & Bunting, B. (2013). Impact evaluation of a school-based counselling intervention in Northern Ireland: Is it effective for pupils who have been bullied? *Child Care in Practice, 19*(1), 4–22. doi:10.1080/13575279.2012.732557

Menesini, E., Codecasa, E., Benelli, B., & Cowie, H. (2003). Enhancing children's responsibility to take action against bullying: Evaluation of a befriending intervention in Italian middle schools. *Aggressive Behavior, 29,* 1–14.

Menting, A., Orobio de Castroa, B., & Matthys, B. (2013). Effectiveness of the Incredible Years parent training to modify disruptive and prosocial child behavior: A meta-analytic review. *Clinical Psychology Review, 33,* 901–913. doi:10.1016/j.cpr.2013.07.006

Metz, S. M., Frank, J. L., Reibel, D., Cantrell, T., Sanders, R., & Broderick, P. C. (2013). The effectiveness of the Learning to BREATHE program on adolescent emotion regulation. *Research in Human Development, 10,* 252–272. doi:10.1080/15427609.2013.818488

Miller, D. N., Nickerson, A. B., & Jimerson, S. R. (2014). Positive psychological interventions in U.S. schools: A public health approach to internalizing and externalizing problems. In R. Gilman, E. S. Huebner, & M. J. Furlong (Eds.), *Promoting wellness in children and youth: A handbook of positive psychology in the schools* (2nd ed.; pp. 478–493). Mahwah, NJ: Lawrence Erlbaum.

Mytton, J., DiGuiseppi, C., Gough, D., Taylor, R., & Logan, S. (2007). Cochrane review: School-based secondary prevention programmes for preventing violence. *Evidence-Based Child Health, 2,* 814–891. doi:10.1002/ebch.127

Naylor, P., & Cowie, H. (1999). The effectiveness of peer support systems in challenging school bullying: The perspectives and experiences of teachers and pupils. *Journal of Adolescence, 22,* 467–479.

Newman, D. A., Horne, A. M., & Bartolomucci, L. (2000). *Bully busters: A teacher's manual for helping bullies, victims and bystanders.* Champaign, IL: Research Press.

Nickerson, A. B., Cornell, D. G., Smith, D., & Furlong, M. (2013). School anti-bullying efforts: Advice for policymakers. *Journal of School Violence, 12*, 268–282. doi:10.1080/1 5388220.2013.787366

Nickerson, A. B., & Slater, E. D. (2009). School and community violence and victimization as predictors of suicidal behavior for adolescents. *School Psychology Review, 38*, 218–232.

Nishina, A., & Juvonen, J. (2005). Daily reports of witnessing and experiencing peer harassment in middle school. *Child Development, 76*, 435–450. doi:10.1111/ j.1467-8624.2005.00855.x

Patterson, G. R. (1986). Performance models for antisocial boys. *American Psychologist, 41*, 432–444. doi:10.1037//0003-066X.41.4.432

Pepler, D. J., & Craig, W. (2000). *Making a difference in bullying: Understanding and strategies for practitioners.* Retrieved from http://psycserver.psyc.queensu.ca/craigw/Craig_Pepler_2000_REPORT_Making_a_Difference_in_Bullying.pdf

Perren, S., Ettekal, I., & Ladd, G. (2013). The impact of peer victimization on later maladjustment: Mediating and moderating effects of hostile and self-blaming attributions. *Journal of Child Psychology and Psychiatry, 54*, 46–55. doi:10.1111/j.1469-7610.2012.02618.x

Posthumus, J. A., Raaijmakers, M., Maassen, G., van Engeland, H., & Matthys, W. J. (2012). Sustained effects of Incredible Years as a preventive intervention in preschool children with conduct problems. *Abnormal Child Psychology, 40*, 487–500. doi:10.1007/ s10802-011-9580-9

Rigby, K., & Griffiths, C. (2011). Addressing cases of bullying through the Method of Shared Concern. *School Psychology International, 32*, 345–357. doi:10.1177/0143034311402148

Sainio, M., Veenstra, R., Huitsing, G., & Salmivalli, C. (2010). Victims and their defenders: A dyadic approach. *International Journal of Behavioural Development, 35*, 144–151. doi:10.1177/0165025410378068

Salmivalli, C., Lagerspetz, K., Björkqvist, K., Österman, K., & Kaukiainen, A. (1996). Bullying as a group process: Participant roles and their relations to social status within the group. *Aggressive Behavior, 22*, 1–15. doi:10.1002/(SICI)1098-2337

Shabazian, A. N. (2015). The significance of location: Patterns of school exclusionary disciplinary practices in public schools. *Journal of School Violence, 14*, 273–298. doi:10.108 0/15388220.2014.913254

Sharp, S., & Cowie, H. (1998). *Counseling and supporting children in distress.* London: Sage Publications.

Strawhun, J., Fluke, S., & Peterson, R. (2013, October). *The Target Bullying Intervention Program* [Program brief]. Lincoln: Student Engagement Project, University of Nebraska–Lincoln and the Nebraska Department of Education. Retrieved from http://k12engagement. unl.edu/strategy-briefs/Program%20Targeting%20Bullying%2010-23-2013.pdf

Sukhodolsky, D. G., Kassinove, H., & Gorman, B. S. (2004). Cognitive-behavioral therapy for anger in children and adolescents: A meta-analysis. *Aggression and Violent Behavior, 9*, 247–269. doi:10.1016/j.avb.2003.08.005

Swearer, S. M., Espelage, D. L., & Napolitano, S. A. (2009). *Bullying prevention and intervention: Realistic strategies for schools.* New York: Guilford Press.

Swearer, S. M., & Givens, J. E. (2006). *Designing an alternative to suspension for middle school bullies.* Paper presented at the annual convention of the National Association of School Psychologists, Anaheim, CA.

Ttofi, M. M., & Farrington, D. P. (2009). What works in preventing bullying: Effective elements of anti-bullying programmes. *Journal of Aggression, Conflict, and Peace Research, 1*, 13–24. doi:10.1108/17596599200900003

Ttofi, M. M., & Farrington, D. P. (2011). Effectiveness of school-based programs to reduce bullying: A systematic and meta-analytic review. *Journal of Experimental Criminology, 7,* 27–56. doi:10.1007/s11292-101-9109-1

Ttofi, M. M., Farrington, D. P., Lösel, F., & Loeber, R. (2011). The predictive efficiency of school bullying versus later offending: A systematic/meta-analytic review of longitudinal studies. *Criminal Behaviour and Mental Health, 21,* 80–89.

van Oort, F.V.A., Greaves-Lord, K., Ormel, J., Verhulst, F. C., & Huizink, A. C. (2011). Risk indicators of anxiety throughout adolescence: The trails study. *Depression and Anxiety, 28,* 485–494. doi:10.1002/da.20818

van Starrenburg, M. A., Kuijpers, R. M., Hutschemaekers, G. M., & Engels, R. E. (2013). Effectiveness and underlying mechanisms of a group-based cognitive behavioural therapy-based indicative prevention program for children with elevated anxiety levels. *BMC Psychiatry, 13,* 183. doi:10.1186/1471-244X-13-183

Watson, T. S., & Steege, M. W. (2003). *Conducting school-based functional behavior assessments: A practitioner's guide.* New York: Guilford Press.

Williford, A., Boulton, A., Noland, B., Little, T. D., Kärnä, A., & Salmivalli, C. (2012). Effects of the KiVa anti-bullying program on adolescents' depression, anxiety, and perception of peers. *Journal of Abnormal Child Psychology, 40*(2), 289–300. doi:10.1007/s10802-011-9551-1

Wilson, S. J., Lipsey, M. W., & Derzon, J. H. (2003). The effects of school-based intervention programs on aggressive behavior: A meta-analysis. *Journal of Consulting and Clinical Psychology, 71,* 136–149. doi:10.1037/0022-006X.71.1.136

18

Preventing Bullying in Middle Schoolers by Using the Coping Power Program: A Targeted Group Intervention

Catherine P. Bradshaw, John E. Lochman, Nicole Powell, and Nicholas Ialongo

Although universal approaches to bullying prevention can be effective, consistent with a multitiered system of supports framework, there is a great need for early intervention for youth who are already involved in bullying (Bradshaw, 2015). Such programs help prevent the behavior problems from escalating and resulting in more severe behavioral and mental health problems (O'Connell, Boat, & Warner, 2009). This chapter summarizes a research-based indicated preventive intervention called Coping Power (Lochman & Wells, 2002, 2003), which was recently developmentally adapted to meet the needs of middle school–age youth who are engaging in bullying and other forms of aggressive behavior. Like previous versions of Coping Power, the middle school version includes sessions for parents, teachers, and youth, thereby providing a comprehensive system of support to stem bullying and address related behavioral and mental health concerns. This chapter provides an overview of the recently developed middle school model and some preliminary evidence of its promise as a strategy for addressing the needs of students who are involved in bullying and other forms of aggressive behavior.

RATIONALE FOR A MIDDLE SCHOOL VERSION OF COPING POWER

Behavioral challenges, such as bullying, cause school disruptions and are associated with both short- and long-term academic difficulties as well as a range of mental health concerns (Swearer, Espelage, Vaillancourt, & Hymel, 2010). These issues are particularly significant during the middle school years, when rates of bullying, school violence, and disruption increase and student engagement and parental involvement in school-based programming decline (Eccles & Harold, 1993). Yet there are relatively few school-based prevention programs to address the concerns of middle school students, particularly regarding bullying (Bradshaw, 2015).

One of the relatively few rigorously tested school-based programs currently available to address aggressive behavior problems among children is called Coping Power (Lochman & Wells, 2002, 2003). This multicomponent program includes clinician-facilitated group sessions for youth, separate group sessions for parents, and support to teachers. However, Coping Power had not been tested with youth in grade 7 or above. Moreover, some of the content of the original program required adaptation to meet the shifting developmental issues faced by students in the middle school grades, such as bullying, relational aggression, cyberbullying, social–romantic relationships, parent–youth relationships, parental monitoring, communication, and family stress. Therefore, with pilot funding from the National Institute of Mental Health–funded Johns Hopkins Center for Prevention and Early Intervention, our research team adapted the program to be more developmentally appropriate for middle school–age students displaying high levels of aggressive behaviors, which we called the Early Adolescent Coping Power (EACP) Program.

OVERVIEW OF THE EACP PROGRAM

Similar to the original program, the EACP is based on a contextual social-cognitive developmental model (Lochman & Wells, 2002). It was designed to be an "indicated" (that is, tier 3) prevention program for students with identifiable risk markers of aggressive behavior problems in an effort to prevent later, and possibly worse, school and behavioral adjustment problems (O'Connell et al., 2009). Such programming during the middle school years may afford an opportunity to shift the developmental trajectory of aggressive behavior, thereby reducing rates of aggressive and other high-risk behaviors and preventing subsequent negative outcomes, such as school failure. EACP was designed to be implemented with small groups of six to seven youth in grades 6–8 who display moderate to high levels of aggressive behaviors and are therefore at risk for later problem behaviors (for example, school failure, aggression, and substance abuse).

EACP is a multicomponent program (that is, youth, parent, and teacher supports) that targets processes within the child (for example, social-cognitive, self-regulation) and family (for example, parenting practices) that contribute to aggressive behavior and academic achievement. Youth participants are typically identified by teachers through a screening or referral process based on their pattern of aggressive behavior. Coping Power is based on a social-cognitive model of youth aggression and focuses on known proximal (for example, parenting practices, youth social cognition and self-regulation, peer context) and distal (for example, school context, family context, and child neurobehavioral status) risk factors for adolescent aggression. Like the previous versions of Coping Power, the middle school version targets the following four interrelated predictors of aggression and antisocial behavior in youth and adulthood: social competence, self-regulation, protective bond with school, and parenting practices. Specifically, youth with poor social competence also have deficiencies in their social problem-solving skills and more physical responses to provocation. Aggressive youth believe that aggressive responses will cause others to stop behaving aversely and will enhance their social status (Lochman & Dodge, 1994).

However, aggressive and socially challenged youth are often rejected by prosocial peers and therefore become susceptible to the influence of deviant peer groups in adolescence. Youth's poor capacity for self-regulation of their emotional responses can also contribute to their poor social competence. Notably, reactive aggressive behavior has been shown to be related to unregulated, intense emotional arousal in general and to high levels of anger in particular (Dodge, Lochman, Harnish, Bates, & Pettit, 1997). Youth's ability to develop a protective bond with school is compromised by reactive, aggressive behavior, which is likely to elicit negative reactions from teachers and rejection from prosocial peers beginning in early to middle childhood. Negative interactions with teachers often lead to missed academic time resulting from disciplinary actions, which inhibits academic progress and promotes disengagement. It is especially important for parents and students to maintain a strong school bond in the transition to high school (Bradshaw, O'Brennan, & McNeely, 2008). Furthermore, several risk factors related to parenting practices are directly linked to childhood aggression, including deficient family management practices, poor monitoring, unclear expectations of behavior, high levels of family conflict, and low levels of warmth in parent–child relations (for example, Collins, Maccoby, Steinberg, Hetherington, & Bornstein, 2000). As youth transition into adolescence, appropriate parental monitoring is increasingly important in preventing adolescents' gravitation to deviant peer groups, delinquency, and substance use. Like the previous versions of Coping Power, EACP built on research regarding these core areas and integrated a set of interactive activities and training components for students, parents, and teachers to promote skill development in these four broad areas. Below we describe the components of the program in greater detail.

OVERVIEW OF THE EACP INTERVENTION COMPONENTS

The Youth Component includes 25 group sessions, which take place at the students' schools, typically outside of academic hours (for example, before or after school, during nonacademic homeroom periods, recess, specials, lunch) over the course of a single school year. Group sessions last approximately 45–50 minutes (that is, they are designed to fit within a single class period) and include approximately six to seven students per group. Sessions are co-led by a clinician, counselor, social worker, or school psychologist who is trained in the manualized intervention. Each student also receives a total of eight to 10 individual 30-minute sessions during school hours (for example, once a month) from the clinician to encourage generalization and to monitor and reinforce attainment of classroom and social behavior goals (for example, avoiding fights, resisting peer pressure). The Parent Component consists of 12 parent group sessions of 45–50 minutes each over the same school year with the same co-leaders administering the youth sessions. The Teacher Component consists of professional development sessions and periodic check-ins led by a clinician for teachers of intervention students each year. The Teacher Component was designed to provide opportunities for the promotion of youth' generalization of skills developed in the session to other nonsession contexts, such as the classroom.

EFFICACY OF COPING POWER

Previous trials of the elementary version of Coping Power have shown preventive effects on substance use, aggression, and delinquent behavior; and promotion of social competence, concentration, and achievement (Lochman & Wells, 2002, 2003; Lochman, Wells, Qu, & Chen, 2013). Specifically, randomized controlled efficacy and effectiveness studies have demonstrated reductions in youth substance use and delinquent behavior (Lochman & Wells, 2003), reduction in proactive aggression, improved social competence and concentration, and greater behavioral improvement in comparison to control children (Lochman & Wells, 2002; Lochman et al., 2013). Research has also demonstrated promising effects on academic outcomes (Lochman et al., 2012) as well as bullying. The Youth Component of Coping Power is directly derived from the Anger Coping Program, which has been shown to prevent high levels of adolescent substance use. As a result of these favorable findings, Coping Power is included on several federal and state lists of evidence-based programs (for example, What Works Clearinghouse, Blueprints Promising Program).

PILOT FINDINGS ON EACP

Our team recently conducted a small randomized pilot of the middle school Coping Power program with 30 sixth-grade students (ages 11–13; 50 percent male) in urban middle schools; half of the students were randomized to receive EACP, and the other half were randomized to receive care as usual. Although composed of just 30 students, the pilot was underpowered. Teacher reports on the Behavioral Assessment System for Children Version 2 (BASC-2; Reynolds & Kamphaus, 2006), which includes scales and several items related to bullying and aggressive behavior, suggested that students randomized to receive EACP experienced a positive trend in terms of changes over time for all but one (anxiety) of the 20 BASC-2 standardized scales. For the student self-reported BASC-2 data, 12 of the 21 scales favored the EACP condition. The process data from the pilot also indicated that for the vast majority of the sessions, the clinicians were able to complete core elements, such as journaling (72 percent of the sessions), providing positive feedback (78.1 percent), and goal setting (93.8 percent). The clinicians also indicated that youth appeared very comfortable with the group leader (87.5 percent were "very comfortable"; 12.5 percent were "partially comfortable") and with their peers in the group (90.6 percent were "very comfortable"; 9.4 percent were "partially comfortable"). Most sessions (87.5 percent) proceeded as planned with no disruptions or problems. For all but one session, there was a high level of youth engagement in the session discussions and activities. Taken together, these pilot findings suggest promise of the middle school Coping Power program. These findings also informed an ongoing larger randomized trial in 40 middle schools in Maryland and Alabama, which is currently funded by the Institute of Education Sciences. Preliminary findings from this ongoing trial are also favorable. Specifically, relative to students in the control condition, at the end of the school year following participation in the year-long program students exposed to EACP experienced significant improvements in Adaptive Skills (effect size [ES] = .47), with even stronger effects on the adaptive skills subscale scores for Adaptability (ES = .85) and Leadership (ES = .53). Relative to youth in the control condition, EACP youth displayed decreases in the Externalizing Behavior Composite (ES = 2.38), with significant reductions on the Hyperactivity subscale score (ES = 2.53). Interestingly, the effect sizes were even larger one year postintervention. Another grant from the National Institute of Justice is currently funding the adaptation of the EACP model for use in urban high schools; this version includes school police officers, who receive training to participate in the implementation of select Coping Power group sessions.

CONCLUSIONS

Coping Power is an established indicated prevention program that incorporates youth, parent, and teacher elements in an effort to address aggressive behavior problems. Although the impacts of Coping Power are far-reaching and include multiple behavioral, social, emotional, substance use, and academic effects, the program also appears to be a promising intervention for addressing bullying among youth who are already engaged in high-risk behaviors. An important consideration in facilitating Coping Power or any other group intervention for aggressive youth is careful adult supervision and monitoring to ensure that there is limited opportunity for peer deviance training (Dodge, Dishion, & Lansford, 2007). Further work is needed on the middle school Coping Power program to determine whether it generates similarly favorable effects as have been observed in randomized studies testing the elementary version.

REFERENCES

Bradshaw, C. P. (2015). Translating research to practice in bullying prevention. *American Psychologist, 70*, 322–332.

Bradshaw, C. P., O'Brennan, L. M., & McNeely, C. A. (2008). Core competencies and the prevention of school failure and early school leaving. *New Directions for Child and Adolescent Development, 122*, 19–32.

Collins, W. A., Maccoby, E. E., Steinberg, L., Hetherington, E. M., & Bornstein, M. H. (2000). Contemporary research on parenting: The case for nature and nurture. *American Psychologist, 55*, 218–232.

Dodge, K. A., Dishion, T. J., & Lansford, J. E. (2007). *Deviant peer influences in programs for youth: Problems and solutions.* New York: Guilford Press.

Dodge, K. A., Lochman, J. E., Harnish, J. D., Bates, J. E., & Pettit, G. S. (1997). Reactive and proactive aggression in school children and psychiatrically-impaired chronically assaultive youth. *Journal of Abnormal Psychology, 106*, 37–51.

Eccles, J. S., & Harold, R. D. (1993). Parent-school involvement during the early adolescent years. In R. Takanishi (Ed.), *Adolescence in the 1990s: Risk and opportunity.* New York: Columbia University Teachers College.

Lochman, J. E., Boxmeyer, C. L., Powell, N. P., Qu, L., Wells, K., & Windle, M. (2012). Coping Power dissemination study: Intervention and special education effects on academic outcomes. *Behavioral Disorders, 37*, 192–205.

Lochman, J. E., & Dodge, K. A. (1994). Social-cognitive processes of severely violent, moderately aggressive and nonaggressive boys. *Journal of Consulting and Clinical Psychology, 62*, 366–374.

Lochman, J. E., & Wells, K. C. (2002). Contextual social-cognitive mediators and child outcome: A test of the theoretical model in the Coping Power Program. *Development and Psychopathology, 14*, 971–993.

Lochman, J. E., & Wells, K. C. (2003). Effectiveness study of Coping Power and classroom intervention with aggressive children: Outcomes at a one-year follow-up. *Behavior Therapy, 34*, 493–515.

Lochman, J. E., Wells, K. C., Qu, L., & Chen, L. (2013). Three year follow-up of Coping Power intervention effects: Evidence of neighborhood moderation? *Prevention Science, 14*, 364–376.

O'Connell, M. E., Boat, T., & Warner, K. E. (2009). *Preventing mental, emotional, and behavioral disorders among young people: Progress and possibilities*. Washington, DC: Committee on the Prevention of Mental Disorders and Substance Abuse Among Children, Youth and Young Adults: Research Advances and Promising Interventions; Institute of Medicine; National Research Council; National Academies Press.

Reynolds, C. R., & Kamphaus, R. W. (2006). *BASC-2: Behavior Assessment System for Children* (2nd ed.). Upper Saddle River, NJ: Pearson Education.

Swearer, S. M., Espelage, D. L., Vaillancourt, T., & Hymel, S. (2010). What can be done about school bullying? Linking research to educational practice. *Educational Researcher, 1*, 38–47.

19

The Role of Education Support Professionals in Preventing Bullying

Tracy E. Waasdorp, Lindsey O'Brennan, and Catherine P. Bradshaw

Education support professionals (ESPs) play a crucial role in the daily functioning of schools and the success of students (for example, teachers' aides, secretaries, bus drivers, cafeteria workers, custodians). Yet limited research has examined the extent to which they are involved in bullying prevention and intervention efforts. This is surprising, given that ESPs comprise approximately 40 percent of school-based employees, which makes them a potentially untapped resource within the school. Although research suggests that collaborative schoolwide programs tend to be most effective in preventing bullying (Bradshaw & Waasdorp, 2009; Ttofi & Farrington, 2011), there is a need for better integration of ESPs into school-based prevention efforts. This chapter provides an overview of research-based strategies for involving ESPs in schoolwide bullying programming across elementary and secondary school settings.

WHO ARE EDUCATION SUPPORT PROFESSIONALS?

ESPs are a diverse group of staff members with varied skill sets and professional backgrounds. According to the National Education Association (NEA; http://www.nea.org), nearly half of ESPs are paraeducators (for example, teachers' aides, instructional assistants, playground monitors), approximately 16 percent are in clerical services (for example, secretaries, office

This work was supported in part through a contract with the National Education Association (NEA). The thoughts and opinions expressed in this document are those of the authors and not of the NEA. The authors would also like to acknowledge Joanne Morris of the NEA for her comments and feedback on a draft of this chapter.

assistants), 11 percent are in transportation (for example, bus drivers), 10 percent are in food services (for example, cooks, cafeteria workers), and 15 percent are in other services (for example, maintenance, custodians). Despite differences in their various roles and responsibilities, ESPs have many commonalities related to their involvement in school-based prevention and intervention programs. For example, given that they interact with a wide range of students during transition periods and are often the first and last staff members that students see each day, ESPs are often on the "front line" of bullying prevention and intervention.

Interaction with Students

School staff have varying levels of interaction with students depending on their role in the school. For instance, a teacher spends substantially more time with a core set of students compared with a food service professional, who interacts with the majority of students in a large group setting. Yet the more interactions staff have with students, the more likely they are to have students report bullying to them. A national study of ESPs and teaching staff's perceptions of bullying showed that 45 percent of teachers, compared with 35 percent of ESPs, indicated that a student had reported bullying to them within the past month (Bradshaw, Waasdorp, O'Brennan, & Gulemetova, 2011). The level of student interaction also tended to vary depending on the school setting, such that staff working in elementary schools, as compared with those in middle or high schools, were more likely to have students report bullying incidents to them. In fact, research suggests that younger students are more likely to rely on adults for emotional support, but as students progress into adolescence, they tend to disclose personal struggles to their peers as opposed to school staff or their parents. Perhaps adolescents perceive that seeking help from school staff is a sign of weakness or immaturity. If so, it is not surprising that research suggests that peer bystander interventions are more effective among adolescents than among younger students (Polanin, Espelage, & Pigott, 2012). With this in mind, secondary school staff are encouraged to lead discussions about bullying when talking with students individually and in classroom settings, because students may not feel comfortable raising this issue. In addition, ESPs can create safe spaces where students can feel comfortable talking about bullying incidents, both when working one-on-one with students and in small groups.

Work with Special Populations

Although research has highlighted differences among student reports of bullying in the general student population, some subgroups of students may have more regular interaction with ESPs than with teachers or administrators. ESPs often supervise students in settings where bullying frequently occurs (for example, paraeducators, lunch and playground aides), which means they may have more exposure to bullying than teachers. Similarly, given that students in special education are more likely to be bullied than their peers, ESPs who provide supports to special education students may have more opportunity to witness bullying (for example, O'Brennan, Waasdorp, & Bradshaw, 2014). For example, children with emotion regulation difficulties are at an increased risk of being a bully as well as of being a victim of bullying (Fite, Evans, Cooley, & Rubens, 2014). Likewise, both frequent victimization and higher levels of bullying are associated with recurrent visits to the school nurse, putting nurses in a position to intervene (Vernberg, Nelson, Fonagy, & Twemlow, 2011). ESPs should be more involved in bullying prevention programming, and their role should be tailored to fit staff members' position and their access to different types of students.

Work in Hotspots

Bullying "hotspots" are specific locations where bullying behaviors are more likely to occur. These locations are often open gathering areas in a school, where there is a high student-to-adult ratio and few structured activities (Leff, Power, Costigan, & Manz, 2003). As would be expected, the riskiness of the location varies depending on the age of the youth. For example, the playground is often the most common location for bullying in elementary schools (for example, Fite et al., 2013), whereas the hallways and cafeteria are the most common hotspots in high schools (Vaillancourt et al., 2010). Other hotspots include school buses, libraries, stairwells, and bathrooms. Many ESPs work in these unstructured locations (Leff et al., 2003) where a significant portion of bullying occurs. In fact, a recent study of ESPs indicated that 82 percent had witnessed bullying at least once in the past month (Bradshaw, Waasdorp, O'Brennan, & Gulemetova, 2013). Research also indicates that the presence of adults in the hallway in middle and high school is associated with 26 percent fewer incidents of peer victimization (Blosnich & Bossarte, 2011). However, ESPs are rarely given a central role in bullying prevention or intervention in the areas they supervise (DeLara, 2008; Hendershot, Dake, Price, & Lartey, 2006). Yet ESPs clearly play an important part in increasing supervision in these hotspot areas.

ESPS AND EVIDENCE-BASED BULLYING PROGRAMMING

Much of the research to date on ESPs comes from small-scale studies of particular ESP groups. For example, one qualitative study of transportation staff by DeLara (2008) revealed that although ESPs witnessed a considerable amount of bullying, most felt that they were not included in the district's school safety planning efforts. Most schoolwide bullying prevention models emphasize the inclusion of all staff in prevention efforts, but this is rarely the case in practice. Moreover, a recent study revealed that compared with teachers, ESP workers were more likely to report a greater need for additional training related to intervening in bullying situations and specifically when the bullying is related to sexual orientation, being overweight, or having a disability (Bradshaw et al., 2013). Results from that study revealed that, compared with teachers, ESPs are equally likely to have parents report bullying situations to them. ESPs are often the first point of contact for families (for example, clerical staff, bus drivers), and it is crucial that ESPs are prepared to respond to and guide parents in accordance with a school's bullying policies (for example, who to report to, how to document the situation; Bradshaw et al., 2013).

Given the importance of including ESPs in bullying prevention and intervention programming, it is surprising that antibullying efforts seldom incorporate ESPs (Bradshaw et al., 2011). If they are included, ESPs are rarely given a central role in prevention or intervention with bullying behaviors. For instance, whole-school programs, such as the Olweus Bullying Prevention Program (Olweus, Limber, & Mihalic, 1999) and Positive Behavioral Intervention and Supports (Ross & Horner, 2014), advocate for representative members of the nonteaching staff and other paraeducators to serve on the school committees. But because of logistical issues (see below), ESPs are often not able to attend monthly meetings where intervention strategies are discussed. Likewise, most programs for bullying rarely assess ESPs' perceptions of what would be effective or essential for them to best prevent or intervene in problem behaviors. In order for all school personnel, including those who oversee high-risk areas for bullying, to feel invested in the prevention and intervention efforts, it would be essential to have a whole-school model of prevention in which ESPs are valued members of the planning and implementation. To date, there are few preventative intervention programs for bullying designed to address the specific needs of ESPs.

Despite the scant programming that provides training specific to the issues of ESPs, there are some programs and studies that distinctly incorporate ESPs. Leff et al. (2003) designed a measure that was explicitly intended to assess the bullying climate on the playground and the lunchroom (Playground and Lunchroom Climate Questionnaire). This measurement tool is among the first to highlight the importance of the perceptions of those personnel who oversee these high-risk areas; the findings from this measure also underscore the importance of collaboration between teaching and nonteaching staff. Similarly, an assessment of school nurses' perceptions of bullying revealed that nurses perceive many barriers when dealing with bullying, such as a need for more information regarding how to identify bullies and victims, as well as which behaviors to report to administrators (Hendershot et al., 2006).

To further illustrate the significance of including ESPs, research examining the effectiveness of programs including ESPs has shown positive results. In a program designed to reduce bullying on the playground, Leff, Costigan, and Power (2004) found that allowing the playground staff (that is, paraeducators) to tailor the intervention to best meet their perceived needs resulted in staff feeling more motivated and empowered to implement the intervention. Another example of ESPs being integrated into the schoolwide prevention program is a study by McCurdy, Lannie, and Barnabas (2009), who adapted a behavior management program, the Good Behavior Game (GBG; Barrish, Saunders, & Wolf, 1969; Embry, 2002), for use in the cafeteria. The GBG is a widely researched classroom management strategy that has been shown through randomized controlled trials to reduce bullying (Ialongo, Werthamer, & Kellam, 1999) and to produce multiple long-term behavioral, mental health, and academic outcomes (see, for example, Bradshaw, Zmuda, Kellam, & Ialongo, 2009). Although only a preliminary study, McCurdy et al. (2009) found a decrease in disruptive behaviors and, notably, that the GBG was rated as highly acceptable by the lunchroom staff. Although the GBG was not designed to specifically target bullying behaviors, this study illustrated the importance of a concerted focus on high-risk areas and the inclusion of ESPs, such as lunchroom staff, for universal prevention programming to be most effective.

Other curricula, such as *Bus Discipline: A Positive Approach* (Sprick & Colvin, 1992) and *In the Driver's Seat: A Roadmap to Managing Student Behavior on the Bus* (Sprick, Schwartz, & Schroeder, 2006), have been used by bus drivers to manage problem behaviors, like bullying on the bus. Similar curricula, developed by Sprick, Garrison, and Howard (2000), aim to aid teachers and ESPs in managing discipline problems in the cafeteria and playground (see http://safeandcivilschools.com). Although there is some promising anecdotal evidence of their effectiveness, there has been little systematic research testing the impacts of these programs on student outcomes. Another possible way to include nonteaching staff and paraeducators in targeted prevention activities could be through the use of school-based mentoring programs, as there is some preliminary evidence of the effectiveness of such programs with victimized youth (Herrera, 2004). Additional research is needed to determine effective ways for including ESPs in targeted and schoolwide bullying prevention programming, especially given that more than 40 percent of adults working within a school are ESPs (National Education Association, 2009).

OVERCOMING LOGISTICAL CHALLENGES TO INCLUDING ESPS IN PREVENTION PROGRAMMING

It is important to consider some possible logistical barriers when incorporating ESPs into bullying prevention efforts. For instance, approximately 25 percent of ESPs are part-time employees and many work at multiple schools (Bradshaw et al., 2011); therefore, they may have limited time to participate in schoolwide meetings focused on bullying or to attend school-based trainings focused on prevention policies and procedures. In fact, most of the professional development they receive is job-specific (for example, records management for clerical staff, safety and sanitation for cafeteria workers) rather than related to schoolwide prevention and intervention (National Education Association, 2003). Yet, a study of school nurses revealed that they perceived several other barriers to dealing with bullying, such as a need for more information regarding policies and procedures for how to identify bullies and victims and which behaviors to report to administrators (Hendershot et al., 2006).

ESPs have generally been perceived as lower-status employees relative to teachers because of the credentials typically required for the position, the salaries they earn, and the relatively limited autonomy and control ESPs have over their work (Bradshaw & Figiel, 2012). As a result of their lower perceived status, ESPs may be vulnerable to feeling bullied by other staff and possibly students. Perceived personal experiences with victimization are important to understand in light of staff roles within a school, as they may also influence staff members' willingness to intervene in bullying situations or engage in bullying prevention efforts. In fact, research suggests that staff who feel more connected to the school are more likely to intervene in bullying situations (O'Brennan et al., 2014).

Despite these and other potential challenges to engagement, ESPs are in a unique position to both prevent and intervene in bullying, particularly bullying that occurs among high-risk groups and in hotspots across the school. This makes them valuable potential partners for assisting youth with bullying and helping administrators implement evidence-based programs. Given the growing interest in whole-school approaches to prevention, it is critical that we identify strategies for scaffolding ESPs' involvement in bullying prevention. Toward that end, Table 19.1 summarizes some recommendations for different opportunities for ESPs to get involved in prevention and intervention programing. These recommendations are based on the Bully Free: It Starts with Me! campaign developed by the National Education Association (http://www.nea.org).

CONCLUSIONS AND NEXT STEPS

A large proportion of teachers and ESPs witness bullying on a weekly basis (approximately 40 percent and 36 percent, respectively); yet ESPs receive less training on their districts' bullying policy, are less likely to be involved in bullying prevention efforts at school, and are less likely to feel that it is their responsibility to intervene in bullying (Bradshaw et al., 2013). A clear next step for schools is to provide additional training to ESPs and increase their involvement in schoolwide prevention and intervention programs. At present, few youth violence programs specifically address ESP involvement. However, schools are encouraged to adapt bullying curricula to meet the specific professional needs of ESPs (see Table 19.1), for example, by increasing adult supervision in bullying hotspots and better addressing bullying among special populations of students, such as students in special education, and sexual minority youth. Involving all school staff in prevention programming is likely to result in enhanced staff cohesiveness, cross-communication, and overall feelings of connectedness to their school community.

Table 19.1: Bullying Prevention and Intervention Strategies Specific to Each Education Support Professional

Education Support Professionals	Bullying Prevention	Bullying Intervention
Bus drivers	Set clear and consistent rules for expected bus behavior. Use the schoolwide reward system to reinforce positive behaviors.	Start with verbal warnings, and if the behavior escalates then stop the bus in a safe place to address the bullying. Talk to school staff and students about the bullying happening before/after school so they are informed.
Clerical and administrative	Encourage students and staff to report bullying incidents to you. Maintain a log of incidents and help identify patterns of bullying schoolwide.	Learn and share information with all staff about bullying policies. Alert school staff about bullying you witnessed and possible retaliation.
Custodial	Inform administrators of areas in the school that need increased adult supervision. Talk with administrators about the importance of custodial staff participating in bullying training.	Help monitor less supervised areas such as hallways, stairways, and bathrooms. Talk with administrators about how you should intervene and where to report students involved in bullying.
Food service	Help consistently enforce rules for the cafeteria. Suggest a reward program for classrooms meeting the behavioral expectations during their lunchtime.	Remind students of the cafeteria rules if disruptive behavior starts escalating. Talk with administrators about lunch periods that are high-risk for bullying and need additional supervision.
Health and student services	Ask about bullying when conducting health check-ups, especially among "frequent flyer" students who routinely come into the health office. Talk with school staff and parents about students at risk for bullying.	Help victimized students safely get back to class and check in with students as needed. Seek out additional student mental health resources for students frequently involved in bullying.
Paraeducators	Emphasize empathy and respect when working with students. Talk with students about the different types of bullying. Role-play bullying scenarios and teach students how to defuse the situation.	Work alongside classroom teachers and remove a bully or victim from the class if an incident occurs. Teach bystanders how they could intervene next time.

Adapted from the National Education Association (http://www.nea.org).

REFERENCES

Barrish, H. H., Saunders, M., & Wolf, M. M. (1969). Good behavior game: Effects of individual contingencies for group consequences on disruptive behavior in a classroom. *Journal of Applied Behavior Analysis, 2*(2), 119–124. doi:10.1901/jaba.1969.2-119

Blosnich, J., & Bossarte, R. (2011). Low-level violence in schools: Is there an association between school safety measures and peer victimization? *Journal of School Health, 81*(2), 107–113. doi:10.1111/j.1746-1561.2010.00567.x

Bradshaw, C. P., & Figiel, K. (2012). *Prevention and intervention for workplace bullying in schools.* Washington, DC: National Education Association.

Bradshaw, C. P., & Waasdorp, T. E. (2009). Measuring and changing a "culture of bullying." *School Psychology Review, 38*, 356–361.

Bradshaw, C. P., Waasdorp, T. E., O'Brennan, L., & Gulemetova, M. (2011). *Findings from the National Education Association's nationwide study of bullying: Teachers' and staff members' perspectives on bullying and prevention.* Report prepared for the National Education Association, Washington, DC.

Bradshaw, C. P., Waasdorp, T. E., O'Brennan, L., & Gulemetova, M. (2013). Teachers' and education support professionals' perspectives on bullying and prevention: Findings from a National Education Association (NEA) survey. *School Psychology Review, 42*(3), 280–297.

Bradshaw, C. P., Zmuda, J. H., Kellam, S. G., & Ialongo, N. A. (2009). Longitudinal impact of two universal preventive interventions in first grade on educational outcomes in high school. *Journal of Educational Psychology, 101*, 926–937.

DeLara, E. W. (2008). Bullying and aggression on the school bus: School bus drivers' observations and suggestions. *Journal of School Violence, 7*(3), 48–70.

Embry, D. D. (2002). The good behavior game: A best practice candidate as a universal behavioral vaccine. *Clinical Child and Family Psychology Review, 5*, 273–297.

Fite, P. J., Evans, S. C., Cooley, J. L., & Rubens, S. L. (2014). Further evaluation of associations between attention-deficit/hyperactivity and oppositional defiant disorder symptoms and bullying-victimization in adolescence. *Child Psychiatry and Human Development, 45*(1), 32–41. doi:10.1007/s10578-013-0376-8

Fite, P. J., Williford, A., Cooley, J. L., DePaolis, K., Rubens, S. L., & Vernberg, E. M. (2013). Patterns of victimization locations in elementary school children: Effects of grade level and gender. *Child & Youth Care Forum, 42*, 585–597.

Hendershot, C., Dake, J. A., Price, J. H., & Lartey, G. K. (2006). Elementary school nurses' perceptions of student bullying. *Journal of School Nursing, 22*(4), 229–236. doi:10.1177/10598405050220040801

Herrera, C. (2004). *School based mentoring: A closer look. Public private ventures.* Retrieved from http://www.ppv.org/ppv/publications/assets/180_publication.pdf

Ialongo, N. S., Werthamer, L., & Kellam, S. G. (1999). Proximal impact of two first-grade preventive interventions on the early risk behaviors for later substance abuse, depression, and antisocial behavior. *American Journal of Community Psychology, 27*, 599–641.

Leff, S. S., Costigan, T., & Power, T. J. (2004). Using participatory research to develop a playground-based prevention program. *Journal of School Psychology, 42*(1), 3–21. doi:10.1016/j.jsp.2003.08.005

Leff, S. S., Power, T. J., Costigan, T. E., & Manz, P. H. (2003). Assessing the climate of the playground and lunchroom: Implications for bullying prevention programming. *School Psychology Review, 32*(3), 418–430.

McCurdy, B. L., Lannie, A. L., & Barnabas, E. (2009). Reducing disruptive behavior in an urban school cafeteria: An extension of the good behavior game. *Journal of School Psychology, 47*(1), 39–54. doi:10.1016/j.jsp.2008.09.003

National Education Association. (2003). *The ESProfessionals: An action guide to help you in your professional development.* Washington, DC: Author.

National Education Association. (2009). *Education support professionals.* Retrieved from http://www.nea.org/home/1604.htm

O'Brennan, L. M., Waasdorp, T. E., & Bradshaw, C. P. (2014). Strengthening bullying prevention through school staff connectedness. *Journal of Educational Psychology, 106,* 870–880. doi:10.1037/a0035957

Olweus, D., Limber, S. P., & Mihalic, S. F. (1999). Blueprints for violence prevention: Book nine—Bullying prevention program. In D. S. Elliott (Series Ed.), *Blueprints for violence prevention series.* Boulder, CO: Center for the Study and Prevention of Violence, Institute of Behavioral Science, University of Colorado.

Polanin, J. R., Espelage, D. L., & Pigott, T. D. (2012). A meta-analysis of school-based bullying prevention programs' effects on bystander intervention behavior. *School Psychology Review, 41*(1), 47–65.

Ross, S. W., & Horner, R. H. (2014). Bully prevention in positive behavior support: Preliminary evaluation of third-, fourth-, and fifth-grade attitudes toward bullying. *Journal of Emotional and Behavioral Disorders, 22*(4), 225–236. doi:10.1177/1063426613491429

Sprick, R. S., & Colvin, T. (1992). *Bus discipline: A positive approach.* Retrieved from http://www .safeandcivilschools.com

Sprick, R., Garrison, M., & Howard, L. (2000). *ParaPro: Supporting the instructional process.* Eugene, OR: Pacific Northwest Publishing.

Sprick, R. S., Schwartz, L., & Schroeder, S. (2006). In *the driver's seat: A roadmap to managing student behavior on the bus.* Retrieved from http://www.safeandcivilschools.com.

Ttofi, M. M., & Farrington, D. P. (2011). Effectiveness of school-based programs to reduce bullying: A systematic and meta-analytic review. *Journal of Experimental Criminology, 7*(1), 27–56. doi:10.1007/s11292-010-9109-1

Vaillancourt, T., Brittain, H., Bennett, L., Arnocky, S., McDougall, P., Hymel, S., et al. (2010). Places to avoid: Population-based study of student reports of unsafe and high bullying areas at school. *Canadian Journal of School Psychology, 25*(1), 40–54.

Vernberg, E. M., Nelson, T. D., Fonagy, P., & Twemlow, S. W. (2011). Victimization, aggression, and visits to the school nurse for somatic complaints, illnesses, and physical injuries. *Pediatrics, 127,* 842–848.

20

Youth Engagement in Bullying Prevention Efforts: History, Current Applications, and the Born Brave Bus Tour

Susan M. Swearer, Michelle Howell-Smith, Sara E. Gonzalez, Zachary R. Myers, Heather Schwartz, Jenna Strawhun, Theresa McKinney, and Cynthia Germanotta

Youth empowerment and engagement are necessary components of violence-prevention efforts (Zeldin, 2004) and positive youth development (Debnam, Johnson, Waasdorp, & Bradshaw, 2013). The focus on youth empowerment and youth engagement is an intuitive and appealing heuristic, but it has been lacking in the context of bullying prevention and intervention efforts. Many bullying prevention and intervention programs focus on the behaviors of bystanders who witness bullying. Researchers and practitioners recognize that bullying often takes place in the peer context (Rodkin, Espelage, & Hanish, 2015) and is witnessed by peers (Pepler, Jiang, Craig, & Connolly, 2008), but the question of how to engage and empower youth to respond effectively to bullying situations remains underexplored. In this chapter, we discuss the necessary elements for engaging youth and the history of two popular movements in the United States. Then we describe two examples of youth development programs (gay–straight alliances [GSAs] and 4-H clubs), which can be leveraged to address issues of bullying and youth connectedness. We then focus on a novel multimedia campaign called the Born Brave Bus Tour, which is a signature project of the Born This Way Foundation (BTWF; http://www.bornthiswayfoundation.org) designed to create opportunities for positive youth engagement. We summarize some qualitative findings from the Born Brave Bus Tour and conclude with some recommendations for community and school-based youth engagement efforts.

ENGAGING YOUTH IN BULLYING PREVENTION: PREREQUISITE FACTORS

For positive youth development and the facilitation of healthy social relationships to occur, three interrelated factors must first be firmly in place in youth's lives: (1) a social support system; (2) skills to empower healthy cognitive and social development; and (3) opportunities for meaningful engagement in academics, extracurricular activities, and community involvement (Checkoway & Gutierrez, 2011). In this section, we discuss these prerequisite factors and the mission of BTWF that cultivates these necessary conditions for youth engagement.

Youth Social Support

Human beings are essentially social creatures. An individual's need for belonging must be met before addressing higher-order needs such as self-esteem and self-actualization (Maslow, 1943). Baumeister and Leary (1995) suggested that this fundamental need to belong relates to the existence of groups. Individuals' group membership profoundly influences their behaviors and self-concept, shaping how they think, feel, and behave within their groups (Hogg & Cooper, 2007), even without direct reinforcement (Bandura, 1977). The influence of group membership on individual behavior can have a cascading effect as observed behaviors are repeated throughout the social system (Fowler & Christakis, 2010). Because group membership is a particularly salient component of an individual's identity, as youth develop their own identity independent of their family of origin, their peer group becomes an important source of social support.

In the same way that group membership influences individual behavior, it also provides support essential for healthy development. For youth, social supports not only enrich the development of self-esteem, self-concept, social skills, and relationships with parents, teachers, and peers but also safeguard against negative outcomes such as depression, anxiety, and conduct problems, particularly for at-risk youth (Demaray & Malecki, 2013). There is a clear relationship between the perceived level of social support and involvement in bullying (Demaray & Malecki, 2010). Research has consistently found that bullies, victims, and bully–victims perceive less social support than those not involved in bullying (Demaray & Malecki, 2003), whereas higher levels of perceived social support are related to lower levels of victimization (Kendrick, Jutengren, & Stattin, 2012). In other words, youth who perceive that they have a strong social support system may be less likely to engage in bullying behaviors or to be targets of bullying.

Youth Empowerment

Empowerment is a psychological construct that includes the feeling of control over one's life and the agency to actively engage in one's community (Rappaport, 1981). Although empowerment theory addresses multiple levels and contexts of empowerment (Peterson, 2014), psychological empowerment is most directly related to individual behavior change and is composed of intrapersonal, interactional, and behavioral components (Zimmerman, 1990; Zimmerman, Israel, Schulz, & Checkoway, 1992). The intrapersonal dimension includes one's sense of self-efficacy and motivation for engagement; the interaction dimension includes an awareness of one's environment and decision making and problem solving; and the behavioral dimension includes the specific actions related to engagement. Thus, psychological empowerment includes both cognitive and behavioral components.

There are numerous components necessary for facilitating empowerment in youth (Russell, Muraco, Subramaniam, & Laub, 2009). The positive youth development framework suggests five components that are essential in developing socially healthy young adults: (1) competence, (2) confidence, (3) connection, (4) character, and (5) caring (Bowers et al., 2010; Wilson, Minkler, Dasho, Wallerstein, & Martin, 2008). These five C's map onto the three components of psychological empowerment. However, for youth to acquire the skills and confidence needed to translate into youth empowerment, they must be given ample opportunities to gain mastery and experience success. Although evaluations of youth empowerment programs have found positive effects for self-efficacy (Gullan, Power, & Leff, 2013), motivation to volunteer (Sharma, Suarez-Balcazar, & Baetke, 2003), and reduced drug use (Berg, Coman, & Schensul, 2009), there is limited experimental research empirically testing the effectiveness of these programs in improving adolescents' self-efficacy and self-esteem (Morton & Montgomery, 2013).

Youth Engagement

Engagement typically refers to active participation in working toward the betterment of the community and society (Sherrod, 2007; Voight & Torney-Purta, 2013). Engagement includes both behavioral and attitudinal factors with individuals displaying various levels of each (da Silva, Sanson, Smart, & Toumbourou, 2004). In an investigation of civic engagement among middle school students, Voight and Torney-Purta (2013) found three distinct combinations of civic engagement behaviors and attitudes: (1) social justice actors, who present high levels of behavior and attitudes; (2) social justice sympathizers, who present low levels of attitudes and high levels of behavior; and (3) civic moderates, who present low levels of attitudes and behaviors. Is it is important to recognize not only the actions that youth take to be engaged but also their attitudes toward their society and creating change. If individuals feel hopeful about creating change, they are more likely to participate in bettering their homes, schools, and communities.

Although examples of youth engagement vary by context, several forms of civic engagement have been identified in the literature, including volunteering, participating in student government, and taking part in school-diversity and youth groups (Checkoway & Aldana, 2013; Geller, Voight, Wegman, & Nation, 2013). In addition, youth engagement has been associated with positive school climate, better psychological adjustment, and positive identity achievement (Geller et al., 2013; Pancer, Pratt, Hunsberger, & Alisat, 2007). Although these positive results provide support for the importance of youth engagement, a lack of opportunities to participate meaningfully in organized groups or feelings of being disconnected from one's community may hinder the promotion of civic engagement among the very youth who may benefit the most from group connections (that is, disconnected youth; Zeldin, 2004). Therefore, for youth to be engaged, they must be given opportunities and guidance to develop the necessary skills and expertise to feel confident in their ability to cause change. The research findings on social support, youth empowerment, and youth engagement suggest that effective youth programs need to address these three areas. There are several examples that can serve as models for effective youth engagement efforts in the United States.

MODELS OF YOUTH ENGAGEMENT

Several organizations have created programs for youth that provide opportunities to develop a sense of social support from their peers and program staff, deepen their feelings of control of and influence over their own lives, and inspire them to make a difference in their communities. In this section, we describe two models of youth engagement that have positively empowered youth to stand up to bullying and other negative behaviors: GSAs and 4-H programs.

GSAs

Much of the research on lesbian, gay, bisexual, transgender, and questioning (LGBTQ) youth has centered on peer victimization and the negative mental and physical health consequences associated with these sexual orientations (Toomey & Russell, 2013). In contrast, research on GSAs as a positive and supportive vehicle for youth development, engagement, and empowerment is an emerging area of research inquiry. GSAs are typically constructed as student-led organizations in high school and college settings to create positive partnerships and supportive spaces for LGBTQ youth and to ally students and staff who are supportive and inclusive (Toomey, Ryan, Diaz, & Russell, 2011).

GSAs may be involved in a number of school and community-based activities that catalyze youth empowerment (Russell et al., 2009), such as advocating for a safer and more supportive school climate; offering counseling and support services; connecting youth with LGBTQ community members; increasing the visibility of LGBTQ students in schools; and providing education to the school students and administration on LGBTQ issues and experiences (Russell et al., 2009; St. John et al., 2014). GSAs can also serve to combat anti-LGBTQ ideologies and bias-based language in school settings (Russell et al., 2009), reduce school absenteeism (Walls, Kane, & Wisneski, 2010), increase school belongingness and grade point averages, and buffer against the effects of bias-based victimization (Toomey et al., 2011).

The presence of a GSA in high schools has been found to affect students in meaningful ways, such as promoting positive attitudes toward LGBTQ individuals, even when controlling for variables such as gender, race, and age (Worthen, 2014), and more positive health outcomes in college, including reduced alcohol use and depressive symptoms (Heck, Flentje, & Cochran, 2013). In addition, research has found that including LGBTQ-inclusive curricula in schools is related to lower levels of bullying at the school level (Snapp, McGuire, Sinclair, Gabrion, & Russell, 2015). These findings illustrate the extended positive impacts of inclusive curricula and GSAs not only in high schools but also as students transition to other settings.

4-H Clubs

4-H clubs allow youth to interact with positive adult mentors to facilitate four pillars of growth, including head (that is, managing and thinking), heart (that is, relating and caring), hands (that is, giving and working), and health (that is, physical and mental), through after-school programs, summer camps, and community clubs (D'Onofrio, Moskowitz, & Braverman, 2002). An eight-year longitudinal study that surveyed 7,000 adolescents across 42 states found that boys and girls involved in 4-H were four times more likely to make contributions to their communities, two times more likely to be civically active, two times more likely to make healthier choices, and two times more likely to participate in science, engineering, and computer technology programs during out of school time. Relatedly, girls participating in 4-H were two to three times more likely to take part in science programs compared with girls not involved in 4-H programming (Lerner & Lerner, 2013). 4-H club participation has also been linked to decreased cigarette smoking, improved knowledge of the addictive properties and prevalence of smoking, (D'Onofrio et al., 2002), and increases in positive youth development (Lerner & Lerner, 2013). Thus, research on involvement in 4-H has reported that positive relationships with caring adults, a safe and inclusive environment, opportunity for mastery, service, engagement in learning, opportunity to see oneself as an active participant in the future, and opportunity for self-determination are all positive outcomes of participation in 4-H.

The two aforementioned youth engagement movements have a distinguished history. In 1902, youth clubs were formed as a way to connect public school education to farming and communities, and by 1924, 4-H clubs had formed across the United States (4-H, n.d.). The first GSAs were formed in 1998 in two private schools in Massachusetts and have since spread across private and public schools, with the goal of creating inclusive and accepting school climates (GSAday, n.d.). The United States has a long history of recognizing the importance of healthy youth development and engagement; yet research efforts have not developed in an equal trajectory. We now focus on a more recent and novel application of these core principles of positive youth development to an innovative multimedia campaign called the Born Brave Bus Tour. This effort had the overarching goal of promoting greater connections and social support among youth and their communities and also reducing bullying and intolerance through promoting kindness and bravery.

THE BORN BRAVE BUS TOUR: A VEHICLE FOR YOUTH ENGAGEMENT PROMOTION

To create a youth engagement movement, Lady Gaga's Born This Way Foundation sought to create a youth experience while also studying the factors youth need to create a kinder and braver world. Born This Way Foundation developed a three-pillar model, which included a focus on safety, skills, and opportunities. These three pillars have guided the foundation's work. The mission of Born This Way Foundation is "committed to supporting the wellness of young people and empowering them to create a kinder and braver world. We achieve this by shining a light on real people, quality research, and authentic partnerships" (https://bornthisway.foundation/). The philosophy of collaboration is threefold: (1) online through the Web site and an interactive map of resources for young people world-wide; (2) on the road through the Born Brave Bus Tour; and (3) down the street through the youth advisory board, Born Brave retreat, partnership with Westfield shopping centers, and commitment to research. The projects supported by Born This Way Foundation put into practice the nexus of social support, youth empowerment, and youth engagement. To evaluate the impact of support, empowerment, and engagement on reducing bullying and creating a kinder, braver world, the research advisory board of Born This Way Foundation designed a mixed-methods research study to understand these relationships. Below we summarize some of the findings from this study and highlight implications of this work for youth-led bullying prevention efforts.

The Born Brave Bus Tour was launched as a way to create a safe space outside concert venues where participants connect with local and national partners, learning skills of engagement and accessing opportunities for volunteering in their local communities. The

Born Brave Bus Tour started in January 2013 and consisted of a tour bus, three tents with representatives from local and national collaborators, and a space that included games, music, food, and spaces for people to socialize. The tour partnered with more than 50 organizations in cities across the United States and attracted over 150,000 participants from 2013 to 2014. The Born Brave Bus was a physical space where youth could meet one another, learn about mental health resources in their communities, sign up for volunteer opportunities, and be inspired to become ambassadors of kindness and bravery in their homes, schools, and communities.

Overview of the Study Design

Spurred by a desire to learn more about youth engagement and empowerment, the research advisory board of Born This Way Foundation designed a mixed-methods study to explore what youth between the ages of 13 and 25 need "to create a kinder and braver world." The quantitative component of the mixed-methods study involved collection and analysis of responses to an online survey, accessed through Born This Way Foundation's Web site. The qualitative component of the study involved collection and analysis of in-depth interviews conducted with youth and young adults in the fall of 2014 in Kansas City, Missouri ($n = 6$); Lincoln, Nebraska ($n = 5$); Los Angeles ($n = 10$); and New York ($n = 9$). In this chapter, we focus on the qualitative findings from the larger study.

With regard to the sample, we conducted interviews with 30 youth and young adults between the ages of 15 and 23. The interviews were guided by a semistructured protocol that aimed to elicit participants' thoughts, feelings, and experiences of kindness, bravery, and the Born Brave Bus (if they had attended). Our participants, who were all fans of Lady Gaga, were a diverse group in terms of gender identity, sexual orientation, ethnicity, and experiences with bullying. The interviews were transcribed verbatim, and we used MAX-QDA software to manage the transcripts during coding and analysis. For the purpose of this chapter, we conducted a general thematic analysis (Guest, MacQueen, & Namey, 2011), looking specifically for participants' conceptualizations of social support, empowerment, and engagement.

Summary of Qualitative Findings

Social Support. The Born Brave Bus Tour was described by participants as being a place where youth and young adults felt a sense of unconditional acceptance by everyone at the event. Whether it was feeling comfortable to be themselves or to be "whoever you wanna be," participants described feeling supported not just by an individual or a small group but by an entire community. The inclusiveness was palpable for the participants. They felt like they were "loved and supported by everyone there." The feeling of acceptance and inclusion permeated the event as evidenced by descriptions of the Bus as a "giant family dinner table" or a "sanctuary." One participant had a particularly vivid description of how it felt to be at the Born Brave Bus Tour: "It was a good aura. Like, I didn't feel one bad vibe there."

The Born Brave Bus Tour was also a space where youth and young adults cultivated, reinforced, and enlarged their social supports. Participants shared experiences of meeting new friends and connecting with people they met on social media prior to the event. One participant appreciated the opportunity that the Bus provided to connect with others and talk about "the music, the Foundation itself, what Gaga's message means to us, and just 'fangirling' [that is, a fan's emotional reaction] the whole time. And it was cool, 'cause the Born Brave Bus brought us all together into one spot." Many friendships formed at the Bus endured long after the event was over. Participants reported keeping in touch with these friends online via social networks like Facebook, Twitter, and Little Monsters.com. They also "hung out" with friends who lived nearby and traveled to visit friends in other places. One participant described a trip to New York City, where he did not know anyone except for friends he had made at the Bus and through Little Monsters (that is, a community of Lady Gaga fans). He commented that "they just took me underneath their wing and showed me the city."

In addition to the social support they received at the Born Brave Bus Tour, participants received information about local community-based supports, such as mental health providers and bullying prevention programs. The presence of the community organizations was valued by participants, who saw these organizations as not just providing individual information about their services but as partners who "are on the same mission—to empower youth."

Empowerment. Empowerment was another core theme expressed by the Born Brave Bus Tour participants. Some participants discussed empowerment indirectly, in terms of their appreciation for the Born Brave Bus Tour and its efforts to empower youth. The appreciation was directed toward the community partners who were "providing tools and resources" to help empower the youth and young adults at the event. Appreciation was also directed toward Lady Gaga for creating the Born Brave Bus Tour. As one participant said, "Like, who else would do that for their fans? Who else would start this and like, absolutely try to change the lives of their fans from the inside out, like, making them feel like a superstar?"

Many of the participants described profound and personal feelings of empowerment as a result of attending the Born Brave Bus Tour. The sense of empowerment participants felt at the Bus helped one participant to "break out of my shell" and to "feel safe to be myself." Another participant was empowered by the realization that there were other people "just like me out there," which in turn marked the "beginning of the end of my depressing state." The empowerment that resulted from attending the Bus helped yet another participant "feel in control" of his life. This sense of empowerment radiated from others; as one participant noted, "It's on the inside. I mean if you're brave, I feel like it'll shine from you. You'll feel empowered. You can see the empowerment."

For one participant, it was several months after she attended the Born Brave Bus Tour when she realized how the experience affected her sense of empowerment. While listening to Lady Gaga's impassioned plea at the event to "let go of all your insecurities," this participant thought, "Oh, Gaga, I'm still going to be self-conscious and care what people think." However, over the course of the next two or three months, she slowly started to notice that her inner voice had changed. Now she tells herself, "Wait. Who cares? Who are these people? They're not going to affect my life."

Engagement. Attending the Born Brave Bus Tour not only inspired feelings of support and empowerment of youth and young adults but also served as a catalyst for participants to become more engaged in their communities. They described being motivated to do something after interacting "with all these people that care about the same things that you care about, that want to make a change, that wanna do something good." Participants were no longer content to "sit here and just let the world pass by." They wanted to make a difference in the lives of others the way Lady Gaga had made a difference in their own lives.

For some participants, this engagement occurred on a very personal level, in day-to-day interactions with others. One participant shared that prior to attending the Bus she used to be scared and timid around other people. But now she tries to "be one of those people that reaches out to everybody at my school. It's made me be more open." Another participant described how she used to feel that she did not need to get "in-depth" with the youth she was mentoring through a community-based theater arts program. But after attending the Bus, she realized she was missing an opportunity to truly help kids who were shy or afraid or were just not in the best place in their lives. She felt a personal responsibility to them: "We have to help them grow."

Other participants reported that they were inspired to get involved through community organizations and appreciated the variety of resources that were available at the Bus. These resources were viewed by one participant as a form of support that would make getting involved easy, "because you supported me with everything I needed." Another participant shared how the information he received at the Bus inspired him to act: "The Bus gave [me] more information, and then I started looking it up, and then that's what inspired me more to want to be involved with Born Brave Nation and get involved with that." He became an ambassador of the program and started a Born Brave Nation club at his school.

The youth-reported impact of the Born Brave Bus was not limited to the people who attended the event. As a result of the social support they received and the empowerment they felt, many participants shared stories of how they engaged with their communities to make a difference in the lives of others. One participant reported that she befriended a girl in school who was being bullied for being a lesbian. She stood up for this girl, telling the bullies, "Whoa. You can't do that. She's a really nice person." Another participant shared how he helps others who are bullied by reaching out to them on his Tumblr blog or other social media by sending them personal messages of encouragement, such as "Hey, don't listen to that. That's not true. Don't let that bring you down." The three pillars of the Born This Way Foundation, safety, skills, and opportunities, inspired one participant who was a teacher to incorporate them in his classroom to ensure that his students have a comfortable place to come and talk about any problems that they might have.

CONCLUSION

This chapter summarized research highlighting the importance of prerequisite factors for youth involvement in bullying prevention efforts. Applying a youth support and engagement framework, we emphasized the significance of traditional programs such as GSAs and 4-H programs for promoting positive youth development and youth support. These programs have deep historical roots in the youth development movement and support the importance of creating supportive environments where youth can thrive. We then provided a deeper dive into the findings from the recent multimedia Born Brave Bus Tour sponsored by the Born This Way Foundation. The qualitative findings suggested that the tour achieved its goals of affecting social support, youth empowerment, and youth engagement. These data further suggest that the Born Brave Bus Tour was an inspiring, uplifting experience that led to greater engagement with nonprofit groups in each community (that is, YMCA, Gay, Lesbian & Straight Education Network, Boys and Girls Clubs, and so on). In addition, opportunities to engage in an experience like the Born Brave Bus served as a catalyst for youth empowerment and youth engagement. With supportive scaffolding from adults and community organizations, youth will have the support needed to create a kinder and braver world. Such efforts may also prove to have an impact on bullying behavior and improve tolerance for difference and diversity among youth.

REFERENCES

Bandura, A. (1977). *Social learning theory.* New York: Prentice Hall.

Baumeister, R., & Leary, M. (1995). The need to belong: Desire for interpersonal attachments as a fundamental human motivation. *Psychological Bulletin, 117,* 497–529. doi:10.1037/00332909.117.3.497

Berg, M., Coman, E., & Schensul, J. J. (2009). Youth action research for prevention: A multi-level intervention designed to increase efficacy and empowerment among urban youth. *American Journal of Community Psychology, 43,* 345–359. doi:10.1007/s10464-009-9231-2

Bowers, E. P., Li, Y., Kiely, M. K., Brittian, A., Lerner, J. V., & Lerner, R. M. (2010). The Five Cs model of positive youth development: A longitudinal analysis of confirmatory factor structure and measurement invariance. *Journal of Youth and Adolescence, 39,* 720–735. doi:10.1007/s10964-010-9530-9

Checkoway, B., & Aldana, A. (2013). Four forms of youth civic engagement for diverse democracy. *Children and Youth Services Review, 35,* 1894–1899. doi:10.1016/j.childyouth.2013.09.005

Checkoway, B. N., & Gutierrez, L. M. (Eds.). (2011). *Youth participation and community change.* New York: Routledge.

da Silva, L., Sanson, A., Smart, D., & Toumbourou, J. (2004). Civic responsibility among Australian adolescents: Testing two competing models. *Journal of Community Psychology, 32,* 229–255. doi:10.1002/jcop.20004

Debnam, K. J., Johnson, S. L., Waasdorp, T. E., & Bradshaw, C. P. (2013). Equity, connection, and engagement in the school context to promote positive youth development. *Journal of Research on Adolescence, 24,* 447–459. doi:10.1111/jora.12083

Demaray, M. K., & Malecki, C. K. (2003). Perceptions of the frequency and importance of social support by students classified as victims, bullies, and bully/victims in an urban middle school. *School Psychology Review, 32,* 471–489.

Demaray, M. K., & Malecki, C. K. (2010). The role of social support in the lives of students involved in bullying. In D. Espelage & S. Swearer (Eds.), *Bullying in North American schools* (2nd ed., pp. 182–190). New York: Routledge.

Demaray, M. K., & Malecki, C. K. (2013). Best practices in assessing and promoting social support. In P. Harrison & A. Thomas (Eds.), *Best practices in school psychology: Student level services* (pp. 239–250). Bethesda, MD: National Association of School Psychologists.

D'Onofrio, C. N., Moskowitz, J. M., & Braverman, M. T. (2002). Curtailing tobacco use among youth: Evaluation of Project 4-Health. *Health Education & Behavior, 29,* 656–682. doi:10.1177/109019802237937

4-H. (n.d.). *4-H history.* Retrieved from http://www.4-h.org/about/4-h-history

Fowler, J. H., & Christakis, N. A. (2010). Cooperative behavior cascades in human social networks. *Proceedings of the National Academy of Sciences, 107,* 5334–5338. doi:10.1073/pnas.0913149107

Geller, J. D., Voight, A., Wegman, H., & Nation, M. (2013). How do varying types of youth civic engagement relate to perceptions of school climate? *Applied Developmental Science, 17,* 135–147. doi:10.1080/10888691.2013.804377

GSAday. (n.d.). *Gay-straight alliance history.* Retrieved from http://gsaday.org/info/gay-straight-alliance-history

Guest, G., MacQueen, K. M., & Namey, E. E. (2011). *Applied thematic analysis.* Thousand Oaks, CA: Sage Publications.

Gullan, R. L., Power, T. J., & Leff, S. S. (2013). The role of empowerment in a school-based community service program with inner-city, minority youth. *Journal of Adolescent Research, 28,* 664–689. doi:10.1177/0743558413477200

Heck, N., Flentje, A., & Cochran, B. N. (2013). Offsetting risks: High school gay-straight alliances and lesbian, gay, bisexual, and transgender (LGBT) youth. *Psychology of Sexual Orientation and Gender Diversity, 1,* 81–90. doi:10.1037/2329-0382.1.S.81

Hogg, M. A., & Cooper, J. (2007). *The Sage handbook of social psychology: Concise student edition.* Thousand Oaks, CA: Sage Publications.

Kendrick, K., Jutengren, G., & Stattin, H. (2012). The protective role of supportive friends against bullying perpetration and victimization. *Journal of Adolescence, 35,* 1069–1080. doi:10.1016/j.adolescence.2012.02.014

Lerner, R. M., & Lerner, J. V. (2013). *The positive development of youth: Comprehensive findings from the 4-H study of positive youth development.* Chevy Chase, MD: National 4-H Council.

Maslow, A. H. (1943). A theory of human motivation. *Psychological Review, 50,* 370–396. doi:10.1037/h0054346

Morton, M. H., & Montgomery, P. (2013). Youth empowerment programs for improving adolescents' self-efficacy and self-esteem: A systematic review. *Research on Social Work Practice, 23,* 22–33. doi:10.1177/1049731512459967

Pancer, S. M., Pratt, M., Hunsberger, B., & Alisat, S. (2007). Community and political involvement in adolescence: What distinguishes the activists from the uninvolved? *Journal of Community Psychology, 35,* 741–759. doi:10.1002/jcop.20176

Pepler, D., Jiang, D., Craig, W., & Connolly, J. (2008). Developmental trajectories of bullying and associated factors. *Child Development, 79,* 325–338. doi:10.1111/j.1467-8624.2007.01128.x

Peterson, N. A. (2014). Empowerment theory: Clarifying the nature of higher-order multidimensional constructs. *American Journal of Community Psychology, 53,* 96–108. doi:10.1007/s10464-013-9624-0

Rappaport, J. (1981). In praise of paradox: A social policy of empowerment over prevention. *American Journal of Community Psychology, 9,* 1–25. doi:10.1007/BF00896357

Rodkin, P. C., Espelage, D. L., & Hanish, L. D. (2015). A relational framework for understanding bullying: Developmental antecedents and outcomes. *American Psychologist, 70,* 311–321.

Russell, S. T., Muraco, A., Subramaniam, A., & Laub, C. (2009). Youth empowerment and high school gay-straight alliances. *Journal of Youth and Adolescence, 38,* 891–903. doi:10.1007/s10964-008-9382-8

Sharma, A., Suarez-Balcazar, Y., & Baetke, M. (2003). Empowerment evaluation of a youth leadership training program. *Journal of Prevention & Intervention in the Community, 26,* 89–103. doi:10.1300/J005v26n02_07

Sherrod, L. (2007). Civic engagement as an expression of positive youth development. In R. Silbereisen & R. Lerner (Eds.), *Approaches to positive youth development* (pp. 59–75). doi:10.4135/9781446213803.n3

Snapp, S. D., McGuire, J. K., Sinclair, K. O., Gabrion, K., & Russell, S. T. (2015). LGBTQ-inclusive curricula: Why supportive curricula matter. *Sex Education: Sexuality, Society, and Learning, 15,* 580–596. doi:10.1080/14681811.2015.1042573

St. John, A., Travers, R., Munro, L., Liboro, R., Schneider, M., & Grieg, C. L. (2014). The success of gay–straight alliances in Waterloo region Ontario: A confluence of political and social factors. *Journal of LGBT Youth, 11,* 150–170. doi:10.1080/19361653.2014.878564

Toomey, R. B., & Russell, S. T. (2013). Gay-straight alliances, social justice involvement, and school victimization of lesbian, gay, bisexual, and queer youth: Implications for school well-being and plans to vote. *Youth & Society, 45,* 500–522. doi:10.1177/0044118X11422546

Toomey, R. B., Ryan, C., Diaz, R. M., & Russell, S. T. (2011). High school gay–straight alliances (GSAs) and young adult well-being: An examination of GSA presence, participation, and perceived effectiveness. *Applied Developmental Science, 15*, 175–185. doi:10.1080/10888691.2011.607378

Voight, A., & Torney-Purta, J. (2013). A typology of youth civic engagement in urban middle schools. *Applied Developmental Science, 17*, 198–212. doi:10.1080/10888691.2013.836041

Walls, N. E., Kane, S. B., & Wisneski, H. (2010). Gay–straight alliances and school experiences of sexual minority youth. *Youth & Society, 41*, 307–332. doi:10.1177/0044118X09334957

Wilson, N., Minkler, M., Dasho, S., Wallerstein, N., & Martin, A. C. (2008). Getting to social action: The Youth Empowerment Strategies (YES!) Project. *Health Promotion Practice, 9*, 395–403. doi:10.1177/1524839906289072

Worthen, M. (2014). The interactive impacts of high school Gay-Straight Alliances (GSAs) on college student attitudes toward LGBT individuals: An investigation of high school characteristics. *Journal of Homosexuality, 61*, 217–250. doi:10.1080/00918369.2013.839906

Zeldin, S. (2004). Preventing youth violence through the promotion of community engagement and membership. *Journal of Community Psychology, 32*, 623–641. doi:10.1002/jcop.20023

Zimmerman, M. A. (1990). Taking aim on empowerment research: On the distinction between individual and psychological conception. *American Journal of Community Psychology, 18*, 169–177. doi:10.1007/BF00922695

Zimmerman, M. A., Israel, B. A., Schulz, A. J., & Checkoway, B. (1992). Further explorations in empowerment theory: An empirical analysis of psychological empowerment. *American Journal of Community Psychology, 20*, 707–727. doi:10.1007/BF01312604

21

Policies Related to the Prevention of Bullying

Anna Heilbrun and Dewey Cornell

Although school bullying is not a new problem, American schools had no established legal obligation to protect students from peer aggression until 1999 (Stein, 1999). That year, the U.S. Supreme Court ruled in *Davis v. Monroe County Board of Education* that school authorities were liable for the sexual harassment of a fifth-grade girl by her classmate. The girl had experienced months of verbal and physical forms of sexual harassment, yet school authorities had taken no decisive action. The court held that schools must intervene to stop harassment when "the behavior is so severe, pervasive, and objectively offensive that it denies its victims equal access to education that Title IX is designed to protect" (*Davis v. Monroe County Board of Education*, 1999, p. 21). Additional court decisions, legislative actions, and government initiatives since *Davis* have produced substantial and rapidly evolving changes in school policy and practice. This chapter provides an overview of federal, state, and local policies on bullying, including relevant judicial decisions and steps taken by the U.S. Department of Education. We conclude by making policy recommendations for schools to meet these new legal expectations.

FEDERAL BULLYING POLICIES

Bullying is not explicitly recognized in federal law, but the closely related concept of harassment is a central concern in federal antidiscrimination laws. Under state law, harassment is characterized as unwanted behavior that demeans, threatens, or offends another and results in a hostile environment for the victim (Sacco, Silbaugh, Corredor, Casey, & Doherty, 2012; U.S. Department of Education, 2011). Multiple federal laws protect students from discriminatory harassment. These are complex laws passed for various purposes, but court decisions that interpret how the laws should be applied and periodic revisions of federal regulations have shaped public education. Most notably, Title VI of the Civil Rights Act of 1964 (Title VI) prohibits discrimination on the basis of race, color, or national origin; Title IX of the Education Amendments of 1972 (Title IX) prohibits discrimination on the basis of sex; Section 504 of the Rehabilitation Act of 1973 (Section 504) and Title II of the Americans with Disabilities Act of 1990 (Title II; U.S. Department of Education, 2011) prohibit discrimination on the basis of disability. Students with disabilities have special protections under the 1975 Education of All Handicapped Children Act, which introduced the key concept that these students have a right to free and appropriate public education. This law, commonly referred to as IDEA (Individuals with Disabilities Education Act), was most recently revised in the Individuals with Disabilities Education Improvement Act of 2004 (P.L. 108-446). The U.S. Department of Education has extensive information on IDEA on its Web site: http://idea.ed.gov/explore/home.

Antidiscrimination laws were widely understood to protect students from discriminatory treatment by adults at school, but the *Davis* case expanded their application to student-on-student harassment. The case, as mentioned previously, involved a fifth-grade girl who was repeatedly sexually harassed by a male classmate (*Davis v. Monroe County Board of Education*, 1999). After school authorities failed to stop the harassment, her grades dropped and she wrote a suicide note. Her parents contacted the police and pressed charges, and subsequently the student perpetrator pled guilty to sexual battery. The girl's mother sued the school district for sexual discrimination and harassment. The lower courts sided with the school, but the U.S. Supreme Court held that the school district had violated Title IX of the Education Amendments of 1972, which prohibits a student from being "excluded from participation in, being denied the benefits of, or being subjected to discrimination under any education program receiving Federal financial assistance" (*Davis v. Monroe County Board of Education*, 1999, p. 22). The Court identified four conditions that must be met for a school to be held liable: (1) the student must be harassed because of membership in a protected category; (2) the harassment at school must be "so severe, pervasive, and objectively offensive that it denies the victims the equal access to education that Title IX is designed to protect" (*Davis v. Monroe County Board of Education*, 1999, p. 21); (3) authorities must be aware of the harassment; and (4) schools must have failed to make a "reasonable effort" to stop the harassment, demonstrating that they were "deliberately indifferent" to it.

There are now numerous court decisions holding schools accountable for failure to stop the bullying or harassment of a student under various circumstances (Sacco et al., 2012). Two notable examples illustrate these kinds of cases. In *Scruggs v. Meriden Board of Education* (2005), the U.S. District Court of Connecticut held that a school was liable for the suicide of a 12-year-old boy, who killed himself after enduring years of bullying. In the wake of the *Scruggs* decision, the Connecticut legislature passed antibullying legislation (Connecticut Commission on Children, n.d.). In *Shore Regional High School Board of Education v. P.S. 41* (2004), the United States Court of Appeals for the Third Circuit ruled on a case in which a boy who was receiving special education services for emotional disturbance was bullied by his peers because of his perceived "girlish" appearance and called names such as "gay" and "faggot." The court held that the school district's failure to stop the bullying was a denial of his right to a free and appropriate public education under IDEA (1990).

BULLYING VERSUS HARASSMENT

"Harassment" and "bullying" are often used interchangeably, but there are important conceptual as well as legal differences. Although the conventional definition of bullying requires a power imbalance between aggressor and victim, acts of harassment have no such requirement. However, in order for harassment to constitute legal discrimination, the behavior must be based on certain characteristics of the victim, such as gender, race, religion, or disability status. Harassment based on a student's size or weight, for example, would not constitute discrimination because size and weight are not legally protected categories. In contrast, bullying has no such boundaries and can be applied to any form of derogatory behavior (Cornell & Limber, 2015; U.S. Department of Education, 2011). These distinctions can make it difficult to interpret federal and state laws.

In an effort to clarify the distinctions between harassment and bullying, the U.S. Department of Education (U.S. Department of Education, Office of Civil Rights, 2010) issued a series of *Dear Colleague* letters to all public school authorities in the United States, noting that school authorities should be aware that some forms of bullying constitute discriminatory harassment under federal law. As the *Dear Colleague* letter advised, bullying of an individual on the basis of race, color, national origin, sex, or disability is a civil rights violation when it interferes with a student's educational services, activities, or opportunities (U.S. Department of Education, Office for Civil Rights, 2010). Furthermore, the letter advised schools to do more than stop the bullying. When a student's bullying constitutes a federal civil rights violation, the school must "eliminate any hostile environment and its effects" as well as take steps to "prevent the harassment from recurring" (U.S. Department of Education, Office for Civil Rights, 2010, pp. 2–3). These obligations suggest a broader and sustained effort to change student behavior and to improve the school climate. The OCR also encouraged schools to establish policies and procedures for dealing with harassment and bullying, to train their staff on the school's civil rights obligations, and to educate students and families so that they would recognize and seek help for harassment.

In 2011, the OCR advised school authorities that their obligation to protect students from gender-based harassment included students harassed on the basis of their perceived sexual orientation (U.S. Department of Education, 2011). This was an important clarification because lesbian, gay, bisexual, and transgender (LBGT) youth experience particularly high levels of bullying and are at a higher risk of suicide (Olsen, Kann, Vivolo-Kantor, Kinchen, & McManus, 2014). A small body of correlational research suggests that targeted state and school policies can reduce some of the negative outcomes for LGBT youth. For example, one study of high school students in Oregon found that LGBT students reported fewer suicide attempts when their school had an antibullying policy that specifically included sexual orientation as a protected status (Hatzenbuehler & Keyes, 2013). The Department of Education has emphasized that schools are required under the Equal Access Act to allow gay–straight alliances and similar clubs for LGBT youth (U.S. Department of Education, 2011).

In 2013, the U.S. Department of Education's Office of Special Education and Rehabilitative Services (OSERS) reminded schools that disability-based harassment could result in a denial of equal educational opportunities under Section 504 of Title II, IDEA (U.S. Department of Education, OSERS, 2013). Furthermore, OSERS pointed out that even if the bullying was not related to a student's disability (and thus was not discriminatory), if it was severe enough to deny the student his or her right to a free and appropriate education, the school must intervene. Overall, the *Dear Colleague* letters make a complex but compelling case for schools to address bullying and harassment in various forms and to be proactive in maintaining a positive school climate that protects students' educational rights.

STATE POLICIES ON BULLYING

Prior to 1999, no states had laws explicitly covering bullying. Around the same time as the *Davis* decision, another event in 1999 served as an even more powerful impetus for states to adopt antibullying measures: the shooting at Columbine High School. The Columbine massacre, perpetrated by two students who claimed to have been victims of bullying, was perhaps the most infamous of a series of school shootings that stimulated a wave of bullying-related legislation (Alley & Limber, 2009). The first state bullying laws were passed in 1999, and by 2015, every state had legislation directing schools to address the problem of bullying (Sacco et al., 2012; U.S. Department of Education, 2011).

Most (42) state antibullying laws direct schools to prohibit bullying (General Accounting Office, 2012), but they vary widely in their requirements. Two-thirds of states require schools to investigate bullying, and more than one-third mandate schools to report levels of bullying on school grounds. Half (25) of states require training for school personnel (http://www.stopbullying.gov). Ten states mandate or encourage the use of task forces or committees to oversee bullying prevention initiatives. The Web site stopbullying.gov is a valuable resource and provides more comprehensive information about each state's bullying policies (http://www.stopbullying.gov/laws/index.html).

The disparate state-adopted approaches to bullying present some policy challenges. One problem is that many state definitions of bullying do not match the conventional definition of bullying that requires intentional aggression, a power differential between aggressor and victim, and repetition of the aggressive behavior (Gladden, Vivolo-Kantor, Hamburger, & Lumpkin, 2014; Olweus, 2010, 2013). In an attempt to standardize the measurement of bullying, the Centers for Disease Control and Prevention (CDC) released a consensus definition of *bullying* as "any unwanted aggressive behavior by another youth or group of youths who are not siblings or current dating partners that involves an observed or perceived power imbalance and is repeated multiple times or is highly likely to be repeated" (Gladden et al., 2014, p. 7). State definitions typically ignore the power imbalance criterion and use the term interchangeably with harassment. Some state definitions focus on the motivation or intent of the aggressor, the severity of the harm inflicted, or specific categories of victims (for example, bullying based on gender or perceived sexual orientation; General Accounting Office, 2012). This means that state legislative definitions of bullying do not necessarily align with the conventional definitions used in standard surveys of bullying and evidence-based programs such as the Olweus Bullying Prevention Program (Olweus, 2013).

State antibullying policies also vary in the guidance they provide to schools. Perhaps the most comprehensive and prescriptive state law is the New Jersey Anti-Bullying Bill of Rights Act (Cerf, Hespe, Gantwerk, Martz, & Vermeire, 2011), which requires that every school train all teachers and administrators to identify and respond to bullying. The state also requires each district board of education to develop its own harassment, intimidation, and bullying policy through a process that includes representation of parents and other community members, school employees, school volunteers, students, and school administrators. The chief school administrator (superintendent of the school district) must appoint a district antibullying coordinator, and principals in each school designate a school antibullying specialist. In addition, all board of education members and school employees are required to report any possible bullying incident to the principal on the same day that it is witnessed.

RECOMMENDED ELEMENTS OF ANTIBULLYING PROGRAMS

Although nearly all states currently require schools to develop and implement a bullying policy, there is little available information on how these directives are followed and to what effect (Sacco et al., 2012; Sherer & Nickerson, 2010). A large number of bullying prevention programs and motivational speakers have appeared in the commercial education marketplace, but schools should be cautious about adopting programs that claim effectiveness without scientific evidence (Nickerson, Cornell, Smith, & Furlong, 2013). Many authorities have recommended schoolwide staff training as a starting point for antibullying efforts (Gladden et al., 2014; Nickerson et al., 2013). A typical training program includes teaching everyone a common definition of bullying, the impact of bullying on victims, and strategies for identifying bullying and intervening with victims, aggressors, and bystanders (Luxenberg, Limber, & Olweus, 2014).

Schools also need clear policies and school rules about bullying (Gladden et al., 2014; Nickerson et al., 2013). Rigby (2010) advised that antibullying policies be guided by input from parents, teachers, school employees, and students to increase collective commitment to implement the policy. A school's antibullying policy should be widely disseminated through a variety of outlets and forums, including booklets, newsletters, assemblies, and student handbooks (Rigby, 2010). Schools should monitor their progress in reducing bullying through student and staff surveys and use this information to evaluate their program and address school climate needs (Nickerson et al., 2013).

Schoolwide programs typically establish school rules against bullying and classroom meetings and lessons intended to convince students not to bully others or allow their peers to engage in bullying. Ttofi and Farrington's (2011) meta-analysis of bullying prevention programs identified several key components of effective programs. The most successful programs were more comprehensive in scope and included extended training for students, teachers, school personnel, and community stakeholders. Interventions with the largest effect sizes included parent meetings and, for younger grades, close playground supervision (Ttofi & Farrington, 2011). Effective programs tended to monitor the prevalence of bullying, most often with a student survey, and use a protocol for responding promptly to reported incidents. Other important factors associated with a reduction in bullying were firm but fair disciplinary sanctions for students who bullied and positive behavioral interventions. Successful antibullying programs must also be delivered consistently with a high degree of fidelity to the program's requirements.

OTHER EVIDENCE-BASED PRACTICES

Research has found that schools have lower levels of bullying when the school climate is characterized by supportive teacher–student relationships and structured, strict, but fair discipline (Cornell, Shukla, & Konold, 2015; Gregory et al., 2010; Konold et al., 2014). These two characteristics of student support and disciplinary structure define an authoritative school climate that can be distinguished from schools that are authoritarian (strict discipline but not supportive) or permissive (supportive but not strict discipline) (Gregory & Cornell, 2009). Students in an authoritative school are more engaged in school and less likely to engage in aggressive misbehavior directed at peers or teachers (Berg & Cornell, 2016). This model provides an overarching conceptual framework from which school authorities can measure and identify goals for improving school climate.

Reductions in bullying may be achieved through programs that have a broader focus on school improvement. Social and Emotional Learning (SEL) programs are designed to teach students to manage negative emotions, set and achieve positive goals, and handle interpersonal situations effectively (Durlak, Weissberg, Dymnicki, Taylor, & Schellinger, 2011). Studies have indicated that SEL programs integrated into the school day with high fidelity produce benefits to student behavior, academic performance, and social-emotional development (Durlak et al., 2011). Positive Behavioral Intervention and Supports (PBIS) is another approach associated with reductions in school bullying. A randomized controlled trial in 37 elementary schools found that PBIS created sustained changes in how Maryland public schools managed discipline and significantly reduced bullying (Bradshaw et al., 2012).

THREAT ASSESSMENT

Threat assessment is a form of risk assessment and intervention that is conducted when an individual makes threats of violence or engages in some other form of threatening behavior. Although threat assessment originated as a law enforcement practice to protect public officials, schools were advised to use this approach by several studies of school shootings (Cornell, Sheras, Gregory, & Fan, 2009). One example of school-based threat assessment is the Virginia Student Threat Assessment Guidelines, an evidence-based practice that uses a set of procedures and a decision tree to help school authorities evaluate the seriousness of a student's threatening behavior and take appropriate action (Cornell & Sheras, 2006). In practice, most student threats do not pose a serious risk of violence and can be easily resolved without suspending the student from school, but the process often brings attention to incidents of bullying and other student conflicts that merit intervention (Cornell, 2013). Several controlled studies found that schools using the Virginia Student Threat Assessment Guidelines had reductions in bullying infractions and that students reported greater willingness to seek help for bullying and threats of violence (Cornell et al., 2009).

One purpose of the Virginia Student Threat Assessment Guidelines is to provide schools with an alternative to zero-tolerance suspension practices (JustChildren & Cornell, 2013). After training in the Virginia Student Threat Assessment Guidelines, school administrators, counselors, psychologists, and resource officers showed a decrease in concerns about school violence and a shift away from zero-tolerance policies (Cornell, Allen, & Fan, 2012). A randomized controlled study found that students in schools using the Virginia Student Threat Assessment model were less likely to be suspended or transferred from school and more likely to receive counseling services and parental involvement in addressing their threat behavior (Cornell et al., 2012). A statewide study of threat assessment practices in Virginia schools found that use of the Virginia threat assessment model was associated with overall lower school suspension rates and a smaller racial disparity in long-term suspensions (JustChildren & Cornell, 2013).

CONTROVERSIAL POLICIES

In response to nationwide concern about gun violence in schools, the Gun-Free Schools Act of 1994 required all schools to adopt zero-tolerance policies for firearms. Zero-tolerance discipline expanded to become a more general disciplinary philosophy that mandates strict, uniform punishment—typically long-term suspension or expulsion from school—for an increasingly wide range of infractions (American Psychological Association, Zero Tolerance Task Force, 2008). There is no evidence that zero-tolerance policies increase school safety or improve student behavior but substantial evidence that these policies have had unintended negative consequences, most notably a national increase in school suspensions (American Psychological Association, Zero Tolerance Task Force, 2008; Morgan, Salomen, Plotkin, & Cohen, 2014). Suspension has been associated with a host of negative student outcomes, including lost instructional time, school failure, dropout, and juvenile justice involvement (Fabelo et al., 2011). This process has had high impact on minority students, who are at a disproportionately high risk of being suspended and are more likely than white students to be suspended for minor, relatively subjective offenses (Fabelo et al., 2011).

Efforts to criminalize bullying and other school misbehavior are also questionable (Cornell & Limber, 2015; Morgan et al., 2014). A national report has identified a variety of problems associated with prosecuting students for school misbehavior (Morgan et al., 2014). Most forms of bullying can be dealt with through school discipline without resorting to law enforcement intervention and prosecution. The sheer numbers of bullying make criminalization seem impractical. For example, national results from the CDC's Youth Risk Behavior Survey found that approximately one in five students (grades 9–12) reported being bullied at school in the past 12 months (Kann et al., 2014). Another survey study found that more than 40 percent of U.S. students (ages 11, 13, and 15) admitted occasional bullying of a peer (Molcho et al., 2009). In the relatively few severe or persistent cases where school discipline seems insufficient, bullying behavior will likely meet criteria for more serious offenses such as assault and battery, stalking, threatening, or extortion.

FUTURE DIRECTIONS

The wave of bullying legislation over the past decade represents an important step forward in the management and prevention of bullying. Nearly every state requires school policies on bullying or harassment. However, we still know little about the efficacy of different policies (Cornell & Limber, 2015), and there is little evidence to show what, if any, direct impact these laws have had on the prevalence of bullying. There is a need for more comprehensive legislation grounded in evidence-based practice, as the existing legislation comprises a patchwork of coverage that does not systematically protect the rights of all children.

A number of steps need to be taken to extend these protections. Cornell and Limber (2015) recommended that state laws distinguish harassment and peer aggression from bullying because research suggests that they have a differential impact and warrant different intervention approaches. Another important step is ensuring that school policies include provisions for reporting bullying. There is evidence that anonymous reporting methods, such as peer nomination, can encourage children to report and seek help for incidents of bullying that they witness or experience (Cornell & Huang, 2014; Cornell & Limber, 2015).

CONCLUSION

The widespread movement to reduce school bullying is part of a broader civil and human rights movement to give children in school the rights to safety and protection from harm that are afforded to adults in the workplace (Cornell & Limber, 2015). Recent interpretations of federal laws against discrimination, new state legislation, and a wave of civil lawsuits have mandated that school authorities take responsibility for protecting students from bullying and harassment by their peers. Schools are advised to train their staff and implement evidence-based antibullying programs. Schools should also strive to improve school climate through broader programs aimed at reforming discipline strategies, establishing positive teacher–student relations, and teaching students social and emotional skills that foster healthy student development.

REFERENCES

Alley, R., & Limber, S. P. (2009). Legal issues for school personnel. In S. M. Swearer, D. L. Espelage, & S. A. Napolitano (Eds.), *Bullying prevention and intervention: Realistic strategies for schools* (pp. 53–73). New York: Guilford Press.

American Psychological Association, Zero Tolerance Task Force. (2008). Are zero tolerance policies effective in the schools? An evidentiary review and recommendations. *American Psychologist, 63*, 852–862.

Berg, J., & Cornell, D. (2016). Authoritative school climate, aggression toward teachers, and teacher distress in middle school. *School Psychology Quarterly, 31*(1), 122–139. doi:10.1037/spq0000132

Bradshaw, C., Pas, E., Bloom, J., Barrett, S., Hershfeldt, P., Alexander, A., et al. (2012). A state-wide partnership to promote safe and supportive schools: The PBIS Maryland Initiative. *Administrative Policy Mental Health, 39*, 224–237.

Cerf, C., Hespe, D., Gantwerk, B., Martz, S., & Vermeire, G. (2011). Guidance for schools on implementing the anti-bullying Bill of Rights Act. *New Jersey Department of Education, P.L.2010, c.122.*

Connecticut Commission on Children. (n.d.). *Bullying.* Retrieved from http://www.cga.ct .gov/coc/bullying.htm

Cornell, D. (2013). The Virginia Student Threat Assessment Guidelines: An empirically supported violence prevention strategy. In N. Böckler, T. Seeger, W. Heitmeyer, & P. Sitzer (Eds.), *School shootings: International research, case studies and concepts for prevention* (pp. 379–400). New York: Springer.

Cornell, D., Allen, K., & Fan, X. (2012). A randomized controlled study of the Virginia Student Threat Assessment Guidelines in grades K-12. *School Psychology Review, 41*, 100–115.

Cornell, D., & Huang, F. (2014). School counselor use of peer nominations to identify victims of bullying. *Professional School Counseling, 18*(1), 191–205. doi:10.5330/2156-759X-18.1.191

Cornell, D., & Limber, S. (2015). Law and policy on the concept of bullying at school. *American Psychologist, 70*, 333–343.

Cornell, D., & Sheras, P. (2006). *Guidelines for responding to student threats of violence.* Longmont, CO: Sopris West.

Cornell, D., Sheras, P., Gregory, A., & Fan, X. (2009). A retrospective study of school safety conditions in high schools using the Virginia Threat Assessment Guidelines versus alternative approaches. *School Psychology Quarterly, 24*, 119–129. doi:10.1037/a0016182

Cornell, D., Shukla, K., & Konold, T. (2015). Peer victimization and authoritative school climate: A multilevel approach. *Journal of Educational Psychology, 107*, 1186–1201. doi:10.1037/edu0000038

Davis v. Monroe County Board of Education, 526 U.S. 629 (1999).

Durlak, J., Weissberg, R., Dymnicki, A., Taylor, R., & Schellinger, K. (2011). The impact of enhancing students' social and emotional learning: A meta-analysis of school-based universal interventions. *Child Development, 82*, 474–501.

Fabelo, T., Thompson, M. D., Plotkin, M., Carmichael, D., Marchbanks, M. P., & Booth, E. A. (2011). *Breaking schools' rules: A statewide study of how school discipline relates to students' success and juvenile justice involvement.* New York: Council of State Governments Justice Center.

General Accounting Office. (2012). *School bullying: Extent of legal protections for vulnerable groups needs to be more fully assessed.* Retrieved from http://www.gao.gov/products/GAO-12-785T

Gladden, R. M., Vivolo-Kantor, A. M., Hamburger, M. E., & Lumpkin, C. D. (2014). *Bullying surveillance among youths: Uniform definitions for public health and recommended data elements, version 1.0.* Atlanta: National Center for Injury Prevention and Control, Centers for Disease Control and Prevention, and U.S. Department of Education.

Gregory, A., & Cornell, D. (2009). "Tolerating" adolescent needs: Moving beyond zero tolerance policies in high school. *Theory into Practice, 48*, 106–113.

Gregory, A., Cornell, D., Fan, X., Sheras, P., Shih, T., & Huang, F. (2010). Authoritative school discipline: High school practices associated with lower student bullying and victimization. *Journal of Educational Psychology, 102*, 483–496.

Hatzenbuehler, M. L., & Keyes, K. M. (2013). Inclusive anti-bullying policies and reduced risk of suicide attempts in lesbian and gay youth. *Journal of Adolescent Health, 53*, S21–S26. doi:10.1016/j.jadohealth.2012.08.010

Individuals with Disabilities Education Act, P.L. 101-476, 20 U.S.C. §§ 1400–1487 (1990).

Individuals with Disabilities Education Improvement Act of 2004, P.L. 108-446, 118 Stat. 2647 (2004, December 3).

JustChildren & Cornell, D. (2013). *Prevention v. punishment: Threat assessment, school suspensions, and racial disparities.* Retrieved from http://curry.virginia.edu/uploads/resourceLibrary/UVA_and_JustChildren_Report_-_Prevention_v._Punishment.pdf

Kann, L., Kinchen, S., Shanklin, S., Flint, K., Hawkins, J., Harris, M., et al. (2014). Youth Risk Behavior Surveillance: United States, 2013. *Morbidity and Mortality Weekly Report, 63*(SS-4), 1–168.

Konold, T., Cornell, D., Huang, F., Meyer, P., Lacey, A., Nekvasil, E., et al. (2014). Multi-level multi-informant structure of the Authoritative School Climate Survey. *School Psychology Quarterly, 29*, 238–255. doi:10.1037/spq0000062

Luxenberg, H., Limber, S. P., & Olweus, D. (2014). *Bullying in U.S. schools: 2013 status report.* Center City, MN: Hazelden.

Molcho, M., Craig, W., Due, P., Pickett, W., Harel-Fisch, Y., Overpeck, M., & the HBSC Bullying Writing Group. (2009). Cross-national time trends in bullying behavior 1994-2006: Findings from Europe and North America. *International Journal of Public Health, 54*, S225–S234.

Morgan, E., Salomen, N., Plotkin, M., & Cohen, R, (2014). *The school discipline consensus report: Strategies from the field to keep students engaged in school and out of the juvenile justice system.* New York: Council of State Governments Justice Center. Retrieved from http://csgjusticecenter.org/wp-content/uploads/2014/06/The_School_Discipline_Consensus_Report.pdf

Nickerson, A. B., Cornell, D. G., Smith, J., & Furlong, M. (2013). School antibullying efforts: Advice for education policymakers. *Journal of School Violence, 12*, 268–282.

Olsen, E. O., Kann, L., Vivolo-Kantor, A., Kinchen, S., & McManus, T. (2014). School violence and bullying among sexual minority high school students, 2009–2011. *Journal of Adolescent Health, 55*, 432–438.

Olweus, D. (2010). Understanding and researching bullying: Some critical issues. In S. R. Jimerson, S. M. Swearer, & D. L. Espelage (Eds.), *Handbook of bullying in schools: An international perspective* (pp. 9–33). New York: Routledge.

Olweus, D. (2013). School bullying: Development and some important challenges. *Annual Review of Clinical Psychology, 9*, 14.1–14.30.

Rigby, K. (2010). *Bullying interventions in schools: Six basic approaches.* Victoria, Australia: Acer Press.

Sacco, D. T., Silbaugh, K., Corredor, F., Casey, J., & Doherty, D. (2012). *An overview of state anti-bullying legislation and other related laws.* Retrieved from https://cyber.harvard.edu/publications/2012/state_anti_bullying_legislation_overview

Scruggs v. Meriden Board of Education (2005). U.S. District Court of Connecticut WL 2072312 (D. Conn. 2005).

Sherer, Y. C., & Nickerson, A. B. (2010). Anti-bullying practices in American schools: Perspectives of school psychologists. *Psychology in the Schools, 47*(3), 217–229.

Shore Regional High School Board of Education v. P.S. 41 (2004). United States Court of Appeals for the Third Circuit No. 03-3438. Retrieved from http://www2.ca3.uscourts.gov/opinarch/033438p.pdf

Stein, N. (1999). *Classrooms and courtrooms: Facing sexual harassment in K-12 Schools.* New York: Columbia Teachers College Press.

Ttofi, M. M., & Farrington, D. P. (2011). Effectiveness of school-based programs to reduce bullying: A systematic and meta-analytic review. *Journal of Experimental Criminology, 7*(1), 27–56. doi:10.1007/s11292-010-9109-1

U.S. Department of Education. (2011). *Analysis of state bullying laws and policies.* Washington, DC: Author.

U.S. Department of Education, Office for Civil Rights. (2010). *Dear colleague letter: Harassment and bullying.* Retrieved from http://www2.ed.gov/about/offices/list/ocr/letters/colleague-201010.pdf

U.S. Department of Education, Office of Special Education and Rehabilitative Services. (2013). *Dear colleague letter: Bullying of students with disabilities.* Retrieved from http://www2.ed.gov/policy/speced/guid/idea/memosdcltrs/bullyingdcl-8-20-13.pdf

22

Promoting Relationships to Prevent Bullying: A Network Approach

Wendy Craig, Debra J. Pepler, Joanne Cummings,
and Kelly Petrunka

The World Health Organization (WHO) has identified interpersonal violence as "an insidi-ous and frequently deadly social problem [and noted that] the direct and indirect financial costs of such violence are staggering, as are the social and human costs that cause untold damage to the economic and social fabric of communities" (WHO, 2004, p. vii). The WHO initiated a global violence prevention campaign calling for "prevention efforts which target the root causes and situational determinants of interpersonal violence" (WHO, 2004, vii). Canada does poorly on the international stage on critical early indicators of interpersonal violence, as it ranks in the bottom third on bullying and victimization (that is, in the top third of countries in terms of prevalence of bullying and victimization) (Craig et al., 2009). Bullying is an early indicator of risk for interpersonal violence (dating aggression, sexual harassment, violent crime) (Farrington & Ttofi, 2011; Pepler, Jiang, Craig, & Connolly, 2008). In Canada, 12 percent of boys and 6 percent of girls are engaged in severe bullying (more than two or three times a week); 15 percent of boys and 13 percent of girls report being chronically victimized (Molcho et al., 2009). The most effective strategy to prevent youth violence is to promote healthy relationships; however, Canada fares poorly on the quality of family and peer relationships (that is, trust, commitment, intimacy, and connectedness), ranking 25th out of 28 developed nations (UNICEF Office of Research, 2013). Despite sci-entific knowledge about preventing violence by promoting healthy relationships, there is a substantial knowledge mobilization gap between science and practice. Adults responsible for children and youth are not receiving evidence-based knowledge, strategies, and pro-grams to effectively prevent bullying.

The consequences of failing to protect children and youth from violence and failing to support them in developing healthy relationships are significant, costly, and lifelong (CDC, 2010). In a longitudinal study, bullying at age 14 predicts violent convictions between ages 15 and 20, self-reported violence at age 15–18, low job status at age 18, drug use at age 27–32, and an unsuccessful life at age 48 (Farrington & Ttofi, 2011). Bullying, violence, mental and physical health problems, substance abuse, school dropout, and unemployment are all outcomes rooted in experiences within violent relationships (CDC, 2010). Poor social relationships are as big a contributor to early death as smoking, drinking, and obesity (Holt-Lunstead, Smith, & Layton, 2010). The cost of a single youth whose troubled relationship context leads to a life of crime has been estimated to be $2.6 to $4.4 million (Cohen & Piquero, 2009). Conversely, by preventing violence and promoting relationships, we can optimize children's healthy physical, emotional, and cognitive development—all of which underlie well-being, citizenship, and productivity.

In response to growing concerns about youth in Canada, PREVNet (Promoting Relationships and Eliminating Violence Network) was established in 2006. PREVNet comprises 129 researchers and their 145 graduate students, from 27 universities representing 15 disciplines, and 63 national organizations working with children and youth. Since 2006, PREVNet has established our reputation as Canada's authority on research and resources for bullying prevention. Our partnership model is unique in the world; we know of no other country with a network of leading researchers and leading youth-serving partners who exchange knowledge on a national scale to promote the well-being of children. With partners' dissemination channels, we have the capacity to reach every child, adult, and community in Canada.

PREVNet's goal was to co-create sustainable knowledge mobilization (KMb) projects by engaging researchers, students, and leaders from six key sectors of society (government, nongovernment, industry, education, health, and youth) to connect with stakeholders to prevent violence and promote healthy relationships. We provided adults and youth with evidence-based knowledge, strategies, tools, and programs to prevent violence and promote healthy relationships. By working with established organizations, we have developed a comprehensive and coordinated KMb strategy to promote innovative, effective, and ongoing uptake by end users for enhanced practice.

For the first phase of PREVNet, we focused on 10 signature KMb projects that leveraged partners' expertise and connections to disseminate evidence-based knowledge, strategies, resources, and programs to prevent bullying. The KMb projects were designed to reach diverse audiences, such as professionals and volunteers, parents, and youth. Knowledge and resources from projects were further mobilized to achieve broader penetration into receptor communities through our national partners. We engaged in innovative KMb practices through a new model of shared leadership for projects (researchers and partner representatives), new cross-sector networking (for example, government, corporations), new receptor communities (for example, Aboriginal communities), and innovative technologies (for example, electronic magazine).

The short-term goal of these KMb projects was the uptake of evidence-based violence prevention knowledge, strategies, tools, and programs. The medium-term goal was (a) to implement evidence-based knowledge, strategies, tools and programs; and (b) with the evaluation tools, for stakeholders (for example, participating schools and communities) to demonstrate program effectiveness with decreased rates of children's bullying and increased positive social behaviors and relationships. New knowledge and technology transfer products derived from the signature KMb projects enhanced the abilities of

PREVNet partners to promote the social capacity and well-being of Canadians to lay the foundation for long-term economic, health, and social benefits. By 2015, PREVNet had met its short- and medium-term goals of

- Creating a model of excellence in governance, network composition, training of students, knowledge mobilization, and measuring impact, which has been recognized by the National Centres of Excellence.
- Creating strong multisectoral partnerships with broad reach for rapid KMb from research to impact.
- Creating an ethos in which our partners value research and our researchers value partners' practical expertise and research contributions.
- Demonstrating gold standard excellence in co-creating knowledge, tools, and resources for practices and policies.
- Engaging in over 5,000 KMb activities and developing over 240 evidence-based tools and resources.
- Developing strong metrics for evaluation of impact.
- Building awareness—the beginning of social-cultural change. Last year alone, we reached 22.7 million stakeholders.
- Sharing our one-of-a-kind partnership model internationally in more than 20 countries through over 250 dissemination activities.

PREVNET'S FRAMEWORK FOR KMB

Prior to PREVNet, Canadian youth-serving organizations had few resources and opportunities to connect with research. PREVNet's KMb strategy is designed to maximize the social and economic benefits of newly generated research by accelerating the flow of knowledge and innovative resources to partners and receptor communities. A significant challenge in achieving research impact is in moving research findings beyond their original academic contexts into accessible formats that are useful and actionable for practitioners and receptor communities. There is also a challenge in moving from knowledge dissemination to uptake and implementation. Drawing from the health sector, passive dissemination takes an average of 17 years to reach 14 percent uptake in clinical practice. In contrast, with implementation support it takes an average of three years to reach 80 percent uptake (Fixsen, Blase, Timbers, & Wolf, 2001). To address these challenges and facilitate the flow of knowledge and resources into partners' practices to optimize impact, PREVNet has been developing a co-creation partnership model of KMb. PREVNet's co-created Pathway to Impact model maintains collaboration throughout all stages of the process. This creates iterative interactions between researchers and partners while sustaining the progression from research development to discovery to ultimate impact.

Co-creation occurs at each stage of PREVNet's KMb model and accelerates the impact of research. For example, co-creation at the research stage ensures partners' readiness to uptake findings because of their input on the nature of the research questions, methods, and interpretations. Co-creation in the research stage enhances partners' motivation and engagement with research content—the new knowledge will be relevant to them. At the dissemination stage, the research findings are tailored to meet the partners' needs in KMb products. These products are in an accessible format for the partners. Different partners can tailor the same research findings into their own relevant and actionable KMb products, which further heightens network engagement and increases dissemination. Partners also enhance dissemination through their organizational channels with a breadth and depth that researchers cannot achieve. Consequently, subsequent stages of uptake and implementation are accelerated. The ongoing mutual and reciprocated support and collaboration between the researchers and partners in the uptake and implementation stages enables organizational transformation in response to the new research findings.

Traditionally, as research moves to KMb, there is a decrease in engagement across the four stages of KMb (research, dissemination, uptake, and implementation); hence, engagement of the academic partners is lowest in ultimate impact stage. Unlike the traditional process of research dissemination with research "handed" to partners, our framework supports an ongoing relationship through the KMb processes. With ongoing assessment, there are critical feedback loops at each stage of the Pathways to Impact model. Each stage of the model confers benefits for both researchers and partners, leading to new research questions, knowledge, and potential KMb products. These iterations can enhance processes at every stage, leading to increased impact. The Pathways to Impact model supports PREVNet's mission of creating social-cultural change in preventing bullying by promoting positive relationships. Below, we describe an example of how PREVNet is currently implementing this model with a corporate partner.

Research

In our model, researchers and partners identified their new questions for research and practice members. In a partnership with a leading telecommunications company, PREVNet conducted research to identify parental attitudes and behaviors to adolescent social media use. The following were key research highlights (Primus, 2015):

- **Cyberbullying outranks drug use, teenage pregnancy, and alcohol use as a major concern for parents.** Parents are more concerned about cyberbullying (48 percent) than they are about teenage pregnancy (44 percent), drug use (40 percent), or alcohol use (38 percent).
- **The majority of parents wait for children to report cyberbullying.** The majority of Canadian parents were overly optimistic that their children would take the first steps to report being bullied online. In fact, 89 percent of parents surveyed feel their children would tell them if they were being cyberbullied.
- **Parents believe they are most responsible for their child's online safety.** The majority of parents (81 percent) feel that they are most responsible for protecting their children from cyberbullying. When parents were asked who else should be responsible for protecting their child, they responded schools (54 percent), social media companies (41 percent), the government (31 percent), and friends (30 percent).
- **Parents who were victimized themselves were significantly more concerned that their children will be bullied.** Half of Canadian parents surveyed admitted to being bullied in some capacity during their lives. In fact, 62 percent of parents who were bullied or cyberbullied reported emotional distress (43 percent), long-term impact on self-esteem (25 percent), reclusiveness (20 percent), and depression (20 percent) as key effects. Parents who themselves had been cyberbullied also showed greater concern that their child could be or could become a cyberbully (42 percent versus 24 percent for parents who never experienced online bullying).

- **Parents of girls were more concerned about cyberbullying; mothers were more concerned than fathers.** When expressing levels of concern about important issues affecting children and teenagers today, more than half (53 percent) of Canadian parents with girls between the ages of eight and 16 showed concern about the issue of online bullying, compared with 43 percent of parents with young sons. Although there are gender differences in the type of cyberbullying to which children may be exposed (girls receive more negative comments than boys), boys are just as much at risk as girls. Female parents are also significantly more likely to be concerned than male parents about exposure to sexual content online (64 percent versus 50 percent), body image (55 percent versus 47 percent), fitting in (50 percent versus 42 percent), and being good people (48 percent versus 43 percent).

Dissemination

KMb supports dissemination beyond traditional academic publishing. Innovative and effective dissemination can include (a) publishing activities, such as press releases, clear language research summaries, and social media; and (b) research events where researchers engage actively with organizations (that is, networking opportunities like conferences, working group meetings).

The research results from our partnership were disseminated broadly across Canada, with over five million media hits. In addition, given the significance of these results, the company and PREVNet have engaged in a new activity to develop an interactive educational Web site for parents (https://primus.ca/cyberbullying/). This Web site will provide evidence-based education, assessment, and prevention and intervention strategies for parents to interact with their youth about social interactions that occur online. We will evaluate the dissemination of this Web site with the following indicators: number of parent visits to the site, number of PREVNet partners disseminating the link, and number of corporate clients who share the Web site.

Uptake

Uptake occurs when receptor communities take knowledge or resources from a dissemination activity into its organization. The critical question for uptake is whether the research knowledge or resource is interesting to stakeholders and useful for practice, programming, or services. Uptake benefits enable consistent evidence-based practice and programming within the partner organizations. The uptake for our corporate partner in our example is the interest in developing the interactive Web site to translate the research into a KMb product. The company has increased its interest and its support to a new corporate social responsibility initiative that derives directly from the research, with the goal of educating, supporting, and proving strategies to parents to promote their children's healthy online relationships. This effort is a new one that is still in its initial stages. We have conducted a working group with researchers, students, and the employees of the company to develop the content for the interactive Web site. The interactive Web site will translate research on cyberbullying for parents and youth. Parents will learn the best practices in discussing cyberbullying, which will be assessed within the Web site. Public awareness will be increased through media outreach. The uptake of research has been the development of a new evidence-based product (that is, the Web site) that will be research informed; vetted by youth, researchers, and parents; piloted with the company's employees who are parents; and then broadly disseminated. There is also uptake in the level of the company's continued in-kind and financial investment. Other uptake indicators of this Web site will include the number of parents completing the module, parents' performance on the assessment, and media hits.

Implementation

Implementation refers to an internal activity in which partners use research to inform organizational decisions. For PREVNet, implementation activities involve actual changes in practices, programs, or policies within partner organizations. Implementation benefits are evidence-informed practice, programming, and policy that reach and affect a greater number of children and youth. The development of the interactive Web site is an example of the implementation of the research. We will assess the implementation benefits of the interactive Web site by using the following indicators with parent reports of how they implemented knowledge from modules.

Impact

Impact is the effect that the research-informed KMb products have on partners and receptor communities. For PREVNet, the indicators of impact can be measured proximally within partner organizations or nationally with the Health Behaviours School-Aged Survey of Children and Youth. Indicators of impact for the co-created interactive Web site will include improvements in rates of bullying problems, the quality of youth's relationships, life satisfaction, health and well-being outcomes, and, in the longer term, the productivity, social, health, and economic well-being of citizens.

PREVNet's KMb Pathway to Impact model provides a framework for monitoring and assessing KMb process and the associated impact. By developing the goals and indicators of each stage of the model, PREVNet has assessed the benefits of KMb accruing along the pathway. The example provided illustrates how the process is conducted, as well as how it is evaluated. Below we provide some examples of how PREVNet has successfully co-created KMb resources through four strategy pillars: education and training, assessment and evaluation, prevention and intervention, and policy.

EDUCATION AND TRAINING

In working with PREVNet's partners, Big Brothers Big Sisters, Scouts, and Red Cross, we discovered a substantial gap in training for those who work with children and youth in Canada. To fill this gap, we co-created the Healthy Relationships Training Module (HRTM). The content of the training was based on a review of the literature on developing positive relationship skills. After the review, we developed several drafts of the module that were revised after focus groups with the agencies involved and also from the working group composed of researchers, graduate students, and members from all of the involved organizations. The module includes pre- and postevaluations of knowledge of the module content, skills, and confidence in executing many of the skills addressed in the intervention. The impact of the HRTM is that we have changed professional practice in more than 100 organizations that train over 75,000 adults and reach more than 330,000 youth each year. Key messages from the HRTM are also now part of training programs with Big Brothers

Big Sisters in Australia, Ireland, New Zealand, and Russia. PREVNet (n.d.-a, n.d.-b) also has generated two developmentally tailored resources on preschool aggression and bullying for parents. The AboutKidsHealth Web site launched these two resources. We also published an article in an online parenting magazine, *ParentsCanada*, to help promote these tip sheets (Low, 2015).

PREVNet also organized and hosted a series of conferences. Specifically, we hosted two meetings with our researchers and partners, followed by a full-day conference for community professionals. Approximately 700 attended the conferences. The conferences enhanced the professional practice of conference attendees and were seen as valuable networking opportunities to make new connections. We also co-hosted the 46th Banff International Conference on Behavioural Science. More than 110 attended, representing stakeholders from academia, federal and provincial governments, nongovernmental organizations, and industry. The impact was that 84 percent of surveyed participants agreed that the information from the conference motivated them to adopt new evidence-based practices. In addition, we cohosted the 4th Annual Think Tank on Bullying with the Bullying Research Network, an international network of researchers.

ASSESSMENT AND EVALUATION

PREVNet also has commercialization experience in developing an online bullying assessment and reporting tool (Bullying Evaluation and Strategies Tool, or BEST). BEST was developed through input of over 20 researchers and graduate students. This assessment tool has been implemented in more than 55 schools with 7,500 students across the country. It provides assessments of bullying and related problems, with a report for principals that identifies key areas for improvement and school-specific evidence-based strategies for them to use. PREVNet's National Youth Advisory Committee (NYAC) has recently been involved in a research initiative aimed at understanding how young people use social media, especially regarding online safety and bullying. More than 770 youth have participated from 15 countries. NYAC summarized key messages from our survey that were highlighted in a media campaign.

PREVENTION AND INTERVENTION

With regard to prevention and early intervention, PREVNet created a Model Bullying Prevention Toolkit for the Ontario Ministry of Education. It was translated into French and released to all 72 school boards (with nearly 5,000 schools) in Ontario. PREVNet created innovative, high-quality, accessible, and evidence-based tools and resources to prevent bullying and promote healthy relationships. PREVNet has also partnered with *MyHealth*, an online magazine for youth, on bullying prevention and healthy relationships modules. Schools subscribe to *MyHealth* so that teachers and students can read articles, written by youth, on health topics. Last year, *MyHealth* reached over 200,000 youth and 175,000 teachers throughout Canada and the United States. Similarly, PREVNet partnered with the Wynford Group to evaluate and create an educators' guide and to help disseminate the Build Character, Build Success program. The program has grown from two to 73 schools.

UNICEF Canada established a partnership with PREVNet for expertise in program evaluation and in program reviews. PREVNet has reviewed the program and developed evaluation tools and an evaluation plan to test the efficacy of UNICEF's Rights Respecting Schools Initiative and joined a community of practice to support the expansion, reach, and impact. The Canadian Red Cross program Walking the Prevention Circle (WTPC) provides education to enable Aboriginal communities to create nurturing and stable environments for children and youth by integrating an understanding of violence prevention and relevant community and historical knowledge. Together, PREVNet and WTPC have created tools and a framework for evaluation that are relevant and appropriate for Aboriginal communities.

In light of research showing that most educators choose bullying prevention programs on the basis of word of mouth, and despite the fact that research shows that approximately 15 percent of these programs do more harm than good (Craig, Pepler, Murphy, & McCuaig-Edge, 2010), PREVNet has worked with the Public Health Agency of Canada (PHAC) to develop the Preventing Violence Stream (PVS). PVS is an online collection of evidence-based violence prevention programs suitable for schools, community organizations, and other users. It is available on PHAC's Canadian Best Practices Portal. Approximately 72 percent of users have shared information from the site with others to effect change. PREVNet researchers have presented information on PVS to more than 10,000 educators, social workers, and others. The impact of this effort is measured by the demonstration that the portal is gaining recognition as an important tool to help stakeholders find evidence-based prevention programs.

PREVNet has also been a key partner in the dissemination of the WITS (Walk Away, Ignore, Talk It Out, and Seek Help) programs, which are designed to prevent bullying and promote positive relationships for children from kindergarten to grade 6. This literacy-based bullying prevention program comprises a whole-school approach involving community members, classroom curricula, and schoolwide initiatives to create a supportive and caring school climate. In the first funding cycle, more than 136,500 students were involved and almost 1,300 teachers and 160 community leaders took the online training. PREVNet also collaborated with Family Channel to deliver the most current bullying research, strategies for prevention, and statistics to teachers across Canada through Family Channel's Stand UP! annual bullying awareness campaign. For the 2014 campaign, media reach was more than 4.7 million impressions.

POLICY

Through a research project, PREVNet was able to influence the direction of policy in PHAC. PREVNet conducted a trend analysis of Canadian data in the 2002, 2006, and 2010 WHO Health Behaviours of School-Aged Children (HBSC) survey. There was a decrease in the proportion of youth who reported a high-quality relationship with their parents, with their schools, and with their neighborhoods from 2002 to 2010. There were strong links between the quality of relationships and a wide range of health outcomes. The impact of this work is that PHAC's Youth Policy Division has included healthy relationships as one of five key foci. PREVNet also launched a Provincial/Territorial Bullying Prevention Legislation and Policies Resource on its Web site. This resource provides accessible and easy to understand information for parents, educators, and youth-serving organizations and outlines the roles and responsibilities of school personnel and parents, so that bullying problems can be effectively resolved.

CONCLUSIONS

In summary, bullying is a significant public health issue and of significant concern to the majority of adults in Canada and worldwide (Craig et al., 2009). The individual, health, social, and economic costs associated with bullying are enormous. As in most other countries, the current bullying prevention efforts in Canada are disjointed, inconsistent, and only moderately successful. Implementation of evidence-based bullying strategies is unevenly distributed across Canadian communities. The lack of effectiveness arises from a need to have research inform education and training, assessment and evaluation, prevention, and intervention through effective knowledge mobilization. By implementing PREVNet's KMb Pathways to Impact model, with partners in education, health, justice, community and social services, and corporations, PREVNet has conducted new research, developed new knowledge, mobilized this knowledge, and developed a new generation of graduate students who bring science to practice and practice to science. Through partners and co-creation, we are effectively finding solutions and making a significant impact on the serious problem of on- and offline bullying for children and youth and society as a whole.

REFERENCES

Centers for Disease Control and Prevention. (2010). Adverse childhood experiences reported by adults. *Morbidity and Mortality Weekly Report, 59*(49), 1609–1613.

Cohen, M. A., & Piquero, A. R. (2009). New evidence on the monetary value of saving a high risk youth. *Journal of Quantitative Criminology, 25*, 25–49.

Craig, W., Harel-Fisch, Y., Fogel-Grinvald, H., Dostaler, S., Hetland, J., Simons-Morton, B., & Pickett, W. (2009). A cross-national profile of bullying and victimization among adolescents in 40 countries. *International Journal of Public Health, 54*(Suppl. 2), 216–224.

Craig, W. M., Pepler, D. J., Murphy, A., & McCuaig-Edge, H. (2010). What works in bullying prevention? In E. Vernberg & B. Biggs (Eds.), *Preventing and treating bullying and victimization* (pp. 215–242). New York: Oxford University Press.

Farrington, D., & Ttofi, M. (2011). Bullying as a predictor of offending, violence and later life outcomes. *Criminal Behavior and Mental Health, 31*, 90–98.

Fixsen, D. L., Blase, K. A., Timbers, G. D., & Wolf, M. M. (2001). In search of program implementation: 792 replications of the Teaching-Family Model. In G. A. Bernfeld, D. P. Farrington, & A. W. Leschied (Eds.), *Offender rehabilitation in practice: Implementing and evaluating effective programs* (pp. 149–166). London: Wiley.

Holt-Lunstead, J., Smith, T. B., & Layton, J. B. (2010). Social relationships and mortality risk: A meta-analytic review. *Public Library of Science Medicine, 7*(7), e1000316. doi:10.1371/journal.pmed.1000316

Low, A. (2015, March 3). How to deal with aggression in preschoolers. *ParentsCanada*. Retrieved from http://www.parentscanada.com/articles/how-to-deal-with-aggression-in-preschoolers

Molcho, M., Craig, W., Due, P., Pickett, W., Harel-Fisch, Y., Overpeck, M., & the HBSC Bullying Writing Group. (2009). Cross-national time trends in bullying behaviour 1994–2006: Findings from Europe and North America. *International Journal of Public Health, 54*, 1–10.

Pepler, D., Jiang, D., Craig, W., & Connolly, J. (2008). Developmental trajectories of bullying and associated factors. *Child Development, 79*, 325–338.

PREVNet. (n.d.-a). *Aggression in preschoolers* [Parent tip sheet 1]. Retrieved from http://www.aboutkidshealth.ca/En/Assets/PDF_PN_Tips_Preschool_Aggression.pdf

PREVNet. (n.d.-b). *Preschool bullying* [Parent tip sheet 2]. Retrieved from http://www.aboutkidshealth.ca/En/Assets/PDF_PN_Tips_Preschool_Bullying.pdf

Primus. (2015, January 13). *How times have changed: Cyberbullying outranks drugs, teenage pregnancy and alcohol as a top concern of Canadian parents* [Press Release]. Retrieved from: http://www.marketwired.com/press-release/how-times-have-changed-cyberbullying-outranks-drugs-teenage-pregnancy-alcohol-as-top-1982373.htm

UNICEF Office of Research. (2013). Child well-being in rich countries: A comparative overview. *Innocenti Report Card 11.*

World Health Organization. (2004). *Preventing violence: A guide to implementing the recommendations of the world report on violence and health.* Geneva: Author.

23

The Role of Physicians and Other Health Providers in Bullying Prevention

Sarah Lindstrom Johnson, Catherine P. Bradshaw, Tina Cheng, and Joseph Wright

With youth homicides and assault-related injuries totaling an estimated $16 billion in medical and work loss costs (Centers for Disease Control and Prevention, 2010), it is clear that interpersonal violence is expensive. Acute health care providers, particularly emergency department clinicians, are often involved in the treatment of these individuals and therefore see the cost of violence both fiscally and in terms of mortality and morbidity. Primary care clinicians promote positive health and screen for conditions that may be associated with an increased likelihood of victimization (for example, mental health problems, behavioral disorders). They build relationships with patients over time and are often consulted about problems including bullying. In addition, because of their location, school-based health providers are likely to build relationships with students and potentially have more awareness of bullying.

The effects of bullying on youth and adult behavioral and mental health have been well documented. Moreover, recent work has explored physical health impacts of bullying, such as headaches, stomach pains, and other psychosomatic complaints (Gini & Pozzoli, 2013); these effects are more common among younger children, highlighting the need for sensitivity to the child's development. As a result, there is increased interest in bullying prevention that involves health care clinicians. Both the American Academy of Pediatrics and the Society for Adolescent Health and Medicine have policy statements that support the role of medical professionals in the prevention of bullying (American Academy of

Pediatrics, 2009; Eisenberg & Aalsma, 2005). For example, the Society for Adolescent Health and Medicine suggests that

> Health care providers should be familiar with the characteristics of youth that may be involved in bullying, either as aggressors or victims. They need to be sensitive to signs and symptoms of bullying, victimization, their influences and their sequelae. Health care providers are encouraged to intervene early when either bullying or victimization behaviors are noted. Discussing possible interventions with the adolescent and parent is appropriate. Additionally, referral for co-occurring mental health disorders (for example, conduct disorder, depression, anxiety) is recommended. Lastly, health care providers and school personnel can provide leadership and education to community organizations on these issues. (Eisenberg & Aalsma, 2005, pp. 89–90)

This statement highlights the range of responsibilities for health care clinicians, including identification, intervention and treatment, and advocacy. Unfortunately, the reality for many health care providers is that they already face time constraints in their visits with patients and lack training on effective counseling and intervention strategies around bullying prevention. This can create a large gap between suggested best practices and the actual application of these practices (Wright, 2005).

This chapter focuses on ways in which health care clinicians conceptualize and are involved in bullying prevention at various points across the life course. Given the salience of bullying prevention in childhood and adolescence, we have particular interest in the role of pediatric providers. We consider two broad dimensions of medical involvement related to bullying prevention: (1) opportunities for prevention and intervention in primary care settings, including schools; and (2) opportunities for prevention and intervention in acute care settings. We examine research and practice guidelines in these two areas. We also provide some examples of evidence-based programs to prevent violence involvement in both primary and acute care settings. We conclude with some recommendations for future research and training related to medical professionals.

PRIMARY CARE AS A SETTING FOR BULLYING PREVENTION

The fields of pediatrics and pediatric nursing have traditionally been grounded in human development. Thus, it is a natural connection for health care providers to discuss and promote healthy and successful development among their patients. Current recommendations for preventive pediatric health care include psychosocial and behavioral screening from infancy through adolescence with counseling (that is, anticipatory guidance) on developmentally relevant topics provided. The American Academy of Pediatrics' *Bright Futures* guidelines provides sample questions and suggestions for anticipatory guidance to promote well-being and ensure safety; in this context, *Bright Futures* recommends that providers have a conversation about friendship and bullying at each visit with children beginning at age five (Hagan, Shaw, & Duncan, 2008). Suggested questions such as "Do you know what signs to look for if your child is being bullied?" provide opportunities for both dialogue and advice (Hagan et al., 2008). Likewise, practice recommendations encourage family physicians to screen for bullying as a part of the HEEADSSS assessment, which is a comprehensive psychosocial evaluation including assessment of environmental, educational, and personal factors (that is, **H**ome, **E**ducation/Employment, **E**ating/Exercise, **A**ctivities/

Hobbies/Peer Relationships, Drug Use, Sexual Activity/Sexual Relationships, Suicide/ Depression/Mental Health, Safety/Risk) that could negatively influence health. As part of the safety component, physicians are encouraged to ask questions like, "Some teens have told me about feeling bullied or picked on at school or online. What has happened with you or your friends?" (Klein, Myhre, & Ahrendt, 2013, p. 87). Unfortunately, studies have shown that few pediatric and family physicians and residents routinely provide anticipatory guidance for patients and parents around violence prevention, partially because of a lack of comfort with the topic (Borowsky & Ireland, 1999; Sege, Hatmaker-Flannigan, De Vos, Levin-Goodman, & Spivak, 2006).

These screening questions and opportunities for anticipatory guidance are particularly important for children with special health care needs (that is, ADHD, learning disabilities) who are at higher risk for involvement in bullying (Twyman et al., 2010; Van Cleave & Davis, 2006). By definition, children with special health care needs require health or health-related services at a greater level than other children. Therefore, children with special health care needs and their families may be even more likely to view their health care providers as trusted advisors (Van Cleave & Davis, 2006). This fact combined with the higher risk of bullying among this population suggests that providing bullying screening for children with special health care needs at every visit may be an important intervention strategy.

School health suites and school-linked or school-based health centers can also be leveraged to support bullying prevention efforts. These resources, along with their staff, are often underused when it comes to promoting healthy relationships as well as identifying and seeking treatment for students involved in bullying. School health providers may have a different relationship with students than other staff in the school as they do not provide direct instruction and are not in a disciplinary role. This combined with the fact that students involved in bullying are more likely to seek care at school suggests that school health providers could play an important role in both the prevention and treatment of bullying (Cooper, Clements, & Holt, 2012). Many schools have committees designed to address school climate or implement bullying prevention initiatives. Given the important role of health in children's safety and bullying, it is essential that the school-based health providers be included in schoolwide bullying prevention and school climate promotion efforts.

PREVENTION AND INTERVENTION IN THE PRIMARY CARE SETTING

Given the link between bullying, youth violence, and mental health, some clinic-based efforts have aimed to reduce youth involvement in violence by diagnosing and treating mental health problems. One such initiative provided clinicians with tools to support violence prevention, including access to positive screens from the Pediatric Symptom Checklist (Borowsky, Mozayeny, Stuenkel, & Ireland, 2004). Data from a randomized controlled trial indicated that after nine months, children in the intervention condition (that is, those whose clinician had received support) had lower rates of parent-reported bullying and child-reported victimization by bullying (Borowsky et al., 2004). Physicians reported referring 27 percent of children for mental health services, scheduling follow-up appointments with 34 percent of children, and providing information on a parenting curriculum with 70 percent of parents. This study demonstrated that a youth violence prevention intervention can be successfully implemented in primary care with minimal disruption to practice as usual.

Another opportunity for intervention in primary care focuses on the provision of ancillary support services. The *Healthy Futures* intervention provided adolescent and young adult patients with access to a career coach, a master's-level professional trained in motivational interviewing. Patients were invited for three sessions, with intervention activities providing opportunities for the participants to discuss their goals for the future, identify barriers to accomplishing these goals (including involvement in risk behaviors), practice the skills necessary to accomplish these goals (for example, research careers, jobs and educational programs, develop their résumé, complete applications), and link them to community resources. Results from a randomized controlled trial found that at six months, adolescents and young adults in the intervention arm experienced a 63 percent decrease in fighting compared with those not receiving the intervention (Lindstrom Johnson, Jones, & Cheng, 2015). Primary care therefore may represent a novel location for positive youth development interventions promoting positive educational and health outcomes. Part of recommended pediatric practice is the provision of clinician guidance around academic competence and the skills and behaviors necessary to transition to adulthood (Hagan et al., 2008), which, as this study shows, may have relevance for reducing youth involvement in violence.

PREVENTION AND INTERVENTION IN ACUTE CARE SETTINGS

The 2004 National Institutes of Health State-of-the-Science Conference on Preventing Youth Violence suggested that acute care visits, particularly visits to the Emergency Department (ED), may be important settings in which to initiate secondary violence prevention (National Institutes of Health, 2004). In fact, all trauma centers require a coordinated violence prevention initiative. Injuries resulting from violence represent a substantial number of ED visits, particularly for adolescents; 25 percent of adolescent ED visits were the result of violence (Melzer-Lange & Lye, 1996). Some research suggests that the ED visit should be used as a "teachable moment"—a time of introspection and vulnerability following an injury event—as more than 40 percent of adolescents and young adults treated for a violent injury return to the ED as a result of other violent incidents (Cunningham et al., 2009). In a study of adolescents and their parents presenting to the ED for assault-related injuries, 59 percent of adolescents and 65 percent of parents reported that they thought there was something they could do to prevent another injury (Johnson et al., 2007). In addition, because many assault-injured patients may not be strongly connected to schools or other programs, intervening in the ED offers a unique opportunity to provide support around bullying experiences. Two recent reviews of ED-based violence prevention efforts suggest that case management and brief interventions are the two most common interventions in acute care settings and show some promise of effectiveness (Mikhail & Nemeth, 2015; Snider & Lee, 2009). However, similar to primary care clinicians, a study of emergency medicine physicians found that although the majority supported the role of the clinician in identifying risk for repeat injury and providing treatment, less than half regularly addressed the risk of a repeat injury or plans for retaliation or provided information about violence prevention resources (Fein et al., 2000).

As is evidenced by the emergence of the National Network of Hospital-Based Violence Intervention Programs (NNHVIP; n.d.), a growing number of violence prevention interventions are being situated in hospitals. Currently, 22 programs are a part of the network, with a mission to engage "patients during the window of opportunity when they are recovering in the hospital after a violent injury, to reduce the chance of retaliation and recurrence" (NNHVIP, n.d.). This group has also been an advocate of a trauma-informed approach to working with violently injured patients, as studies have suggested that the majority present with symptoms of acute stress (Fein, Kassam-Adams, Vu, & Datner, 2000). One hospital-based program, Caught in the Crossfire, paired adolescents and young adults with a staff member from the community who had been in a similar situation (that is, injured by violence or criminal involvement) who both served as a positive role model and provided tangible support in the form of referral to services, educational and job skills training, and legal assistance for up to a year post-hospitalization (Becker, Hall, Ursic, Jain, & Calhoun, 2004). An evaluation of this program showed that intervention participants were 70 percent less likely to be arrested and 60 percent less likely to have any criminal involvement than participants who did not receive the intervention. Unfortunately, no significant results were found for re-injury rates.

Another mentoring-based intervention pairs adolescents who present in the ED with peer assault injuries with a Big Brothers Big Sisters mentor who received specialized training in a violence prevention curriculum. Over the first six months of the relationship, the mentor completes one session a month focused on topics such as future orientation, self-regulation, conflict resolution, and gun safety. Parents also receive three sessions that serve to reinforce the conversations between their child and their mentor. A randomized controlled trial of this intervention is currently under way in two major urban city centers. However, a prior randomized controlled trial of a similar mentoring intervention showed promise for improved self-efficacy in avoiding violence, decreased aggression, and problem behavior at six months (Cheng et al., 2008).

Based on the success of other brief interventions in the ED, the SafERteen intervention was designed to explore the effectiveness of a brief intervention around violence prevention for adolescents who presented with either a medical illness or an assault injury. Patients could be randomized to receive a computerized brief intervention, a therapist brief intervention, or an informational packet. The brief interventions used adapted motivational interviewing to enhance motivation to change, modify norms about violence involvement, and improve conflict resolution skills. Results showed that brief interventions around violence are feasible in the ED context, are well received by adolescents, and are effective in changing attitudes and improving self-efficacy for violence prevention (Cunningham et al., 2009). Most important, findings show decreased youth involvement in peer violence that extended 12 months after the initial ED visit (Cunningham et al., 2012).

CONCLUSION AND RECOMMENDATIONS

The health care clinician has great opportunities to aid bullying prevention through the support of developmental milestones (such as positive peer and parent relationships) and appropriate referral services for victimized children, adolescents, and young adults. Although many of the programs cited in this chapter focused more broadly on violence prevention, the fact that they all aimed to support positive development suggests that they would be relevant for bullying prevention. We also tried to highlight the critical role that clinicians play in addressing and mitigating the implications of mental health concerns, which may be present for youth involved in bullying. In addition, although not necessarily the focus of this chapter, it is clear that clinicians may encounter victims of bullying when addressing more severe mental health consequences, such as attempted suicide or panic attacks. For effective treatment, it is critical to be aware of the potential for these health presentations to be related to bullying. This chapter focused largely on primary and acute care settings, which can supplement the prevention services provided in schools. However, we also highlighted the importance of incorporating school-based health providers into the ongoing bullying prevention efforts occurring in schools.

It is also clear that physicians need more training to address violence-related issues, be they in acute or primary care settings. Although time constraints are a real barrier, there is evidence that relatively modest efforts, such as screening or parent and youth referral to services, can have significant impacts in decreasing future incidents of violence and increasing mental health service utilization (for example, Borowsky et al., 2004; Cunningham et al., 2012). More bullying and youth violence prevention programing needs to be embedded into primary and acute care settings, and it is imperative that health staff recognize the important role they play in violence prevention. This shift is starting to occur, as illustrated in the recently expanded *Bright Futures* program, which now includes more information on bullying and youth violence–related issues. There is also a need for more attention to these issues through continuing education as well as during medical training. We cannot expect physicians and other health providers to initiate these conversations if they have not been trained to do so or if there are not clear expectations that this is part of their job as health providers.

The connection pediatric clinicians have with both children and their parents can also be leveraged to address bullying, not only directly with the child, but also by encouraging parents to engage in dialogues about bullying and violence and to monitor their children's behavior. In fact, recent research highlights the significance of the family dinner in offsetting the potentially devastating impacts of cyberbullying (Elgar et al., 2014). As such, clinicians should take an active role in bullying and youth violence prevention, directly through their own medical and health-related interactions with youth and indirectly through parent supports and referrals. They can also serve as advocates and educators by helping others to understand that bullying can have physiological impacts on youth, which over the life course can create a vulnerability to self-harm, a tendency to harm others, and behavioral and mental health problems (see chapter 3 and Swearer & Hymel, 2015).

REFERENCES

American Academy of Pediatrics. (2009). Policy statement: The role of the pediatrician in youth violence prevention. *Pediatrics, 124*(1), 393–402.

Becker, M. G., Hall, J. S., Ursic, C. M., Jain, S., & Calhoun, D. (2004). Caught in the crossfire: The effects of a peer-based intervention program for violently injured youth. *Journal of Adolescent Health, 34*(3), 177–183.

Borowsky, I. W., & Ireland, M. (1999). National survey of pediatricians' violence prevention counseling. *Archives of Pediatrics & Adolescent Medicine, 153*, 1170–1176.

Borowsky, I. W., Mozayeny, S., Stuenkel, K., & Ireland, M. (2004). Effects of a primary care-based intervention on violent behavior and injury in children. *Pediatrics, 114*, e392–e399.

Centers for Disease Control and Prevention, National Center for Injury Prevention and Control. (2010). *Web-based injury statistics query and reporting system (WISQARS)*. Retrieved from http://www.cdc.gov/injury

Cheng, T. L., Haynie, D., Brenner, R., Wright, J. L., Chung, S. E., & Simons-Morton, B. (2008). Effectiveness of a mentor-implemented, violence prevention intervention for assault-injured youths presenting to the emergency department: Results of a randomized trial. *Pediatrics, 122*, 938–946.

Cooper, G. D., Clements, P. T., & Holt, K. E. (2012). Examining childhood bullying and adolescent suicide implications for school nurses. *Journal of School Nursing, 28*(4), 275–283.

Cunningham, R. M., Chermack, S. T., Zimmerman, M. A., Shope, J. T., Bingham, C. R., Blow, F. C., & Walton, M. A. (2012). Brief motivational interviewing intervention for peer violence and alcohol use in teens: One-year follow-up. *Pediatrics, 129*, 1083–1090.

Cunningham, R., Knox, L., Fein, J., Harrison, S., Frisch, K., Walton, M., et al. (2009). Before and after the trauma bay: The prevention of violent injury among youth. *Annals of Emergency Medicine, 53*, 490–500.

Eisenberg, M. E., & Aalsma, M. C. (2005). Bullying and peer victimization: Position paper of the Society for Adolescent Medicine. *Journal of Adolescent Health, 36*(1), 88–91.

Elgar, F. J., Craig, W., Napoletano, A., Saul, G., Poteat, P., Dirks, M. A., et al. (2014). Cyberbullying victimization and mental health in adolescents and the moderating role of family dinners. *JAMA Pediatrics, 168*, 1015–1022.

Fein, J. A., Ginsburg, K. R., McGrath, M. E., Shofer, F. S., Flamma, J. C., & Datner, E. M. (2000). Violence prevention in the emergency department: Clinician attitudes and limitations. *Archives of Pediatrics & Adolescent Medicine, 154*, 495–498.

Fein, J. A., Kassam-Adams, N., Vu, T., & Datner, E. M. (2001). Emergency department evaluation of acute stress disorder symptoms in violently injured youths. *Annals of Emergency Medicine, 38*, 391–396.

Gini, G., & Pozzoli, T. (2013). Bullied children and psychosomatic problems: A meta-analysis. *Pediatrics, 132*, 720–729. doi:1-0.1542/peds.2013-0614

Hagan, J. F., Shaw, J. S., & Duncan, P. (Eds.). (2008). *Bright Futures: Guidelines for health supervision of infants, children, and adolescents*. Elk Grove Village, IL: American Academy of Pediatrics.

Johnson, S. B., Bradshaw, C. P., Wright, J. L., Haynie, D. L., Simons-Morton, B. G., & Cheng, T. L. (2007). Characterizing the teachable moment: Is an emergency department visit a teachable moment for intervention among assault-injured youth and their parents? *Pediatric Emergency Care, 23*, 553–559.

Klein, D. A., Myhre, K. K., & Ahrendt, D. M. (2013). Bullying among adolescents: A challenge in primary care. *American Family Physician, 88*(2), 87–92.

Lindstrom Johnson, S., Jones, V., & Cheng, T. L. (2015). Promoting healthy futures to reduce youth involvement in risk behaviors: A randomized controlled trial. *American Journal of Community Psychology, 56*(1–2), 36–45.

Melzer-Lange, M., & Lye, P. S. (1996). Adolescent health care in a pediatric emergency department. *Annals of Emergency Medicine, 27*, 633–637.

Mikhail, J. N., & Nemeth, L. S. (2015). Trauma center based youth violence prevention programs: An integrative review. *Trauma, Violence, & Abuse, 17*(5), 500–519. doi:10.1177/1524838015584373

National Institutes of Health. (2004, October 13–15). *Preventing violence and related health-risking social behaviors in adolescents* [State-of-the-Science Conference Statement]. Retrieved from http://consensus.nih.gov/2004/2004YouthViolencePreventionSOS023html.htm

National Network of Hospital-Based Violence Intervention Programs. (n.d.). *About: Mission.* Retrieved from http://nnhvip.org/mission/

Sege, R. D., Hatmaker-Flanigan, E., De Vos, E., Levin-Goodman, R., & Spivak, H. (2006). Anticipatory guidance and violence prevention: Results from family and pediatrician focus groups. *Pediatrics, 117*, 455–463.

Snider, C., & Lee, J. (2009). Youth violence secondary prevention initiatives in emergency departments: A systematic review. *Canadian Journal of Emergency Medicine, 11*(2), 161–168.

Swearer, S. M., & Hymel, S. (2015). Understanding the psychology of bullying: Moving toward a social-ecological diathesis–stress model. *American Psychologist, 7*, 344–353. doi:10.1037/a0038929

Twyman, K. A., Saylor, C. F., Saia, D., Macias, M. M., Taylor, L. A., & Spratt, E. (2010). Bullying and ostracism experiences in children with special health care needs. *Journal of Developmental and Behavioral Pediatrics, 31*(1), 1–8.

Van Cleave, J., & Davis, M. M. (2006). Bullying and peer victimization among children with special health care needs. *Pediatrics, 118*, e1212–e1219.

Wright, J. L. (2005). Training healthcare professionals in youth violence prevention: Closing the gap. *American Journal of Preventive Medicine, 29*(5), 296–298.

Index

middle childhood bullying, 23
See also school-age bullying
Miller, S., 87
mindfulness interventions, 204
minority stress model, 94
"Mix It Up" program, 106
Moffitt, T., 37, 38
Molnar-Main, S., 193, 195
Monda-Amaya, L., 116
Monks, C., 12
Moss, A., 116
multisystemic therapy (MST), 207–208
MyHealth, 257

N
Namie, G., 143
Namie, R., 143
National Center on Safe Supportive Learning
    Environments, 169
National Crime Victimization Survey, 104
National Education Association (NEA), 143,
    221–222, 225
National Network of Hospital-Based Violence
    Intervention Programs (NNHVIP),
    264–265
National School Climate Center, 166
National Violent Death Reporting System, 60
Neckerman, H., 50
neighborhoods, 26
    See also community involvement
network approach. *See* PREVNet (Promoting
    Relationships and Eliminating
    Violence Network)
New Jersey Anti-Bullying Bill of Rights Act,
    244–245
Newgent, R., 206
Nielsen, M., 11, 14, 145–146
Nishii, L., 105
nonteaching staff, bullying by, 155–156
nurses. *See* school nurses

O
Obama, B., 114
Office of Civil Rights (OCR), 95, 115, 243
Office of Special Education and Rehabilitative
    Services (OSERS), 115, 243–244
Ogle, N., 206
Olweus, D., 8, 17, 190, 192, 193
Olweus Bullying Prevention Program (OBPP),
    11, 172, 189–199, 223
Ormel, J., 40
Ostrov, J., 26
Ouellett-Morin, I., 41

P
paraeducators. *See* education support
    professionals (ESPs)
parent bullying, 156–157
parent involvement. *See* families and
    caregivers
parent trainings, 106, 108, 181–182, 206–207
parental attitudes, 254–255
parent–child relationships, 25–26, 36
Pathway to Impact model, 253, 254
Pediatric Symptom Checklist, 263
peer helpers, 206
peer nominations, 11–12, 16
peer victimization, neurobiology of, 35–47
Pellegrini, A., 87
Pepler, D., 86, 87
physicians, 262–263, 264, 266
Pitula, C., 40
Playground and Lunchroom Climate
    Questionnaire, 224
playgrounds, 223, 224
Polanin, J., 120
policies. *See* federal policies; state policies
polyvictimization, 24–25
popularity, relational aggression and, 54–55
Positive Behavioral Interventions and
    Supports (PBIS), 120, 172, 177–188,
    203, 223, 246
Power, T., 224
prejudice, 156
    See also racial–ethnic bullying
prejudice reduction programs, 106–107
preschool bullying. *See* early childhood
    bullying
Preventing Suicide: A Toolkit for High Schools, 63
Preventing Violence Stream (PVS), 258
prevention programs. *See* antibullying
    programs
PREVNet (Promoting Relationships and
    Eliminating Violence Network),
    252–256, 257–258
Price, L., 41
primary care settings, 262–264
Principal Mistreatment-Abuse Inventory,
    153
protective factors, 36, 61–62, 96, 118–119, 202,
    204
Protor, L., 86
psychopathology, 23
    See also mental health issues
Public Health Agency of Canada (PHAC),
    258
public health approaches, 61–64